BUDDHIST AND ISLAMIC
ORDERS IN SOUTHERN ASIA

BUDDHIST AND ISLAMIC ORDERS IN SOUTHERN ASIA

Comparative Perspectives

Edited by R. Michael Feener and Anne M. Blackburn

UNIVERSITY OF HAWAI‘I PRESS
Honolulu

Paperback edition 2021

Printed in the United States of America

26 25 24 23 22 21 6 5 4 3 2 1

Library of Congress Cataloging-in-Publication Data

Names: Feener, R. Michael, editor. | Blackburn, Anne M., editor
Title: Buddhist and Islamic orders in southern Asia : comparative perspectives / edited by R. Michael Feener and Anne M. Blackburn.
Description: Honolulu : University of Hawai‘i Press, [2019] | Includes bibliographical references and index.
Identifiers: LCCN 2018006253 | ISBN 9780824872113 (cloth ; alk. paper)
Subjects: LCSH: Buddhism—South Asia—History—Case studies. | Islam—South Asia—History—Case studies. | Buddhism—Southeast Asia—History—Case studies. | Islam—Southeast Asia—History—Case studies.
Classification: LCC BQ322 .B83 2019 | DDC 294.3/65095—dc23
LC record available at https://lccn.loc.gov/2018006253

ISBN 978-0-8248-9249-4 (paperback)

University of Hawai‘i Press books are printed on acid-free paper and meet the guidelines for permanence and durability of the Council on Library Resources.

Cover photos: *Top*, Buddhist devotional monuments at Monywe, Burma (Anne Blackburn); *bottom*, shrine of a Sufi saint at Kozhikode, India (R. Michael Feener)

CONTENTS

PREFACE

Recent work on religion and society in Southern Asia has highlighted the dynamic ways in which translocal traditions move across and take root in the region's diverse cultural contexts. These broad dynamics have been of interest to historians of both Buddhism and Islam, producing work that has explored different aspects of the networks linking coreligionists across premodern Southern Asia. Despite shared academic interests, researchers working in these two distinct subfields of the history of religions have rarely engaged each other in a focused or sustained way. Although scholars of both Buddhist studies and Islamic studies share interests in similar processes and focus on contexts that overlap in terms of both periodization and geography, little has been done to share investigative approaches and methods of interpretation.

There is, however, much that scholars working in these two fields could learn from each other to support our evolving understandings of the circulation and localization of religious traditions. For example, historians of Muslim societies can benefit from recent work in Buddhist studies on aspects of material culture as well as from perspectives on dimensions of ritual practice that stretch beyond canonical literature and narrowly doctrinal definitions of the tradition. Approaches that direct attention toward the intentionality of participants in localized forms of devotion and that examine where protective and/or salvific power is attributed by practitioners can and should stimulate new thinking about the diverse modes of Muslim ritual practice in Southern Asia. Likewise, scholars of Buddhism could learn from their colleagues in Islamic studies who have been developing models of circulation and connected histories, bringing into view transregional dimensions of institutional and intellectual history. Moreover, studies of Islam in Southern Asia offer thought-provoking treatments of smaller-scale contexts of reception and localization. Working together, scholars of Islam and Buddhism can develop more nuanced and integrated analytical frameworks for conceptualizing the coproduction of polity, ritual forms, intellectual currents, and material cultures.

To facilitate such work, we must first create spaces for constructive engagement between the fields of Islamic and Buddhist studies. This volume aims to create one such space by drawing analytic perspectives developed by both fields into discussions of one major dimension of the history of religion in Southern Asia. The focus is on "religious orders"—conceptualized here as a comparative category for discussion of Sufi brotherhoods and Buddhist monastic and ritual lineages. Both Buddhism and Islam historically developed institutional mechanisms that facilitated the expansion and maintenance of liturgical, literary, and clerical/ritual specialist connections. These were important factors in the historical development of both traditions—particularly during the period from the sixteenth through the nineteenth centuries.

This volume brings together contributions by scholars engaged in cutting-edge work in the study of Islam and Buddhism in Southern Asia in conversation about the ways in which "orders" have functioned within these two traditions to expand and sustain transregional religious networks. Orders have presented particular traditions and their human representatives as attractive and authoritative, and have established means by which far-flung local communities could come to be recognized and engaged with as part of a broader world of coreligionists. This volume opens new spaces of creative interaction between scholars in both fields in order to develop a better understanding of the complex roles played by religious networks in the history of Southern Asia.

This book is the fruit of exchanges launched at the conference "Orders and Itineraries: Comparative Religious Networks in Southern Asia," convened on February 21 to 22, 2013, at the National University of Singapore's Asia Research Institute. We are immensely grateful for the generous support of the institute and its staff, and especially to Valerie Yeo for her outstanding work in organizing the event. We would also like to extend our thanks to all those who joined the discussions in Singapore and shared their thoughts, especially to Prasenjit Duara, Rick Weiss, Nola Cooke, Ramani Hettiarachchi, Iain Sinclair, Gerrit de Vylder, Ines Zupanov, Oona Paredes, Lim Peng Han, Carolina Dionco, Masao Imamura, and Andrea Acri. We are also grateful to Adora Elisapeta Jones for her kind assistance with copyediting and formatting the final manuscript for publication.

BUDDHIST AND ISLAMIC ORDERS IN SOUTHERN ASIA

1

SUFIS AND *SAṄGHA* IN MOTION

Toward a Comparative Study of Religious Orders and Networks in Southern Asia

ANNE M. BLACKBURN AND R. MICHAEL FEENER

The multidisciplinary study of transregional networks has seen remarkable growth over recent decades. Following approaches developed by Fernand Braudel in his path-breaking work on the Mediterranean world,[1] scholars have developed an impressive body of work on the *longue durée* economic and social histories of other regions.[2] Work along such lines on the complex seascapes and shorescapes connecting diverse parts of southern Asia—including the major contributions by K. N. Chaudhuri and Patricia Risso for the medieval and early modern periods as well as those by Thomas Metcalf, Sugata Bose, and Sunil Amrith for the modern—has done much to map out major dynamics of trade and state relations across the Indian Ocean.[3] The work of Anthony Reid, Denys Lombard, Janet Abu-Lughod, and Roderich Ptak has added important dimensions to our understanding of the integrated histories of the eastern end of the Indian Ocean world and its connections to the South China Sea through the waters of the Indonesian archipelago.[4]

COMPARATIVE PERSPECTIVES ON RELIGIOUS NETWORKS

Against this background, other scholars working in diverse fields of history have sought to uncover new data and highlight its relevance for understanding varied modes of connectivity across South and Southeast Asia.[5] To date, they have mined rich sources for identifying connections and tracking commodities, individuals, and ideas along complex paths crisscrossing the region. Students of the history of religions have also been active on parallel fronts in recent years, making considerable advances in mapping shifting pathways and patterns of connection along maritime and land routes that linked the members of religious communities across Asia and beyond.[6] The wealth of data brought to light by these studies makes it clear that for centuries modes of transregional connection played an important role in shaping local communities, their patterns of religious practice, and their forms of collective identification.

At the same time, however, such richly detailed examinations of particular networks have tended toward a significant degree of specialization, mapping the transregional movement of individuals and institutions within frameworks of particular communities and diasporas. These analyses have rarely been developed in substantial communication with adjacent fields or through a comparative orientation involving more than one religious tradition. This volume demonstrates the benefit of collaboration between scholars in the fields of Islamic studies and Buddhist studies. By highlighting points of structural and chronological comparison and contrast, this comparative exercise on Buddhist and Islamic networks and institutions allows for critical reflections on the conceptual frameworks used across different fields in the comparative history of religions. As we have pursued our work in this direction during recent years, we have found our approach to comparison resonant with that elaborated in the recent work of Peter van der Veer, who argues that "comparison should be conceived not primarily in terms of comparing societies or events, or institutional arrangements across societies, although this is important, but as a reflection on our conceptual framework as well as on the history of interactions that have constituted our object of study."[7] This volume as a whole demonstrates the ways in which developing robust comparison between analogous developments in Buddhist and Islamic traditions can be mutually illuminating for both fields of study.

Historians of Buddhism and of Islam can both benefit from a more substantial engagement with the work being pursued by their counterparts. Such engagement, however, requires shared awareness of the scholarly conversations within each subfield—something that we as editors have tried to develop through our collaboration on this volume. The contributions to this volume focus on one category of comparative analysis, that of religious "orders," with a geographic focus on the region of Southern Asia in which Buddhism and Islam have had a long and substantial presence. The comparative exercises collected in the volume help us to better appreciate the historical dynamics involved in the ongoing reconfiguration of Buddhist lineages and Sufi "brotherhoods." Some of these studies direct attention toward the roles of polities in patronage of religious networks and their localization in specific settings, revealing patterns shared across Islamic and Buddhist contexts. Others point the way toward a comparatively informed periodization of changes in the character of orders and their relationship to wider communities within the traditions of Islam and Buddhism. Moreover, by developing exemplary cases from three different Buddhist "subtraditions," oriented respectively toward authoritative texts in Classical Chinese, Classical Tibetan, and Pali, and characterized by strikingly different institutional arrangements, this volume underscores the fruitfulness of intra-Buddhist comparison across thematic axes. All chapters draw attention to the fact that networked persons in both traditions were not always strongly institutionalized; members of Buddhist lineages and Islamic *ṭuruq* often moved through the Southern Asian region and developed local bases without being involved in complex corporate organizations.

ON "ORDERS" WITHIN AND ACROSS TRADITIONS

The terminology of religious orders, derived from Christian religious traditions, has been deployed within the academic study of religion to identify forms of association among religious specialists across diverse traditions. These lines of scholarly discussion are situated within a long legacy of scholarship in which Christian traditions have provided not only foundational categories, but also implicit bases for comparison in the academic study of religion. This volume deliberately attempts to develop a different kind of comparative exercise, working across two non-Christian traditions—Islam and Buddhism—while paying close attention to the diverse and historically contingent forms of institutionalized association in which religious specialists participated.

The idea of orders has been central to discussion of Islam and its diverse traditions of Sufi lineage. Although the term "Sufism" has been used by modern scholars with reference to things ranging from metaphysics and poetry to ritual practice and technologies of invulnerability, discussion of Sufi orders focuses more specifically on mechanisms for the transmission of teachings in a lineage associated with a particular "master" (Arabic *shaykh*; Persian *pir*). The Arabic term frequently translated as "order" or "brotherhood" here, *ṭarīqa* (pl. *ṭuruq*), might more literally be rendered as "path" or "way." By the twelfth century, however, it had emerged as a technical term for more formalized lineages of authority, often identified posthumously with an eponymous founder.[8] Mark Sedgwick has cautioned against assumptions about institutional continuity that Christian models of religious orders might encourage when looking comparatively at other traditions. In particular, he highlights the extent to which Sufi orders have historically remade themselves in diverse forms through cyclical dynamics of disruption and stabilization.[9] This dynamic history of internal Sufi reconfigurations complicates simplistic comparisons with more institutionalized forms of Christian monasticism.

The institutional dimensions of Sufi orders have nevertheless sometimes been overplayed in modern scholarship on the early history of Sufism. As Nile Green has recently argued against such overdetermined images of orders, "while some aspects of these mechanisms were organizational and corporate in the sense that the term brotherhood usually suggests, they were both enabled by and subject to the intangible but ultimately more weighty operations of tradition as a conceptual and symbolic mechanism. We should not then expect the brotherhoods . . . [of the early period] to comprise complex organizations with card-carrying members and efficient managerial hierarchies."[10]

Indeed, more fluid structures for the transmission of Sufi traditions have proved remarkably resilient as mechanisms for connecting Muslims across both time and space. Marshall Hodgson powerfully highlighted the importance of Sufi orders (alongside the mechanisms of Islamic legal scholarship) as one of the primary means by which a rapidly expanding Islamic world maintained a degree of integration despite the political fragmentation of the post-Abbasid period.[11] More recently, an increasing number of scholars have expanded on the importance of *ṭuruq* in the formation of networks linking far-flung regions of the Muslim world from West Africa to Southeast Asia. For example, in an essay on "transregional interactions," John Voll, drawing on the terminology of Christopher Bayly, has discussed Sufi orders as a prime example of "archaic globalizers."[12] Neither of these two authors, however, went into great detail on exactly how *ṭuruq* actually functioned in this capacity or attempted to situate these aspects of Sufi orders in comparison to contemporaneous formations of religious networks within other traditions.

Scholars of Buddhism have likewise devoted attention to associational groups involved in the internal differentiation and expansion of the tradition. Foundational works on Buddhist history made explicit use of the term "order" to refer to the Buddhist monastic community (*saṅgha*), revealing an implicit conceptual debt to studies of Christianity among an early generation of scholars.[13] Over the course of the twentieth century, a variety of other terms came into use among scholars of Buddhism. The terms used to refer to more narrowly delineated associational groups of textual and ritual specialists—who may be monastic or nonmonastic—include "order," "fraternity," "school," "sect," and "lineage."[14] Such terms figure in scholarly accounts of the historical and geographic expansion of Buddhism across Asia, with emphasis on the role played by textual and ritual specialists in channeling selected philosophical/doctrinal positions, textual corpora, and potent ritual practices across the region—often in symbiotic relationships with commercial, military, and administrative elites.[15]

Across its diverse usages within Buddhist and Islamic studies, the concept of an "order" has encompassed a range of broadly shared features identified among many scholars working within these distinct subfields of the academic study of religion. Prominent among these features are conceptions of lineage or genealogy. In the case of Islam, the Sufi *ṭarīqa*, structured according to a lineage of religious authority (Ar. *silsila*) comprises one of a number of forms of defining tradition grounded in the teachings of the Prophet. Sufi genealogies structured according to *silsila* and the Sufi orders (Ar. *ṭuruq*) that came to be built around them developed alongside other, parallel mechanisms for the transmission of tradition, including those of *ḥadīth* scholarship focused on "chains of transmission" (Ar. *isnād*, pl. *asānid*) and the established schools (Ar. *madhhab*, pl. *madhāhib*) of Islamic jurisprudence.

There are likewise plural conceptions of lineage within Buddhist traditions. Buddhist textual and ritual specialists identify themselves and are identified by others in relation to both ordination lines and bonds of teacher-student relationships, including links formed through the transmission of specific ritual (including meditation) techniques. Buddhist monastics (both male and female) undergo an ordination ritual that emplots the ordinand within Buddhist institutional and associational space. The ritual location of ordination itself indicates the ordinand's participation within a distinctive subsector of the Buddhist monastic establishment within a particular polity or geographic region, usually one to which the ordinand has gained access through his or her primary teacher. The ordinand is also understood to stand within a lineage relationship to the preceptor (*upajjhāya/upajjhāyā*), who presents the candidate for ordination. Historically, it was common for Buddhist monastics to study with multiple teachers, before and subsequent to their ordination. Teachers and students could thus report their place within their lineages in a number of ways, providing an extremely flexible means of expressing intellectual and material inheritance, loyalty, and other bonds.

The breadth and flexibility of such teacher-student bonds and lineage claims characterized nonmonastic teacher-student networks as well. Especially in the Himalayan and Central Asian worlds of Vajrayāna Buddhism, but also elsewhere in Asia, nonmonastic textual and ritual specialists typically studied and forged ritual bonds with more than one teacher, generating a broad and flexible web of lineage relationships as well as nested forms of collective identification. In relation to the transregional mobilities examined within this volume, it is important to recognize that the claim to—and recognition of—participation within a shared Buddhist lineage could facilitate (often in very practical material ways) the movement of Buddhists across geographic space. For instance, lineage claims (and sometimes documents affirming them) were shaped by the acceptance of Buddhist travelers within new geographic and Buddhist institutional domains as well as the success of diplomatic projects originating from state centers. Where Buddhists competed with one another for recognition, social authority, and material well-being, especially at geographic frontiers and/or in rapidly changing political environments, the ability to be recognized as a participant within a well-recognized, historically venerable Buddhist lineage could be central to success. As Amy Holmes-Tagchungdharpa's chapter shows powerfully, many factors contributed to such recognition.

Those connected to such lineages are also distinguished by particular patterns of practice and aesthetic markers that are constitutive signs of belonging within these genealogical traditions. For example, Buddhist ritual and textual specialists are often distinguished from one another visually by vestment practices, according to which ordination and other forms of teacher-student lineages are identified through patterns of robe wearing, and the use of sartorial accessories. Indeed, competition among Buddhist textual and ritual specialists—both monastic and nonmonastic—has often been expressed centrally through a discourse linking ways of dressing to hierarchies of purity and authority. In such contexts, disputes over appropriate dress are closely linked to an evaluation of specialists' comportment and their right to occupy positions within eminent and powerful Buddhist institutional establishments.[16] Although historically members of some Sufi orders have sometimes been distinguished by particular styles and colors of robes and headdress, such visual markers of adherence to a particular lineage have been relatively less pronounced in Islamic traditions. Rather, attachment to different orders has tended to be most clearly marked in the performance of specific forms of ritual practice, such as in preferences for particular forms of vocal or silent performance of the ritual remembrance of God (*dhikr*) or the recitation of particular litanies.[17]

Perhaps the most obvious point of comparison between Islamic and Buddhist orders—and one of central concern within this volume—is their role in the creation and maintenance of transregional networks. As noted earlier, scholars of Buddhism and Islam have devoted considerable attention to the relationship between orders and the geographic expansion of Islam and Buddhism across Southern Asia and beyond. Although in both scholarly traditions such geographic extension was initially treated without much nuance, recent work in both fields has begun to critically examine the chronology of the expansion of orders and their members across the Asian region and to develop more fine-grained pictures of the dynamics of localization involved in such expansionary processes, including what Holmes-Tagchungdharpa here calls "technologies of transmission." Scholars of Buddhism have begun to investigate in more detail how Buddhist ideas, institutions, and forms of practice were localized within particular arenas of Southern Asia. These investigations have drawn attention to the fact that the transregional extension of Buddhism in Asia should be understood as a multidirectional networked process rather than a unilinear extension of Indic Buddhism.

In this regard, Prapod Assavavirulhakorn draws attention to the historical complexity that characterized the extension of Buddhism beyond India:

> The introduction of Buddhism [to Southeast Asia] did not occur in a single moment, nor as a single act, but during a long process of time. . . . It is likely that there was more than simply one introduction, but rather, multiple introductions. And, there was not the introduction of just one single kind of Buddhism, but of numerous schools of Buddhism. This fact, together with the extensive area exposed to Indian cultures to which Buddhism belongs, makes the issue even more complicated, because this allows for the possibility that different places were exposed to different types of Buddhism at the same time. And it is probable that some regions did not adopt Buddhism directly from India.[18]

In addition to emphasizing that Buddhism and Buddhist orders extended their reach in the Southern Asian region through long and historically complex processes characterized by multiple locations of origin, it must be noted that contingent local circumstances also shaped the reception and patronage of members of Buddhist orders within new territories. These histories require much more detailed research than they have tended to receive.[19] As the work of Alexey Kirichenko in this volume suggests, it may be fruitful to conceptualize the expansion of religious orders as occurring on a spectrum of institutionalization. At the extreme end of deinstitutionalization we find sporadic transmission of objects, texts, ordinations, and so on, moving separately from the circulation of lineages and their specialists. The opposite pole is characterized by the substantial expansion and localization of lineages along with distinctive practices and corporate institutional forms. Kenneth Dean, in his chapter on Chinese networks in Malaya, refers to these as "formal religious orders." Perhaps more common than scholars have realized, but well attested by this volume, was the circulation of lineages separately from complex corporate institutions. Such lineages offered forms of collective identification and aspirations to practice that could be flexibly deployed in diverse local contexts, compatible with existing local practices and social and institutional dynamics.

At the same time, historians of Islam have come to substantially revise previously dominant narratives of the spread of Islam in Southern Asia. Recent scholarship on the history of Islam in the Indonesian archipelago, for example, has been marked by the development of increasingly nuanced and contextualized views on the roles Sufi orders played in processes of Muslim expansion during the premodern period.[20] Michael Laffan has sounded a strong cautionary note in the face of the paucity of evidence that we actually have for organized *ṭarīqa* activity during the earliest phases of the Islamization of the Indonesian archipelago. Moreover, even after affiliation to particular orders appears more prominently in the seventeenth century, this appears in connection with elite court circles rather than as mechanisms for the spread of Islam among the broader population.[21] Such close connections between Sufism and the structures of empire were to remain important in several parts of Southern Asia over the centuries that followed.[22] What is clear through all this is that, in the premodern history of Islam in Southern Asia, Sufi orders functioned not primarily as expansionary beachheads, but rather as contextualized loci that helped to redefine modes of belief and practice for religious elites under state patronage.

Several of the contributions to this volume pursue particulars of how certain orders took shape in Southern Asia over the course of the nineteenth century. Torsten Tschacher, for example, presents an insightful perspective on the ways in which two Sufi traditions, the Qādiriyya and the Shādhiliyya, developed in southern India and Laṅkā in interaction with broader reconfigurations of orders across the Indian Ocean world during that period. In his contribution to this volume, Martin van Bruinessen critically explores the development of more popular forms of localized *tarekat* affiliation through his examination of the formation of confessional communities centered on rural Islamic schools and devotional communities in Java and Sumatra. His chapter highlights how "corporate" forms of Sufi traditions appear in Indonesia only from the nineteenth century, a period in which other types of Muslim communities that might be viewed as "orderlike formations" were also emerging. The work of Kenneth Dean similarly directs attention to the historically late monasticization of Chinese Buddhist associations within the region, shaped by British colonial policies in Malaya as well as new intellectual and institutional directions taken by Buddhists on the southern Chinese mainland. These affected Southern Asia through South China Sea Buddhist networks.[23]

SOUTHERN ASIA

In order to delimit the scope of our comparative exercise, this volume is organized around a regional focus on "Southern Asia." This region—stretching from India, Sri Lanka, and the Himalayas through mainland Southeast Asia and across the Indonesian archipelago—has long been a site of dynamic and overlapping interaction between Buddhist and Muslim communities in motion. It thus forms a unit of analysis that is not only geographically contiguous, but also marked by a historically high degree of economic and cultural integration. The mobile persons and communities investigated in the chapters that follow understood themselves to function within a broad transregional geography that transcends the boundaries of modern academic area studies frameworks of "South Asia" and "Southeast Asia."

Similarities in the ways in which both Buddhism and Islam were localized within this Southern Asian region stem in part from long centuries of interaction between these two traditions, although this interactive history requires much further scholarly investigation than it has received to date.[24] Buddhists and Muslims, with their own various lineages and institutions, acculturated themselves in recognizably similar ways to a shared regional landscape characterized by deep historical dynamics of circulation. This regional landscape was constituted by patterns of political formation and the employment of supramundane power within human territory that extended in similar ways across Southern Asia. Buddhism and Islam underwent comparable processes of deep regional localization, and within both traditions the members of orders played significant roles in these processes. There are also substantial similarities in the dynamics through which orders were localized in Southern Asia in close relationship to regional polities.

This volume builds on our own previous work toward conceptualizing new approaches to religious connections across Southern Asia. Michael Feener has argued elsewhere for the importance of looking beyond established paradigms of "Indianization" and "influence" between "South" and "Southeast" Asia in order to better recognize the interconnected processes of social transformation that animated the connected histories of Islamization across this broader region.[25]

Anne Blackburn's study of eighteenth- and nineteenth-century transregional Buddhist projects involving Laṅkā underscores the deeply connected monastic itineraries and imaginations of Buddhist community negotiated by Southern Asian monks across the boundaries of present-day South and Southeast Asia, often exceeding national and protonational geographic limits.[26] Such work serves to highlight the extent to which Cold War–era area studies optics can impede, as much (if not more) as they may facilitate, understandings of interactions between societies of "South Asia" and "Southeast Asia" in earlier periods.

Across this broader geography, local religious specialists within orders of both traditions remained in constant communication for centuries through dynamic circulations of people, ideas, texts, objects, and practices. As we see especially in the chapters by Dean, van Bruinessen, and Alatas, circulations brought diverse currents of internal reform and notions of ritual and lineage purity to the Southern Asian region from distant locations, and these moved across Southern Asia with considerable speed. At the same time, distinctive reconfigurations within the region could produce reverberations across networks of Buddhist and Islamic orders and the broader religious traditions of which they were part. Read together, the chapters in this volume draw attention to similarities across Islam and Buddhism—both within and beyond Southern Asia—in the ways that orders were shaped and reshaped through transregional processes under way within their respective traditions. In addition, they allow us to specify more closely significant points of chronological convergence between the formative dynamics of orders in both traditions, with changes in the forms of institutional structures as well as in the ideological conception of community defined in relation to particular orders. As the ensuing chapters demonstrate, comparative examinations of religious orders in Southern Asia must take into account the deep and continuing history of increasingly rapid and intense communication and mobility across the wider Buddhist and Muslim worlds, as well as the contemporaneous production of new forms of religious practice and authority at multiple points within changing religious networks during the nineteenth and twentieth centuries.

NETWORKS IN HISTORY

Scholars of Islam have yet to address fully the challenge poignantly proposed by Carl Ernst and Bruce Lawrence more than a decade ago to "figure out how to understand . . . [Sufi orders] as historical developments."[27] There is thus a clear need for the continuing development of more dynamic, diachronic approaches to understanding the shifting forms and features of Islamic religious orders across diverse contexts. Scholars of Sufism continue to struggle with considerable historiographic problems. Devin DeWeese has insightfully identified two aspects of the challenges faced here: "both because we know so little of the actual role of Sufis in Islamization, and because our image of Sufis themselves has been shaped by later textual sources."[28] This is a powerful reminder of our need to develop more nuanced readings of the literary texts of the Sufi traditions in historical context.

Nancy Florida pursues such work in her contribution to this volume on vernacular Sufi traditions of the Shaṭṭāriya order in nineteenth-century Java. Her discussion of this textual tradition demonstrates the continued association of certain forms of Sufism with court culture in the nineteenth century even as the new political realities of European imperialism reconfigured the nature of the sultanate. Through her close, historically contextualized reading of a Javanese Sufi poem (*suluk*), Florida reveals the complex nature of both distinctly local aesthetics and connections to a transregional discursive tradition in the conceptualization of a Sufi order. In her presentation of the history of the *tarekat* within courtly circles of the Surakarta palace, she explores the ways in which the literary lineages defining the order navigated both colonial reconfigurations of political power and internal movements of Islamic reform over a tumultuous period of its history. Florida's work thus provides a compelling case for the continuing importance of particular lines of Shaṭṭārī textual tradition even during a period in which—as Martin van Bruinessen highlights in his chapter—at more popular levels the teachings of that order had become more "diffused" through folk cosmologies and practices of magic.

Other chapters in this volume further develop new approaches to the historical configurations of *ṭuruq* in the nineteenth century. As Ismail Alatas demonstrates with regard to the 'Alawiyya in the Netherlands Indies, the period saw an increased emphasis on standardization in conceptions of Islamic orthopraxy among some Sufi orders. Focusing on the career of ʿAbdallāh b. ʿUmar ibn Yaḥyā (d. 1849), he explores the microhistorical interactions between this itinerant Sufi scholar, Dutch colonial authorities, and local royal houses. His work highlights the material infrastructure and contingent historical circumstances that informed the reconfiguration of a particular religious order within a single tradition.

Over two decades ago, Frank Reynolds and Charles Hallisey proposed an approach to a large-scale periodization of Buddhist history. This was an invitation to bring greater diachronic precision to the study of Buddhism in Southern Asia and beyond and to do so through an examination of changing interrelationships among polities, Buddhist orders, ritual practice, textual forms, and languages.[29] A striking feature of this work was its early attempt to recognize and analyze historical changes in Buddhist conceptions of the geographic space that constituted a perceived Buddhist world as well as ways in which Buddhist communities were understood by their members to map onto cultural, national, and other political geographies.[30]

However, the conceptual naturalness of contemporary nation-state boundaries has exerted a powerful force within the field, making it difficult for scholars of Buddhism to recognize Buddhist socio-institutional projects occurring at scales larger and smaller than that of the nation. At the same time, the rich philological and philosophical orientation that characterized several generations of scholarship on Buddhism in Southern Asia has often abetted—if not always intentionally—a tendency to examine textual/doctrinal developments separately from institutional contexts.[31] Thus, despite an important call to consider the transregional collective constituted by shared participation in a particular Buddhist textual-conceptual system such as the "Pāli imaginaire,"[32] the study of premodern and precolonial Buddhist orders and the networks related to them has proceeded somewhat slowly,[33] and sometimes with too great a reliance on the narratives of monastic "missions" articulated by Buddhist texts themselves.[34] Studies of the Himalayan-Tibetan world have offered a valuable corrective to this, with considerable comparative potential for other parts of Southern Asia.[35] Moreover, inspired partly by the expanding field of Indian Ocean studies as well as by an explosion of data from the "Silk Road" connecting central, southern, and eastern Asia, other recent scholarship attends more closely to the ways in which Buddhist institutions and the members of Buddhist orders participated within and helped to shape the transregional ecosystems of Southern Asia.[36]

As in studies of Sufism, understanding the history of Buddhist orders requires more work to clarify how specific Buddhists operated within particular frameworks of organization and action. One significant challenge faced by scholars working along such lines is that of negotiating literary portrayals of orders and their individuals that often obscure historical contexts and conditions. Alexey Kirichenko's chapter in this volume points out new types of textual evidence, including that emanating from royal and monastic bureaucracies, that may be explored fruitfully in order to reconstruct the lives and itineraries of mobile Buddhists who participated in one or more orders within the Southern Asian region. In addition, Kirichenko develops a diachronic and intertextual strategy that can be used to reveal how members of orders negotiated their movement across institutional boundaries and secured patronage and authority in diverse locations, while accommodating themselves to historically and geographically shifting expectations of specialist behavior and experience. His study of Sāralaṅka's (b. ca. 1730) movement between rapidly shifting political formations in Ayutthaya, Tenasserim, and Ava—like Ismail Alatas' on the Sufi shaykh Ibn Yaḥyā in his chapter—helps us to appreciate the role of highly mobile individuals in the creation, maintenance, and transformations of orders through their negotiation of diverse social, political, and economic relationships.

Beyond court circles, orders were also reconfigured in relation to patterns of religious patronage by merchant communities in several parts of Southern Asia during the eighteenth and nineteenth centuries. In his contribution to this volume, Torsten Tschacher calls attention to the ways in which the organization of Sufi networks and lineages shifted over the course of the eighteenth century with new dynamics of support and sponsorship taking hold among merchant elites in the Tamil regions of India and Laṅkā. The type of order that characterized this period, however, was not one of institutionalized structures of lineage (*silsila*), but rather of ritual complexes associated with shrines and the communities that supported them. As Tschacher points out, more institutionalized forms of Sufism appear there only in the nineteenth century with new dynamics of consolidation arising out of encounters and entanglements between the Qādiriyya and the Shādhiliyya orders. The resonance and attraction of the kinds of Sufi reform promoted by these two orders in the nineteenth century contributed to significant transformations in conceptions of transregional networks across the far-flung coasts of the Indian Ocean.[37]

COLONIAL MODERNITY AND THE FURTHER REMAKING OF RELIGIOUS ORDERS

The studies produced for this volume highlight important shifts in conceptions of what constitutes a religious order in diverse but interconnected locations across Southern Asia over the past three centuries. The eighteenth and nineteenth centuries were characterized by a number of significant developments across the religious networks of both traditions in Southern Asia. As the nineteenth century progressed, new dynamics were introduced into the ongoing reconfiguration of religious orders across Southern Asia and beyond. The context was powerfully shaped by the expansion and consolidation of European imperial power along the coasts of the Indian Ocean as well as within the Indo-Tibetan highlands. As colonial authorities expanded their power across the region in the early nineteenth century, however, the expansion of both Buddhist and Islamic religious orders accelerated apace—with both the development of new orders in the region and the introduction of others from elsewhere.[38]

Encounters between religious orders and colonial officials were by no means universally antagonistic during this period. Indeed, colonial policies sometimes created (albeit often inadvertently) conditions conducive to the expansion and/or restructuring of religious orders in the region. In the Himalayan sphere, as Holmes-Tagchungdarpa's chapter on Sikkim and Bhutan demonstrates, British interruption of earlier Sikkimese practices of royal-lama patronage opened that kingdom to a wider range of Buddhist teaching lineages. As Dean's contribution reveals, southern Chinese Buddhist orders in the Straits Settlements became more prominent in the later nineteenth century when increasing colonial pressure on Triads encouraged Buddhist entrepreneurs and other commercial elites in the region to transfer patronage from Triad-linked temples dedicated to regional deities of diverse migrant communities and clan associations to emerging Buddhist monastic establishments. Although monastic Buddhism has a long history on the Chinese mainland, distinctive patterns of overseas Chinese commercial expansion into the Straits Settlements initially favored nonmonastic Buddhist institutions—a phenomenon encouraged by the fact that what became Malaya had no prior history of royal support for Buddhist orders. The case presented by Dean here also reveals how the local forms taken by orders—and the practices they encouraged—were both shaped by and constitutive of changes of emphasis within the wider religious tradition. The Mahāyāna Buddhist monasteries that developed in places like Singapore, Penang, and Malacca owed much to southern Chinese reformist trajectories favoring monastic forms of Buddhist institutional life. They also helped to naturalize this new emphasis through the circulation of Buddhist teachers and discourses within the Southern Asian and southern Chinese regions.

The colonial period interplay among rapidly changing economies, polities, institutional forms, and conceptions of "religion," as well as discourses circulating within specific religious traditions, contributed to the emergence of a more formal sense of institutionalization and more bounded forms of organization and administration among orders in Islam and Buddhism. An important factor in such developments was an interconnected set of innovations within transportation and communications technologies. These allowed religious orders to explore new modes of connectivity over the second half of the nineteenth century.[39] Steam-driven transport over rail and sea facilitated not only the itineraries of monks, shaykhs, and other ritual specialists across Southern Asia, but also opened up possibilities for new forms of mass pilgrimage to shrines and other religious sites.[40] The rapid proliferation of print technology during this same period also had diverse impacts on the understandings and experiences of religion for many Muslims, Buddhists, and others all across Southern Asia. Indeed, such impacts were felt even in parts of the region that were not brought under full colonial administrative control, such as Thailand and Himalayan kingdoms like Tibet and Bhutan.[41] Holmes-Tagchungdarpa's contribution to this volume exemplifies how colonial period expansions of infrastructure created new conditions of possibility for the development of Buddhist orders, even outside domains governed completely by colonial authorities. As her research shows, the new royal line installed in Bhutan with British support became an avid patron of the Buddhist Tantric order of Shakya Shri, originating from eastern Tibet. Bhutanese royal knowledge and patronage of Shakya Shri's order was facilitated by the expanding infrastructure for travel and print communication in the Himalayan region and across Southern Asia, helping to distinguish the new Wangchuck dynasty from its Zhabdrung predecessor. The chapters gathered here begin to suggest that the changing ecosystems of lineages, orders, and royal patronage found in Himalayan states during the British colonial period offer ground for fruitful comparison with the sultanates and princely states of India, Malaya, and the Dutch East Indies.

ORDERS, PATRONS, AND AUDIENCES

In the Himalayas, as in other parts of Southern Asia, the late nineteenth and early twentieth centuries were marked by an expansion of religious orders within both Buddhism and Islam. Contributions to this volume reveal that in both traditions religious orders developed widening social bases in the nineteenth and early twentieth centuries. In the process, broader segments of some communities developed ideological investments in the structures of lineage and the forms of practice that were associated with particular orders. The chapters that follow explore this expansion of patronage patterns for Islamic and Buddhist orders. In many parts of Southern Asia, royal houses continued to play significant roles in the patronage of orders. However, changes in political formations and communications technologies as well as the collective norms guiding reflections on an individual's obligations vis-à-vis his or her religious tradition all contributed to widening engagement of Buddhists and Muslims in the institutional spaces of religious orders—either as participating members, or as observers evaluating the public profiles and activities of particular orders in their communities.

Thus, in both the Buddhist and the Islamic contexts, the sense of community with a stake in orders, their definition, and their claims to authority grew significantly over the course of the nineteenth and twentieth centuries. Comparative investigation and analysis illuminates the broader ecology of religious organization that informed discrete developments within different confessional communities. This volume as a whole demonstrates that careful specialist examinations of the microdynamics of institutional expansion, sponsorship, devotionalism, and competition can be successfully placed in critical, comparative perspective. Identifying analogous processes in play across both traditions facilitates new understandings of processes of transmission, reception, and localization. It also brings into sharper relief internal reconfigurations of religious institutions and the changing relationships between orders and particular forms of patronage and power. Thus, the contributions to this volume not only provide empirically rich studies of particular religious orders in the history of Southern Asia, but also clearly attest to the benefit gained through more sustained engagement between scholars of Buddhism and Islam. Controlled comparison across religious traditions in this volume has been achieved through three phases of analysis. First, we identified zones of apparent commonality within textual and institutional practice as well as in historical circumstance, searching for cases across the contexts of Islam and Buddhism that appear to bear some family resemblance to one another. A second phase involved the detailed investigation and contextualization of each case identified within the initial comparative field, seeking a more nuanced understanding of these contexts and a sharper analysis of the processes under way within them. Finally, this introduction and the chapters that follow have drawn on the data and interpretations emerging from the second phase to propose a more refined framework of comparison for further investigation within and across traditions. We hope that this work will inspire further comparative exercises of this type, sharpening our understanding of other eras and dimensions of the historical development of these expansive and dynamic religious traditions.[42]

NOTES

1. Fernand Braudel, *The Mediterranean and the Mediterranean World in the Age of Philip II* (Berkeley: University of California Press, 1995). The original French edition appeared in 1949, but the work did not appear in English translation until 1972.

2. For a critical overview of such work on the "Atlantic World," see Michael A. McDonnell, "Paths Not Yet Taken, Voices Not Yet Heard: Rethinking Atlantic History," in *Connected Worlds: History in Transnational Perspective*, edited by Ann Curthoys and Marilyn Lake (Canberra: ANU E Press, 2005), pp. 45–62.

3. K. N. Chaudhuri, *Trade and Civilisation in the Indian Ocean: An Economic History from the Rise of Islam to 1750* (Cambridge, UK: Cambridge University Press, 1985); Patricia A. Risso, *Merchants and Faith: Muslim Commerce and Culture in the Indian Ocean* (Boulder: Westview Press, 1995); Thomas Metcalf, *Imperial Connections: India and the Indian Ocean Arena, 1860–1920* (Berkeley: University of California Press, 2007); Sugata Bose, *A Hundred Horizons: The Indian Ocean in the Age of Global Empire* (Cambridge, MA: Harvard University Press, 2009); Sunil S. Amrith, *Crossing the Bay of Bengal: The Furies of Nature and the Fortunes of Migrants* (Cambridge, MA: Harvard University Press, 2013).

4. Anthony Reid, *Southeast Asia in the Age of Commerce, 1450–1680*, vol. 1: *The Lands Below the Winds* (New Haven: Yale University Press, 1988); Anthony Reid, *Southeast Asia in the Age of Commerce, 1450–1680*, vol. 2: *Expansion and Crisis* (New Haven: Yale University Press, 1993); Denys Lombard, *Le Carrefour Javanais: Essai d'histoire globale*, 3 vols. (Paris: Éditions de l'École des hautes études en sciences sociales, 1990); Janet L. Abu-Lughod, *Before European Hegemony: The World System, A.D. 1250–1350* (Oxford: Oxford University Press, 1989); Roderich Ptak, *China's Seaborne Trade with South and Southeast Asia, 1200–1750* (Burlington, VT: Ashgate, 1999); and Angela Schottenhammer, ed., *The East Asian Mediterranean: Maritime Crossroads of Culture, Commerce, and Human Migration* (Wiesbaden: Harrasowitz Verlag, 2008).

5. A comprehensive list of such work would require a series of substantial bibliographies for several subfields and is beyond the scope of this essay. Major works of scholarship contributing to our current understanding of multiple modes of connection across maritime Asia in the areas of literature, art history, and archaeology include Sheldon Pollock, *The Language of the Gods in the World of Men: Sanskrit, Culture, and Power in Premodern India* (Berkeley: University of California Press, 2009); Ronit Ricci, *Islam Translated: Literature, Conversion, and the Arabic Cosmopolis of South and Southeast Asia* (Chicago: University of Chicago Press, 2012); Elizabeth Lambourn, "From Cambay to Samudera-Pasai and Gresik: The Export of Gujerati Grave Memorials to Sumatra and Java in the Fifteenth Century, C.E.," *Indonesia and the Malay World* 31.90 (2003): 221–284; Elizabeth Lambourn, "Borrowed Words in an Ocean of Objects: Geniza Sources and New Cultural Histories of the Indian Ocean," in *Irreverent History: Essays for M. G. S. Narayanan*, edited by Kesavan Veluthat and Donald R. Davis, Jr. (Delhi: Primus Books, 2014), pp. 215–242; Pierre-Yves Manguin, A. Mani, and G. Wade, eds., *Early Interactions between South and Southeast Asia: Reflections on Cross-Cultural Exchange* (Singapore: Institute of Southeast Asian Studies Press, 2011); Himanshu Prabha Ray and Jean François Salles, eds., *Tradition and Archaeology: Early Maritime Contacts in the Indian Ocean* (Singapore: ISEAS Press, 2012); and John Miksic, *Singapore and the Silk Road of the Sea, 1300–1800* (Singapore: NUS Press, 2013).

6. See, for example, Azyumardi Azra, *The Origins of Islamic Reformism in Southeast Asia* (London: Allen and Unwin, 2004); Francis Bradley, "The Social Dynamics of Islamic

Revivalism in Southeast Asia: The Rise of the Patani School, 1785–1909" (Ph.D. diss., University of Wisconsin, 2010); Tansen Sen, *Buddhism, Diplomacy and Trade: The Realignment of Sino-Indian Relations, 600–1400* (Honolulu: University of Hawai'i Press, 2003); Toni Huber, *Holy Land Reborn: Pilgrimage and the Tibetan Reinvention of Buddhist India* (Chicago: University of Chicago Press, 2008); John Holt, *The Buddhist Vishnu: Religious Transformation, Politics, and Culture* (New York: Columbia University Press, 2004); and D. Christian Lammerts, ed., *Buddhist Dynamics in Premodern and Early Modern Southeast Asia* (Singapore: Institute for Southeast Asian Studies, 2015).

7. Peter van der Veer, *The Value of Comparison* (Durham: Duke University Press, 2016), p. 28.

8. J. Spencer Trimingham, *The Sufi Orders in Islam* (Oxford: Oxford University Press, 1971); Alexander Knysh, *Islamic Mysticism: A Short History* (Leiden: Brill, 2000), pp. 169–170.

9. Mark Sedgwick, *The Making and Remaking of the Rashīdī Aḥmadi Sufi Order, 1799–2000* (Leiden: Brill, 2005).

10. Nile Green, *Sufism: A Global History* (Malden, MA: Wiley-Blackwell, 2012), p. 82.

11. Marshall Hodgson, *The Venture of Islam: Conscience and History in a World Civilization*, vol. 2 (Chicago: University of Chicago Press, 1974).

12. See, for example, John Voll, "Sufi Brotherhoods: Transcultural/Transstate Networks in the Muslim World"; Christopher Bayly, "From Archaic Globalization to International Networks, circa 1600–2000," in *Interactions: Transregional Perspectives on World History*, edited by Jerry H. Bentley, Renate Bridenthal, and Anand A. Yang (Honolulu: University of Hawai'i Press, 2005), pp. 30–47, 14–29.

13. See, for instance, T. W. Rhys Davids, *Indian Buddhism: Lectures on the Origin and Growth of Religion as Illustrated by Some Points in the History of Indian Buddhism* (London: Williams and Norgate, 1891), and Max Weber, *Gesammelte Aufsätze zur Religionssociologie II* (Tubingen: J. C. B. Mohr, 1921).

14. Histories of Buddhism often narrate the proliferation of divisions within the *saṅgha* by referring to the emergence of and relationships between "sects," "schools," "fraternities," and "lineages." See, for example, Richard Gombrich, *Theravada Buddhism: A Social History from Ancient Benares to Modern Colombo* (London: Routledge, 1988); Peter Harvey, *An Introduction to Buddhism: Teachings, History and Practices* (Cambridge, UK: Cambridge University Press, 1990); and Rupert Gethin, *The Foundations of Buddhism* (Oxford: Oxford University Press, 1998). "Fraternity" continues to evoke (albeit distantly) the comparative framework of Christian traditions, whereas "school" and "lineage" remain closer to indigenous Southern Asian usage (e.g., *darśana, vāda, paraṃparā*), with differences of emphasis. "School" typically foregrounds doctrinal and philosophical distinctions among specialist groups; "lineage" refers to specialists related through any process of transgenerational transmission. "Order" may also be used to refer to subdivisions of the *saṅgha*, partly to foreground social-historical or historical-sociological comparison to Islam and Christianity (e.g., Anne M. Blackburn, *Buddhist Learning and Textual Practice in Eighteenth-Century Lankan Monastic Culture* [Princeton: Princeton University Press, 2001]). When referring to monastic lineages in what are now Sri Lanka, Thailand, and Burma, scholars generally prefer to use the contemporary emic terms.

15. See, for instance, Ryuichi Abe, *The Weaving of Mantra: Kukai and the Construction of Esoteric Buddhist Discourse* (New York: Columbia University Press, 1999).

16. See, for instance, Anne Hansen, *How to Behave: Buddhism and Modernity in Colonial Cambodia, 1860–1930* (Honolulu: University of Hawai'i Press, 2007); and Patrick Pranke,

"The Treatise on the Lineage of Elders (Vaṃsadīpanī): Monastic Reform and the Writing of Buddhist History in Eighteenth-Century Burma" (Ph.D. diss., University of Michigan, 2004).

17. Indeed, such markers of affiliation are prominently highlighted in traditional biographical literature of Sufis written in the Arabic genre of *ṭabaqāt*. For an English translation of one example in the account of a Sufi from Sumatra active in the Yemeni city of Zabid in the eighteenth century, see R. Michael Feener, "Abd al-Samad in Arabia: The Yemeni Years of a Shaykh from Sumatra," *Southeast Asian Studies* 4.2 (2015): 259–277.

18. Prapod Assavavirulhakorn, *The Ascendancy of Theravāda Buddhism in Southeast Asia* (Chiang Mai: Silkworm Publications, 2010), p. 45.

19. See, for instance, Peter Skilling, "The Advent of Theravāda Buddhism to Mainland South-east Asia," *Journal of the International Association of Buddhist Studies* 20.1 (1997): 1–17; Assavavirulhakorn, *Ascendancy of Theravāda Buddhism*; and Anne M. Blackburn, "Buddhist Connections in the Indian Ocean: Changes in Monastic Mobility, 1000–1500," *Journal of the Economic and Social History of the Orient* 58 (2015): 3. See also the chapters by Alexey Kirichenko, Kenneth Dean, and Amy Holmes-Tagchungdarpa in this volume.

20. A striking example of this reevaluation of earlier views on the subject can be found in the work of Anthony Johns, who published a poignant, self-reflective piece on his own earlier work, demonstrating this change in scholarly perspective on the early history of Islam in Southeast Asia. See Anthony Johns, "Islamization in Southeast Asia: Reflections and Reconsiderations with Special Reference to the Role of Sufism," *Southeast Asian Studies* 31.1 (1993).

21. Michael F. Laffan, *The Makings of Indonesian Islam: Orientalism and the Narration of a Sufi Past* (Princeton: Princeton University Press, 2011).

22. Nile Green, *Indian Sufism since the Seventeenth Century: Saints, Books, and Empires in the Muslim Deccan* (London: Routledge, 2006).

23. Jack Meng-Tat Chia, "Diasporic Dharma: Buddhism and Modernity across the South China Sea" (Ph.D. diss., Cornell University, 2017).

24. Although nothing similar yet exists for the maritime world of Southern Asia that is the focus of this volume, work along these lines has been done for the overland corridors of Central Asia in Johan Elverskog, *Buddhism and Islam on the Silk Road* (Singapore: Institute of Southeast Asian Studies, 2013).

25. R. Michael Feener, "Issues and Ideologies in the Study of Regional Muslim Cultures," in *Islamic Connections: Muslim Societies in South and Southeast Asia*, edited by R. Michael Feener and Terenjit Sevea (Singapore: ISEAS Press, 2009), pp. xiii–xxiv.

26. Blackburn, *Buddhist Learning and Textual Practice*; Anne M. Blackburn, *Locations of Buddhism: Colonialism and Modernity in Sri Lanka* (Chicago: University of Chicago Press, 2010).

27. Carl W. Ernst and Bruce Lawrence, *Sufi Martyrs of Love: The Chisti Order in South Asia and Beyond* (New York: Palgrave MacMillan, 2002), p. 11.

28. Devin DeWeese, *Islamization and Native Religion in the Golden Horde: Baba Tükles and Conversion to Islam in Historical and Epic Tradition* (University Park, PA: Pennsylvania State University Press, 1994), p. 137.

29. Frank Reynolds and Charles Hallisey, "Buddhist Religion, Culture, and Civilization," in *Buddhism and Asian History*, edited by Joseph M. Kitagawa and Mark D. Cummings (London: Macmillan, 1989).

30. See also R. A. L. H. Gunawwardana, "The World of Theravada Buddhism in History: Relevance of a Territorial Category as a Conceptual Tool in the Study of History," in *Dhamma*

Vinaya: Essays in Honor of Venerable Professor Dhammavihari (Colombo: Sri Lanka Association for Buddhist Studies, 2005).

31. See Gregory Schopen, "Archaeology and Protestant Presuppositions in the Study of Buddhism," *History of Religions* 31 (1991): 1.

32. Steven Collins, *Nirvana and Other Buddhist Felicities* (Cambridge, UK: Cambridge University Press, 1998).

33. See, for instance, Donald K. Swearer and Sommai Premchit, "The Relationship Between the Religious and Political Orders in Northern Thailand (14th–16th Centuries)," in *Religion and the Legitimation of Power in Thailand, Laos, and Burma*, edited by Bardwell L. Smith (Chambersburg: Anima Books, 1978); Kanai Lal Hazra, *History of Theravada Buddhism in South-East Asia* (New Delhi: Munshiram Manoharlal, 1982); Jonathan Walters, "Buddhist History: The Sri Lankan Pali Vamsas and Their Commentary," in *Querying the Medieval*, edited by Ronald Inden, Jonathan Walters, and Daud Ali (Oxford: Oxford University Press, 2000), pp. 99–164; and Anne M. Blackburn, "Localizing Lineage: Importing Higher Ordination in Theravādin South and Southeast Asia," in *Constituting Communities: Theravada Buddhism and the Religious Cultures of South and Southeast Asia*, edited by John Holt, Jonathan Walters, and Jacob Kinnard (New York: State University of New York Press, 2003), pp. 131–150.

34. See Jonathan Walters, "Rethinking Buddhist Missions" (Ph.D. diss., University of Chicago, 1992); Anne M. Blackburn, "Sīhaḷa Saṅgha and Laṅkā in Premodern and Early Modern Southeast Asia," in Lammerts, ed., *Buddhist Dynamics*, pp. 307–332.

35. For example, see Matthew Kapstein, *The Tibetan Assimilation of Buddhism: Conversion, Contestation, and Memory* (Oxford: Oxford University Press, 2002); Jacob Dalton, *The Gathering of Intentions: A History of a Tibetan Tantra* (New York: Columbia University Press, 2016).

36. See Sen, *Buddhism, Diplomacy and Trade*; Indrani Chatterjee, *Forgotten Friends: Monks, Marriages, Memories of Northeast India* (Oxford: Oxford University Press, 2013); and Elverskog, *Buddhism and Islam on the Silk Road.*

37. For contemporary developments among the Qādiriyya and the Shādhiliyya orders as they established local forms in more westerly sections of the Indian Ocean world, see Anne K. Bang, *Islamic Sufi Networks in the Western Indian Ocean, c. 1880–1940* (Leiden: Brill, 2014), pp. 47–41.

38. For Buddhism, see Craig Reynolds, "The Buddhist Monkhood in Nineteenth Century Thailand" (Ph.D. diss., Cornell University, 1972); Kitsiri Malalgoda, *Buddhism in Sinhalese Society, 1750–1900: A Study of Religious Revival of Change* (Berkeley: University of California Press, 1976); Anne Hansen, *How to Behave: Buddhism and Modernity in Colonial Cambodia, 1860–1930* (Honolulu: University of Hawai'i Press, 2007); and Amy Holmes-Tagchungdarpa in this volume. For Islam: Werner Kraus, *Islamische mystische Bruderschaften im heutigen Indonesien* (Hamburg: Institut für Asienkunde, 1990); Martin van Bruinessen, *Tarekat Naqsyabandiyah di Indonesia* (Bandung: Mizan, 1992); Sedgwick, *Making and Remaking of the Rashīdī Aḥmadi Sufi Order*; Marc Gaboriau, *Le Mahdi incompris: Sayyid Ahmad Barelwî (1786–1831) et le millénarisme en Inde* (Paris: CNRS Éditions, 2010); as well as the contributions by Torsten Tschacher, Ismail Alatas, and Martin van Bruinessen in this volume.

39. R. Michael Feener, "New Networks and New Knowledge: Migrations, Communications and the Refiguration of the Muslim Community in the Nineteenth and Early Twentieth Centuries," in *The New Cambridge History of Islam*, vol. 6, edited by Robert Hefner (Cambridge, UK: University Press, 2010), pp. 39–68; James L. Gelvin and Nile Green, eds., *Global Muslims in the Age of Steam and Print* (Berkeley: University of California Press, 2013);

Mark Frost, "'Wider Opportunities': Religious Revival, Nationalist Awakening and the Global Dimension in Colombo, 1870–1920," *Modern Asian Studies* 36.4 (2002): 937–967; and Steven Kemper, *Rescued from the Nation: Anagarika Dharmapala and the Buddhist World* (Chicago: University of Chicago Press, 2015).

40. Ian J. Kerr, "Reworking a Popular Religious Practice: The Effects of Railways on Pilgrimage in 19th and 20th Century South Asia," in *Railways in Modern India*, edited by Ian J. Kerr (Oxford: Oxford University Press, 2001), pp. 304–327; and Elizabeth Nissan, "The Sacred City of Anuradhapura: Aspects of Sinhalese Buddhism and Nationhood." (Ph.D diss., London School of Economics and Political Science, 1985).

41. Thongchai Winichakul, *Siam Mapped: A History of the Geo-Body of the Nation* (Honolulu: University of Hawai'i Press, 1994); Toni Huber, *The Holy Land Reborn: Pilgrimage and the Tibetan Reinvention of Buddhist India* (Chicago: University of Chicago Press, 2008).

42. One area of future comparative work that could be particularly fruitful would be debates over projects of "modernizing" religious reform in both traditions—looking comparatively, for example, at developments in Buddhist Burma and Muslim Indonesia in the twentieth century.

2

A ḤADRAMĪ SUFI TRADITION IN THE INDONESIAN ARCHIPELAGO

The Itineraries of Ibn Yaḥyā (1794–1849) and the Ṭariqa ʿAlawiyya

ISMAIL FAJRIE ALATAS

The nineteenth century has been regarded by some scholars as marking the end of the dominance of Sufism and Sufi orders in the propagation and expansion of Islam in the Indonesian archipelago.[1] The end of the eighteenth and the beginning of the nineteenth centuries, however, should not be seen as a mere transitory phase that bridges the period of early Islamization and the era of modern Islamic reformism. To the contrary, this period witnessed consolidations of Islamic thought and practices in the various regions where Islam had been adopted.[2] Such processes were facilitated by the rise in the numbers of pilgrims to Mekka from the Indonesian archipelago, expanding networks of Islamic study centers and circulation of religious scholars as well as dynamic reconfigurations of Sufi "orders."[3]

In this chapter, I examine the role of a Sufi tradition, the Ṭarīqa ʿAlawiyya, in the transmission of Islam in the Malay-Indonesian archipelago at the beginning of the nineteenth century.[4] I do this by focusing on an itinerant Ḥaḍramī scholar, ʿAbdallāh b. ʿUmar ibn Yaḥyā (1209/1794–1265/1849), who visited the Malay-Indonesian archipelago in 1832 and stayed there until 1835. Although recent works dealing with state formation in Ḥaḍramawt have highlighted the crucial role played by Ibn Yaḥyā, not much is known about his sojourn in Java.[5] One reason for this is the scarcity of sources. Neither his hagiography (*manāqib*) nor his biographies (*tarājim*) substantially discuss his visit to Java. To address this lacuna, I reconstruct Ibn Yaḥyā's travel to Java by using available documentary evidence including his poems and epistles.

I will suggest that a reconstruction of Ibn Yaḥyā's Javanese itinerary provides a contextualized glimpse into the development and expansion of the Ṭarīqa ʿAlawiyya in the early nineteenth-century Malay-Indonesian world, one that has implications for our broader understanding of religious "orders" in Southern Asia during the later colonial period. The consolidation of Dutch colonial authority and the defeat of the indigenous political and religious leadership following the Java War (1825–1830) provided Bā ʿAlawī scholars from Ḥaḍramawt the opportunity to broaden their involvement in the region. The travels of Ibn Yaḥyā illustrate the gradual movements of Bā ʿAlawī itineraries into more established stations during a period marked by major sociopolitical reconfigurations. The shifting Islamic landscape that resulted from these political dynamics opened up spaces through which itinerant Bā ʿAlawī scholars were able to transmit their understanding of Islamic tradition in new ways. The hallmark of the Ṭarīqa ʿAlawiyya during this period, as I will illustrate in this chapter, was a spirited sharīʿa-oriented Sufism with a strong commitment to the implementation of Islamic law, the spread of simplified theological and legal knowledge, and the creation of peace and security through what they understood as a strong and legitimate political order.

In this chapter, I adopt Nile Green's definition of a *ṭarīqa* (Sufi "order") as a formal and cultural mechanism of tradition. That is, a *ṭarīqa* is a conceptual and practical apparatus that reproduces standardized and consistent Sufi practice and doctrine through time and space.[6] The notion of *ṭarīqa* enabled the Sufi-oriented Muslims to conceive their doctrine and practices as something inherited, "as a cross-generational system of inheritance" or lineage capable of distinguishing one tradition from another within an encompassing religious community.[7] Positing *ṭarīqa* as a practical mechanism of tradition allows us to trace the changing forms and shapes of a *ṭarīqa* as it encounters novel contexts and challenges in shifting historical contexts. Although participants in *ṭarīqa* (Ar. pl. *ṭuruq*) stressed the reproduction of standardized doctrine and practices within their orders as something inherited through lineal transmission, in actuality, what was reproduced varied across historical circumstances. In the case of the Ṭarīqa ʿAlawiyya in the early nineteenth-century Malay-Indonesian world, this order, or mechanism of tradition, involved three dimensions that I elaborate in this chapter: trade, royal power, and scholarly networks bounded by a shared textual canon. These three dimensions served to promote and reproduce a distinct and standardized sharīʿa-oriented Sufism as a nineteenth-century articulation of the Alawiyyā tradition, establishing a distinct identity that could be accentuated to different degrees across changing historical contexts.

Reconstructing the itinerary of Ibn Yaḥyā from Ḥaḍramawt in South Arabia to the Malay-Indonesian archipelago highlights the need to situate these separate regions as part of a historically cohesive space of diverse mobilities and intercultural transmissions and translations. Following Anne Blackburn and Michael Feener, I use the term "Southern Asia" to describe this "broad transregional geography that transcends the boundaries of modern academic area studies frameworks of 'South Asia' and 'Southeast Asia.'"[8] Whereas Feener and Blackburn define Southern Asia as a region "stretching from India, Sri Lanka, and the Himalayas through mainland Southeast Asia and across the Indonesian archipelago," in this chapter, I extend this useful geographic term to include South Arabia, where Ḥaḍramawt is located.[9] Incorporating South Arabia as part of Southern Asia means situating the former as part of the historical circulation of people, ideas, objects, texts, and practices that made up the latter. As will be shown here, the development of a Sufi "order" like the Ṭarīqa ʿAlawiyya in the Malay-Indonesian archipelago cannot be separated from its contemporaneous development in Ḥaḍramawt and vice versa. This fact in turn reinforces the need to observe (1) the role of itinerant actors—like Ibn Yaḥyā—in forming religious networks that linked these otherwise distant regions and in performing the work of transmission, and (2) the apparatus of religious "orders"—like the Ṭarīqa ʿAlawiyya—in maintaining coherence in what was transmitted across time and space by structuring them in the framework of a lineage.

NETWORKS AND ORDERS

Recent works on Sufism have moved away from the notion of "religious order" that was employed by earlier scholars who analyzed Sufi *ṭarīqa* in relation to perceived similarities between *ṭarīqa* and the Christian monastic institutions of the medieval period.[10] Shahzad Bashir, for instance, opts for the term "network" rather than "order" for its relative neutrality. The notion of "order," according to Bashir, "has led scholars to misapprehend the type of internal cohesion and discipline than can be attributed to the Sufi communities."[11] Bashir's use of "network" to supplant "order" is geared toward understanding Sufi *ṭarīqa* on their own terms as a form of sociality that is historically contingent.

Although the term "network" captures the complex, nebulous, and historically contingent horizontal relations among adherents of a particular *ṭarīqa*, it does not in my view capture the ways in which *ṭarīqa* have created their own modes of *vertical* interaction that have allowed them to produce a sense of coherence across time for their participants. And although Bashir's argument for the importance of embodied beliefs and practices as mechanisms that unite people into a moral community devoted to charismatic exemplars is well taken, religious groups assume a more complex and institutionalized form, such as a Sufi *ṭarīqa*, for example, "when the group finds it needs to acquire a representation of itself that can incorporate the idea of its continuity beyond the immediate context of its members' interrelating."[12] Equally important is the fact that the informal connotation of the term "network" downplays the various techniques of boundary making that have historically been deployed by the adherents of a particular *ṭarīqa* to separate themselves from others. If we seek to comprehend the mechanisms of reproduction and authentication that have enabled each *ṭarīqa* to formulate a lineage that sustains a distinct identity vis-à-vis other *ṭarīqa*, we require an analytical framework that captures this temporal depth, which in my view is not adequately provided by the concept of "network."

I suggest that the notion of "order" should be refined rather than completely abandoned as Bashir suggests. One reason for this is precisely because the term "order" is useful for comparative purposes. It allows constructive comparison across religious traditions that can shed light on the similarities and differences in the features of these traditions. Such features include their organizational infrastructure, conception of affinities, and mechanisms of reproduction, self-representation, authentication, and lineage making. To this end, the case of Ibn Yaḥyā is developed in this chapter to highlight the formal, material, and organizational infrastructure of the Alawiyyā *ṭarīqa* as a religious order. Moreover, I use the case of Ibn Yaḥyā to suggest important features that should be considered in refining and developing further the "religious order" as a comparative category. "Orders" are sustained by networks. Networks, however, are not stable over time, but are defined and organized through mechanisms that establish lineage and historical continuity, including the "chains of memory"—often in objectified forms like shrines or bodies of texts—that establish continuity within the order beyond the interpersonal encounters between its participants.[13] The shape and character of an order's networks at particular moments in time are related to formal, material, and organizational infrastructure within and beyond the order. Even within a single religious tradition, such as Islam, the institutional infrastructure shaping and shaped by orders will differ significantly across time and place. Analytically, the notion of "order" is able to capture the intricate constructions of temporal continuity and geographic connectivity that enabled each tradition to develop a distinct lineage and coherent identity. Employing this concept, in turn, allows us to compare similar mechanisms across different religious traditions. With this in mind, let us now turn to Ibn Yaḥyā.

IBN YAḤYĀ AND THE ṬARĪQA ʿALAWIYYA IN ḤAḌRAMAWT

Ibn Yaḥyā was born in the town of Ghuraf āl-Shaykh—a settlement founded by his ancestor Shaykh b. Aḥmad ibn Yaḥyā—on 20 Jumād I 1209 (December 13, 1794).[14] He studied under his parents and two maternal uncles, Ṭāhir (d. 1229/1814) and ʿAbdallāh b. Ḥusayn ibn Ṭāhir (d. 1272/1855). It was ʿAbdallāh who first formally initiated him into the Ṭarīqa ʿAlawiyya. Ibn Yaḥyā also studied under influential Bā ʿAlawī scholars of Ḥaḍramawt, including ʿUmar b. Saqqāf al-Saqqāf (d. 1216/1801) and his brother ʿAlawī (d. 1235/1819), al-Ḥasan b. Ṣāliḥ al-Baḥr al-Jufrī (d. 1273/1856), and Aḥmad b. ʿUmar ibn Sumayṭ (d. 1258/1842).[15] His teachers from among the non–Bā ʿAlawī Ḥaḍramī scholars included ʿAbdallāh b. Aḥmad Bā Sawdān (d. 1266/1849) and ʿAbdallāh b. Saʿad ibn Sumayr (d. 1262/1846).[16] Ibn Yaḥyā also studied with ʿAbd al-Raḥmān b. Sulaymān al-Ahdal (d. 1250/1834) in Zabīd, Yemen, and ʿUmar b. ʿAbd al-Karīm b. ʿAbd al-Rasūl al-Aṭṭār (d. 1249/1833) in Mekka.

Ibn Yaḥyā's biographical account illustrates how the transmission of Islamic knowledge and practices in Ḥaḍramawt took place in informal study circles that revolved around a particular teacher.[17] There is no mention of Ibn Yaḥyā enrolling in a formal educational institution or in Sufi lodges (*zawāyā; arbiṭa*) despite their existence throughout South Yemen since the seventh/thirteenth century.[18] In Ḥaḍramawt, however, the first formal educational institution was only founded as late as 1878.[19] Ibn Yaḥyā's initiation into the *ṭarīqa* was thus accomplished by studying with and being in the company of scholars who had been initiated into the *ṭarīqa* by their predecessors. The education also involved visiting the tombs and mosques of the Bā ʿAlawī predecessors, where Sufi audition and concert (*samāʿ*) were performed on a regular basis.[20] In the absence of formal educational institutions or Sufi lodges, such practices enabled scholars like Ibn Yaḥyā to conceive the standardized Islamic doctrines and practices he was immersed in as something coherent and inherited through lineal transmission, thereby providing them with temporal depth and distinct genealogical identity.

The hagiography describes how the young Ibn Yaḥyā traveled from one place to another to read texts under different scholars, all of whom had their own followings. From these scholars he acquired the proper authorizations (*ijāza*) and initiations into the *ṭarīqa* (*taḥkīm*), providing him with tangible links to previous masters that also created social bonds with his fellow students. The Ṭarīqa ʿAlawiyya in Ḥaḍramawt did not, however, develop the elaborate economic and institutional structures that characterized large organized Sufi orders found in some other areas of the Muslim world. According to Alexander Knysh, this may be attributable to a "lack of resources on the part of Yemeni ruling elites" that barred the rulers from endowing Sufi lodges and economic foundations for the growth of the *ṭarīqa*.[21] In addition, intrinsic political instability and fragmentation due to the absence of a powerful centralized political order may have contributed to this reality.[22] Under such conditions, formal elements like the bond of allegiance (*ʿuqda*) between masters and disciples together with chains of initiations (*silsila*) functioned to generate a sense of both vertical and horizontal identity and solidarity among the initiates. Among the Bā ʿAlawīs, such formal elements intensified vertical and horizontal connections that were already present through kinship ties.

By studying with the leading scholars of his day, Ibn Yaḥyā concurrently formed his spiritual connection to the deceased scholars through grave visitations and was gradually able to emerge as an important node in the intellectual genealogy of the Ṭarīqa ʿAlawiyya himself. The scholar ʿAydarūs b. ʿUmar al-Ḥabashī (d. 1314/1896)—author of the *ʿIqd al-yawāqīt* (A knot of rubies), a compilation of the initiatory chains of the Ṭarīqa ʿAlawiyya—listed Ibn Yaḥyā as one of the nineteen crucial nodes that linked Bā ʿAlawī scholars of the eighteenth century to those of the nineteenth and twentieth centuries. Al-Ḥabashī described how he studied several texts under Ibn Yaḥyā's guidance, including the legal primer *al-Minhaj* of the Syrian jurist al-Nawāwī (d. 676/1278) and the Bā ʿAlawī Sufi manual *Fath al-khallāq* of ʿAbd al-Raḥman b. ʿAbdallāh

Bilfaqīh (d. 1162/1748). Ibn Yaḥyā initiated al-Ḥabashī into the *ṭarīqa* in 1845 and renewed the initiation in 1848 at the mausoleum of the eponymous ancestor of the Bā ʿAlawī. He also gave al-Ḥabashī the authorization to recite a collection of Bā ʿAlawī litanies and prayers (*adhkār wa awrād*) compiled by Ibn Yaḥyā's teacher and uncle Ṭāhir.[23]

Al-Ḥabashī's account reveals the dynamics of educational practice and ritual socialization among the Bā ʿAlawī in early nineteenth-century Ḥaḍramawt. Learning consisted mainly of reading Islamic legal texts in conjunction with Bā ʿAlawī Sufi manuals under the direction of senior scholars, who in turn bestowed the *licentia docendi* (*ijāza*) to the students. In some cases, it also involved initiation into the *ṭarīqa*, usually formalized by the bestowal of a cloak of investiture (*khirqa*).[24] Equally important were visits to the graves of those perceived to be the luminaries of the *ṭarīqa*. The *ṭarīqa* also stressed the recitations of litanies and prayers, usually compiled and organized by the Bā ʿAlawī predecessors to facilitate guided ritual recitations. Together with other formal elements, these litanies served as proprietary practices that differentiated the adherents of the *ṭarīqa* from other Muslims. The *ṭarīqa* therefore provided an institutional rubric binding a historical community—consisting of both the dead and the living—through a sense of shared canonical texts, practices, rituals, sacred spaces, and litanies. These elements were reproduced through a chain of master-disciple relationships, thereby forming a perceivable lineage and historical continuity with clear boundaries.

Most of Ibn Yaḥyā's teachers were working under the reformed paradigm of the *ṭarīqa* set by the influential eighteenth-century scholar ʿAbdallāh b. ʿAlawī al-Ḥaddad (d. 1132/1720). Motivated by a drive to reform society, al-Ḥaddād reshaped the teachings of the *ṭarīqa* from their earlier emphasis on individual devotional efforts into a set of moral and ethical guidelines for both the elites and the masses.[25] Following al-Ḥaddād, the *ṭarīqa* in the early nineteenth century was marked by a combination of the commitment to the sacred law and its implementation, the spread of simplified legal and theological knowledge, and the creation of peace and security through a strong and legitimate political order. Such a vision was by no means unique to the Ṭarīqa ʿAlawiyya. In fact, since at least the sixteenth century, different Sufi orders placed a great emphasis on the law-abiding moral rectitude of the Sufis as a social role model for Muslims in general, an emphasis that made Sufism attractive to state administrators. Sufism as it developed in different parts of the Muslim world at that time had grown into "a powerful idiom of collective organization and communal solidarity," which went hand in hand with the systematic attempts of several Islamic polities to demote "the nomadic, charismatic, and 'anarchistic' Sufism associated with rural tribal groups."[26] The reformed paradigm of al-Ḥaddād should therefore be situated in relation to these broader developments.

Ibn Yaḥyā himself was known for his mastery of Islamic law, especially the Shāfiʿī legal school.[27] Appointed as the mufti of Ḥaḍramawt at a relatively young age, Ibn Yaḥyā emphasized the learning and teachings of Islamic law as the most crucial step to the attainment of a higher spiritual state.[28] Rather than seeing the law and Sufism as two different entities, he posited Sufism as an intensification of the law ultimately geared toward emulation of the Prophet, a position that had a long precedent in the history of Sufism. In Ibn Yaḥyā's view, spiritual wayfaring is a process of emulating the Prophet and, as such, knowing the correct forms of practices pursued along this path constitutes the first crucial step.

In Ḥaḍramawt the Ṭarīqa ʿAlawiyyā developed as sporadic kinship and scholarly networks. Rather than seeing it as an exclusive Sufi fraternity that emerged from a particular lodge, it is more accurate to comprehend the *ṭarīqa* as a mechanism of tradition sustained by a dispersed network of master-disciple relationships devoted to the promotion of a sharīʿa-oriented Sufism. This mechanism of tradition involved rituals, sacred spaces, and liturgies to develop concrete bonds of vertical and horizontal connectivity. It also comprised formal apparatuses including *ʿuqda* (pledge of allegiance between a disciple and his or her Sufi master), *khirqa* (ritual robe of investiture, usually of distinctive design or color), and *silsila* (chain of spiritual genealogy of master-disciple links), all of which functioned to constitute its discursive boundaries and define its historical and lineal identity. The shape and character of a particular *ṭarīqa*, however, was also intricately linked to the formal, material, and organizational infrastructure available to it at a particular time or in a particular region. In what follows, I will turn to Ibn Yaḥyā's travel to the Indonesian archipelago to examine the development of the Ṭarīqa ʿAlawiyyā in that region.

ISLAM, TRADE, AND POLITICS IN THE INDONESIAN ARCHIPELAGO

Beginning as early as the seventeenth century, the Bā ʿAlawīs began to emigrate in increasing numbers to different places in Southern Asia, including India, Malaya, and the Indonesian archipelago.[29] Internal strife and limited opportunities in Ḥaḍramawt together with the ample economic opportunities abroad drove many Bā ʿAlawī to leave their homeland. Thriving port cities including Malacca, Aceh, and several Javanese port cities became the preferred destinations for many. These cities became the bases from which the migrants traveled both inland and to other islands, where they established trading ventures. Before the consolidation of British and Dutch colonization, the Bā ʿAlawīs had already established themselves in prominent positions in the regions, with some even assuming the position of sultans.[30]

Advances in maritime transportation in the early nineteenth century resulted in the increasing presence of Ḥaḍramī Arabs in the region.[31] The sphere of Ḥaḍramī mercantile activities was for the most part centered on the sea and the littorals. Shipping was their dominant economic activity until the middle of the nineteenth century. Beginning in the mid-1750s, Ḥaḍramīs specialized in sailing from Java to Palembang and Malacca, with an average ship size of over fifty tons. William G. Clarence-Smith has noted that "from 22% of the registered tonnage of square-rigged ships in 1820, Arabs went to just over 50% in 1850, compared to 29% for the Chinese, 9% for the Dutch, 9% for the British, and 3% for 'natives.'"[32] This expanding world of Ḥaḍramī merchants provided the foundation for the expansion of the Ṭarīqa ʿAlawiyya, as will be shown in the next section.

When Ibn Yaḥyā arrived in Java in 1833, the island had just recovered from an extended war between the composite forces that made up the supporters of Prince Dipanegara and the Dutch colonial regime.[33] The Java War had begun in 1825 and ended in 1830 with the victory of the colonial forces. The conclusion of the war left the colonial regime with no serious competitor to its increasing power, allowing it to refocus on profit acquisition. The new governor general, Johannes van den Bosch (d. 1844), enacted an agricultural reform plan to facilitate the extraction of agricultural products from Java in quantities and at prices that would make the Netherlands Europe's biggest supplier of tropical products, especially coffee.[34] The cultivation system helped the Dutch to rebuild Holland's economy following the ravages of the Napoleonic war and the Belgian secessionists. In Java, it led to a neofeudalization, converting and buttressing a *priyayi* class of Javanese elites to colonial intermediaries.[35]

The monetization of the agricultural economy resulted in flourishing trade, which then led to an increase in the number of Javanese pilgrims to Mekka.[36] By the 1850s and 1860s, an average of approximately 1,600 pilgrims set out from the Netherlands Indies annually, despite the colonial authority's attempt to discourage them from going.[37] In Mekka, they were exposed to diverse visions of Islamic reform and the revival movements of the early nineteenth century. On their return to Java, many of these pilgrims challenged the social positions of established rural teachers and attempted to carve a niche for themselves and their enthusiastic transmission of what they had learned in Mekka to their fellow Javanese Muslims. Nineteenth-century Java was a conflictual and competitive "religious marketplace" where competing visions of Islam vied against each other while state patronage and resources were rapidly diminishing.[38]

One Islamic vision gaining ground during the period was sharīʿa-oriented Sufism. By the early 1800s, the works of Egyptian Sufi-oriented scholars, emphasizing the dissemination of simplified texts on legal and ethical guidance, had begun to replace the earlier Medinese tradition of Sufism with its emphasis on Sufi philosophical teachings.[39] This new trend worked to restrict the dissemination of the more speculative Sufi treatises to a small religious elite, while laying the foundation for what later became the standard Islamic curriculum in Java and across other areas of the Indonesian archipelago. This curriculum situates a thorough immersion in relatively simplified legal and theological tradition under the guidance of a competent teacher as a prerequisite to mystical training. The gradual process of curricular standardization in turn demanded a cohort of trained scholar-instructors.

The dissemination of this sharīʿa-oriented Sufism was facilitated by the emergence of new Islamic educational institutions, the *pesantren* (rural Islamic religious schools), across Java. The aftermath of the Java War witnessed the movement of Muslim scholars—many of whom were involved with the insurrection—away from the royal court into the countryside and the littoral, resulting in the rapid increase of new *pesantren*.[40] According to the colonial survey of education in Dutch Java, Cirebon, Semarang, and Surabaya had the largest number of *pesantren*. In 1831, Cirebon had 190 with a total of nearly 2,800 pupils; Semarang had 180 with a total of almost 3,000; and Surabaya, a total of 2,600 pupils.[41] The Great Post Road, linking the western to the eastern tip of Java, was completed in 1808, facilitating greater communication between *pesantren* and allowing students to move more easily from one institution to another.[42] These *pesantren* served as the nodes of intellectual exchanges through which a new Islamic curriculum—based on sharīʿa-oriented Sufism—was developed.

Central to this emerging Islamic vision was an insistence on the performance of the five daily prayers along with heightened observation of other "pillars of Islam." These practices, according to Ricklefs, became key elements during this period differentiating the reformed Muslims from the adherents of the prior and long-established Islamic tradition in Java. Ricklefs argues that among the adherents of the old religious tradition—what he describes as "the mystic synthesis"—"those who practiced the 'perpetual *salat* [prayer]' did not see a need to perform 'the (ordinary) *salat*' with ablutions." [43] Ibn Yaḥyā should be placed within the development of this diverging vision of a reformed Islam that historians like Ricklefs and Laffan have detailed. As noted above, Bā ʿAlawī Sufi scholars of Ḥaḍramawt, including Ibn Yaḥyā himself, were influenced by the wider turn of Sufi thought in the Middle East toward legal-oriented Sufism.

The itineraries of wandering Ḥaḍramī scholars like Ibn Yaḥya should therefore be situated alongside the expansion of trade networks and other Sufi traditions that paved the way for the emergence of a new vision of sharīʿa-oriented Islam. At the same time, such a dynamic landscape was often marked by conflicts, contestations, and competitions among different scholars representing different Sufi traditions. As such, a distinct religious order like the Ṭarīqa ʿAlawiyya should not be examined in isolation from other intellectual developments in overlapping networks within the encompassing religious community of Javanese Islam. With this shifting historical context in mind, I will now turn to the three dimensions of the Ṭarīqa ʿAlawiyya in the early nineteenth-century Indonesian archipelago that I have identified through my reconstruction of Ibn Yaḥyā's journey, namely, trade, royal power, and scholarly networks bound by a shared canon of texts. I will illustrate how these three dimensions served to create and reproduce a distinctly Bā ʿAlawī vision of a standardized sharīʿa-oriented Sufism.

TRADE

When Ibn Yaḥyā traveled to Singapore in 1832, he was entering the expanding and prosperous world of the Ḥaḍramī diaspora. Since its establishment in 1819, Singapore had attracted merchants from various ethnic communities, including Ḥaḍramīs from all over Malaya and the Indonesian archipelago. Among them was the wealthy Bā ʿAlawī merchant ʿUmar b. ʿAlī al-Junayd (d. 1269/1852), with whom Ibn Yaḥyā stayed during his sojourn in the port city. Al-Junayd had come to Singapore from Palembang shortly after Raffles established Singapore. He brought his accrued wealth from Sumatra and invested in Singapore, buying lands and developing properties that led to the substantial expansion of his family's fortune. He built what today is known as the first mosque in downtown Singapore in 1820. He was also in the habit of sending money for the maintenance and renovation of the tombs and mosques of the Bā ʿAlawī ancestors.[44] Al-Junayd's wealth together with his philanthropic passion and enthusiasm for the Ṭarīqa ʿAlawiyya attracted several members of the Ḥaḍramī scholarly elites to Singapore. It is no surprise that al-Junayd became Ibn Yaḥyā's destination in Singapore.

Among the Ḥaḍramī scholarly elites in Singapore who revolved around al-Junayd was the jurist Sālim b. ʿAbdallāh ibn Sumayr (d. 1853). Ibn Sumayr had migrated to Singapore several years before Ibn Yaḥyā and had begun teaching there, presumably with the financial support of al-Junayd. His study circle attracted advanced students from Singapore and Java.[45] Ibn Sumayr was a close friend of Ibn Yaḥyā; the former's father was one of the latter's teachers. Ibn Sumayr had traveled to the Hijāz and India before settling down in Batavia and Singapore. He was the author of a legal abridgment (*mukhtaṣar*), the *Safīnāt al-najāḥ* (Ark of salvation), which became popular in Southeast Asia as a basic primer for the study of Islamic law. This short text continues to be studied in Islamic boarding schools across Java today.[46] Ibn Sumayr was also known for his active condemnation of Sufi teachers who initiated "ignorant masses" into their *ṭarīqa* without basic knowledge of Islamic law. While such a position exemplified the reformed paradigm of the Ṭarīqa ʿAlawiyya, it also provided incoming Ḥaḍramī scholars with the necessary discursive arsenal to criticize other Sufi orders active in the religious marketplace of the early nineteenth-century Malay-Indonesian archipelago. At the same time, it allowed scholars like Ibn Yaḥyā and Ibn Sumayr to introduce their *ṭarīqa* as being strictly based on Prophetic teachings. Accessible Ḥaḍramī legal primers, like that of Ibn Sumayr, gradually became popular all over Malaya and the Indonesian archipelago and more so as Singapore became a major center of Islamic publication in the late nineteenth and early twentieth centuries.[47] These texts constituted one way through which the Bā ʿAlawī vision of sharīʿa-oriented Sufism spread in the region.

Apart from establishing connection with the wealthy Ḥaḍramī community of Singapore, Ibn Yaḥyā also visited the Ḥaḍramī merchant elites of Java.[48] Among the poems he wrote during his sojourn in Java were four poems naming and dating the construction of new boats owned by Ḥaḍramī merchants in Surabaya.[49] Interestingly, Ibn Yaḥyā named these vessels after Bā ʿAlawī saints. In one poem, he named a vessel *al-Saqqāf*, adding that "the named will be under the protection of the name," referring to the Bā ʿAlawī saint ʿAbd al-Raḥmān b. Muḥammad al-Saqqāf (d. 819/1416), who instituted many of the ritual practices of the Ṭarīqa ʿAlawiyya.[50] Ibn Yaḥyā also used these poems to counsel the owners of the vessels in basic Islamic teachings, especially on spending their accrued wealth in accordance with the teachings of the *ṭarīqa*. Designating trading vessels with the names of Bā ʿAlawī saints established historical connections between the boats, their owners, the wealth that these boats generated, and the saints' tombs in Ḥaḍramawt. Like the tombs, the boats constituted "chains of memory" that produced a sense of historical continuity. This historical connection in turn provided the trajectory through which profits generated by the boats could be channeled into the maintenance of the *ṭarīqa*'s infrastructure, such as the conservation of al-Saqqāf's tomb in Ḥaḍramawt. It allowed the reproduction of the Bā ʿAlawī saints' memory among the merchant elites, establishing semiotic ties that diachronically connected them to the saints. Such a practice also reproduced horizontal connectivity in the form of network and social bonds among these merchants and other adherents of the *ṭarīqa*, including scholars like Ibn Yaḥyā and their brethren in Ḥaḍramawt. Just as an initiation ceremony *formally* inducts a living body into a religious order and adopts him or her into its lineage, such symbolic gestures *formally* imbued these vessels with clear pedigrees, thereby repositioning them as the material apparatus of the *ṭarīqa*. Such activities exemplify the process identified earlier in this chapter in which the shape of a religious order, in this case the Ṭarīqa ʿAlawiyya, at particular moments owes much to the available material and organizational infrastructure in which it functions, which, in turn, allows for different practices of lineage making.

The expanding and prosperous world of the Ḥaḍramī economic diaspora, therefore, constituted one dimension of the Ṭarīqa ʿAlawiyya in this period. It acted as an important mechanism of tradition that allowed the reproduction of a standardized Bā ʿAlawī Sufi practice and doctrine with a distinct historical identity and lineage. The Ḥaḍramī merchants assumed the role of patrons for traveling Bā ʿAlawī scholars like Ibn Yaḥyā and Ibn Sumayr, who then articulated the sharīʿa-oriented doctrines and practices of Bā ʿAlawī Sufism. Financially supported by the Ḥadramī merchant elites, these scholars were able to provide spiritual guidance, instructing these merchant families and other Muslims in the basic teachings of the *ṭarīqa*. Although today legal abridgments like *The Ark of Salvation* are used in Islamic boarding schools throughout the Indonesian archipelago, it may also be the case that they were initially composed to provide accessible teachings of the *ṭarīqa* to these merchant elites and their families. Proper education for the children of these merchant elites seems to have been a central preoccupation of Ibn Yaḥyā. In a poem written during his stay in Singapore, Ibn Yaḥyā implores al-Junayd to send his children to Ḥaḍramawt for proper education that they might become acquainted with the *ṭarīqa* of their ancestors.[51] Without proper education and ritual socialization, it was feared that the children of these wealthy Ḥaḍramī merchants would lose their attachment to the *ṭarīqa*.

At the same time, interactions between traveling scholars and the Ḥaḍramī merchant elites reshaped the *ṭarīqa*. Such networks allowed the construction of new material infrastructures, like merchant boats, that were mechanisms for the identification and unification of the order. Whereas some Sufi orders during this era were characterized by landholdings, lodges, and caravanserais, Bā ʿAlawī sharīʿa-oriented Sufism depended on a different kind of infrastructure, the multilocal and prosperous world of the Ḥaḍramī economic diaspora and its merchant patrons. For merchant elites and their families, the Ṭarīqa ʿAlawiyya and connections to its scholarly elites offered a sense of prestigious history, inherited tradition, social bonds, and translocal geographic connectivity. These provided a distinct lineage and coherent identity, thereby differentiating them from other merchant communities, Muslim and non-Muslim.

ROYAL POWER

As previously noted, the aftermath of the Java War witnessed the movement of Muslim scholars away from the royal courts and into rural Islamic religious schools (Jv. *pesantren*). This shift provided an opportunity for Ḥaḍramī scholars to take over prominent religious positions, which would enable them to extend their influence through attaining prominent positions within the reconfiguration of courts of Southeast Asian sultanates in the colonial period. There is a long historical precedent attesting to the relationship between Sufi *ṭarīqa* and ruling structures. Sufi *ṭarīqa* have historically been able to develop their institutional structure through royal patronage. Rulers have traditionally sought legitimacy through the patronage of influential Sufi scholarly families who held sway among the populace. These rulers acted as grantors of pious endowments (*waqf*) supporting the infrastructural development of *ṭarīqa*. They also accorded Sufi scholars prominent posts in the bureaucratic administration. These scholars in turn connected sultans to wider Islamic intellectual currents and enhanced their positions as legitimate leaders of their communities.[52]

Such dynamics are clearly articulated in the letters that Ibn Yaḥyā wrote to local rulers in the Indonesian archipelago. The compilation of Ibn Yaḥyā's correspondence includes three extant letters addressed to different rulers. The first was addressed to the Bā ʿAlawī sultan Uthmān b. ʿAbd al-Raḥmān al-Qadrī of Pontianak, Borneo. The second letter was addressed to the Pakunataningrat, the hereditary ruler of Sumenep on the island of Madura, off the northeast coast of Java. A third was addressed to Sultan ʿAbd al-Qādir b. ʿAbd al-Raḥmān Tjakraadiningrat II (d. 1847) of Bangkalan, also on Madura.[53] As the form and content of the three letters are similar, in what follows I will limit myself to a close reading of the letter written to the ruler of Bangkalan.[54]

Written in Surabaya in 1833, the text is framed as a letter of scholarly advice and counsel (*munāṣaḥā wa tawāṣī*) to a ruler in an epistolary genre that goes back to the classical period of Islam.[55] In the letter, Ibn Yaḥyā explained his motivation for writing to the sultan in such terms:

> And the thought surfaced to address this writing [*al-kitāb*] to your high stature [*ʿalī al-janāb*] to fulfill the task ordered by the Lord of the lords [*rabb al-arbāb*] on those who were given knowledge and the Book [*al-kitāb*] to instruct it to the people and explain it to them [*bayyanūh*] without circumventing or concealing it from them [*yuktamūh*] and to strive to counsel the brethren [*al-ikhwān*] from all the people of the faith [*al-īmān*] especially those with power [*dhā sulṭān*] as stated by the most distinguished creation of the Most-Merciful [*al-raḥmān*]. Religion is counsel [*al-naṣīḥa*] for the sake of God, His messenger, His books, and to the leaders of the Muslims and their common folk.
>
> In that *ḥadīth*, the Prophet specifically refers to the leaders and judges, because when they are counseled, it becomes possible to reform the conditions of both the elites and the masses, thereby perfecting the [social] structure. If one turns away from advising them, then the worst condition will befall the state and its people. So know, may God strengthen and guide you, that our master the Prophet—peace be upon him—initially invited everyone to embrace Islam. He then instructed them to perform prayers and made it incumbent upon them. *But if they repent and establish regular prayers and practice regular charity, then open the way for them* [Q. 9:5].[56]

Consequently, Ibn Yaḥyā continues, it is incumbent upon any ruler to instruct and even to compel his subjects and those under his authority to perform prayers. Failure to do so would result in the calamities experienced by people of the past:

> So it is incumbent upon every ruler to instruct his Muslim subjects who live in his dominion to perform prayers. And to force them if they decline to do so even if they have to be killed, in accordance to what has been explained by the scholars in following the footsteps of the Prophet, and to maintain what has been instructed by his Lord. And verily God commanded us to follow the Prophet and to hold fast to his laws. *Follow what has been sent down unto you by your Sustainer, and follow no masters other than Him.*

> *How seldom do you keep this in mind! And how many a community have We destroyed, with Our punishment coming upon it by night or while they were resting at noontide!* [Q. 7:3–4].[57]

Ibn Yaḥyā further advised the sultan to honor and implement the sacred law, especially the obligation to perform collective prayers five times a day and to have the call to prayer (*adhān*) be clearly heard in the streets and the markets:

> What we requested from your lordship—may God advance his condition and aid his religion by strengthening its pillars—is for you to strive truly with utmost perfection in resuscitating Islam's greatest symbol. And that symbol is the injunction and commandment for both the elites and the masses of his dominion and all of his subjects to perform the five obligatory prayers in the beginning of their times. And that you make the call to prayer manifest and organize communal prayers in every village. Verily, prayer is the pillar of religion. It is a mark that differentiates the Muslims from the infidels. It *restrains from shameful and unjust deeds* [Q. 29:45], elevates the ruler, and affords him victory over his foes. *Allah will certainly aid those who aid his [cause]; for verily Allah is full of Strength, Exalted in Might; those who, if We establish them in the land, establish regular prayer and give regular charity enjoin the right and forbid wrong* [Q. 22:40–41].[58]

He ended the letter with a warning:

> So hasten to this honor [*makārim*] and execute it with strong determination and resolution [*ʿazāʾim*]. Attain aspiration [*al-munā*], esteem, and splendor [*sanā*] in the hereafter and here [*hunā*]. Thank God for what He has bestowed upon you in the form of kingdom and delight [*niʿma*] by upholding what is incumbent upon you in terms of service [*khidma*]. For what is truthfully required from the ruler is the improvement of religion and teaching the ignorant [*juhhāl*] while instructing them to perform righteous deeds [*aʿmāl*]. Verily, if he thanks God by commanding his subjects to pray [*ṣalāt*] and [to observe] all that has been ordained by his Lord [*mawla*], God's bounty will abide with him [*niʿma*] and repel his enemies and those who are envious of him [*aʿdāh*]. But if he becomes lenient in these biddings [*aʿmāl*] and leans toward the path of ignorant kings [*al-mulūk al-juhhāl*], then he jeopardizes the delights to wither [*liʾl-zawāl*] *if you are grateful, I shall give you more; but if you are ungrateful, verily, my chastisement will be severe indeed* [Q.14:7]. So hurry, hurry [*fā al-badār al-badār*] to that which will provide us with pride [*al-fakhkhār*] and complete esteem and zenith [*al-manār*] in this abode and in the final abode [*dār al-qarār*].[59]

Like the other two letters to local rulers, this letter to Sultan ʿAbd al-Qādir of Bangkalan exemplifies an explicit moral discourse communicated eloquently. The potential sting of the advice is removed by the deployment of poetic language ornamented with Qurʾānic verses and rhymed prose. The formal composition of the letter itself is a moral performative, demonstrating the proper way of addressing a ruler. Hence, the letter frames the interaction as that between an Islamic scholar and a powerful ruler, both having moral obligations and responsibilities. Such a framing was especially important when the actual power of local kingdoms was rapidly diminishing in the face of the Dutch colonial expansion. The performative dimension of the letter thus functioned to safeguard the dignity of the increasingly weakened monarchs by fostering particular types of ethical interactions.

Ibn Yaḥyā's correspondence to local rulers can thus be read as attempts to persuade these power holders to implement and realize the Bā ʿAlawī sharīʿa-oriented vision of Islam more forcefully in their dominions. Note, however, that Ibn Yaḥyā did not invite the rulers to pledge their allegiance to the Ṭarīqa ʿAlawiyya. Rather, he was more interested in communicating the practical teachings of the *ṭarīqa* than in dwelling on its institutional structures and composition. His correspondence thus illustrates the crucial point that the dissemination of the Ṭarīqa ʿAlawiyya in the early nineteenth century took on the form of the expansion—ideally with the assistance of royal power—of the sharīʿa-based vision of Islam, which is not necessarily based on formal affiliation to an order. In this fact, we can glimpse an important dimension of the history of Islam in the region that would be difficult to appreciate if one viewed the *ṭarīqa* as an "order" only in the sense of an institutional structure.

Ibn Yaḥyā's engagement with local rulers was thus part of an ongoing effort by the Bā ʿAlawī sayyids to gain influence and position in the region. Indeed there seems to be an increase in their penetration of royal courts in the archipelago from the late eighteenth century onwards. One famous example was Ibn Yaḥyā's contemporary, the Bā ʿAlawi scholar Shaykh Aḥmad Bā Faqīḥ (d. 1289/1872). Born in the port of al-Shiḥr on the coast of Ḥaḍramawt, Bā Faqīḥ traveled to Surabaya before moving to the Maluku Islands to set up trade. He later became acquainted with the ruler of Sumenep, Madura—the Pakunataningrat—who invited Bā Faqīḥ to become the personal religious tutor to his family. Bā Faqīḥ spent twenty-five years in Sumenep, where he commanded considerable influence in the royal court.[60]

Attachment to the royal courts and the ability to influence society that came with it allowed Bā ʿAlawī scholars to disseminate their teachings more forcefully. Although there was certainly a degree of status and financial stability to be gained from being connected to royal courts—even at a time of diminishing royal power—Ibn Yaḥyā's attempt to influence local rulers should also be situated in a longer trajectory of Bā ʿAlawī commitment to the implementation of the sacred law, the spread of simplified legal and theological knowledge, and the promotion of a strong and legitimate political order. Such engagements placed local ruling structures in the service of the Bā ʿAlawī Sufi order. Royal power functions as a significant mechanism for the reproduction and implementation of particular forms of Islamic doctrine and practices. This second dimension of the Ṭarīqa ʿAlawiyya in the early nineteenth-century Malay-Indonesian archipelago is thus marked by engagement with, rather than disassociation from, royal power. As Sufi orders like the Shaṭṭāriya, the Sammaniyya, and the Khalwatiyya were moving away—albeit without fully detaching themselves—from the royal courts and were developing in various sites of learning closer to the general population from the mid-eighteenth century onwards, Bā ʿAlawī scholars continued to make inroads into the circles of the local ruling elites.[61] The sharīʿa-oriented Sufism envisioned by Bā ʿAlawī scholars like Ibn Yaḥyā offered ideological means of reinforcing royal authority. Aside from providing rulers with powerful idioms of collective organization and ruling ideology, as members of wider Islamic scholarly networks, traveling Bā ʿAlawī scholars were, to a certain extent, able to validate their aspiration and claim to the mantle of "defenders of Islam."

SCHOLARLY NETWORKS

The last dimension of the Ṭarīqa ʿAlawiyya in this period was the establishment of Islamic scholarly networks connected by a shared canon of texts. The dissemination of sharīʿa-oriented Sufism in the Indonesian archipelago was facilitated by the proliferation of *pesantren* across the region in the nineteenth century. At the same time, new infrastructure, including the Great Post Road, allowed the intensification of communication between Muslim scholars living in different places. Ibn Yaḥyā attempted to tap into these networks and use them to transmit the Bā ʿAlawī vision of a sharīʿa-oriented Sufism to the broader public.

Such an endeavor can be observed through the *tadhkira* (reminder), he wrote at the request of a number of Javanese scholars who studied with him in Surabaya.[62] This short text illustrates Ibn Yaḥyā's engagement with local scholars and his attempt to redefine the canon of Islamic texts while establishing an intellectual genealogy between local scholars and the Bā ʿAlawī scholars of Ḥaḍramawt. In short, it shows Ibn Yaḥyā's attempt to create another apparatus that could serve as a mechanism for the consolidation of the ʿAlawī order in the early nineteenth century. As this is an important document, I translate it in its entirety:

> In the name of God most Gracious, most Merciful
>
> *O ye who believe! Fear Allāh and be with those who are true* [Q. 9:119].
>
> All praise be to Allāh who has made piety [*taqwā*] as a cause for goodness in this world and the next. God's salutation be upon our master Muḥammad, His prophet and His chosen one [*muṣṭafāhu*], and his elevated

family and companions. This is a reminder from him who is in need of God's mercy, ʿAbdallāh b. ʿUmar, to our brethren, the pilgrims [*al-ḥujjāj*] residing in Surabaya. [They have] requested [from] me this [reminder]. I have seen their commitment to goodness, their acceptance of the truth, and their assistance in reviving the symbols [*shaʿāʾir*] of the religion. May God further them and us in this, and lead them and us to the best path. Know, O brothers, that this religion is built on five things:

First, beneficial knowledge, that which introduces you to your Lord and His commandments and prohibitions; and [teaches] abstention from the world, desire for the hereafter, and humility; and discourages you from great sins, jealousy, envy, the desire for respect in the hearts of men, and being removed from the truth. Any knowledge that results in these [spiritual/psychological] states is beneficial knowledge to our condition and possessions. Any knowledge that does not result in what we have described is harmful knowledge. It will not result in anything in the two abodes except disgrace and decay. This [beneficial] knowledge is divided into two: exoteric and esoteric. As for the exoteric: [it is] the knowledge of the law [*fiqh*]. And among its sources are beneficial books for every seeker: *Mukhtaṣar bā faḍl* and *ʿUmdat al-sālik*, *Mukhtaṣar al-anwār*, and the *Minhāj* of Imām al-Nawawī. As for the esoteric: the *Bidāya al-hidāya* of al-Ghazālī, the *Naṣāʾiḥ al-dīniyya* of al-Ḥabīb ʿAbdallāh b. ʿAlawī al-Ḥaddād, also *Risāla al-muʿāwana* and *Risāla al-mudhākara* by the same author, and the *Minhāj al-ʿābidin* of al-Ghazālī.

Second, teaching this knowledge to those who are ignorant, especially his [al-Ghazālī's] selected writings on creeds [*al-ʿaqāʾid*], the creeds of al-Ghazālī [*ʿaqīda al-ghazālī*], and other abridged treatises on theology such as the *matn Jawharat al-tawḥīd* and *Taʿlīm al-ʿishrīn al-ṣifa*, without learning the [*ʿUmm*] *al-barāhīn*. As for the last book, it is forbidden to learn it, except for those who have mastered several sciences and have the intelligence and acumen as cautioned by the imams, such as al-Ghazālī and Shaykh Ibn Ḥajar. They asserted the interdiction of teaching the book to the ordinary people. And the people of this age are ordinary [*ʿawām*]. We have mentioned earlier the selections of books in the legal sciences and Sufism. However, the novice should start by learning short and gentle abridged manuals. Of particular importance is the *Sullam al-tawfīq* of our master and shaykh my maternal uncle ʿAbdallāh b. Ḥusayn bin Ṭāhir Bā ʿAlawī. Our lover [*muḥibbunā*] Ḥajji Muḥammad Ḥāshim has received the text and we have read it in the Ampel mosque in the presence of our lover Ḥajji Muḥammad Arshad for the most part.[63] Beware, and beware of occupying oneself with learning any knowledge before learning these short manuals, as these texts have collected a lot of important things that have to be put before the others.

Third, being truthful to God with sincerity in knowledge and work. Truthful to God's creations in advising, teaching, and instructing them in the good, while prohibiting them from any evil, first with gentleness and soft speech, then with warnings and reminders, and finally with pressure and anger freed from whims and debased passions.

Fourth, leaving any pretension of being a man of knowledge and positioning oneself as a teacher to the ignorant while having no ability on such matters. As it will only bring calamities to the person and his followers. The Prophet, may peace and blessing be upon him and his family, said:

> God does not snatch away knowledge from the chests of His servants, but He takes away knowledge by the death of scholars, until, when there are no more scholars remaining, the people take ignorant leaders [as scholars]. And these leaders will be asked [by the people], and they will respond without any knowledge, and they will be misguided and misguide others.

This is narrated by al-Bukhārī and Muslim. There seem to multiply in this land those whom the master of all masters [*sayyid al-sādāt*] had warned. Many occupy themselves with teaching and giving legal opinion [*fatwā*] without the necessary knowledge and mastery, resulting in destruction and catastrophe. Many people are led astray because of them, and the sins that result from such confusions remain continuously and accrue upon them even after their death. And among the disasters of those phony men is their preoccupation with learning great tomes that no one has the ability to master except the *ʿulamāʾ* and the erudite sages [*jahābadha al-mubarrizīn*], and as a result they make mistakes in comprehending their intended meanings. This has led to the obfuscation of [legal] boundaries. Thus, what is suitable for them is to occupy themselves with simple texts [*al-mukhtaṣarāt*] so that they can gain some knowledge that will lead them to its conclusions. As such, they will learn what is obligatory for them. And among the calamities is their preoccupation with uncommon problems without any finality. There is no benefit in learning about every situation. They hope that, in discussing such matters in their gatherings, they will be seen as illustrious *ʿulamāʾ*. They do not know that the Prophet—may God and peace and blessings be upon him—prohibited [them] from *al-aghlūṭāt* [irresolvable questions of doctrine]. So beware, and beware [occupying oneself with] such matters, as it constitutes something without benefits [*al-fuḍūl*], which only results in anger and discord. It is an approach by which Satan led people to pride and arrogance.

Fifth, inviting [people] to the collective performance of the five obligatory prayers, calling [people] to it in the markets and streets, and

> reverberating the *adhān* [call to prayer]. Such acts are among the symbols [*shaʿāʾir*] of Islam and *imān* [faith]. Commit to it with perseverance, and invite every Muslim to it. When they gather, teach them interactively, and summarize for them the commandments of the religion. This is because the ordinary people do not benefit from the reading of books. They do not fully understand the arguments and explanations [of these books]. And those who are teaching them [the masses] should approach them in their gatherings, their congregations, their fathers, and their mothers. By doing so, they will revive Islam, and they will gain God's mercy. I ask the almighty God to secure you and us in all goodness, and to protect us from all evils. May God's salutation and blessing be upon our master Muḥammad, his family, and his companions. And all praise belongs to God the lord of the two universes.

The *tadhkira* illustrates another apparatus of the Ṭarīqa ʿAlawiyya in this period, that is, scholarly networks consisting of both Ḥaḍramī and local scholars bound by a particular textual canon that incorporated the works of the Bā ʿAlawī luminaries. Several important points can be adduced from this document. First, the document clearly shows that Ibn Yaḥyā was involved in the establishment of intellectual networks tying Bā ʿAlawī scholars in Ḥaḍramawt with scholars and students in various parts of the Indonesian archipelago, facilitated also by the Ḥaḍramī merchant network discussed above. The document illustrates how he himself had taught the *Sullam al-tawfīq*—a Sufi-oriented legal abridgment authored by his maternal uncle and teacher ʿAbdallāh b. Ḥusayn bin Ṭāhir—to his local students. It is likely that Ibn Yaḥyā was the first person to bring this now popular text to Southeast Asia.[64] Other texts that he recommended for the Muslims of Java consisted mostly of short legal and Sufi texts written by Ḥaḍramī scholars including Bā Faḍl and al-Ḥaddād. He also criticized the established practice of teaching intricate theological texts like the *ʿUmm al-barāhīn* of al-Sanūsī (d. 895/1490). Ibn Yaḥyā was therefore involved centrally in the broader transformation of the Islamic curriculum in Java discussed above. In the period when the teachings of the Egyptian Sufi-oriented scholars were gaining ground in the Indonesian archipelago, Ibn Yaḥyā introduced and disseminated teachings with similar outlooks produced by scholars affiliated with the Ṭarīqa ʿAlawiyya. By transmitting the works of the Ḥaḍramī scholars affiliated with the Ṭarīqa ʿAlawiyya, Ibn Yaḥyā was not only disseminating the teachings of the *ṭarīqa*; he was also forming intellectual ties between the Javanese and the Bā ʿAlawī Sufi scholars of Ḥaḍramawt, thereby establishing a particular lineage that served to define and structure these networks.

Second, while Ibn Yaḥyā was actively propagating the teachings of the Ṭarīqa ʿAlawiyya, he apparently did not take oaths of allegiance (*ʿuqda*) from the people. Although such formal elements have historically functioned to generate a sense of both vertical and horizontal identity and solidarity within a *ṭarīqa*, they were not the only mechanism of lineage formation that reproduces a *ṭarīqa*. It appears that Ibn Yaḥyā's approach to the consolidation of the Ṭarīqa ʿAlawiyya focused on the redefinition of the textual canon used by the order's adherents rather than other mechanisms of social incorporation. In this way, curriculum reproduced a particular and recognizable configuration of Sufi doctrine and practice, one with a perceivable pedigree. It also worked as a boundary marker, defining a textual canon for students of Islamic knowledge to the exclusion of other texts. Such a canon together with establishment of an intellectual genealogy through teacher-disciple relationship facilitated the emergence of a particular kind of religious order. These expanding networks and the proliferating educational institutions that they generated functioned to reproduce a coherent body of religious doctrine and practice. As such, they should be identified as one key dimension of the Ṭarīqa ʿAlawiyya, insofar as they promoted a distinctly Bā ʿAlawī vision of sharīʿa-oriented Sufism even when they did not necessarily involve formal elements of *ṭarīqa* affiliation like *ʿuqda* or *khirqa*.

Aside from propagating a new Islamic curriculum, Ibn Yaḥyā was also involved in the production of simplified legal and theological texts that represented the teachings of the Ṭarīqa ʿAlawiyya. He wrote three short legal manuals on (1) the correct performance (*manāsik*) of pilgrimage to Mekka, (2) the proper etiquette (*ādāb*) for visiting the Prophet's tomb, and (3) the righteous division (*tafrīq*) of alms. He also issued legal opinions (*fatwā*) on various issues he witnessed in the Malay-Indonesian world, including the performance of *dabus*, payment of religious officials, alimony, and the marriage between a woman from the Prophet's family and a non-sayyid.[65] He argued that imitating the dress and language of the colonial rulers did not constitute unbelief as long as no religious commitment was involved.[66] He also composed a short creedal statement during his time in Java on the meaning of the *shahāda*. That short text, titled *ʿAqīda jāmiʿa nāfiʿa* (The complete beneficial creed), was written so as to facilitate oral recitation and dictation in gatherings—thus reflecting Ibn Yaḥyā's injunction to teach the masses interactively and mnemonically. In addition, he wrote a short treatise called *Risāla fī ibṭāl bidaʿmunkarāt* (Epistle on nullifying reprehensible innovations), comprising a diatribe against what he witnessed as erroneous innovations in local commemorations of the martyrdom of the Prophet's grandson Ḥusayn (*ʿāshūra*). In the treatise, he attacked those who demonstrated excessive grief over the event as well as those who were pleased with it. The focus of Ibn Yaḥyā's criticism is on practices such as wailing, outburst of emotion, self-flagellation, and the tearing of one's garments.[67]

The available historical sources do not permit us to fully discern the success of Ibn Yaḥyā's attempt to tap into local scholarly networks. In a period marked by the proliferation of competing visions of Islamic knowledge, Ibn Yaḥyā's vision was certainly not the only one. Ibn Yaḥyā's curriculum resonated with the broader sharīʿa-oriented Islamic visions that were gaining ground during the period, while at the same time incorporating key texts written and lineally transmitted by the luminaries of the Ṭarīqa ʿAlawiyya including al-Ḥaddād and Ibn Ṭāhir. The fact that these texts have been incorporated into the course of study of the traditional *pesantren* hint at the significant success of Bā ʿAlawī scholars including Ibn Yaḥyā in redefining Islamic curriculum in the region.[68] However, the fact that texts excluded by Ibn Yahyā, such as al-Sanūsī's *ʿUmm al-barāhīn*, remain central in the curriculum of the *pesantren* suggests that Ibn Yaḥyā's aims were not completely realized.

In this chapter, I have partially reconstructed Ibn Yaḥyā's sojourn to observe the development of the Ṭarīqa ʿAlawiyya in the early nineteenth-century Malay-Indonesian world. I have shown that the shifting sociopolitical context enabled the gradual movement of Bā ʿAlawī scholars into more established positions. This process was facilitated by the broader rise of sharīʿa-oriented Sufism transmitted by returning pilgrims and scholars who were exposed to the intellectual currents prevalent in places like the Hijaz. This religious orientation was akin to that promulgated by Bā ʿAlawī scholars in Ḥaḍramawt—many of whom studied in the Hijaz, where they were exposed to such currents—and brought to different parts of Southern Asia and East Africa by Ḥaḍramī merchants and itinerant scholars.[69] The convergence of these multiple itineraries resulted in the emergence of a strong vision of sharīʿa-oriented Sufism in the region. Within this complex and competitive religious economy, where different Sufi orders and competing visions of Islam vied against each other for societal influence, Ḥaḍramī scholars like Ibn Yaḥyā attempted to transmit Bā ʿAlawī sufism as encapsulated in the Ṭarīqa ʿAlawiyya.

I have shown that the Ṭarīqa ʿAlawiyya in this period was characterized by a strong commitment to the implementation of the sharīʿa, the spread of simplified legal and theological knowledge, and the promotion of particular forms of political order. As a formal and cultural mechanism of tradition, the *ṭarīqa* functioned as an order, involving formal, conceptual, and practical apparatuses that reproduced standardized practice and doctrine, maintaining consistency and coherence. The *ṭarīqa* enabled its adherents to perceive these intellectual and practice components in the framework of a lineage, that is, as something inherited from previous scholarly generations and thus possessed of a distinct historical identity, differentiated from other *ṭarīqa*. In Ḥaḍramawt, this sense of identity was shaped through kinship and scholarly networks bound by shared rituals, sacred spaces, and liturgies, solemnized by formal elements including *ʿuqda*, *khirqa*, and *silsila* that constituted its discursive boundaries and defined its identity. In the Indonesian archipelago, the Ṭarīqa ʿAlawiyya order retained coherence and distinctiveness within a social ecology markedly different from that of the order's origins in southern Arabia. Three dimensions of the ʿAlawiyya order made this possible: the Ḥaḍramī merchant diaspora, royal power in the archipelago, and scholarly networks consisting of both Ḥaḍramī and local scholars bound by a particular textual canon that incorporated key Bā

ʿAlawī texts. These three dimensions served as mechanisms that promoted a Bā ʿAlawī vision of sharīʿa-oriented Sufism.

The case of the Ṭarīqa ʿAlawiyya developed in this chapter attests to the value of retaining the term "order" as an analytic category. The term allows the development of comparative perspectives on the organizational infrastructure, conception of affinities, and mechanism of reproduction of diverse religious lineages and formations. Such comparisons can, in turn, highlight the dynamic formal, material, and organizational infrastructures that, together with shifting historical contexts, enable a religious order to function across time and space.

NOTES

I would like to thank Sayyid Zayd b. ʿAbd al-Raḥmān ibn Yaḥyā, the director of the Markaz al-Noor Research Center, Tarim, Ḥadramawt, for providing me with access to the primary sources used in this chapter. Webb Keane, Engseng Ho, Nancy Florida, and Nico Kaptein have all read the chapter in draft and provided helpful comments. Ahmad al-Habsyi helped me with the translation of several difficult passages. Last but not least, I would like to thank R. Michael Feener and Anne Blackburn for their critical reading of the chapter and their valuable feedback.

1. See, for example, Clifford Geertz, *Islam Observed: Religious Development in Morocco and Indonesia* (New Haven: Yale University Press, 1968); Christine E. Dobbin, *Islamic Revivalism in a Changing Peasant Economy: Central Sumatra, 1784–1847* (London: Curzon Press, 1983); and Deliar Noer, *The Modernist Muslim Movement in Indonesia, 1900–1942* (Singapore: Oxford University Press, 1973). For more elaborate discussion and critique of this perception, see Michael Laffan, *The Makings of Indonesian Islam: Orientalism and the Narration of a Sufi Past* (Princeton: Princeton University Press, 2011).

2. Peter G. Riddell, *Islam and the Malay-Indonesian World: Transmission and Responses* (Singapore: Horizon Books, 2001).

3. M. C. Ricklefs, "The Middle East Connection and Reform and Revival Movements among the *Putihan* in 19th-Century Java," in *Southeast Asia and the Middle East: Islam, Movement, and the Longue Durée*, edited by Eric Tagliacozzo (Singapore: NUS Press, 2009), pp. 111–134; Laffan, *Makings of Indonesian Islam*, pp. 25–64; Christian Pelras, "Religion, Tradition, and the Dynamics of Islamization in South Sulawesi," *Indonesia* 57 (April 1993): 133–154; A. H. Johns, "Sufism in Southeast Asia: Reflections and Reconsiderations," *Journal of Southeast Asian Studies* 26.1 (1995): 169–183.

4. The Ṭarīqa ʿAlawiyya originated among the Bā ʿAlawī *sāda* (sing. *sayyid*), the descendants of the Prophet Muḥammad who had long settled in the Ḥadramawt valley of southern Yemen. Initially articulated in the thirteenth century by Muḥammad b. ʿAlī Bā ʿAlawī (d. 653/1255), also known as al-Faqīh al-Muqaddam (the preeminent jurist), The *ṭarīqa* combines two spiritual genealogies (*silsila*): that of the Prophet's family (*ahl al-bayt*) transmitted through the Prophet's descendants and that of the renowned sufi master of the Maghrib, Shuʿayb Abū Madyan (d. 594/1198). The *ṭarīqa* provides a particular model of spiritual wayfaring, a set of sharīʿa-oriented guidelines for those climbing the ladder of spiritual stations (*maqāmāt*). Its practical underpinning is articulated in the doctrine of emulating the

Prophet inwardly and outwardly by following the footsteps of his family and descendants, in particular the Bā ʿAlawī. See Ismail Fajrie Alatas, "[al-]ʿAlāwiyya (in Ḥaḍramawt)," in *Encyclopaedia of Islam*, vol. 3, edited by Kate Fleet, Gudrun Krämer, Denis Matringe, John Nawas, and Everett Rowson (Brill Online, 2014), http://referenceworks.brillonline.com/entries/encyclopaedia-of-islam-3/al-ala-wiyya-in-h-ad-ramawt-COM_23830, accessed August 6, 2014.

5. Ulrike Freitag, *Indian Ocean Migrants and State Formation in Hadhramaut* (Leiden: Brill, 2003).

6. Nile Green, *Sufism: A Global History* (Chichester: Wiley-Blackwell, 2012), p. 81.

7. Ibid.

8. See Anne Blackburn and Michael Feener's introduction to this volume in Chapter 1. See also R. Michael Feener, "Issues and Ideologies in the Study of Regional Muslim Cultures," in *Islamic Connections: Muslim Societies in South and Southeast Asia*, edited by R. Michael Feener and Terenjit Sevea (Singapore: ISEAS Press, 2009), pp. xiii–xxiv; Anne M. Blackburn, *Buddhist Learning and Textual Practice in Eighteenth-Century Lankan Monastic Culture* (Princeton: Princeton University Press, 2001).

9. See Anne Blackburn and Michael Feener's introduction to this volume in Chapter 1.

10. For a prominent example, see, J. S. Trimingham, *The Sufi Orders in Islam* (Oxford: Clarendon Press, 1971).

11. Shahzad Bashir, *Sufi Bodies: Religion and Society in Medieval Islam* (New York: Columbia University Press, 2011), p. 11.

12. Danièle Hervieu-Léger, *Religion as a Chain of Memory* (New Brunswick: Rutgers University Press, 2000), pp. 151–152.

13. Ibid., pp. 106–107.

14. ʿAbd al-Raḥmān b. ʿUbaydillāh al-Saqqāf, *Idām al-qūt fī dhikr buldān ḥaḍramawt* (Sana'a: Dār al-minhaj 2005), p. 824.

15. ʿAqīl b. ʿAbdallāh ibn Yaḥyā, *Tadhkira al-aḥya' bi-manāqib sayyidinā wa imaminā al-sayyid al-sharīf ʿabdallāh b. ʿumar bin yaḥyā bā ʿalawī*, edited by Zayd b. ʿAbd al-Raḥmān ibn Yaḥyā (privately printed, n.d.), p. 32.

16. Abdallāh b. Saʿad ibn Sumayr was the father of the jurist Sālim bin Sumayr (d. 1270/1853), the author of the popular text on jurisprudence *Safīnat al-najāh* (Arc of salvation) and a close friend of Ibn Yaḥyā. Today, the text is still in use as an elementary text in *pesantren* (Islamic boarding schools) throughout Java.

17. The summary of Ibn Yaḥyā's life is based on his *manāqib* (hagiography), titled *Tadhkira al-aḥyā' bi-manāqib sayyidinā wa imaminā al-sayyid al-sharīf ʿAbdallāh bin ʿUmar ibn Yaḥyā Bā ʿAlawī* (Reminder for the living with the hagiography of our master and our imam the sayyid and *sharīf* ʿAbdallāh bin ʿUmar ibn Yaḥyā Bā ʿAlawī), written by his son ʿAqīl (d. 1294/1877). The text summarizes the birth, upbringing, education, and teachers of Ibn Yaḥyā. It also illustrates his many virtues and noble characters together with several anecdotes of miracles that he performed. Aqīl concludes the *manāqib* with a detailed exposition of Ibn Yaḥyā's chain of initiation into the *ṭarīqa* together with the chain of his cloak of investiture (*khirqā*). I thank Sayyid Zayd b. ʿAbd al-Raḥmān ibn Yaḥyā for sending me a typescript of the unpublished *manāqib* together with a collection of Ibn Yaḥyā's discourse, correspondence, and poems that he edited and compiled from various manuscripts in Ḥaḍramawt. For a shorter version of Ibn Yaḥyā's biography as well as the biographies of his descendants, see Muḥammad ʿAlawī b. Aḥmad ibn Yaḥyā al-ʿAlawī al-Ḥaḍramī, *Sharaf*

al-muḥayyā fī tarājim ʿadad min ʿulamāʾ wa udabāʾ āl yaḥyā (Tarīm: Tārīm lidirāsāt wa al-nashr, 2007), pp. 25–48.

18. Alexander Knysh, "A Tale of Two Poets: Sufism in Yemen during the Ottoman Epoch," in *Le Soufisme à l' époque Ottomane*, edited by Rachida Chih and Catherine Mayeur-Jaouen (Cairo: Institut française d'archéologie orientale, 2010), p. 338.

19. This was the *ribāṭ* (pl. *arbiṭa*) in Sayʾūn founded by the charismatic Bā ʿAlawī scholar and poet ʿAlī b. Muḥammad al-Ḥabashī (d. 1914). See Freitag, *Indian Ocean Migrants*, pp. 278–281.

20. Engseng Ho, *The Graves of Tarim: Genealogy and Mobility across the Indian Ocean* (Berkeley: University of California Press, 2006), pp. 43–44.

21. Knysh, "Tale of Two Poets," p. 338.

22. Ibid., p. 339.

23. ʿAydarūs b. ʿUmar al-Ḥabashī, *ʿIqd al-yawāqīt al-jawhariyya wa simṭ al-ʿayn al-dhahabiyya bi-dhikr ṭarīq al-sādat al-ʿalawiyya* (Jakarta: privately printed, n.d)., vol. 1, p. 127.

24. For further elaborations on these formal elements of a *ṭarīqa*, see Jamal J. Elias, "The Sufi Robe (*khirqa*) as a Vehicle of Spiritual Authority," in *Robes and Honor: The Medieval World of Investiture*, edited by S. Gordon, (New York: St. Martin's Press, 2000), pp. 275–289.

25. Ismail Fajrie Alatas, "ʿAbdallāh b. ʿAlawī al-Ḥaddād," *Encyclopaedia of Islam*, vol. 3, edited by Fleet, Krämer, Matringe, Nawas, and Rowson, http://www.paulyonline.brill.nl/entries/encyclopaedia-of-islam-3/abdalla-h-b-alawi-al-h-adda-d-COM_24682, accessed August 6, 2014.

26. Green, *Sufism*, p. 175. For this development in the Ottoman Empire, see Cemal Kafadar, *Between Two Worlds: The Construction of the Ottoman State* (Berkeley: University of California Press, 1995). For similar development in the Safavid Empire, see Kathryn Babayan, "The Safavid Synthesis: From Qizilbash Islam to Imamite Shiʿism," *Iranian Studies* 27.1–4 (1994): 135–161. For the Mughal Empire, see Muzaffar Alam, "The Mughals, the Sufi Shaikhs and the Formation of the Akbari Dispensation," *Modern Asian Studies* 43.1 (2009): 135–174.

27. For instance, the *Nayl al-waṭar*, a biographical dictionary of the Yemeni scholars of the thirteenth Islamic century, mentions Ibn Yaḥyā as a scholar and jurist without specifying his role as a shaykh of the Ṭarīqa ʿAlawiyya. See Muḥammad Zubāra, *Nayl al-waṭar min tarājim rijāl al-Yaman fi-l-qarn at-thālith ʿashr* (Sanaa: al-Maṭbaʿa al-Salafīya, 1931), pp. 91–92.

28. Ibn Yaḥyā, *Tadhkira al-aḥya'*, pp. 39–40.

29. For detailed accounts on this expanding world of Ḥaḍramī diaspora in Southeast Asia, see Freitag, *Indian Ocean Migrants*, chap. 1; Ho, *Graves of Tarim*, chap. 6.

30. Ho, *Graves of Tarim*, chap. 6; Omar Farouk Bajunied, "Arabs and the Nation-State in Southeast Asia," *al-Mahjar* 2.1 (1997): 4–6.

31. R. Michael Feener, "New Networks and New Knowledge: Migration, Communication, and the Refiguration of Muslim Community in the Nineteenth and Early Twentieth Centuries," in *The New Cambridge History of Islam*, vol. 6, edited by Robert Hefner (Cambridge, UK: Cambridge University Press, 2010), pp. 39–68; James L. Gelvin and Nile Green, "Introduction," in *Global Muslims in the Age of Steam and Print*, edited by James L. Gelvin and Nile Green (Berkeley: University of California Press, 2014), pp. 1–24.

32. William Gervase Clarence-Smith, "Entrepreneurial Strategies of Hadhrami Arabs in Southeast Asia, c. 1750s–1950s," in *The Hadhrami Diaspora in Southeast Asia: Identity*

Maintenance or Assimilation? edited by Ahmed Ibrahim Abushouk and Hassan Ahmed Ibrahim (Leiden: Brill, 2009), pp. 139–140.

33. Peter Carey, *The Power of Prophecy: Prince Dipanagara and the End of an Old Order in Java, 1758–1855* (Leiden: KITLV Press, 2008).

34. Robert Van Niel, "Measurement of Change under the Cultivations System in Java, 1837–1851," *Indonesia* 14 (Oct. 1972): 89–109.

35. The term *priyayi* originally referred to the younger siblings of the king. Subsequently it came to denote the bureaucratic or administrative elite of Java. See Heather Sutherland, *The Making of a Bureaucratic Elite* (Singapore: Heinemann, 1979).

36. Eric Tagliacozzo, *The Longest Journey: Southeast Asians and the Pilgrimage to Mekka* (Oxford: Oxford University Press, 2013), pp. 63–82.

37. Ricklefs, "Middle East Connection and Reform," p. 114.

38. The term "religious marketplace" is Nile Green's. See Nile Green, *Bombay Islam: The Religious Economy of the West Indian Ocean, 1840–1915* (Cambridge, UK: Cambridge University Press, 2011), p. 47.

39. Laffan identifies the role of traveling scholars like ʿAbd al-Samad al-Palimbānī (d. 1789) and Muḥammad Arshad al-Banjarī (d. 1812), both of whom studied with the Medinese shaykh Muḥammad Samman (d. 1776), as the forerunners of this shift. Samman cultivated links with the Cairene tradition of Sufism that emphasized the writings of the medieval Sufi theologian and jurist Abū Ḥāmid al-Ghazālī (d. 1111) and his Egyptian commentators like ʿAbd al-Wahhāb al-Shaʿrānī (d. 1565). See Laffan, *Makings of Indonesian Islam*, p. 33. On al-Shaʿrānī's role in the reconfiguration of Sufi thought, see Richard J. A. McGregor, "Notes on the Transmission of Mystical Philosophy: Ibn ʿArabī According to ʿAbd al-Wahhāb al-Shaʿrānī," in *Reason and Inspiration in Islam*, edited by Todd Lawson (London: I. B. Tauris, 2005), pp. 380–394.

40. This, however, does not mean that Muslim scholars were not active in the countryside before the Java War. Evidence suggests that they were already spread across the countryside and establishing *pesantren*, like the famous *pesantren* of Tegalsari. Sources like the 1815 *Serat Centhini* suggest that the royal court, the countryside, and Muslim scholars were in dialogue. Similarly, one should not assume that the royal court was not actively involved in the *pesantren* of the countryside. Nancy Florida has shown how several key court luminaries, particularly literati and court poets—including the veritable literati family of Yasadipura—were educated in rural *pesantren*. In addition, when Chinese rebels overran the court of Pakubuwana II in 1742, the king fled the royal court and took shelter with the Islamic scholar Kyai Ageng Imam Besari of Panaraga, East Java. In sum, available historical sources suggest that (1) Muslim scholars were already active in the countryside before the Java War and (2) luminaries from the royal court were not imprisoned behind palace walls. Rather, there seems to have been circulation of people and ideas between rural Islamic establishments and the royal court. Nevertheless, the end of the Java War did result in the proliferation of new *pesantren* across Java. See Nancy K. Florida, "Writing Traditions in Colonial Java: The Question of Islam," in *Cultures of Scholarship*, edited by S. C. Humphreys (Ann Arbor: University of Michigan Press, 1997), pp. 187–217. See also Florida's contribution in this volume.

41. M. C. Ricklefs, *Polarizing Javanese Society: Islamic and other Visions, c. 1830–1930* (Singapore: NUS Press, 2007), pp. 52–53.

42. Peter J. M. Nas and Pratiwo, "Java and De Groote Postweg, La Grande Route, the Great Mail Road, Jalan Raya Pos," *Bijdragen tot de Taal-, Land- en Volkenkunde* 158.4

(2002): 707–725; Pramoedya Ananta Toer, *Jalan Raya Pos, Jalan Daendels* (Jakarta: Lentera Dipantara, 2005).

43. Ricklefs, *Polarizing Javanese Society*, p. 81.

44. ʿAbd al-Qādir b. ʿAbd al-Raḥmān al-Junayd, *al-ʿUqūd al-ʾAsjadiyya fī nashr manāqib baʿdh afrād al-usra al-junaydiyya* (Singapore: al-Mahdudah, 1994), pp. 167–168, 178–180; Ho, *Graves of Tarim*, pp. 82–83.

45. Al-Saqqāf, *Idām al-qūt*, pp. 601–602; L. W. C. van den Berg, *Hadramaut dan Koloni Arab di Nusantara*, translated by Rahayu Hidayat (Jakarta: INIS, [1886] 1989), p. 106.

46. Laffan, *Makings of Indonesian Islam*, p. 48; Martin van Bruinessen, *Kitab Kuning, Pesantren dan Tarekat* (Bandung: Mizan, 1995), p. 122.

47. Azyumardi Azra, *Islam Nusantara: Jaringan Global dan Lokal* (Bandung: Mizan, 2002), p. 141; William R. Roff, "The Malayo-Muslim World of Singapore at the Close of the Nineteenth Century," *Journal of Asian Studies* 24 (1964): 75–90; Michael Laffan, "The New Turn to Mekka: Snapshots of Arabic Printing and Sufi Networks in Late 19th Century Java," *Revue des mondes musulmans et de la Méditerranée* 124 (2008): 113–131.

48. One report from 1848 suggests that the Arab population in the coastal region was not big but was large enough to have significant impacts. In Tegal, for instance, out of a total population of 317,446, there were at least 2,275 Arabs and other Asian Muslims. See Ricklefs, *Polarizing Javanese Society*, p. 81.

49. Ibn Yaḥyā, *Tadhkira al-aḥya'*, pp. 376–381.

50. Ibid., p. 378. For al-Saqqāf, see Ho, *Graves of Tarim*, pp. 43–44.

51. Ibn Yaḥyā, *Tadhkira al-aḥya'*, p. 325.

52. Azyumardi Azra, *The Origins of Islamic Reformism in Southeast Asia: Networks of Malay-Indonesian and Middle Eastern ʿUlamaʾ in the Seventeenth and Eighteenth Centuries* (Honolulu: University of Hawai'i Press, 2004); R. S. O'Fahey, "'Small World': Neo-Sufi Interconnexions between the Maghrib, the Hijaz and Southeast Asia," in *The Transmission of Learning in Islamic Africa*, edited by Scott S. Reese (Leiden: Brill, 2004), pp. 274–288.

53. Arabic letters circulated around the Indonesian archipelago and beyond between rulers who had scribes and translators for such correspondence. Writing a few decades later, the Dutch colonial official L. W. C. van den Berg described how the princes of the Madurese royal family were solidly educated in Arabic. An Arabic speaker himself, van den Berg was impressed by the Arabic proficiency of the Madurese princes as well as the Arabic holdings of the royal libraries. Such a conscious effort to be more attuned to the wider Muslim world had opened up lucrative positions for Ḥaḍramī scholars as Arabic instructors to the Madurese royal families. See van den Berg, *Hadramaut dan Koloni Arab*, p. 108.

54. Claiming descent from the last king of Majapahit, the Tjakraningrat family had ruled Madura since the sixteenth century. In the seventeenth century, they were appointed to govern Madura under the suzerainty of the Mataram Sultanate. Following the Javanese-Chinese War of 1741–1743, Tjakraningrat IV took the opportunity to shake off his vassal obligation to Mataram with the help of the Dutch East India Company (VOC). Recognizing the importance of the alliance, the VOC decided in 1762 to raise the title of Tjakradiningrat V to Panembahan Tjakra-adi-ningrat V. During the reign of Tjakradiningrat VII (1780–1815), the kingdom began to send troops to support the colonial authority on its military campaigns, a practice that continued until the Java War. In 1816, the sultan signed a contract with the Dutch relieving the sultanate of taxation in return for the supply of military manpower. In recognition of their military role, the Dutch reorganized the Madurese troops into a permanent armed corps, the *barisan*, consisting

of infantry, cavalry, and artillery. Despite the general commitment to reducing the power of the sultan, the Dutch continued to confer various decorations and privileges on the Madurese ruler. By the 1820s, the Sultanate of Madura was referred to not as *zelf-bestuurders* (self-administrators) but as *onafhankelijk bondgenoten* (independent allies). The honors, however, were not bestowed purely out of generosity, as successive Dutch authorities wished to prevent Madurese defections in the tumultuous first decades of the nineteenth century. In 1808, Tjakraadiningrat VII elevated his title and prestige to become the first sultan of Madura. His son, ʿAbd al-Qādir, succeeded his father as Sultan Tjakraadiningrat II. See Kuntowijoyo, *Perubahan sosial dalam masyarakat agraris Madura, 1850–1940* (Jogjakarta: Matabangsa, 2002); Heather Sutherland, "Notes on Java's Regent Families: Part II," *Indonesia* 17 (1974): 1–42.

55. For an extended discussion of Islamic epistolary tradition, see Jaakko Hämeen-Anttila, "The Essay and Debate (*Al-Risāla and al-Munāẓara*)," in *Arabic Literature in the Post-Classical Period*, edited by Roger Allen and D. S. Richards (Cambridge, UK: Cambridge University Press, 2006,) pp. 134–144; Samer Akkach, *Letters of a Sufi Scholar: The Correspondence of ʿAbd al-Ghanī al-Nābulusī (1641–1731)* (Leiden: Brill 2010).

56. Ibn Yaḥyā, *Tadhkira al-aḥya'*, p. 209.

57. Ibid.

58. Ibid., p. 210.

59. Ibid.

60. Van den Berg, *Hadramaut dan Koloni Arab*, p. 109.

61. Laffan, *Makings of Indonesian Islam*, pp. 25–39.

62. The original copy of this manuscript is kept in the Markaz al-Noor archive in Tarim, Ḥaḍramawt. I thank Zayd bin Yaḥyā for providing me with a copy of this precious document.

63. In Sufi knowledge culture, the term *muḥibbīn* (lovers) is usually contrasted with the term *murīdīn* (disciples). The former refers to the "untutored enthusiasts" of a Sufi master, whereas the latter denotes the "formally initiated disciples." See Vincent J. Cornell, *Realm of the Saint: Power and Authority in Moroccan Sufism* (Austin: University of Texas Press, 1998), p. 197. In Ḥaḍramawt, the term *muḥibbīn* is also used to refer to the non–Bā ʿAlawī followers and devotees of the Bā ʿAlawī sayyids.

64. Together with the *Safīnāt al-najāḥ* of Ibn Sumayr (see above), the *Sullam al-tawfīq* is one of the two most recited and taught elementary legal abridgments in Java to the present day. Both texts are recited not only in the *pesantren*, but also in neighborhood and village prayer halls (Jv. *langgar*).

65. Nico J. G. Kaptein, *Islam, Colonialism and the Modern Age in the Netherlands East Indies: A Biography of Sayyid ʿUthman (1822–1914)* (Leiden: Brill, 2014), p. 66. *Dabus* is a dance with roots in Sufi tradition common in several places in Sumatra, Malaya, and Banten. The word *dabus* in Arabic means "iron awl with a handle." The Sufi dance was probably called *dabus* because it was performed with sharply pointed iron awls. After reaching a trance-like state, the dancers stab their bodies and arms with the awls without physically injuring themselves. See Jacob Vredenbregt, "Dabus in West Java," *Bijdragen tot de Taal-, Land-en Volkunde* 129.2/3 (1973): 302–320; Martin van Bruinessen, "Shari'a Court, Tarekat and Pesantren: Religious Institutions in the Banten Sultanate," *Archipel* 50 (1995): 165–199.

66. The issue of Muslims adopting non-Muslim dress has long been a subject of intense debate among Muslim scholars. Central to this contention is the definition of *tashabbuh* (imitation) as stated in a saying attributed to the Prophet Muḥammad: "whosoever imitates a particular group, he is from among them" (*man tashabbaha bi qawmin fā huwā minhum*). Some

scholars argue that adopting European dress constitutes *tashabbuh* of non-Muslims and can lead to apostasy. The term *tashabbuh* refers to the adoption of customs and habits that are deemed to be peculiar to a particular group. According to this perspective, the adoption of dietary and sartorial habit constitutes *tashabbuh*. Learning a foreign language, however, does not constitute *tashabbuh*. Ibn Yaḥyā's opinion regarding the imitation of European fashion and language is thus more lenient than most scholars'. In 1904, another Bā ʿAlawī scholar from the same family as Ibn Yaḥyā, who also happened to be one of his students, Sayyid ʿUthmān (d. 1914), authored a small brochure forbidding Muslims from imitating European dress, as by wearing a cravat or necktie. See Kaptein, *Islam, Colonialism and the Modern Age*, pp. 66, 137–138.

67. Ibn Yaḥyā, *Tadhkira al-aḥyaʾ*, pp. 299–304.

68. By the time L. W. C. van den Berg had compiled a list of fifty texts studied in the *pesantren* of Java and Madura in 1887, a clear and consistent program of study was already discernible, albeit with slight variations from one institution to the next. Van den Berg's survey demonstrates that the texts recommended by Ibn Yaḥyā had been incorporated into the established curriculum. See L. W. C. van den Berg, "Her Mohammedaansche Godsdienstonderwijs op Java en Madoera: En de Daarbij Gebruikte Arabische Boeken," *Tijdschrift voor Indische Taal-, Land- en Volkenkunde*, 31 (1887): 1–38. See also Bruinessen, *Kitab Kuning, Pesantren dan Tarekat*, pp. 112–171.

69. For the activism of Bā ʿAlawī scholars in East Africa, see Anne K. Bang, *Islamic Sufi Networks in the Western Indian Ocean, c. 1880–1940* (Leiden: Brill, 2014). For their religious activism in South Asia, see Muḥammad Abū Bakr ʿAbdallāh Bā Dhīb, *Ishāmāt ʿulamā ḥaḍramawt fī nashr al-islām wa ʿulūmihi fī al-hind* (Amman: Dār al-fatḥ lil-dirāsāt wa-l-nashr, 2014).

3

THE ITINERARIES OF "SĪHAḶA MONK" SĀRALAṄKĀ

Buddhist Interactions in Eighteenth-Century Southern Asia

ALEXEY KIRICHENKO

Since the early stages of academic work on Buddhist traditions for which Pāli is a canonical language, the task of analyzing Buddhist monastic orders in specific historical contexts has been a difficult one. Vinaya regulations of monastic behavior and observances that form part of the authoritative collections of foundational Buddhist teachings (*tipiṭaka*) essentially see all ordained practitioners who follow the doctrine and discipline of the Buddha as an aggregate body of monastics (*saṅgha*). Empirical studies, in contrast, identify a multitude of local communities with their respective ordination lineages, practical canons, interpretations of discipline, and so on. As testified by the historical evidence, monastics moved as individuals or in groups within the wider Buddhist world, thus transcending the divide between the two scales of macro- and micro-communities. Yet, for scholars, a significant challenge lies in understanding how these movements worked. That is, how did persons identified generally with the wider Buddhist monastic *saṅgha* also function within and across specific local Buddhist and monastic communities? How did local monastic communities interact with each other? Were there impediments to monastic mobility from one area or country to another?

For earlier generations of scholars, it appears that the very notion of macro-community, an ideal *saṅgha* defined in the Vinaya, created an expectation that encounters between local varieties or branches of the Buddhist monastic order oriented toward a shared Pāli-language *tipiṭaka* would be guided by mutual recognition. This perception was strengthened by several known instances of the reintroduction of higher ordination (*upasampadā*) from Laṅkā to Southeast Asia and vice versa in the second millennium. Thus, in his survey of Pāli literature, K. R. Norman noted that, owing to such imports of *upasampadā* and the transmission of manuscripts, "the traditions of each country have become to some extent interwoven."[1] Addressing Burma's contacts with Laṅkā, U Bokay, Kanai Lal Hazra, and Tilman Frasch laid much emphasis on the argument that both countries relied on each other for monastic ordination and maintained what are rather vaguely called "institutional linkages," "strong bonds," and "close religious ties."[2] Some scholars, such as Niharranjan Ray, Charles Godakumbura, Hazra, and Emmanuel Guillon, interpreted the limited data on monastic reordinations as evidence for the expansion of one subregional *saṅgha*—"the Sinhalese form of Buddhism," or "Mahāvihāra Buddhism"—to Burma and other parts of mainland Southeast Asia after the twelfth century, overtaking other local monastic institutions.[3]

However, more recent studies discussing Buddhist monastic contacts in Southern Asia are much more cautious in their conclusions. In particular, Peter Skilling and Anne Blackburn have argued that monastic lineages that arose as a result of imported ordination invoked their origin as a way to prove ritual purity and efficacy but developed their own independent identities, quite distinct from the monastic communities as practiced and organized at the geographic source of the ordination.[4]

The present chapter focuses on new evidence on transregional ordination lineages in early modern Southern Asia. This new evidence generally supports arguments for independent development (such as those by Skilling and Blackburn), showing that importation of an ordination—an act of using transregional monastic intermediaries to enable local initiators of reordination to start a new monastic lineage—did not necessarily entail the transplantation of the lineage of the intermediary or any features associated with that lineage in its location of origin. Though the transplantation of such external features as forms of dress, monastic administration, educational practice, and textual preferences did occur between monastic communities in Burma, Laṅkā, and Thailand since the late nineteenth century, it would be wrong to assume that such transfers were the norm in the earlier periods as well.

Moreover, movements of Buddhist itinerants between local communities within a wider Buddhist world did not necessarily forge lasting operational ties and networks between these communities. The case presented and analyzed in this chapter suggests that clear distinctions should always be made between different types of transmission and mobility among Buddhists. At one end of the spectrum of possibilities, we find sporadic transmission of objects (such as relics, images, and manuscripts) and persons. Another possibility was religious networking involving more regular communication between different nodes. This communication might include a relatively regular use of imported religious specialists for ritual or prestige purposes without a larger expansion of orders. At the other end of the spectrum, we find lasting forms of transfer, resulting in the spread of common practices and social structures. Though all of these possibilities are found at different points in time and space, one has to be very specific in analyzing the extent of historical monastic interactions.

This chapter follows the definition of Southern Asia as suggested by the editors of the present volume. At the same time, it recognizes that the introduction of such a term is unlikely to exhaust the need for refining historical geographic terminology, since important economic and cultural links existed not only between South and Southeast Asia but between Southeast and East Asia and elsewhere. During the period in question here, long-distance mobility at the scale of the entirety of Southern Asia was extraordinary or even exceptional. Therefore, this space might be called a macroregion made of many smaller sub- and microregions (at the scale of individual polities, principalities, and other historical units recognized by Southern Asian peoples and cultures). In this way, the movements of religious itinerants within this macroregion transcended geographic and polity boundaries. It would perhaps have been recognized as transregional by eighteenth-century Burmese, Thai, or Sinhalese had their conceptual vocabulary included such a term.

My general argument and analysis of mobility of Buddhist itinerants in early modern Southern Asia derives from a case study in the eighteenth-century revival of Buddhist contacts between Laṅkā, Siam, and Burma. It is centered on the monk Sāralaṅkā, a Tai from Tenasserim who was involved in one of the Siamese missions to Kandy in the 1750s that led to the establishment of Siyam Nikāya, one of the three currently major Lankan monastic fraternities. Later on, Sāralaṅkā traveled to Upper Burma and resided there for more than a decade. During that time, he gave at least four or five testimonies on his travels, copies of which remained in circulation in Burma until the late nineteenth century.

Following the travels of an individual actor involved in the transmission of monastic ordination offers a rare perspective on the institutionalization of a Buddhist lineage. Sāralaṅkā's testimonies and the alterations to his narratives made over time provide a striking view of the contingencies accompanying the movement of a Buddhist monk from life within a particular local community to functioning within the wider space of Southern Asia, encompassing several sub- and microregions and cultures. The chapter draws attention to Sāralaṅkā's interstitiality as a social actor and argues that it was hardly unusual or insignificant in its time. As the imperial cultures of the region were exclusivist and conceptually incompatible in certain aspects, the malleability of mobile figures such as Sāralaṅkā proved a valuable asset, allowing royal courts to communicate—and sometimes cooperate—across the greater Buddhist world.

IMPORTING MONASTIC ORDINATION AND THE ROLE OF THE "MISSIONARY"

Sāralaṅkā's travel to Laṅkā occurred as a result of attempts made by the royal court at Kandy to reestablish a formally ordained (through *upasampadā*) monastic community on the island.[5] For reasons that are not clear, from the sixteenth century onwards standard forms of Buddhist monasticism yielded to specific types of nonordained monastic practice. A reformist religious movement led by Välivița Saraṇaṃkara (1698–1778) managed to get the support of the Kandyan court, sending off envoys to Southeast Asia with the help of the Dutch East India Company (VOC). In 1753, a monastic mission sent from Ayutthaya was enthusiastically received by Kandyan king Kīrti Śrī Rājasiṃha (r. 1747–1782) and ordained a large number of monks and novices in different parts of the island. Another mission arrived three years later and might have been followed by a third one in the late 1750s. The interchange of missions between Siam and Laṅkā then stopped until the early nineteenth century.

The reestablishment of monastic ordination and the revival of centralized Buddhist ecclesiastical structure achieved by Saraṇaṃkara and his associates had a lasting impact on Sinhalese Buddhism, monastic education, and textual practices.[6] However, little, if any, of this success could be ascribed to Ayutthayan *bhikkhus* (fully ordained monks) who were invited as officiators to Laṅkā. Besides several names and a few celebratory but vague remarks, Sinhalese and Thai sources mention almost nothing about them. Accounts of Kandyan envoys provide limited information about missionaries that were sent to Laṅkā, concentrating instead on details of the journey, description of the Siamese court, local ceremonies they witnessed, and sacred sites near Ayutthaya.[7] The *Mahāvaṃsa*, a major Lankan chronicle first composed in the early sixth century and supplemented serially, including by a prominent Siyam Nikāya monk in the 1780s, is equally silent on the lineage of Siamese missionaries, as noted by Anne Blackburn.[8]

In a coincidence that is quite telling, a similar lack of interest in profiling the source of imported ordination is also evident in the case of Northern Thai monastic histories tracing the ordination of Thai monks on Laṅkā in the fifteenth century.[9] In the same way, the Amarapura Nikāya, a competitor to Siyam Nikāya established as a result of bringing new ordination from Burma to coastal areas of Laṅkā between 1800 and 1813, cherished little memory of Aggasāra and other Burmese monks who officiated at the ordinations carried out after the return of Aṁbagahapiṭiyē Ñāṇavimala, the first of Sinhalese novices ordained in Burma.[10] In fact, it is only from the second half of the nineteenth century that a substantial traffic of ideas, arguments, and modes of practice as well as lasting forms of communication are traceable between Sinhalese and Southeast Asian monks.[11]

In terms of the distinctions introduced above, the emergence of Siyam Nikāya should be understood as a case in which a transfer of ordination within the Southern Asian Buddhist world occurred without the transplantation of monastic order, lineage, or external forms of monasticism. Blackburn's work shows that the success of a new community was secured by its ability to position itself as perpetuating "pre-existing local understandings of prestigious monasticism."[12] She notes a high degree of selectivity by early leaders of Siyam Nikāya with respect to Siamese Buddhist practices. According to Blackburn, in almost every case, when Siyam Nikāya monks had a choice to make between local ritual forms and expressions (styles of chanting, curriculum, administrative models, and so on) and forms and arrangements recommended or personified by Ayutthaya monks, they displayed a clear preference for local Buddhist traditions.[13] Although manuscripts were brought from Ayutthaya and entered Siyam Nikāya collections, there is no evidence that these texts were used in Kandy according to systems of education and practice characteristic of Buddhist monastic orders at Ayutthaya.[14]

Although the Ayutthayan missions to Kandy appear not to have expanded Ayutthayan Buddhist monastic orders to the island, the testimonies of Sāralaṅkā, a monk involved in this transmission of ordination offer a rare opportunity to examine the personality and subjectivity of historical "missionaries." They also offer insights into the context in which Buddhist mobility in historical Southern Asia occurred and the extent of religious networking that such mobility could support. Moreover, since Sāralaṅkā was not a central actor in Ayutthayan missions (and his testimonies result only from his unexpected subsequent relocation to Upper Burma), his perspective on the Ayutthayan connections to Kandy do not reflect the polemical needs of the Ayutthayan or the Kandyan *saṅgha* but, rather, a more distant perspective on the establishment of Siyam Nikāya in particular and the workings of religious travel in eighteenth-century Southern Asia more generally.

SĀRALAṄKĀ'S TESTIMONIES AND CAREER

Of several testimonies taken during Sāralaṅkā's residence in Upper Burma, at least two survive. The first was recorded in 1767 by Ranma Thiri Kyawhtin, officer in charge of the Mahamingalabon royal manuscript library, a service obligation for which he was rewarded with revenues accruing from the village of Khadaw.[15] The record appears to have been made soon after Sāralaṅkā's arrival in Upper Burma. A copy of this testimony survives in the Zetawun monastery in Monywe village. It is undated, but, judging by the manuscript's layout and handwriting, it seems to be nearly contemporary with the original record. The second available testimony was taken before Sāralaṅkā's return to Tenasserim. The document is dated December 1787, but the date appears to be wrong (see notes 18 and 29 below).[16] An undated copy of this document is now kept in the Universities' Central Library in Yangon, and its provenance cannot be ascertained.[17] The manuscript can be assigned a tentative date falling between the 1850s and the early 1900s.

All data on Sāralaṅkā come solely from these testimonies that are not fully reliable. Sāralaṅkā himself gave conflicting information as he was adapting his biography over the time of his stay in Burma. In addition, there seem to be scribal errors in the manuscripts. Therefore, working out a precise chronology of Sāralaṅkā's life and travels poses difficulties.[18] Since the purpose of this chapter is to explore the case of Sāralaṅkā in relation to Buddhist networking and the importation of monastic ordinations, I leave a detailed analysis of testimonies and their chronology for another essay, while providing in this chapter a synoptic reconstruction of Sāralaṅkā's career.

Sāralaṅkā was likely born in the late 1720s or 1730s. According to the 1767 testimony, his place of birth was Pin-o village near Tenasserim.[19] Between the early seventeenth century and 1760, Tenasserim functioned as one of the principal ports controlled by Ayutthaya, so Sāralaṅkā originated from a key spot on the Siamese maritime frontier.[20] In his testimony providing an ethnic identification in accordance with Burmese usage, Sāralaṅkā described himself as Taninthayi Shan (Tai from Tenasserim).[21] The Ayutthayan polity granted his father the revenues accruing from a village of Bakaung near Tenasserim, which suggests that he had been a minor official.[22] Sāralaṅkā grew up at the court of Ayutthaya, for he was summoned there (as he stated in 1767) or moved there accompanying a son of a Mottama (Martaban) princess who became an Ayutthayan queen (as he testified in the 1780s).[23]

When this prince became a novice at an Ayutthayan royal temple (unidentified in the testimonies), Sāralaṅkā followed suit and later became a monk at the same temple.[24] In 1753 and 1756, when two missions were sent to reestablish ordination on Laṅkā, Sāralaṅkā's monastic preceptor was chosen to head the second one. Sāralaṅkā accompanied him to Laṅkā, lived there for a few years, and then returned to Ayutthaya (in 1764, it appears) for a brief period. Later, he moved back to Tenasserim, perhaps in 1765. At that time, Tenasserim fell from Siamese control. In early 1760, the town was captured by the Burmese king Alaungmintaya (r. 1752–1760). After brief restoration of Siamese rule over the Tenasserim coast in the early 1760s, in 1764 a new Burmese king, Hsinbyushin (r. 1763–1776), appointed officials to three major ports to the north of Tenasserim, and, in the summer of 1765, Burmese troops under the command of Min Mahanawyahta arrived at Dawe (Tavoy) and secured the coastline.[25]

As the arrival of troops under Min Mahanawyahta to Tavoy is mentioned in the "1787" testimony, Sāralaṅkā seems to have returned to Tenasserim near this time. He attempted to hide in the forest but was captured by Burmese soldiers, perhaps in 1765 or in early 1766. First, he was accommodated at Mergui. However, owing to the scarcity of resources there, he was sent on to Tavoy, which seems to have functioned as Burmese headquarters on the coast. There, Sāralaṅkā had to be reordained as required by the head of the local monastic community.[26] Information about him then circulated to the capital, and he was escorted from Tavoy to Upper Burma sometime between 1766 and 1767.

During his stay in Upper Burma, Sāralaṅkā made a new career for himself, one that shows the value sometimes attributed to monks with exposure to the wider Southern Asian Buddhist world. On his arrival, he was accommodated in a village near Sagaing (one of the cities composing the capital area). After being questioned about his travels, he was transferred into the tutelage of Kyethtungin Hsayadaw (1693–1775), one of the most venerated royal teachers, also considered a model "forest-dwelling" monk. At this point, Sāralaṅkā's benefactor (providing for his maintenance) was the governor of Sagaing, a close ally of the late king Alaungmintaya, the founder of Konbaung dynasty (1752–1885).

Later on, Sāralaṅkā resided in Taungbila, a famous site near Sagaing with an excellent pedigree as a location of "forest-dwelling" monasticism.[27] Finally, Sāralaṅkā became abbot of his own monastery located to the south of Sagaing. The construction of this monastery was started by another courtier, a relative of Alaungmintaya (who appears to occupy a higher position in the court hierarchy than the governor of Sagaing). However, this new sponsor died, and the monastery was completed by the governor of Sagaing, Sāralaṅkā's earlier donor.[28] After staying in Sagaing for some fourteen years, Sāralaṅkā requested permission to return to his native Tenasserim. He was allowed to go, and a new testimony was recorded before his departure. The likely date when the record was made is either 1780 or 1781.[29] Nothing more is known about Sāralaṅkā thereafter.

Sāralaṅkā's growing recognition during his residence in Upper Burma is reflected in the way Burmese officials who recorded his testimonies referred to him. Whereas the 1767 document identifies Sāralaṅkā as a "monk who has been to Sīhaḷa [*sīhuiḷ rok phunḥ krīḥ*] and was brought [to Ava] by a royal inspector [*nāḥ khaṃ*] and clerks [*cā re*] of the town of Dawe," the second testimony presents Sāralaṅkā as a "venerable monk [*phunḥ tau krīḥ*] who had traveled from Jambudīpa to the island of Sīhaḷa for the purpose of taking care of the *sāsana* [Buddhist teaching and tradition]" and as "the most venerable monk [*phunḥ tau krīḥ phurā*]." This rise from a mere "monk" to "the most venerable monk," mentioned in relation to his own achievements, was significant. Although Sāralaṅkā did not enjoy the most prestigious position of a royal teacher (*charā tau*) and did not belong to the top levels of the monastic hierarchy, he and his contribution to the Lankan *sāsana* were recognized by the Burmese court.

Additional documents from the same period that quote the testimonies of Sāralaṅkā further demonstrate his fame. The first reference appears in the *Cetyavaṃsa* (Chronicle of stūpas), a brief work in Pāli accompanied by bilingual translation composed in 1775 by Mun Ko, a writer from Bagan.[30] The *Cetyavaṃsa* traces the construction of major Buddhist monuments in Burma. Mun Ko focuses on the installation of a new umbrella on Shwedagon stūpa (relic monument) by King Hsinbyushin (r. 1763–1776), then jumps back in time to list improvements made to the stūpa throughout its history, dwelling briefly on King Dhammaceti, also known as Rāmādhipati (r. 1473–1492), one of the kings who sponsored such construction. Mun Ko then provides a summary of a testimony given in 1773 by "a monk who was born in the royal city of Ayutthaya called Dvārāvatī and who came from Sīhaḷa."[31] Although the name of the monk is not mentioned and his birthplace is referred to as Ayutthaya (whereas the 1767 testimony refers to Sāralaṅkā as a native of the Tenasserim area), the contents of the testimony leave no doubt that the person in question was Sāralaṅkā. Thus, to Mun Ko, information on Sāralaṅkā's travel to Laṅkā and details the latter provided about the sacred sites of the island were significant enough to be included alongside major milestones in the history of Buddhism and temple construction in Burma.[32]

Another reference to Sāralaṅkā's testimony appears in monastic correspondence dating to 1810. In a reply given by monk Ariyāvaṃsa Ādiccaraṃsī to his disciple Sirimālā and included in the anthology of such replies called *Samantacakkhudīpanī* (The exposition on the eye of all-around knowledge), Ariyāvaṃsa refers to a "record of a spoken testimony of the venerable Sāralaṅkāra, who has been to Sīhaḷa, [made] in the reign of Lord Hsinbyushin, the elder brother [of the present king], who had founded the third city of Yadanapura."[33] The document mentioned by Ariyāvaṃsa could well be a copy of Sāralaṅkā's 1767 testimony that survives at Ariyāvaṃsa's monastery in Monywe village.[34] If indeed the record referred to by Ariyāvaṃsa is reflected by this manuscript, it is worth noting that it does not mention Sāralaṅkā by name. This fact suggests that Sāralaṅkā was sufficiently well known for Ariyāvaṃsa to attribute the testimony.[35]

The references in Mun Ko's chronicle and Ariyāvaṃsa's monastic correspondence (documents compiled a hundred miles to the southwest of Sagaing in Bagan and some fifty miles to the west of Sagaing in Monywe) suggest a fairly wide circulation of testimonies. Hence, in the late eighteenth century, Sāralaṅkā appears to have been one of the monastic celebrities of Upper Burma. At the same time, it is revealing that in both sources he is mentioned only in the context of testimonies. This suggests that Sāralaṅkā's fame derived not from his monastic practice in Burma or his personal charisma, but depended on literary works created by the Burmese interested in Laṅkā and on the Burmese networks of circulation through which manuscript copies of Sāralaṅkā's testimonies spread.

It is worth stressing that, in relation to monastic practice, the very asset Sāralaṅkā transmitted to Laṅkā—namely, his Ayutthayan ordination—was lost as soon as he had been escorted to Tavoy by Burmese officials. To continue as a monk, Sāralaṅkā was obliged to reordain into a local monastic community. Moreover, Sāralaṅkā's testimonies do not show much rigor in accounting for that Ayutthayan ordination or any indication that the Burmese took any interest in Sāralaṅkā's Ayutthayan lineage or were eager to establish a new lineage in Burma originating with Sāralaṅkā. Instead, he was absorbed into a Burmese monastic order and rose to relative prominence within it, capitalizing on his association with Laṅkā and his ability to narrate this association in terms prized by Burmese patrons. This process of adaptation of a narrative to suit his emerging role of successful "missionary" monk is reflected in the ways the "1787" testimony differs from the one recorded in 1767.

THE DEVELOPMENT OF TESTIMONY

The testimony of 1767 is a record of interrogation that lists the questions asked by a Burmese official and the replies provided by Sāralaṅkā. It gives a matter-of-fact account of Sāralaṅkā's travel together with a few details on the monasteries and sacred sites of Laṅkā. The document gives an overall impression of Sāralaṅkā as a person trying to downplay any individual distinction to avoid claims to authority that he might not be able to substantiate. Sāralaṅkā testified that his ordination occurred only few years before the arrival of the Kandyan embassy at Ayutthaya and that even on his return from Laṅkā he was still a "junior monk" (*rahan ṅay*).[36] He did not pretend to have sound scriptural training or expertise.[37] He did not refer to being prominent anywhere he had traveled or to making a personal contribution to the Lankan mission. It is significant that he also made no effort to celebrate his belonging to a particular monastic lineage or order, providing only those details that were necessary to demonstrate that his claim on monastic status was valid in Vinaya terms so as to prove he was not a false monk.

Sāralaṅkā stated that the mission faced severe difficulties on the way back to Ayutthaya. Whereas the travel to Laṅkā occurred with combined Sinhalese, Siamese, and Dutch support, the return journey was a personal initiative, and so the monks had to find the means of survival in an alien environment. Thus, while traveling in India, they had to go from one place to another pretending to be either Malays or Javanese.[38] According to Sāralaṅkā, the majority of monks who participated in the mission died of chickenpox during the sea journey from India to Southeast Asia. Sāralaṅkā also admitted that the return to Siam did not make things easier for him. He explained that, when surviving monks arrived back at Ayutthaya, the king who had sent the mission was already dead and a new king occupied the throne.[39] Since the embassy's leaders had died on the mission, there was no one of influence to claim a state welcome on return to Ayutthaya. The monks only managed to transmit a message to the king.[40] Sāralaṅkā spent one rainy season's retreat in Ayutthaya and then moved to Tenasserim.[41]

In contrast to the 1767 testimony, the one likely dating to 1780–1781 (but generally referred to as dated 1787) is not the product of an interrogation, but rather a lengthy narrative aimed at detailing Sāralaṅkā's itinerary, the situation on Laṅkā, and the history of that island for the benefit of posterity. Besides offering greater detail, this later testimony also strives to explain the context that necessitated a Buddhist mission to Laṅkā. This new conceptual framework was accompanied by a revised chronology of events, a different itinerary (especially of the return journey), and inflated claims about the prominence of the mission. In a later section, I will address the wider Burmese context for the new conceptual framework into which Sāralaṅkā's activities were drawn.

In 1767, Sāralaṅkā failed to report certain details, citing poor memory. By the 1780s, his memory was refreshed to the extent that he could provide an account that looked essentially complete. If in 1767 he managed to name only thirteen out of thirty monks whom he claimed to have participated in the mission, in the second testimony he provided a full list of thirty-two names (the alleged number of missionaries increased by two) together with their native places. Departing from his earlier statements that he went to Laṅkā as a junior monk with only a few years of monastic standing, following his preceptor, Sāralaṅkā now claimed that, after the arrival of Sinhalese envoys to Ayutthaya, the king assembled all monks residing in the area, offered alms food, and requested to select four *mahātheras* who had completed twenty rainy seasons and were forty years old and twenty-eight monks who were thirty years old and had ten years of monastic standing. Thus, instead of being a poorly educated *bhikkhu* accompanying his teacher two years after ordination, Sāralaṅkā became one of the monks who was ordained for ten years and chosen by the entire Ayutthayan *saṅgha* to travel to Laṅkā.[42]

Sāralaṅkā also claimed that, on selection, monks chosen to transmit the ordination to Laṅkā were given special scriptural training lasting for a year and that this scriptural expertise was imparted to newly ordained Sinhalese monks.[43] Almost every detail related to the mission's experience during the journey that did not sit well with the grand purpose of the mission was corrected from the earlier testimony in a way that strengthened the mission's profile. Thus, mention of disguising as Malays, deaths from chickenpox, and lack of interest shown to the survivors on their arrival back in Ayutthaya had all disappeared. Instead, Sāralaṅkā spoke about reverential treatment the VOC extended to the mission during the latter's residence at Batavia on the way to Laṅkā, added new details about the arrangements the Kandyan king Kīrti Śrī made to greet the mission on its approach to Kandy, and recounted the ceremonial welcome the mission received on return to Ayutthaya as well as lavish donations bestowed on its members who chose to travel back to their native cities (like Sāralaṅkā, who returned to Tenasserim).[44]

Sāralaṅkā's facility in manipulating the data for the second testimony is further highlighted by the fictional genealogy he provided for King Kīrti Śrī and the claim that the latter was ordained and lived for one year as a monk following the arrival of the mission in Laṅkā, a story that finds no support in other sources. Another significant instance of retouching was the conflation of two missions from Ayutthaya in 1753 and 1756 into one: the second testimony identified the leaders of both the first and the second missions from Ayutthaya to Kandy as participants of a single mission. This eliminated the possibility that the role of the 1756 mission (in which Sāralaṅkā appears to have participated based on the first testimony) would be interpreted as purely supportive rather than as foundational to the Ayutthayan-Kandyan interaction.

Despite the embellishments and reformulations evident in the second testimony, it is important to note that Sāralaṅkā's testimonies were not completely fictional. They demonstrated a sound knowledge of Lankan geography and sacred sites, navigation routes in the Indian Ocean, and names of Sinhalese officials, and he correctly identified the names of Siamese ministers who were sent to Laṅkā in 1756 as well as the names of monks who headed the missions to the island. These points suggest that discrepancies in the testimonies and fictionalization of the narrative were mostly strategic and served to create an account that would ultimately be intelligible to and perceived as trustworthy by a Burmese audience. Apparently, a testimony that looked complete and described a successful mission that was well received throughout its journey suited the expectations of that audience better than a more straightforward report that included more signs of risk, contingency, and failure. The circulation and survival of copies of the testimonies prove that Sāralaṅkā managed to pass the tests of intelligibility and trustworthiness within the Upper Burmese Buddhist monastic context. Both the adjustment of Sāralaṅkā's testimonies and the importance accorded to them in Burmese manuscript circulation shed light on one of the forms of circulation identified in the first section of this chapter. Sāralaṅkā's experience in Upper Burma is a striking example of the transmission and localization of things and persons within the Southern Asian Buddhist world in contexts that did not involve the transplantation of either monastic lineage or a monastic order but did involve an adaptation to local circumstances. Thus, the processes of localization involving mobile monastics can be examined both at the scale of monastic ordination lineages and the Buddhist orders that they shape (as noted by Blackburn) as well as at the scale of individuals.[45]

LOCALIZATION AND INTELLIGIBILITY

At first glance, the career of Sāralaṅkā may seem disjointed—consisting of discrete parts with little logic connecting them—and contradictory, to the extent that no truthful testimony of it could be made. A boy from a village near a remote Siamese port city travels to the royal capital and is ordained there. Soon, while still a junior monk with few qualifications, he becomes a part of an important monastic mission, important at least in retrospect (there are no means of ascertaining how the mission was perceived by those who initiated it). Spending some years in a distant country and surviving the hardships of a perilous journey, Sāralaṅkā returns to Ayutthaya and might be expected to enjoy the accruing glory. Yet Ayutthaya is in decline, and so he chooses to return to his native area. Tenasserim, however, is not a safe haven either, and soon Sāralaṅkā is displaced by the Burmese but manages to reassert himself as a venerable monk in Upper Burma. These ruptures and twists in his career leave one to wonder if Sāralaṅkā was ever in control of his itinerary and career trajectories. To what extent, if at all, did his earlier background and relationships shape his subsequent evolution?

Sāralaṅkā's career as evidenced by his testimonies departs significantly from normative accounts of Lankan or Southeast Asian monasticism as found in such sources as the *Mahāvaṃsa*, an early sixth-century Lankan chronicle, or official Burmese chronicles. It would be unimaginable in modern Sinhalese or Thai narratives of the establishment of Siyam Nikāya or Nikāya Siyamwong (Siamese Lineage), which tend toward a panegyric account of monastic missions. Sāralaṅkā seems an unlikely candidate for the transmission of ordination and a successful monastic career, for he does not possess an exalted lineage, sound education, scriptural expertise, or notable charisma. His corporate status as a fully ordained monk and a cofounder of the Siyam Nikāya in Kandy neither helped him to find a suitable place on return to Ayutthaya nor protected him from deportation to Upper Burma.

In fact, by the nature of his origins and interstitiality, Sāralaṅkā was an ideal candidate for perilous travels, someone who could have been considered expendable by authorities yet also capable of surviving in challenging new settings. Though necessitating reordination at Tavoy in 1765 or 1766, Sāralaṅkā's status as a captive and one of non-Burman background did not preclude his being venerated by the Burmese court and receiving his own monastery in Sagaing. In fact, it was Burma, not Laṅkā or Siam, where Sāralaṅkā achieved greatest personal prominence. Marginality and personal insecurity enhanced Sāralaṅkā's ability to adopt whatever socially approved behavior (including the notions of monasticism) was expected from him. This ability is clear in the way he reshaped his second available testimony vis-à-vis the earlier one to suit his acquired status as an eminent monk and recipient of high-level patronage. And it is likely this ability to adapt that brought Sāralaṅkā closer to prestigious social roles and modes of action. The adaptation displayed by Sāralaṅkā in his testimonies shows how authoritative discourses on Buddhism and monastic activity are shaped by negotiation between those speaking and writing and their audience. In turn, this type of negotiation raises the issue of the role of local audience reception in the context of Buddhist mobility, allowing us to expand our analytical understanding of the processes through which Buddhist travelers were localized in particular settings and drawing attention to the ways in which the receiving culture's or community's goals and needs could take precedence over formal measures of knowledge and experience of mobile Buddhists. Indeed, local Buddhist communities had an impressive ability to capitalize on long-distance contacts within Buddhist *oikumene* and to situate itinerant monks and the connections they might symbolize into local projects and conceptual frameworks.

When examined in relation to other contemporary Burmese documents detailing long-distance religious travel to and from Upper Burma in the late eighteenth century, Sāralaṅkā's case appears representative of a fairly large group of "foreign" religious specialists who provided the Burmese court with information on neighboring countries and facilitated Burma's interactions with them. Such evidence reveals a pattern to these interactions, with the Burmese already having a certain idea about a particular foreign destination and its value, construing the "foreign" actor as able to serve their aims. Accordingly, as in Sāralaṅkā's case, the Burmese absorbed the details provided by a "foreigner," while conveying to the traveler their own understanding of the matter at hand and catalyzing the traveler's adaptation to local circumstances. The fusion of "local" and "foreign" elements in Sāralaṅkā's testimonies is illustrated below.

The development of Sāralaṅkā's testimonies was not limited to enhancing his image. Equally notable is his tendency to refer to locally significant sacred sites and religious practices as well as to adapt Burmese historiographical notions. For instance, one of the features of the testimonies is the mapping of Laṅkā according to an understanding of the Burmese religious landscape, where major Buddhist sites of Laṅkā are compared to stūpas in Burma.[46] We see another example in Sāralaṅkā's use of Burmese monastic curricular terms to frame a description of how Siamese monks from Ayutthaya trained Lankan monastics. According to the testimony, fifty newly ordained Lankan monks who had the ability to preach were assigned to act as preceptors in "all curricular texts studied during the evening and daytime classes [*ñña vā ne. vā saṅ ruiḥ kyamḥ akun*]."[47] This description imposed the structure of monastic education in Upper Burma on the training allegedly given to Sinhalese monks by their fellows from Ayutthaya. The division into daytime (*ñña vā*) and evening (*ne. vā*) classes—the former dedicated to Pāli grammar and Vinaya, and the latter to Abhidhamma—reflected the basic daily routine in Burmese monasteries. The term "curriculum" (*saṅ ruiḥ*) also closely resonated with Burmese notions of monastic training, since by the late eighteenth century a significant share of monasteries in Upper Burma based the education of schoolboys, novices, and junior monks on a similar selection of Pāli and bilingual texts.[48]

Finally, Sāralaṅkā's account of the history of Sinhalese kingship and the situation of the *sāsana* on the island (provided in his second available testimony) displayed an interesting fusion of local, unofficial Burmese historiography with more standard Lankan narratives. Though the sequence of rulers of Laṅkā from Vijaya to Kīrti Śrī given by Sāralaṅkā depended on the *Mahāvaṃsa* to a certain degree, it omitted the majority of kings mentioned in the Lankan chronicle. It did, however, refer to Dharmapāla—a puppet king installed by the Portuguese at Koṭṭē in the sixteenth century who was also in contact with the Burmese king Hsinbyumyashin (r. 1551–1581) who ruled at Hanthawady (Bago). Since at least the early seventeenth century, Burmese sources identified Dharmapāla as a rightful sovereign of Laṅkā who fought "Indian" non-Buddhists (*micchādiṭṭhi*) ruling at Koṭṭē [*sic*], Kandy, and Sītāvaka and finally managed to subdue them and unify the island with the help of Hsinbyumyashin.[49] Strikingly, Sāralaṅkā retells this story—apparently unknown in Kandy or Ayutthaya—in a form diverging from mainstream Burmese court historiography but consonant with local traditions at Sagaing, where he resided in Burma.[50] All the monasteries where Sāralaṅkā resided between 1767 and about 1781 were located in direct proximity to a site that embodied the tradition about Hsinbyumyashin and the king of Laṅkā. Therefore, departures from official Burmese narratives in Sāralaṅkā's testimony indicate that Sāralaṅkā's retelling was based not on Burmese texts, but rather borrowed from some local oral version that Sāralaṅkā likely heard in Sagaing.

SĀRALAṄKĀ, THE BURMESE ROYAL COURT, AND A WIDER BUDDHIST WORLD

Strategic use of idioms comprehensible to the Burmese public undoubtedly contributed to Sāralaṅkā's local intelligibility. Of even greater importance, however, was the fact that Sāralaṅkā's travels were compatible with Burmese notions of Burma's position within a wider Buddhist world. Moreover, Sāralaṅkā's residence in Sagaing coincided with late eighteenth- and early nineteenth-century Burmese royal interest in refining its knowledge of the broader Buddhist world and expanding engagement with it. The success with which Sāralaṅkā localized himself in Upper Burma—although he was not sought after as the officiator to found a new monastic lineage or as a participant in a valued foreign monastic order—reflects the importance of this specific historical moment when mobile monastic elites were particularly valued at the Burmese court.

Scholarship on the reign of King Badon-min (r. 1782–1819) has long referred to multiple Burmese missions sent to India during this period. Modern Burmese works mention in particular 170 Sanskrit texts that were brought from Nabadwip (an important center of Sanskrit learning and a Vaishnava pilgrimage site in West Bengal) and transcribed from Bengali into Burmese Sanskrit. They were then recopied on palm leaves under the supervision of Ñāṇābhivaṃsa (1751–1832), a key court-sponsored monk and the future head of the royal monastic hierarchy, in 1786.[51] Manuscript evidence provides further context for such embassies to the Indian subcontinent. In 1783, the minister for palatial affairs (*atvaṅ van*) Min Letwe Nawyahta U Ne (1723–1791) wrote to Ñāṇābhivaṃsa requesting a list of "works of worldly knowledge" (*lokī kyamḥ*; a common phrase used to refer to Sanskrit and Sanskrit-derived texts) that were unavailable in Burma and should be sought in the "foreign country of sea-vessel-[faring] Indians." This request arose in the context of Badon-min's sponsorship of copies of Pāli Buddhist texts and learned Sanskrit works, leading to the recognition of the inadequate availability of Sanskrit texts in Burma. Ñāṇābhivaṃsa identified forty-eight titles that had been available in Burma in the past but were now lost. A year later, Punshi and Sukāram (two royal Brahmins, of either Bengali or Tamil descent,[52] serving at the Burmese court) were sent to Kolkata accompanied by Yangon-based merchant captain Thiri Sandarat.[53] From Kolkata they were referred to Nabadwip, where they managed to recopy a number of texts, most of which were actually not suggested by Ñāṇābhivaṃsa. A year later, they arrived at Amarapura, inaugurating a transcription project completed by late 1786.[54]

This acquisition of Sanskrit intellectual heritage highlights Burmese participation in wider South Asian religious and intellectual networks as well as the need for information and intermediaries that supported such Burmese goals. In the view of the Burmese elites, the royal corpus of Sanskrit works was authoritative not because of its Indian origins, but as a result of its use in Upper Burma. Min Letwe Nawyahta made no indication of Badon-min's interest in expanding the royally transmitted corpus of Sanskrit texts, and Ñāṇābhivaṃsa was asked to identify only those titles that were recopied in Burma in the past.[55]

Also helpful in contextualizing Sāralaṅkā's reception in eighteenth-century Burma is the evidence on Burmese communications with Laṅkā and Qing China in the late eighteenth century. What seems to be the earliest direct contact between the court of Badon-min and the Sinhalese resulted from sending Thiri Sandarat, the captain who had traveled to Kolkata, Nabadwip, and Laṅkā. In about 1787, he was instructed to check whether Laṅkā still possessed the Buddha's tooth relic, the forehead bone relic, the relic of the hair between the eyebrows, and the Bodhi tree brought from India, as described in the Buddhist historiographical works *Mahāvaṃsa*, *Dīpavaṃsa*, *Bodhivaṃsa*, and *Nalāṭadhātuvaṃsa*. He was also instructed to see whether the conduct of Sinhalese monks and novices was in conformity with the Vinaya.[56] In late 1789, Thiri Sandarat returned to Amarapura accompanied by Sinhalese novice Varakālantē and a senior mason Narāyanapā, bringing a manuscript of *Dhammacakkapavattana Sutta* and its bilingual commentaries as well as messages from an unidentified Sinhalese "king" and high-ranking monastic leader (*anunāyaka*) of Anurādhapura.[57] The message of the *anunāyaka* recounted the ecclesiastical history of Laṅkā, mentioning its prior contacts with other parts of Southern Asia for the purposes of monastic ordination and eulogizing Kandyan monarchs for taking perfect care of the country and the *sāsana*.[58] A message that the Burmese identified as being sent by the Sinhalese king requested a number of Pāli texts.[59]

Badon-min and Ñāṇābhivaṃsa made a selective reading of the messages focusing on three points: that Laṅkā had a recent history of importing monastic ordination from elsewhere in the region, that there was no complete *tipiṭaka* available in Laṅkā, and that the Mahācetiya (Great Relic Monument) in Anurādhapura had no umbrella installed on top. This, in current Burmese understanding, signified a dramatic neglect of the sacred site. Ñāṇābhivaṃsa laid plans to give Varakālantē proper scriptural training, ordain him as a monk, learn Sinhala script from him, prepare a full set of *tipiṭaka* transcribed in Sinhala, and send a mission under Ñāṇābhivaṃsa himself to reestablish the *sāsana* on Laṅkā. In the meantime, Narāyanapā would return to Laṅkā and confirm the favorable reports made by Thiri Sandarat about the flourishing state of the teaching in Burma, and a son of Thiri Sandarat should be sent with the funds to repair major monuments. Such measures were intended to convince Lankan Buddhists that the well-being of the *sāsana* could be entrusted to the care of Badon-min.[60]

This example illustrates the performative or "symptomatic" role the engagement with overseas Buddhist locations played in Southern Asian Buddhist cultures of the period. That is, engagement with valued persons and objects from the wider transregional Buddhist world stemmed from specific local historical circumstances and, as such, highlights key moments of institutional instability and/or ambition within local contexts.[61] Within the Buddhist world of that time and indeed earlier, lay Buddhist patrons and monastic leaders were defined as leaders in part through their ability to contribute to the cause of the *sāsana* on a global level. They portrayed themselves and were seen as participants in a greater Buddhist *oikumene* instantiated by relics, sacred sites, manuscripts, and ordination opportunities, supported by Pāli and Sanskrit literature and their vernacular adaptations, Buddhist art, and, sometimes, accounts of foreign informants such as Sāralaṅkā.[62] Of course, Ñāṇābhivaṃsa may have overstated his aims in offering to reordain the monks on Laṅkā; thinking small was not an option for a person responsible for taking care of the *sāsana* on behalf of a Burmese king, especially one as ambitious as Badon-min.[63]

The interactions of the Konbaung court with China displayed similar willingness of the Burmese to offer their ordination and mastery of Pāli texts to a wider Buddhist world and to patronize "foreign" relics. Communications with the Qing started roughly at the same time as the travels of Thiri Sandarat. By 1787, local rulers (Ch. *tǔsī*) from the Burma-Yunnan border facilitated the delivery of a letter from the Qianlong emperor (r. 1736–1796) to Badon-min. A few years later, they set up the delivery of three princesses identified as Chinese, given as brides to Badon-min, an act potentially signifying in local eyes that the Qianlong emperor might be recognized as a Burmese vassal.[64]

From the beginning of these exchanges, the Burmese court chose to frame them in relation to the well-being of the *sāsana*. Among diplomatic gifts exchanged between the two courts, a prime place was given to religious symbols. At the suggestion of Ñāṇābhivaṃsa, an exhortation to Qianlong to worship the Three Jewels (the Buddha, *dhamma* [teaching], and *saṅgha*) was added to the reply to the 1787 letter mentioned above.[65] Moreover, the Burmese embassy sent to China in 1788 to deliver a reply apparently displayed keen interest in the Buddha's tooth relic that the Burmese believed to be kept at Mt. Wutai. As a result, the embassy returned to Burma bringing the image of the Buddha said to be worshiped by Qianlong and made in the likeness of the Buddha that the Mt. Wutai tooth relic had assumed during a visit of the Kangxi emperor (r. 1661–1722) to the site.[66] Another valuable object brought by the embassy was the replica of the tooth relic. In a message to Badon-min, Ñāṇābhivaṃsa confirmed that he was aware of the story of Kangxi's arrival at Mt. Wutai and that the image constituted a genuine relic.[67] At his suggestion, the image and a copy of the tooth relic were enshrined in Pahtodawgyi in Mingun, a stūpa meant to be Badon-min's chief work of merit.

Ñāṇābhivaṃsa's 1796 correspondence with the monks of Köng-ma (Ch. Gěngmǎ; Bur. Kaingma), a Tai principality on the Burma-Yunnan frontier (in what is now Líncāng Prefecture of Yunnan), also shows Ñāṇābhivaṃsa's vision for the Tai areas. Addressing the monks from the location that played a critical role in the communication between the Qing and Konbaung courts, Ñāṇābhivaṃsa cited Badon-min's good deeds, mentioning, for instance, his Buddhist diplomacy with Kandyan king Rājadhi Rājasiṃha (r. 1782–1798). The message also suggested that Köng-ma monks should emulate the example of monk Ekāmuni from Möng Hsa (Bur. Maingtha, an A-ch'ang town in what is now Déhóng Prefecture of Yunnan), who came to Amarapura in Upper Burma to be reordained and trained in the curriculum promoted by Ñāṇābhivaṃsa and his monastic allies.[68] This recommendation underscores the desire of Upper Burmese court elites to establish stronger symbolic links with those who mediated their interactions with the Chinese administration in Yunnan and the Qing imperial court, while promoting conformity with Burmese notions of the *sāsana* among the Tai.

This evidence of concerted, heavily resourced overtures from the court of Badon-min to key nodal points in the Buddhist ritual and wider geopolitical worlds of Southern Asia (and beyond) helps to clarify the position of Sāralaṅkā in Upper Burma and his ascendance to a high rank within royally sponsored monastic circles. Burmese royal conceptions of a greater Buddhist world created a demand for agents able to affirm and animate these geographies and to provide vital practical information that facilitated strategic royal engagement with subregional locations beyond Burma. Although this chapter has concentrated on the ways in which Sāralaṅkā adapted his reports of the Buddhist world to suit his Burmese audiences, it is also evident from Sāralaṅkā's testimonies (and the way they were quoted in subsequent Burmese texts) that his reports were understood as valuable sources of current information on the condition of particular Buddhist sites and travel routes.

Since the Konbaung court's influence beyond the borders of the Burmese polity was limited, religious initiatives of the Burmese crown on its peripheries outside of Burma proper depended on intermediaries and collaborators in a way similar to the functioning of hybrid or plural political structures on the Burma-Yunnan frontier. Though Sāralaṅkā was not strictly an agent of the Burmese court, the interest in his testimonies and the way they were quoted by contemporaries suggest that he was seen as a source of valuable information about Buddhist institutional locations with which Burmese royal and monastic leaders were concerned.

Facilitation of Burma's religious and diplomatic contacts in the eighteenth and nineteenth centuries involved a broad and nonsectarian mix of actors, operating on sea and land routes across Asia and the Indian Ocean. In addition to Buddhist monks of diverse ethnic origin, these interactions relied on European trade companies and colonial powers as well as on Asian trading, religious, and administrative networks (such as Tamil merchants, port masters, and laborers from Laṅkā and the Coromandel coast; Arakanese and Armenian traders, officials, and entrepreneurs from the Burma-Yunnan frontier; Bengali Brahmins; and even Sufi Muslims).[69] Foreign religious practitioners who found their way to Upper Burma and passed local tests of intelligibility were received as significant social actors. Brahmins, Sufis, and Buddhist monks and novices were associated not with margins, but with political and religious centers outside Burma with which they were familiar and about which they could provide information. Some of them came to be rewarded or patronized by the Burmese royal court, which valued such skills as a command of Persian as a language of diplomacy or proficiency in astrology, alchemy, or medicine.

Research in history and the social sciences during the last twenty years has seen the burgeoning of work on border areas and social agents operating in interstitial spaces between lowland states and polities as well as studies of groups and networks acting on the margins or peripheries of large territorially organized social bodies. In Asian studies, this work has led to the development of such concepts as "the history at the interstices" or Zomia that, among other things, called for rescaling conceptual tools to recognize the subjectivity of regions and people that had not been adequately represented in previous research.[70] In China studies, an important trend has been research on hybrid regimes and "dual sovereignty" that Ming and Qing imperial states employed at their frontiers. This research has focused attention on multiple native collaborators on imperial frontiers as well as other indigenous actors.[71] In research on global trade and colonial expansion in the Indian Ocean, growing attention has been paid to social formations of mobile individuals able to function as entrepreneurial minorities. Gujarati *baniyas*, Julfan Armenians, Peranakan Chinese, Parsis, and participants in many other networks termed "conjoint communities," "communally defined trading groups," and "circulation societies" were the primary Asian actors exploiting the opportunities for long-distance trade, financial, and industrial operations created by indigenous and colonial empires.[72] In the case of Southeast Asia, such research has been complemented by work on Chinese and Arab networks in the region.[73]

In the study of Southeast Asian religions, however, a comparable depth of detail on interstitial actors is yet to materialize, although a substantial literature has emerged on the role of Indian intermediaries in the circulation of Islam in Southern Asia.[74] In the field identified as Theravāda studies, the study of Buddhism oriented toward authoritative texts in Pāli, the mapping of peripheral figures has just begun. The most significant example is the recent work on the activities of pioneer Western Buddhists in Asia,[75] but there are no corresponding studies of indigenous itinerants or of mobile Buddhists before the colonial period.[76] The present chapter on Sāralaṅkā draws attention to this category of actors and shows the ability of a particular monastic itinerant to rise in the Burmese monastic order by virtue of his reception as someone able to contribute to Burmese support for the cause of the *sāsana* within a greater Buddhist world.

Sāralaṅkā's case and other examples referred to more glancingly in this chapter illustrate that mobile Buddhists in eighteenth-century Southern Asia made their careers either by fusing into monastic orders at their destinations or by facilitating the development of these monastic orders, often by providing a monastic ordination. These cases do not reveal the extension of Buddhist monastic orders—with their external features of organizational structure and practice—into new foreign locations.[77] Mobility associated with the import of an ordination, as in the establishment of Siyam Nikāya or movements of Burmese-ordained monks in Tai areas on the Burma-Yunnan frontier, was made possible by awareness of a greater Buddhist world transcending political boundaries, by the hybrid nature of communication networks through which diplomatic activities of regional polities were carried out, and by diverse benefits Southern Asian Buddhists and their patrons could derive from venturing into foreign territories.

Thus, this case invites us to consider when and to what extent ordination lineages play a formative role in the institutionalization of Buddhist monastic communities. In my work on eighteenth- and nineteenth-century Burmese monastic organization, I find lineages largely irrelevant or at least much less relevant than ritual communities, reformist networks built around signature practices, royally supported hierarchies, and educational infrastructure.[78] At the same time, in her analysis of the rise of Siyam Nikāya on Laṅkā and the development of Sīhaḷa Saṅgha in Northern Thailand, Blackburn argues that the invocation of imported lineages provided an avenue for reconfiguring local communities and enhancing their claims for recognition.[79] To me, the perspective on the foundation of Siyam Nikāya offered in Sāralaṅkā-related materials suggests that the ordination brought from Ayutthaya merely fulfilled ritual requirements for inaugurating a new monastic lineage in Kandy and reviving Sinhalese monastic order. Neither the lineage, nor the order in this case could be called "imported" in the strict sense of the term.

The compartmentalization of the Buddhist world into multiple polities created opportunities for itinerant religious specialists, who may have been drawn to mobility by social marginality in their places of origin or other instabilities such as wartime conditions. Navigating these spatial formations required many skills, including those demonstrated by Sāralaṅkā, who was able to mix creatively idioms that were vernacular and local with those that were cosmopolitan and transregional. Barriers to and opportunities for the localization of itinerant religious specialists varied greatly from one location in Buddhist Southern Asia to another. For example, the Upper Burmese situation appears different from Laṅkā in the eighteenth and nineteenth centuries, where the close dependence of the formation of monastic orders on the social organization of Sinhalese society (especially in terms of caste hierarchies) and the exclusivist and centralized nature of the dominant monastic community (Siyam Nikāya), with its strict control over access to monastic ordination and bureaucratic appointments, likely limited the prospects for such actors as Sāralaṅkā.[80] More research is required to develop detailed comparisons and identify structural possibilities for the localization of foreign persons, ideas, and practices into Burmese, Sinhalese, Tai, or Thai monasticism and for long-distance networking within the Southern Asian Buddhist world over time. Localization strategies such as that employed by Sāralaṅkā were used elsewhere in Buddhist interactions in early modern Southern Asia during the eighteenth as well as parts of seventeenth and nineteenth centuries. More research is required, however, to determine how common such strategies were in earlier periods and which social and political features may have shaped the success or failure of itinerants seeking a favorable reception in the Southern Asian Buddhist world. It is equally interesting to see how the processes and strategies involved in receiving and localizing mobile Buddhists might have been transformed when interactions between Buddhist countries intensified during the late nineteenth century, producing a more complex intellectual climate and a broader mix of localization patterns characteristic of the modern period.

NOTES

I am grateful to Anne Blackburn and Michael Feener for numerous discussions relevant to the subject of the present chapter as well as for comments and editorial suggestions on its drafts; to Arina Mikhalevskaya for discussions of sources on Qing-Konbaung interactions; to Ko Than Zaw and Ko Soe Nyunt, whose assistance was indispensable during fieldwork in Monywe village, Burma; to Hsayadaw U Jānadhamma, abbot of the Monywe Zetawun monastery, for allowing me to study the manuscripts in his custody; and to the Myanmar Department of Archaeology and National Museum, Ministry of Culture, as well as to Daw Baby, director, Archaeological Museum of Bagan, for providing access to manuscripts in the museum collections.

1. Kenneth Roy Norman, *Pāli Literature Including the Canonical Literature in Prakrit and Sanskrit of All the Hīnayāna Schools of Buddhism, A History of Indian Literature*, vol. 7, fasc. 2 (Wiesbaden: Otto Harrassowitz, 1983), p. 13.

2. Mon Bokay, "Relations between Ceylon and Burma in the 11th Century AD," in *Essays Offered to G. H. Luce*, edited by U Ba Shin, Jean Boisselier, and A. B. Griswold, vol. 1 (New York and Ascona: Artibus Asiae, 1968), p. 94; Kanai Lal Hazra, *History of Theravāda Buddhism in South-East Asia: With Special Reference to India and Ceylon* (New Delhi: Munshiram Manoharlal, 1982), pp. 89, 92, 103, 111, 130; Tilman Frasch, "A Buddhist Network in the Bay of Bengal: Relations between Bodhgaya, Burma and Sri Lanka, c. 300–1300," in

From the Mediterranean to the China Sea, edited by Claude Guillot, Denys Lombard, and Roderich Ptak, South China and Maritime Asia 7 (Wiesbaden: Harrassowitz, 1998), pp. 83, 85, 89.

3. Niharranjan Ray, *An Introduction to the Study of Theravāda Buddhism in Burma* (Calcutta: University of Calcutta, 1946), pp. 114–115, 171, 190–192; C. E. Godakumbura, "Relations between Burma and Ceylon," *Journal of the Burma Research Society* 49.2 (1966): 147; Hazra, *History of Theravāda Buddhism*, pp. 103, 108, 111; Emmanuel Guillon, "Jalons pour une histoire du Bouddhisme en Asie du Sud-Est," *Péninsule* 8–9 (1984): 124. Others argued that the expansion of Sinhalese monasticism in Southeast Asia manifested competing forms of Sinhalese monastic tradition, especially with respect to ritual practice. See, for instance, Prathip Chumphon, "Khor sanitsathan ruang phra malai," *Wannakhadi wikhro* 1975; François Bizot, *Les traditions de la pabbajjā en Asie du Sud-Est* (Göttingen: Vandenhoeck and Ruprecht, 1988). For an alternative view, see Prapod Assavavirulhakarn, *The Ascendancy of Theravāda Buddhism in Southeast Asia* (Chiang Mai: Silkworm, 2010), pp. 170–172.

4. Peter Skilling, "Theravāda in History," *Pacific World: Journal of the Institute of Buddhist Studies*, third series, 11 (2009): 63–64; Anne M. Blackburn, "Sīhaḷa Saṅgha and Laṅkā in Later Premodern Southeast Asia," in *Buddhist Dynamics in Premodern Southeast Asia*, edited by D. Christian Lammerts (Singapore: Institute for Southeast Asian Studies, 2015), pp. 315–322; Anne M. Blackburn, "Buddhist Connections in the Indian Ocean: Changes in Monastic Mobility, 1000–1500," *Journal of the Economic and Social History of the Orient* 58 (2015): 251–257. See also Jason A. Carbine, "How King Rāmādhipati Handled His Boundary Case: Sīmā, Sāsana, and Buddhist Law," *Buddhism, Law, and Society* 1 (2016–2015): 151–152, which follows Blackburn in her arguments regarding the significance of Laṅkā.

5. For the context of this monastic reform, see Kitsiri Malalgoda, *Buddhism in Sinhalese Society 1750–1900: A Study of Religious Revival and Change* (Berkeley: University of California Press, 1976), pp. 54–58; Anne M. Blackburn, *Buddhist Learning and Textual Practice in Eighteenth-Century Lankan Monastic Culture* (Princeton: Princeton University Press, 2001), pp. 37–38.

6. For an analysis of how Saraṇaṃkara drew on Sinhalese literary and cultural heritage in developing the innovative techniques he used to reshape monastic education and preaching, fashioning the emergence of the Siyam Nikāya as a new Buddhist textual community, see Blackburn, *Buddhist Learning.*

7. P. E. Pieris, "An Account of King Kirti Sri's Embassy to Siam in 1672 Saka (1750 A.D.)," *Journal of the Royal Asiatic Society, Ceylon Branch* 18 (1903): 17–44; P. E. E. Fernando, "An Account of the Kandyan Mission to Siam in 1750 A.D.," *The Ceylon Journal of Historical and Social Studies* 2.1 (1959): 37–83. Both articles are translations of reports on a mission that sailed to Siam in 1750 and returned to Laṅkā in 1753, compiled by two officials who took part in the mission. The first is a translation of the account written by Ällepola Mohoṭṭāla, and the second is a translation of the work of Vilbāgedara Muhandiram.

8. Anne M. Blackburn, "Lineage, Inheritance, and Belonging: Expressions of Monastic Affiliation from Laṅkā," in *How Theravāda Is Theravāda? Exploring Buddhist Identities*, edited by Peter Skilling, Jason Carbine, Claudio Cicuzza, and Santi Pakdeekham (Chiang Mai: Silkworm, 2012), pp. 279–281. Blackburn further suggests that such treatment might be due to the nature of the source and its primary focus on the meritorious deeds of kings, Kīrti Śrī in this case. It might be assumed that Thai sources, linked to the missions' origin, would be better

equipped to shed light on these activities, but so far only a few original documents have been brought to light. See Supaphan na Bangchang, "A Pāli Letter Sent by the Aggamahāsenāpati of Siam to the Royal Court at Kandy in 1756," *Journal of the Pali Text Society* 12 (1988): 185–212; Damrong Rajanubhab, *Ruang praditsathan phrasong sayamwong nai Langkathaweep* (Bangkok: Matichon, 2003).

9. Blackburn, "Sīhaḷa Saṅgha," pp. 214, 220–221.

10. Studies of the formation of Amarapura Nikāya are also silent about the practices that might have been introduced to Laṅkā as a result of imported ordination. Malalgoda, *Buddhism in Sinhalese Society*, pp. 94–100; Masahiro Kitsudo, "A Survey of the Founders of the Amarapura Nikāya in Burma (Myanmar): Their Journeys and Higher Ordinations," *Journal of Sugiyama Jogakuen University: Humanities, Social Sciences, Natural Sciences* 33 (2002): 153–172.

11. Malalgoda, *Buddhism in Sinhalese Society*, pp. 132–172; Anne M. Blackburn, *Locations of Buddhism: Colonialism and Modernity in Sri Lanka* (Chicago: University of Chicago Press, 2010).

12. Anne M. Blackburn, "Localizing Lineage: Importing Higher Ordination in Theravādin South and Southeast Asia," in *Constituting Communities: Theravāda Buddhism and the Religious Cultures of South and Southeast Asia*, edited by John Clifford Holt, Jacob N. Kinnard, and Jonathan S. Walters (New York: State University of New York Press, 2003), pp. 133–140. The quote is from p. 139.

13. Blackburn, *Buddhist Learning*, pp. 136–137.

14. Ibid., pp. 58–59. More recently, Kate Crosby, Andrew Skilton, and Amal Gunasena have argued that texts transmitted to the Kandyan court included works on "traditional" Southeast Asian *kammaṭṭhāna* meditation and that this meditation practice was imparted to Sinhalese monks. Unfortunately, no evidence on the use of this practice and its likely scale of penetration is provided. Kate Crosby, Andrew Skilton, and Amal Gunasena, "*The Sutta on Understanding Death* in the Transmission of Boran Meditation from Thailand to the Kandyan Court," *Journal of Indian Philosophy* 40.2 (2012): 177–198. Lorna Dewaraja mentions that the persuasion of Siamese monks was instrumental in the transformation of Asela Mahā Perahera, a principal Kandyan festival that became focused on the Buddha's tooth relic instead of Hindu deities, yet the evidence for this remains unclear. Lorna Dewaraja, "Thailand's Gift to Sri Lanka: the Establishment of the Siam Nikaya," *The Daily News* (Sri Lanka), May 14, 2003, http://www.budsas.org/ebud/ebdha241.htm, accessed January 10, 2013.

15. Undated palm-leaf manuscript from the Zetawun monastery, Monywe village, Monywa township, folio *ka*[v].

16. Palm-leaf manuscript no. 10551 in the Universities' Central Library (UCL), Yangon, folio *ḍaṃ*[v].

17. Library records show that the manuscript was acquired from Daw Ma Ma Gyi Bell from Yangon, but that person was merely a dealer. No details on its earlier provenance are known.

18. Testimonies provide conflicting dates for Sāralaṅkā's birth (1732 in the 1767 testimony and 1730 in the "1787" testimony; neither date can be reconciled with other data in the documents) as well as his monastic ordination (1754 in the former and 1753 in the latter testimony; both seem questionable). His arrival in Laṅkā is dated to 1757 in the former and to either 1758 or 1756 in the latter testimony (it is ambiguous on that point), with only 1756 historically probable.

His departure from Laṅkā is likewise uncertain, dated to 1763 in the former testimony and to 1762 in the latter. Sāralaṅkā's return to Ayutthaya is dated to late 1764 in the 1767 testimony and to early 1764 in the latter.

19. Ms. from the Zetawun monastery, f. *ka*^{v}.

20. See Michael Smithies, "Seventeenth Century Siam: Its Extent and Urban Centres According to Dutch and French Observers," *Journal of Siam Society* 83.1–2 (1995): 62–78.

21. Ms. from the Zetawun monastery, f. *ka*^{v}.

22. Ibid.; ms. no. 10551 in UCL, f. *ḍaṃ*^{v}.

23. Ms. from the Zetawun monastery, f. *ka*^{v}; ms. no. 10551 in UCL, f. *ḍaṃ*^{v}.

24. Ms. no. 10551 in UCL, ff. *ḍam*^{v}–*ḍāḥ*^{r}.

25. Dutch sources show that, in 1762–1763, Mergui and, most likely, Tenasserim were under the Siamese. See Lorna Dewaraja, *The Kandyan Kingdom of Sri Lanka, 1707–1782* (Colombo: Lake House, 1988), p. 116, n. 131. A Burmese royal chronicle contradicts this, effectively implying that Burmese control over the Tenasserim coastline was unbroken since 1760. See Ūḥ Moṅ Moṅ Taṅ, *Kunḥ bhoṅ chak mahārājavaṅ tau krīḥ* (Yangon: Universities Historical Research Centre, 2005), vol. 1, pp. 268 and 282.

26. Ms. from the Zetawun monastery, f. *kū*$^{r-v}$.

27. Moṅ Moṅ Taṅ, *Kunḥ bhoṅ*, p. 280. Perhaps, this shift was also related to Sāralaṅkā's association with Kyethtungin Hsayadaw (though it is not mentioned in the testimonies), as Kyethtungin is known to have been granted a royal monastery near Taungbila in 1766.

28. Ms. no. 10551 in UCL, ff. *ḍhau*^{v}–*ḍhaṃ*^{r}.

29. The second available testimony bears a date of December 1787, while also claiming to be recorded in the reign of King Ngasingu-min (r. 1776–1782), that is, eleven to five years earlier than 1787 (ms. no. 10551 in UCL, ff. *ḍaṃ*^{r} and *ḍhaṃ*^{r}). The document also states that the testimony was taken after Sāralaṅkā resided in the royal city for fourteen years (f. *ḍhaṃ*^{r}). If this information is correct and if, indeed, Sāralaṅkā was escorted to Ava in 1766 or 1767, the document thus falls between 1780 and 1781 (which corresponds to the reign of Ngasingu-min).

30. The creative work and biography of Mun Ko are almost entirely forgotten. Apparently, none of his works have been published, and, thus, most contemporary scholars of Burmese literature never saw his writings. I have been told that, besides *Cetyavaṃsa*, there exist several poems written by Mun Ko. U Thein Lwin, deputy director general of archaeology (Upper Myanmar), personal communication, November 2013.

31. The date 1773 suggests that Mun Ko had access to another testimony of Sāralaṅkā's that is not available to us.

32. Undated noncataloged palm-leaf manuscript from the collection of U Bo Kay, the late archaeological conservator of Bagan, now kept in the Archaeological Museum, Bagan. The quote from Sāralaṅkā's testimony appears on folios *cū*^{v}–*ce*^{v} in the Pāli text and on folios *cho*^{v}—*chaṃ*^{r} in the *nissaya*.

33. Ariyāvaṃsa Ādiccaraṃsī, *Samantacakkhudīpanī kyamḥ* (Yangon: Sāsanā reḥ u ci ṭṭhāna, 1985), p. 398. Ariyāvaṃsa Ādiccaraṃsī (1766–1834), also known as the Second Monywe Zetawun Hsayadaw, was one of the most erudite Burmese authors of his time. He combined nonscriptural and scriptural knowledge and took particular interest in chronicles, legal texts, and devotional poetry. He was one of the primary official historiographers of the Burmese court in the 1820s and early 1830s, and a teacher of several ministers. In spelling Ariyāvaṃsa's title, I follow the historical Burmese manner.

34. As mentioned above, the manuscript is undated, but was, most likely, copied in the 1760s or 1770s and, if so, should have belonged to the first abbot of the monastery who preceded Ariyāvaṃsa. The nature of reference given by Ariyāvaṃsa in his 1810 message rules out the possibility that he used the "1787" testimony, for the information Ariyāvaṃsa quotes is absent there. Moreover, the "1787" testimony was taken not in the reign of Hsinbyushin but later.

35. It is likely that Sāralaṅkā was the only candidate for attribution, as no other participants in Siamese missions to Laṅkā are known to have resided in Burma.

36. Ms. from the Zetawun monastery, ff. *kā*^{v} and *kū*^{r}.

37. He stated that he had studied only to the extent of knowing the four *pārājikas* (the rules that constitute one of the most basic observances in the *saṅgha*). Ms. from the Zetawun monastery, f. *kā*^{r}. *Pārājika* rules cover a group of transgressions of monastic discipline that lead to a loss of monastic status: noncelibacy, theft, murder, and false claims of supramundane spiritual attainments.

38. The Burmese term *pa shyū* used in the text could signify both. Ms. from the Zetawun monastery, f. *kū*^{r}. It is not clear if that entailed posing as Muslims.

39. Borommakot (r. 1732–1758) was succeeded by Utumphon and in two months by Ekkathat (r. 1758–1767).

40. This translation is based on the reading of the phrase in question as *ca khyvam maṅ kui sā chak ra saññ*. The second syllable could also be read as *chvam*, which with some degree of imagination might be translated as "the king has personally offered rice," but the syntax is unusual and the translation does not fit the context.

41. Ms. from the Zetawun monastery, f. *kū*^{r}.

42. Ms. no. 10551 in UCL, f. *ḍāḥ*^{v}. Sāralaṅkā did not try to reconcile the claim about the choosing of monks of ten years' standing with the chronology he had provided for himself and, as he did previously, testified that he had been ordained less than ten years before departure for Laṅkā.

43. Ibid., f. *ḍha*^{r}.

44. Ibid., ff. *ḍha*^{v}–*ḍhā*^{r}, *ḍhau*$^{r–v}$.

45. See Blackburn, *Buddhist Learning*. For a comparative case of such dynamics, see the chapter by Amy Holmes-Tagchungdarpa in this volume.

46. In the 1767 testimony, Sāralaṅkā mentioned that Mahinda stūpa and the stūpa enshrining Buddha's nails in Tissavihāra in Anurādhapura were similar in shape to Shwezigon in Bagan, that Mahiyaṅgana *cetiya* (shrine complex) and Dīghāvāpī *cetiya* were similar in shape to Shwedagon in Yangon, and that the landscape of Anurādhapura was similar to the old city of Bagan with its multitude of ancient temples and overgrown terrain. The 1773 testimony, as quoted by Mun Ko, compared Mahāmaṅgalavihāra in Trincomalee to Shwezigon in Bagan; the same comparison was also reproduced in the "1787" testimony. This third document also featured other comparisons, some of them revised as compared to the 1767 testimony.

47. Ms. no. 10551 in UCL, f. *ḍho*^{v}.

48. For a discussion of this curriculum, see Alexey Kirichenko, "Local Sources and Micro-Regional Perspectives on the Histories of Buddhism in Nyaungyan and Konbaung Myanmar," paper given at the "New Perspectives on the History of Myanmar" conference, University of Yangon, July 24, 2014.

49. Ussaro, *Haṃsavatī Chaṅ phrū rhaṅ areḥ tau puṃ mau kvamḥ udānḥ*, edited by Ūḥ Tuiḥ Hla (Yangon: Universities Historical Research Centre, 2006), pp. 137–148.

50. Ms. no. 10551 in UCL, f. *ḍhe*ʳ.

51. The list appears in a message sent by Ñāṇābhivaṃsa to Badon-min. Ñāṇābhivaṃsa, *Ameḥ tau phre* (Yangon: Sāsanā reḥ u ci ṭṭhāna, 2012), pp. 176–189. It is referred to, for example, in Than Tun, "The Influence of Occultism in Burmese History with a Special Reference to Bodawpaya Reign," *Bulletin of the Burma Historical Commission* 1.2 (1960): 117–145.

52. The Burmese term *kyaññḥ* used in the document does not properly differentiate between the two possible locations.

53. In the 1780s and 1790s, Thiri Sandarat was one of the key agents in Burma's external communications, traveling to India and Laṅkā on the instructions of Badon-min. His origins and biography are not clear so far, but I assume that he was most likely either an Indian or an Armenian. The name Punshi might be a scribal error for Munshi.

54. Palm-leaf manuscript no. 5747 in UCL, ff. *tū*ᵛ*–to*ʳ.

55. The same pattern of restoring one's collections to their former contents has guided other historical manuscript acquisition efforts in Buddhist Southern Asia. For example, in 1755 the Kandyan court requested from Ayutthaya seventy-five Pāli works lost in Laṅkā. These (and some twenty more) were delivered by the 1756 mission in which Sāralaṅkā participated. In 1789, a similar request for thirty-three Pāli texts was made to Amarapura. See Oscar von Hinüber, "Remarks on a List of Books Sent to Ceylon from Siam in the 18th Century," *Journal of the Pali Text Society* 12 (1988): 175–183; Ñāṇābhivaṃsa, *Ameḥ tau*, p. 331. The objective to strengthen local tradition through external contacts does not imply that no external borrowing or influence occurred as a result. As amply demonstrated by the fact that 170 mostly new manuscript copies were delivered to Amarapura from Nabadwip in 1785 instead of the 48 replacement texts requested, Buddhist interactions in eighteenth-century Southern Asia likely promoted the traffic of new artifacts and practices though did not result in the establishment of shared networks related to religious orders.

56. Ñāṇābhivaṃsa, *Ameḥ tau*, p. 340.

57. The only extant royal court on the island at the time was in Kandy rather than Anurādhapura, but the Burmese likely framed their connection with the island in terms of Anurādhapura since it was a well-known early royal Buddhist center on the island. At that time it was to some extent administered from the Kandyan royal court with the assistance of subregional intermediaries on the island.

58. Palm-leaf manuscript no. 6093 in the research library of the Ministry of Religious Affairs, Yangon, ff. *ḍho*ᵛ*–ṇi*ʳ.

59. Ñāṇābhivaṃsa, *Ameḥ tau*, p. 331.

60. Ibid., pp. 324–326, 331–332, and 340–341.

61. I follow Anne Blackburn in her use of the term "symptomatic" in Blackburn, "Sīhaḷa Saṅgha and Laṅkā," p. 318.

62. See further, Blackburn, "Buddhist Connections."

63. At the same time, although the practical outcomes of Ñāṇābhivaṃsa's grand plans were more limited, they helped to lay the foundation for more substantial cooperation between Buddhist elites of Burma and Laṅkā achieved by the late nineteenth century.

64. A Burmese translation of this letter referred to Qing and Burmese sovereigns as being equals. For the translation of Qianlong's letter, see Ñāṇābhivaṃsa, *Ameḥ tau*, pp. 211–212. For an official account of the reception of princesses, see Moṅ Moṅ Taṅ, *Kunḥ bhoṅ*, vol. 2, pp. 62–64. For discussion of this diplomatic activity, see Sylvie Pasquiet, "Trois princesses chinoises à la cour d'Amarapura: Petite histoire d'une mystification diplomatique (1790)," in

Études birmanes en hommage à Denise Bernot, edited by Pierre Pichard and François Robinne (Paris: Presses de l'École française d'Extrême-Orient, 1998), pp. 245–259; and U Thaw Kaung, "Bogus Chinese Envoys, Spurious Chinese Princesses at the 18th-Century Myanmar Royal Court," *Journal of Burma Studies* 18.2 (2014): 193–221.

65. Ñāṇābhivaṃsa, *Ameḥ tau*, pp. 213–214.

66. Ibid., p. 308.

67. Ibid., p. 309. The story of Kangxi's arrival at Mt. Wutai is detailed in a chronicle compiled under the supervision of the Second Monywe Zetawun Hsayadaw. Undated palm-leaf manuscript of the fourth bundle of Monywe chronicles in the Zetawun monastery, ff. *jā–ji*. I have not yet been able to trace the origins of this particular narrative.

68. A-ch'angs are a Tibeto-Burman ethnic group from Yunnan. Ñāṇābhivaṃsa, *Ameḥ tau*, pp. 601–602.

69. An attempt at a closer examination of this mix of actors is made, for example, in Alexey Kirichenko, "Political Expansion, Maritime Trade, and Religious Practitioners on the Move: Revival of Interactions between Burma and Lanka in the Late Eighteenth and Early Nineteenth Centuries," lecture given as a part of the Nalanda-Sriwijaya Lecture Series, Nalanda-Sriwijaya Center, Institute of Southeast Asian Studies, Singapore, May 21, 2012.

70. Thongchai Winichakul, "Writing at the Interstices: Southeast Asian Historians and Postnational Histories in Southeast Asia," in *New Terrains in Southeast Asian History*, edited by Abu Talib Ahmad and Tan Liok Ee (Athens: Ohio University Press, 2003), p. 23; Willem van Schendel, "Geographies of Knowing, Geographies of Ignorance: Jumping Scale in Southeast Asia," *Environment and Planning D: Society and Space* 20 (2002): 647–668; James C. Scott, *The Art of Not Being Governed: An Anarchist History of Upland Southeast Asia* (New Haven: Yale University Press, 2009).

71. See, for example, C. Patterson Giersch, *Asian Borderlands: The Transformation of Qing China's Yunnan Frontier* (Cambridge, MA: Harvard University Press, 2006); C. Patterson Giersch, "Grieving for Tibet: Conceiving the Modern State in Late-Qing Inner Asia," *China Perspectives* 3 (2008): 4–18; John E. Herman, *Amid the Clouds and Mist: China's Colonization of Guizhou, 1200–1700* (Cambridge, MA: Harvard University Asia Center, 2007), esp. pp. 103–143.

72. Definitions are given in Christine E. Dobbin, *Asian Entrepreneurial Minorities: Conjoint Communities in the Making of the World-Economy, 1570–1940* (London: Curzon Press, 1996); Edward A. Alpers, *The Indian Ocean in World History* (Oxford: Oxford University Press, 2014); and Sebouh David Aslanian, *From the Indian Ocean to the Mediterranean: The Global Trade Networks of Armenian Merchants from New Julfa* (Berkeley: University of California Press, 2011). These provide a few representative examples of the extensive body of research on Asian entrepreneurial communities.

73. See, for example, Ismail Alatas' contribution to this volume as well as Eric Tagliacozzo and Wen-Chin Chang, eds., *Chinese Circulations: Capital, Commodities, and Networks in Southeast Asia* (Durham: Duke University Press, 2011); Jianxiong Ma and Cunzhao Ma, "The Mule Caravans as Cross-Border Networks: Local Bands and Their Stretch on the Frontier between Yunnan and Burma," in *Myanmar's Mountain and Maritime Borderscapes: Local Practices, Boundary-Making and Figured Worlds*, edited by Su-Ann Oh (Singapore: ISEAS Publishing, 2016), pp. 237–257; Engseng Ho, *Graves of Tarim: Genealogy and Mobility across the Indian Ocean* (Berkeley: University of California Press, 2006); and Ulrike Freitag, "Introduction: Inter-Oceanic Migrations from an Indian Ocean Perspective, 1830s to 1930s," in

Connecting Seas and Connected Ocean Rims: Indian, Atlantic, and Pacific Oceans and China Seas Migrations from the 1830s to the 1930s, edited by Donna R. Gabaccia and Dirk Hoerder, Studies in Global Social History 8 (Leiden: Brill, 2011), pp. 67–78.

74. See, for example, Michael Feener and Terenjit Sevea, eds., *Islamic Connections: Muslim Societies in South and Southeast Asia* (Singapore: Institute of Southeast Asian Studies, 2009); Michael Laffan, *The Making of Indonesian Islam: Orientalism and the Narration of a Sufi Past* (Princeton: Princeton University Press, 2011); Christopher M. Joll, "Islam's Creole Ambassadors," in *The Ghosts of the Past in Southern Thailand: Essays on the History and Historiography of Patani*, edited by Patrick Jory (Singapore: NUS Press, 2012), pp. 129–146.

75. Brian Bocking, Phibul Choompolpaisal, Laurence Cox, and Alicia M. Turner, eds., *A Buddhist Crossroads: Pioneer Western Buddhists and Asian Networks, 1860–1960* (London: Routledge, 2014).

76. Note, however, that there is an ongoing research project by Anne M. Blackburn, "Making Buddhist Kingdoms across the Indian Ocean, 1200–1500."

77. Anthropological work on contemporary Tai Buddhists in Déhóng Prefecture of Yunnan suggests that even now the participation of Tai monks from the area in ordination and educational networks in Myanmar does not displace indigenous Tai lay and monastic formations not recognized by official Burmese monastic institutions. See Takahiro Kojima, "Tăi Buddhist Practices on the China-Myanmar Border," in *Myanmar's Mountain and Maritime Borderscapes*, edited by Su-Ann Oh, pp. 369–387.

78. See Alexey Kirichenko, "Dynamics of Monastic Mobility and Networking in Seventeenth- and Eighteenth-Century Upper Burma," in *Buddhist Dynamics in Premodern and Early Modern Southeast Asia*, edited by D. Christian Lammerts (Singapore: Institute of Southeast Asian Studies, 2015, pp. 333–372); Alexey Kirichenko, "The Thathanabaing Project: Monastic Hierarchies and Colonialism in Burma," in *Theravada Buddhism in Colonial Contexts*, edited by Thomas Borchert, Routledge Critical Studies of Buddhism (London: Routledge, 2018, pp. 138–161); Alexey Kirichenko, "Change, Fluidity, and Unidentified Actors: Understanding the Organization and History of Upper Burmese Saṃgha from the Seventeenth to Nineteenth Centuries," paper presented at the joint meeting of the Association for Asian Studies and the International Convention of Asia Scholars, Honolulu, Hawai'i, April 3, 2011.

79. Blackburn, "Sīhaḷa Saṅgha"; Blackburn, *Buddhist Learning.*

80. See Malalgoda, *Buddhism in Sinhalese Society*; Blackburn, *Buddhist Learning.*

4

CHALLENGING ORDERS

Ṭarīqas *and Muslim Society in Southeastern India and Laṅkā, ca. 1400–1950*

TORSTEN TSCHACHER

On June 24, 1889, a reader's letter was published in the Colombo-based Muslim weekly *Muslim Nēcaṉ*. Its author complained of magical practices that were supposedly going on in some *zāwiyas* (Sufi lodges) in Colombo, rhetorically asking whether "such magic practices belong to our religion?"[1] Such criticism of Sufi institutions and practices is hardly surprising in the context of nineteenth-century Muslim discourse. What is noteworthy is that the author of the letter identified himself as "a Qādirī Muslim," that is, as a member of a specific Sufi order (*ṭarīqa*). And it was clear to his audience that the Sufi lodges condemned in the letter were not general Sufi institutions but themselves connected with a particular *ṭarīqa*, the Shādhiliyya, a Sufi order that had been introduced to Laṅkā[2] in the middle of the nineteenth century. Not surprisingly then, followers of the Shādhiliyya accused the writer of the letter and even the editor of the newspaper that published it of slandering their *ṭarīqa* unnecessarily for what was, in their eyes, a minor incident involving some uneducated people.[3] But what precisely did it mean to be part of a Sufi *ṭarīqa* in South India and Laṅkā in the nineteenth century? What kind of institutions were these *ṭarīqas*? What role did they play in Muslim society and in the history of Islam in the region? And how, if at all, did their constitution change over time? Despite the ubiquity of Sufi orders in historical accounts of Muslim societies in the region, there is surprisingly little research on the social history of *ṭarīqas* in southeastern India and Laṅkā.[4]

This is particularly surprising since the Sufi "order," or *ṭarīqa*, has often been treated as the single most important institution in South Asian Sufi traditions, if not in South Asian Islam as a whole. There are few treatments of the history of Islam in South Asia that do not assume the centrality of different *ṭarīqas*, an assumption evidenced in the casual references to collectives, such as Chishtīs or Naqshbandīs, or to "orders" and "brotherhoods" in general as a central part of Muslim religious life in South Asia. Yet, despite the impression of familiarity with Sufi orders that these accounts suggest, precisely what kind of institution a Sufi "order" in South Asia is supposed to have been is far from clear. As Carl Ernst and Bruce Lawrence state in their magisterial study on the Chishtiyya, "We don't understand [Sufi orders], or at least we haven't figured out how to understand them as historical developments."[5] I would suggest that the centrality of *ṭarīqa*s in the history of South Asian Islam is more apparent than real, a product of historiographical preferences in terms of themes and sources.[6] From the perspective of postpartition South Asia, Islam has been treated predominantly as a political phenomenon, with the history of Islam in South Asia being written primarily as a history of empires, dynasties, and states.[7] In this narrative, the Sufi "orders" serve as a kind of parallel structure to the Muslim state—what empires and dynasties are in the "secular" domain is constituted by *ṭarīqa*s and *silsilas* in the spiritual realm. Not surprisingly, Sufi "orders" are usually discussed with regard to how they related to the Muslim state, on the one hand, and to non-Muslims and the "Islamization" of South Asia, on the other hand. That this narrative seems so convincing is not simply because of its ubiquity but because it is rooted in the sources that have usually been used to write the history of Islam in South Asia—that is the Persian, Arabic, and Urdu texts that were composed by the elites of Muslim states, in which the relationship of worldly and spiritual "authority" (*wilāya*), of sultan and Sufi saint, was an established trope.[8]

Any investigation of South Asian Islam and Muslim societies that is genuinely interested in moving away from state-centric (which means, in most cases, Delhi-centric) narratives will therefore also have to question the role of the *ṭarīqa* as a supposedly central institution of Muslim religious life outside the circles of imperial political elites. Yet, at least as far as the Tamil-speaking parts of South India and Laṅkā are concerned, such a questioning has not happened. If anything, only the template of Sufi orders that are listed is changed: if, in northern India, the Chishtiyya, Suhrawardiyya, and Naqshbandiyya are identified as the most important *ṭarīqa*s, the Qādiriyya, Rifā'iyya, and Shādhiliyya are mentioned instead—there is no questioning of the centrality accorded to conventional ideas of the Sufi "order" in local Muslim society and history. This chapter aims toward initiating a discussion on the social role and constitution of Sufi "orders" in South India and Laṅkā between the sixteenth and nineteenth centuries by reviewing the actual evidence in Tamil and Arabic sources from the region. Proceeding from the nineteenth-century encounter of the by-then-well-established Qādiriyya with the newly introduced Shādhiliyya, I discuss the presence of Sufi lineages, practices aimed at the recollection of *ṭarīqa* identities, and patterns of authority and controversy among Sufis in South India and Laṅkā. As I hope to show, there is little to suggest that Sufi "orders" were unchanging elements of Muslim life in the history of the region. Although localized teaching lineages transmitting Sufi thought were certainly part of Muslim society from an early stage, there is little evidence for clear-cut *ṭarīqa* identifications among these lineages or institutions that could be clearly linked with specific orders. By contrast, the rise of Qādirī and Rifā'ī identities in the region in the seventeenth and eighteenth centuries seems to be more closely related to horizontal networks than to vertical lineages. Only in the mid-eighteenth century do patterns emerge that integrate vertical lineages with the horizontal networks in patterns assumed to be characteristic for Sufi orders, raising the question of what social processes led to change in the organization of Sufi networks and lineages.

LINEAGE

At the center of the notion of the Sufi order stands the idea of the lineage (*silsila*), created by the initiation (*bay'a*) of a disciple (*murīd*) by a preceptor (*murshid*) that allows the transmission of teachings as much as the power of blessing (*baraka*) of the preceptor across generations.[9] What is identified as a Sufi order in any given context is thus generally a network of lineages tracing their traditions back to the same eponymous master. In the case of the Shādhiliyya in nineteenth-century South India and Laṅkā, the connection between lineage and order was particularly salient. The Shādhiliyya had not only been introduced very recently, but, for the whole of the nineteenth century, it looked back to a single origin in Mekka and only a few acts of transmission into the region.[10] For South India, the person credited with the first act of transmission is one Abū Bakr Miskīn (d. 1872) from Kayalpattinam, an important center of Muslim religious life in South India and a stronghold of the Qādiriyya order. Abū Bakr Miskīn was initiated into the Shādhiliyya while on pilgrimage to Mekka. When he returned to his homeland, the new order seems to have spread rapidly. The introduction to Laṅkā is less clear. Some websites claim that a certain Sayyid Aḥmad b. Ṣāliḥ al-Yamanī established the first Shādhilī lodge in AH 1284 (1867–1868 CE), but other sources claim that three merchant brothers from Galle were first initiated into the order in 1846. Within a few years, the order spread in the southern parts of the Madras Presidency and the southwestern region of Laṅkā. Over time, individuals from the region would come to travel to the Middle East to seek their own independent initiation into the order, the most important of them being the gem merchant and politician Mohamed Macan Markar (d. 1952), who is sometimes erroneously credited with being the first to introduce the Shādhiliyya to Laṅkā in the early twentieth century.[11] The fact that the presence of the Shādhiliyya in the region goes back to the efforts of only a few individuals has important repercussions for the order and its image in the nineteenth century, one that, as we shall see, it shared with its contemporaneous Qādirī contenders. For what was transmitted was in effect not the Shādhiliyya as a whole, but only one particular branch of it known as the Fāsiyya, after its founder, Muḥammad al-Fāsī (1803/1804–1872), who personally initiated Abū

Bakr Miskīn in Mekka. Born in Fez in Morocco, al-Fāsī had become a follower of a revivalist Shādhilī branch, the Darqāwiyya, which was spreading in the Maghreb and the Ottoman Empire at that time. This provided the Fāsiyya with cohesion both through the common memory of its relatively recent origins, but also through the commonality of ritual that came along with it.[12] The link created between al-Fāsī's lineage and its South Asian followers has since been re-created repeatedly by visits of al-Fāsī's descendants to Sri Laṅkā and South India, beginning with his son and successor Shams al-Dīn al-Makkī.[13]

At first glance, the Qādiriyya had a far less uniform presence in nineteenth-century South India and Laṅkā. Indeed, its very ubiquity seems to make it impossible to arrive at any clear picture of its role in local Muslim society, not to speak of its origins. It often appears as if the Qādiriyya has been around ever since Muslims came to settle in the region. Yet, much as in the case of the Shādhiliyya, during the nineteenth century the local Qādirī landscape was dominated by individual lineages, some more visible than others, that effectively operated on their own even as they claimed a common Qādirī background. Perhaps the most important of these was the ʻArūsiyya, named after Sayyid Muḥammad b. Aḥmad, better known as Māppiḷḷai Leppai or Imām al-ʻArūs (1816–1898) of Kilakkarai near Ramanathapuram, one of the most prolific authors of Muslim prose literature in Tamil in the period. Māppiḷḷai Leppai traveled widely in India and especially Laṅkā, attracting students and founding mosques and hospices. Although his lineage of initiation was local rather than Middle Eastern, it included several highly regarded Sufis from elite backgrounds. Through his own preceptor and father-in-law, Kīḻakkarai Taykā Ṣāḥib (1778–1850/1851), a noted poet, Māppiḷḷai Leppai traced his lineage to Shaykh ʻUmar Walī (1748–1801) of Kayalpattinam and Sayyid Muḥammad Bukhārī Taṅṅaḷ (1731/1732–1792/1793) of Kannur in Kerala.[14] With both the Qādiriyya and the Shādhiliyya, the nineteenth century presents us with precisely the institutional structures that we have come to expect of Sufi "orders": clearly delineated spiritual lineages (*silsila*) linked up to a larger common "order" (*ṭarīqa*) and identified by compounding the names of both, such as Qādiriyya-ʻArūsiyya or Shādhiliyya-Fāsiyya.

Though the nineteenth century may present us with a textbook image of Sufi orders in South India and Laṅkā, a closer look at the available sources would suggest that this state of affairs was of rather recent origins. Whereas the Shādhiliyya is widely known to have been a nineteenth-century introduction to the region, the Qādiriyya is generally believed to have been the dominant Sufi order in the region for centuries before that. The vast majority of saints venerated in the region are claimed to have some connection to the Qādiriyya. Indeed, ʻAbd al-Qādir al-Jīlānī is even claimed to have visited Laṅkā personally.[15] But a closer look at the available evidence suggests that there is little apart from modern hagiographies to suggest a widespread presence of Qādirī networks in the region before the seventeenth century. For example, although names suggesting Qādirī devotion, such as 'Abd al-Qādir or Muḥyī al-Dīn, are common in the town of Kayalpattinam today, none of the more than seventy individuals recorded in local epitaphs of the fourteenth to sixteenth centuries mentioned in the works of Desai and Shokoohy has such a name. The first listed instance of "Qādirī" names in Kayalpattinam epitaphs is of a certain Sayyid Muḥyi al-Dīn b. Sayyid 'Abd al-Qādir, dating to 1796.[16] The situation seems similar in other towns: none of the other pre-seventeenth-century Arabic and Persian inscriptions from Tamil Nadu listed by Desai records individuals with names that could be linked to a *ṭarīqa*.[17] The two earliest Islamic poems in Tamil, dating to 1572 and 1590, are almost unique in earlier Islamic Tamil literature as they lack a stanza in praise of 'Abd al-Qādir al-Jīlānī in their opening sections.[18] The first eulogies of the saint appear only in the seventeenth century, and, even with regard to these eulogies, we have to note that Qādirī devotionalism does not necessarily imply the presence of an institutionalized Qādirī order—even one of the main Tamil Shādhilī hagiographies of the nineteenth century begins with a chapter on the life of 'Abd al-Qādir al-Jīlānī. That al-Jīlānī is part of the *silsila* of many Sufi orders, not only of expressly Qādirī lineages, makes devotional traditions around al-Jīlānī weak evidence for the presence of an institutionalized Qādirī order.[19]

It would not be correct to say, however, that lineages of initiation played no role or were not mentioned in this period. We have a number of examples, mostly dating to around 1700, where several generations of teachers are mentioned, especially when a teacher was well known, but without mentioning a particular order that was transmitted through such teaching lineages. A good example is provided by perhaps the best-known Muslim religious scholar of the Tamil country in the seventeenth century, Shaykh Ṣadaqatullāh b. Sulaymān of Kayalpattinam (1632–1703). Although Ṣadaqatullāh is generally assumed to have been a Qādirī and is frequently mentioned in the Tamil literature of the period, his affiliation to the Qādiriyya does not seem to be mentioned in that literature. It is indeed noteworthy that most present-day Qādirī lineages in the region seem to trace themselves to lineages that entered Tamil Nadu and Laṅkā during the eighteenth century at earliest and not to Ṣadaqatullāh. A prime example of this is Māppillai Leppai, who, as already mentioned, traced his initiation to an eighteenth-century preceptor from Kerala rather than to Ṣadaqatullāh even though he was descended from the latter through both his father and his mother.

It is not that the Qādiriyya or other Sufi orders were absent from the region in the sixteenth and seventeenth centuries. Rather, it seems that affiliation to a specific order was not of particular importance, most probably because individuals were affiliated to several orders and not just to one, or possibly because notions about the meaning of *ṭarīqa* affiliation differed from those that are held nowadays. In the process, the precise lineage and preceptors who bundled affiliation to several orders would have become more important than the historically more distant orders themselves. One such order whose presence beside the Qādiriyya in South India and Laṅkā during the sixteenth and seventeenth centuries is strongly suggested is the Shaṭṭāriyya, given the strong presence of that order in other parts of the southern Asian littoral, such as Gujarat or Java. The region's most celebrated Muslim saint, Shāh al-Ḥamīd of Nagore, was a disciple of the Shaṭṭārī preceptor Muḥammad Ghawth of Gwalior (d. 1563), though much less is nowadays made of Shāh al-Ḥamīd's connection to this order than of his additional initiation into the Qādiriyya. As I have suggested elsewhere, it is possible that Sām Shihāb al-Dīn (1634/1635–1709), a younger brother of Shaykh Ṣadaqatullāh, may have been a disciple of Ibrāhīm al-Kūrānī (1614–1690) and the latter's teacher, Aḥmad al-Qūshāshī (d. 1661). Although both of these scholars were, like Shāh al-Ḥamīd, initiated into multiple Sufi *ṭarīqa*s, al-Qūshāshī is most commonly remembered as a preceptor of the Shaṭṭāriyya, whereas al-Kūrānī has been most prominent as a Naqshbandī teacher.[20] In such contexts of multiple initiation and transmission of orders, it would hardly be surprising if distinct "lineages" became more important as points of identification than those of the broader framework of "orders."

Although specific lineages seem to have played an important role in the early transmission of Sufi discourse in southern India and Laṅkā, individual lineages appear to have played a less conspicuous role in the process that first brought not just a particular lineage but a specific Sufi order into the limelight locally. The first clear mention that I have found of a Sufi order in a text from the region is in the *Vētapurāṇam*, probably composed in the second quarter of the eighteenth century. In a chapter devoted to becoming a disciple of a Sufi preceptor, the text claims that "it means a great blessing if one takes hold of the Qādiriyya."[21] It appears that in this period Qādirī lineages in the region began increasingly to be linked to preceptors operating on the west coast of India, thereby possibly obscuring links to networks of orders, Qādirī or otherwise, that may have existed in the region earlier. The most conspicuous feature of these networks is their close interlinking of the Qādiriyya with another order, the Rifā'iyya. Although this order plays an important part in Muslim religious life in both South India and Laṅkā, it has not attracted the same attention from historians as the Qādiriyya, most likely because the Rifā'iyya is far less visible in written sources than the Qādiriyya, and it is most salient among the ranks of itinerant mendicant groups such as the Bawas.[22] The linkages between such groups and the Rifā'iyya connect this order with the Malangs and similar itinerant groups. Indeed, at Tamil Nadu's largest saint-shrine, the Nagore Dargah, Rifā'īs and Malangs play a central role in the rituals performed during the annual festival.[23] Already in 1805, the Scottish orientalist John Leyden (1775–1811), drawing on informants from Malabar, identified "the sect of Ruffii" as a division of the Madāriyya, the order with which the Malangs are most commonly associated.[24] Lifestyle thereby developed into a marker of affiliation to specific orders so that it is often difficult to establish whether certain individuals were indeed formally affiliated with a specific order or were simply identified as members of these orders owing to their living as itinerant mendicants.

Both Rifāʿiyya and Qādiriyya have historically spread through the same networks of itinerant Sufis centered on the Lakshadweep archipelago off the Indian west coast. The person who "discovered" the site of Jailani in the nineteenth century was from Androth Island in the Lakshadweep archipelago, as are many of the Rifāʿī preceptors still active in the region.[25] The participation of Rifāʿī dervishes in the celebrations of shrines with strong Qādirī connections, such as Nagore or Jailani, similarly points to the closeness of these two orders. Although it is from these common Qādirī-Rifāʿī networks that the most prominent Qādirī lineages of the nineteenth century emerged, lineages seem far less salient in these networks as a whole. Furthermore, although family links appear to be rather important in the lineages we have discussed so far, with transmission from father to son or among brothers playing an important role in succession, such kinship links seem to have been of lesser importance to the itinerant Sufis who connected ordinary Muslims throughout South India and Laṅkā to preceptors in the western archipelagos of Lakshadweep and the Maldives. This conjecture still requires far more investigation, but the point can be illustrated by taking a look at a *silsila* contained in a mid-twentieth-century manuscript in my possession (folios 129r–130r).[26] This manuscript was originally owned by a woman named Balqīs Bī, probably from the vicinity of Nagore, who was initiated into the Qādiriyya in February 1944 by a preceptor from Androth Island. From the *silsila*, it emerges not only that her preceptor, Sayyid Muḥammad Pūkōyā b. al-Sayyid ʿAbd al-Qādir, was initiated into both the Qādiriyya and the Rifāʿiyya, but that his own preceptor, at least in the Qādirī line, was not his father. Although their itinerant lifestyle allowed these Sufis to connect and integrate a larger region through a single network, this network was held together less by loyalty to particular lineages than by memories and practices that identified all those who participated in this network with the larger order that served as a common signifier.

RECOLLECTION

In his recent overview of Sufi traditions, Nile Green cautions us not to overlook that, for much of the history of Sufism, Sufi *ṭarīqas* "were forced to operate largely as conceptual communities in which fellowship was built on bonds of memory and imagination rather than bureaucratic ties and direct communication."[27] It was the memory of the transmission of authority and practices from master to disciple over the centuries that made it possible for Muslims to identify as members of such institutions as the Qādiriyya or Shādhiliyya, both named after the Sufi master who is supposed to have initiated the chain of transmission.

Given the importance of memory to the constitution of separate lineages into orders, it is actually surprising that one of the main technologies for the transmission of such memories, namely, hagiographies of important saints, was almost absent from the repertoire of Islamic writings from southeastern India and Laṅkā before the nineteenth century. Such hagiographies formed an important part of non-Muslim Tamil literature, however, the most important being Cēkkiḻār's twelfth-century *Periyapurāṇam*, a hagiography of the most important Śaiva saints of the region.[28] Although Muslim authors adopted the genres and conventions of Tamil literature and apparently especially of Śaiva literature, they focused their attention almost exclusively on the life of the Prophet and his family. For the most part, references to Sufi saints before the nineteenth century were limited to short stanzas in praise of 'Abd al-Qādir al-Jīlānī or (rarely) other saints at the beginning of longer poems. Thus, Sām Shihāb al-Dīn's *Rasūl mālai*, more than a fifth of which consists of stanzas in praise of scholars and savants of Islam from the Prophet to the poet's own family, lists only five saints connected with establishing Sufi orders: al-Jīlānī (stanza 76), al-Suhrawardī (77), al-Rifā'ī (79), al-Shādhilī (89), and al-'Aydarūs (93).[29] Until the late eighteenth century, only 'Abd al-Qādir al-Jīlānī's life was made the subject of occasional hagiographical texts, and none of these was in the esteemed *kāppiyam* genre in which the life of the Prophet and his family had been told since the late sixteenth century.[30] Long poems in the *kāppiyam* genre concerning the hagiographies of important Sufis were not composed before the early nineteenth century, when there was a sudden efflorescence of such poems about al-Jīlānī (three poems dating to 1810, 1814, and 1816) and local saints (the *Tirukkāraṇappurāṇam* on Shāh al-Ḥamīd of Nagore of 1812, and the *Tīṉviḷakkam* on Sayyid Ibrāhīm of Ervadi of 1821).[31]

Things began to change rapidly with the adoption of print by Tamil Muslims from the 1840s onwards. Not only were further *kāppiyam* poems composed, but publishers increasingly printed poems in praise of both local and Middle Eastern saints. By the end of the nineteenth century, the extension of narrative prose in Tamil also affected the publication of hagiographies, including those of important Sufis. The first prose texts seem to have been composed in honor of local saints, especially Shāh al-Ḥamīd of Nagore, but it is noteworthy that among these earliest prose texts we find two Shādhilī hagiographies, *Hidāyat al-Sālikīn fī Takhlīs al-Hālikīn* (1898) by Muḥammad Ismā'īl of Nagapattinam, and *Nafaḥāt al-'Anbar fī Manāqib al-Quṭb al-Akbar* (1902) by Nūḥ b. 'Abd al-Qādir of Kayalpattinam (1830/1831–1905/1906), a well-known scholar and author.[32] Shādhilī authors seem to have quickly adopted the technology of print for their own purposes: a short poem in praise of al-Shādhilī had already been published in 1871, and, by 1914, a full-fledged *kāppiyam* poem titled *Cātulināyakam* had been composed on al-Shādhilī.[33] But Shādhilī authors were not the only ones who competed for space in the developing market for Muslim publications in Tamil. Thus, in 1915, a printing press in Madras issued a volume containing Arabic panegyrics (composed by the Qādirī Māppiḷḷai Leppai) and a hagiography of Mu'īn al-Dīn al-Chishtī as well as a collection of stories about important Chishtī saints, though the Chishtiyya never attained the same popularity among Tamil-speaking Muslims as the Qādiriyya and the Shādhiliyya.[34]

Literary hagiographies were only part of the process of remembering and commemorating the Sufi masters of the past; stories and biographies also circulated orally among disciples and supporters of Sufi lineages and networks. The pattern of the production of hagiographic texts is nevertheless revealing. Literary texts brought with them prestige, especially if they were composed in highly regarded genres like the *kāppiyam*, as well as aiding the creation of "interpretive communities" that shared a common understanding of their lineages and networks as being grounded in an accepted recollection of the deeds and lives of earlier preceptors.[35] In this context, the historical development of the textual recollection of Sufi saints in the Tamil region is revealing. Until the late seventeenth century, it seems that Muslims in the Tamil-speaking parts of South India and Laṅkā were not particularly concerned about the creation of hagiographical accounts about earlier Sufi masters—the Prophet and his family were the prime focus of narrative poetry. When hagiographic writing emerged around 1700, it focused almost exclusively on 'Abd al-Qādir al-Jīlānī, probably reflecting the rise of the regionwide Qādirī network spreading from the western islands in this period. It is only in the context of the nineteenth century that hagiographies of Sufi saints start to form a major element of Muslim writing in Tamil. It is not surprising that the same period saw Qādirīs discuss the propriety of certain stories about 'Abd al-Qādir al-Jīlānī in the new medium of the newspaper or that some of the earliest catalogs of Sufi orders in Tamil are to be found in the Shādhilī hagiographies.[36] As more Sufi orders and lineages came to compete for followers in South India and Laṅkā, textual production increased and fed into the development of a print market for Muslim publications.

Yet orders were not only constituted and defined through a recollection of their past—the definition of certain practices in the present proved to be of similar importance, especially as many of these practices were themselves connected to the recollection of the place of the *ṭarīqa* and lineage in the divine order of things. To quote Nile Green again, "the method of master-disciple learning and the reading of training texts ensured some degree of standardization in the doctrines and practices held by fellow members of the same brotherhood."[37] Nineteenth-century Sufi discourse in South India and Laṅkā placed a heavy emphasis on the practices enjoined by the *ṭarīqa* in question. The connection between *ṭarīqa* and practice is particularly salient in those practices that are limited to specific Sufi orders, such as the performance of litanies for recollection of God, the Prophet, and the saints, such as *dhikr*, *wird*, or *rātib*. Many of the important nineteenth-century lineages performed their characteristic litanies, such as the *Rātiba Jalāliyya* of the Qādiriyya-'Arūsiyya composed by Māppiḷḷai Leppai or al-Fāsī's *Ṣalāt al-Yāqūtiyya* in the Shādhiliyya-Fāsiyya.

Hagiographies were similarly not limited to extolling the learning, miracles, and lineages of the respective saints and preceptors. Muḥammad Ismā'īl's collection of hagiographies of important Shādhilī preceptors is immediately followed by a 130-page tract on the meaning of *ṭarīqa* and the performance of *dhikr*, and then by about 120 pages of *wird* and other types of Arabic poems for ritual recitation. Thus, more than half of what is purportedly a hagiography is actually filled with information on how to be a practicing Shādhilī. Similarly, in the manuscript of a Qādirī woman of the 1940s that I have mentioned above, a short tract is devoted to the performance of *dhikr* in accordance with Qādirī "customs" (*ādāb*). In this way, the nineteenth-century lineages are comparable to what Jamil Abun-Nasr refers to as "Sufi brotherhoods," that is, centralized and exclusive communities of Sufis following only the distinctive rules and practices set down by the brotherhood's founder. This similarity is not surprising, especially in case of the Fāsiyya. Many of the "brotherhoods" discussed by Abun-Nasr formed in northern Africa and provided the context in which the Darqāwiyya, the branch of the Shādhiliyya to which the Fāsiyya belongs, developed. Furthermore, the development of such exclusive Sufi communities was itself a fairly recent development, usually not dating back beyond the eighteenth century.[38]

It is therefore unsurprising that the connection between practice and a specific order was not always so close. This is not to say that practice and notions about the propriety or impropriety of certain practices played no role in earlier Sufi networks and that the emphasis on proper practice in the nineteenth century is part of a process of "Islamization" in which an earlier, somehow less "Islamic" and compromised situation is replaced by closer attention to proper religious behavior and an increased reception of Arabic texts. Rather, what seems to have been missing in the earlier period was the way in which "order" and "practice" defined and reinforced each other, with an order being defined by particular practices and particular practices being the domain of a specific order. In contrast, some of the earlier Islamic nonnarrative religious literature in Tamil, although drawing profusely on Middle Eastern Sufi authors, does not seem to proclaim its *ṭarīqa* background in any meaningful manner. Thus, Maḥmūd b. Muḥammad Leppai's early eighteenth-century dogmatic tract *Iẓām al-Fawā'id fī Niẓām al-'Aqā'id* explicitly draws on works by al-Ghazālī, al-Nawawī, Ibn al-'Arabī, al-Jīlī, al-Burhānpūrī, and al-Qūshāshī but does not seem to ally with any particular order.[39]

The first texts that explicitly proclaim their affiliation with the Qādiriyya, in contrast, appear rather different from prose tracts like *Iẓām al-Fawā'id*. These are poems often dubbed "songs of gnosis," or *meyññāṉap pāṭalkaḷ* (sing. *meyññāṉap pāṭal*) in Tamil.[40] The peculiarity of these songs is that they combine the vocabulary of a Śaiva poetic tradition, so-called Siddha (Tamil *cittar*) poetry, with esoteric Islamic discourse in a dense and as yet insufficiently studied manner. The already mentioned *Vētapurāṇam* clearly draws on this tradition, whose author is significantly said to have been a disciple of the author of

Izām al-Fawā'id. Similar poetry is connected to later authors with clear-cut Qādirī affiliation, such as Shaykh 'Umar Walī and Kīlakkarai Taykā Ṣāḥib. The latter was not only the preceptor of Māppiḷḷai Leppai, but also the teacher of the most important exponent of this style of Islamic Tamil poetry, Kuṇaṅkuṭi Mastān Ṣāḥib. Although these songs drew considerable criticism from some quarters in the nineteenth century—the *Vētapurāṇam* was apparently refuted in AH 1272 (1855/1856 CE) by a convocation of Islamic religious scholars[41]—it is erroneous to characterize them as the product of a weakly Islamized convert society, as is still sometimes done.[42] A widely read scholar such as Māppiḷḷai Leppai felt no inhibitions about quoting poems by Kuṇaṅkuṭi Mastān Ṣāḥib in his religious manuals, and such poems are commonly encountered in Qādirī contexts in South India and Laṅkā.[43] The 1940s manuscript of a Qādirī devotee that I have referred to similarly contains not only texts recording the woman's lineage and proper Qādirī devotional exercises, but also the text of the *Pismil Kuṟam*, a famous *meyññāṉap pāṭal* by the seventeenth-century poet Pīr Muḥammad of Takkalai. Apparently, Balqīs Bī considered such poetry and its interpretation to be as fundamental a part of her religious life as the performance of *dhikr* or the commemoration of her preceptor.

Thus, the situation observed in South India and Laṅkā casts doubt on common assumptions made in studies of Sufism in South Asia and elsewhere that Sufi orders played an important part in the Islamization of the general Muslim population.[44] There seems little evidence that the Qādiriyya or any other Sufi order aided early processes of Islamization, though for most Muslim authors of the period Sufism was a fundamental part of Islamic practice. Rather than the Qādiriyya simplifying Sufi discourse in vernacular poetry for an uneducated audience, it appears that part of the appeal of the Qādiriyya was provided precisely by the opposite process of drawing local Muslims into an "interpretive community" capable of decoding the complex esoteric poetry that was popular in Qādirī circles and that reached beyond the prose treatises on proper practice that circulated in more localized lineages.[45] Interpretation of such poetry thus came to be a practice that defined the Qādirī networks of the period much as Arabic litanies were to do in the second half of the nineteenth century. Although there were no formalized or even state-backed institutions among local Muslims that could inculcate a set of interpretive practices through an educational curriculum, as was the case in the rise of the Siyam Nikāya in eighteenth-century Lankan monasticism, it is clear that *meyññāṉap pāṭalkaḷ* and the capacity to interpret them in an Islamic framework were part and parcel of the extension of integrative and assimilative networks, networks that, in the course of the eighteenth and nineteenth centuries, increasingly came to define themselves by propagating specific practices of interpretation and recollection, thereby demarcating their boundaries and highlighting their individuality, which in turn allowed followers to identify with particular practices and lineages propagated within the network and thus to distinguish it further from other networks.

AUTHORITY

Although the intersection of initiation lineages with certain practices may have helped to define these lines more clearly, this alone would not have been enough to integrate distinct lineages in different localities into common patterns of practice and identity across space as usually associated with the term "order" (*ṭarīqa*). The barriers of communication and limits of de facto authority meant that in many parts of the Muslim world, Sufi *ṭarīqa*s were linked, if at all, by reproduction of a common memory and identity. But in order for different lineages to become, again in the words of Nile Green, "mechanisms of the reproduction and standardization of tradition,"[46] they required more than just an awareness of those lineages and sets of defining practices. They required networks through which their ideas and practices could circulate. These networks needed to command a certain authority to be able to extend themselves into new contexts, ensure adherence of individual groups and lineages to the network, and contest the claims of rival networks. In order to understand how authority was established in Sufi networks in southern India and Laṅkā, let us turn now to consider developments in the nineteenth century.

In the case of the Shādhiliyya-Fāsiyya, the importance of its network and the speed with which it was able to replicate this network in southern Tamil Nadu and the southwestern regions of Laṅkā is remarkable. Although more research is required to be able to map the extension of this network in the course of the nineteenth century exhaustively, it seems likely that a lot depended on individuals like Abū Bakr Miskīn, who brought the order to the region from Mekka. The participation of religious scholars like Nūḥ b. ʻAbd al-Qādir al-Qāhirī, who could support the growth of the network through the production of texts and their distribution via a growing number of printers and booksellers, similarly may have boosted the prestige and appeal of the Shādhiliyya. A third factor may have been the institution of the lodge, or *zāwiya*. In a region where existing Sufi structures, especially shrines, had a long association with the Qādiriyya, the Shādhilī *zāwiyas* allowed the order to colonize local spaces effectively by creating distinctly Shādhilī cityscapes.

Yet the Shādhiliyya-Fāsiyya provided its followers with something even more attractive. As part of the Darqāwiyya, a larger movement of traditionalist Sufi revival, the Fāsiyya fit well within the religious context of Muslim societies in South India and Laṅkā during the later nineteenth century. The Fāsiyya offered more than a revival of Sufi Islam: in contrast to similar movements among the Qādiriyya in the region, the Fāsiyya was directly connected to the Middle East. Al-Fāsī and his successors resided in Mekka, the religious center of the Muslim world, while his branch maintained close connections with larger Shādhilī networks that spread across northern Africa, including Egypt, to Syria. Ẓāfir al-Madanī (1829–1903), the son of al-Fāsī's own preceptor, had even initiated 'Abd al-Ḥamīd II into the Shādhiliyya before the latter became Ottoman sultan. In the late nineteenth century, Egypt and the Ottoman Empire, much more than North India, were the focus of interest among Tamil-speaking Muslims for their role in the revival of Muslim societies, as they were in other Muslim societies across Southern Asia. This interest was fueled by a growing consciousness among South Indian and Lankan Muslims of being part of not only a religious but also a political community defending itself against encroachments by European powers from the Sudan to Aceh and beyond.[47] That the Shādhilīs were well connected to the Middle East was repeatedly brought home by the announcements they circulated in Tamil newspapers informing the members of the order of the passing away of important preceptors in Egypt and Arabia and the memorial rituals that were to be conducted at local *zāwiya*s. Similarly, Nūḥ b. 'Abd al-Qādir made it a point to mention that his hagiography of al-Shādhilī was based on "pearls [found] in books from Egypt and Mekka."[48]

If its connections to the religious and political centers of the Middle East gave the Shādhiliyya a good measure of authority when it began spreading in South India and Laṅkā in the mid-nineteenth century, Qādirī lineages were able to draw on the already existing authority of a network that had spread throughout South India and Laṅkā one or two centuries earlier. The linchpin of this network lay also to the west, though much closer to Tamil Nadu and Laṅkā, in the Lakshadweep and Maldivian archipelagos off the western coast of India and especially on the Lakshadweep island of Androth. It was from there that itinerant Sufi preceptors traveled throughout present-day Kerala, Tamil Nadu, and Laṅkā and initiated disciples into the fold of the two orders they were spreading—the Qādiriyya and the Rifā'iyya. These itinerant preceptors generally claimed to be descendants of the Prophet (Tamil *taṅkaḷ*; Malayalam *taṅṅaḷ*). Although this often went along with a claim that they ultimately hailed from Yemen or Ḥaḍramawt, the appeal and charisma of these *taṅkaḷ*s were predicated on the fact that their descent from the Prophet endowed them with *baraka*, blessings from God that allowed them to work miracles. An early eyewitness account of faith in the miracle-working capacities of the people from the western islands with linkages to the Qādiriyya and the Rifā'iyya was given by John Leyden. In autumn 1805, Leyden journeyed from the Indian west coast to Penang on board a native vessel. Among the crew, he noted that "the two Mu'allim's or pilots are Maldivians prodigiously addicted to Sorcery and adepts completely [*sic*] in the Elmi Dawat [i.e., medicine]."[49] When the vessel was pursued by pirates off the coast of Sumatra, one of the Maldivians went into a trance and began to work charms to make the ship escape the pirates, "all which time he continued in a more ecstatic manner to howl forth Arabic prayers to God, the Prophet, Ali & the Imams but especially to Ruffii."[50] Yet despite the importance of claims to descent from the Prophet and links to Arabian Sea networks and southern Arabia, this Qādirī-Rifā'ī combine in the seventeenth to nineteenth centuries drew as much authority from is its decidedly vernacular character, embodied in the songs of gnosis, or *meyññāṉap pāṭalkaḷ*, that spread as part of the network and that tied followers into a common interpretive community.

Even in the case of early localized lineages, the authority that they wielded can sometimes be gleaned from the fact that their members were integrated into the highest levels of Muslim mercantile elites in the region. The most obvious example is the family of Shaykh Ṣadaqatullāh, whose daughter married the son of the merchant Māmu Nayiṉār, widely believed to have been the younger brother of the magnate Cītakkāti. One son of this marriage, Leppai Nayiṉār, became the linchpin of power in the Ramnad kingdom during the 1720s to 1730s. It is noteworthy that two *kāppiyam* poems funded by Leppai Nayiṉār mention his maternal descent from Ṣadaqatullāh before his paternal descent from Māmu Nayiṉār, suggesting the repute of his Sufi grandfather.[51]

As Sufi networks, with their claims to distinctive practices and prestigious lineages, encountered each other they also got into conflicts over ideas, practices, and claims to status and lineage. Indeed, the noteworthiness of the Shādhiliyya in the region has been predicated on precisely the fact that it was able to carve out a niche for itself in a "religious marketplace" monopolized by the authority of the Qādiriyya. Like the latter, the Shādhiliyya-Fāsiyya spread among Muslim "householders," often of elite background, rather than among the itinerant dervish groups where the Rifā'iyya was and remains the dominant Sufi order in the region. These social dynamics provided ample opportunity for conflict between adherents of different Sufi orders.

Internal controversies in Muslim societies of Tamil Nadu and Laṅkā generally revolved around the propriety of various practices and claims to authority.[52] It is thus hardly surprising that not only individual Sufis or lineages came to contest each other's claims, but also the followers of *ṭarīqa*s as a whole. This became acutely visible when the Shādhiliyya began to challenge the authority of Qādirī networks in the second half of the nineteenth century. The letters to the editor of *Muslim Nēcaṉ* quoted at the beginning of this chapter are a good example of such exchanges. Concomitantly, the number of letter writers who identified as either Qādirī or Shādhilī Muslims similarly rose.[53] Although little can be said about the exact dynamics of these controversies, it seems that the complaints tended to be leveled in the first place by the Qādirīs against the Shādhilīs, suggesting that the former may have felt threatened by the expansion of the new order. The most important preceptors and scholars of the two orders seem to have maintained cordial relationships. Thus, the Shādhilī scholar Nūḥ b. 'Abd al-Qādir wrote Arabic poetry in praise of both al-Fāsī and the Qādirī Mappiḷḷai Leppai, and a *kāppiyam* poem composed about the life of al-Shādhilī in 1914 acknowledged the seniority of the Qādiriyya in the region by praising the local Qādirī lineage extending from Bukhārī Taṅṅaḷ via Shaykh 'Umar to the latter's son and grandson, Kāyalpaṭṭiṉam Taykā Ṣāḥib and Muḥammad Ṣāliḥ, before praising al-Fāsī, Shams al-Dīn al-Makkī, and Abū Bakr Miskīn.[54]

Nevertheless, their followers appear to have not infrequently viewed each other with suspicion. Particularly irksome for the Qādirīs seems to have been the claim frequently made in Shādhilī writings that the Shādhiliyya was preferable to other *ṭarīqa*s.

The second part of Muḥammad Ismā'īl's collection of hagiographies, tellingly, more or less began with a chapter on the preeminence of the Shādhiliyya (*Faḍl al-ṭarīqa al-shādhiliyya*).[55] The most coherent and (for the Qādirīs) annoying exposition of this topic was a tract penned by al-Fāsī himself, titled "The Lordly Introduction Concerning the Preferability of the Shādhilī Ṭarīqa" (*al-Futuḥāt al-rabbaniyya fī tafḍīl ṭarīqa al-shādhiliyya*), which enumerated twenty-six reasons why the Shādhiliyya was preferable to all other Sufi orders. It is hardly surprising that the Qādirīs sought to counter this tract and ultimately published a rejoinder to it.[56] It also seems noteworthy that these controversies between the two orders appear to have been more pronounced in Laṅkā, where, in the decades around the turn of the nineteenth century, Muslim elites were beginning to formulate and contest political claims both among one another and with Tamil and Sinhala politicians. In this context, the two predominant orders (at least in the politically dominant southwestern parts of the islands) came to be linked up with rival political factions.[57]

There is, however, far less evidence for the role of *ṭarīqa*s in local religious controversies before the nineteenth century. This is not particularly surprising given that, before the advent of print, such controversies were most likely local and left no trace in the written record. Nevertheless, two factors need to be mentioned. The first has to do with the language adopted as the Qādiriyya's dominant idiom of expression, namely poetry in the style and vocabulary of Śaiva religious poetry in general, and Siddha poetry in particular. Siddha poetry is often considered to have been highly critical of the existing social and religious order. Most scholars have interpreted the Muslim adoption of the Siddha idiom as a sign of accommodation, religious sharing, and an ecumenical commitment to "the brotherhood of a universal faith."[58] Yet this view is one-sided, as it only takes into account the appropriation of Muslim poets by Hindu audiences. Looking at the actual poetry makes it clear that not only did Muslims use standard notions and fundamental texts of Sufi Islam, but they also resignified the vocabulary of Siddha poetry for Muslim use—for example, by taking the term *ainteḻuttu*, or "five letters," to refer not to the Śaiva mantra *namaḥ śivāya*, but rather to the five-letter Arabic term *al-ḥamd*.[59] It may therefore be possible that the adoption of the Siddha idiom served a double purpose, namely, appropriating a popular idiom critiquing Hindu orthodoxy while at the same time subverting that very idiom from a Muslim perspective.

The other noteworthy factor is the peculiar dominance that the Qādiriyya and Rifā'iyya had achieved in the region by the beginning of the nineteenth century. This first raises the question of how far this spread was accomplished at the expense of other lineages, such as the Shaṭṭārī or the Naqshbandī, and how far their apparent integration into dominant Qādirī networks was harmonious. It is also surprising that other *ṭarīqa*s that might have spread in southern India and Laṅkā have hardly been able to make inroads. Thus, the Chishtiyya with its pan-Indian networks is hardly present in the region beyond the minority Urdu-speaking communities. That the Chishtiyya was unable to spread beyond its social base while a *ṭarīqa* with no local ties whatsoever like the Shādhiliyya was may hint at what made the latter attractive, namely, its capacity to provide an alternative for Muslim elites (or, perhaps better, "householders") to the predominant Qādirī network(s) while at the same time not being associated with any other established elite social formation in the region, as was clearly the case with the Chishtiyya. The Shādhiliyya was well equipped to offer an alternative to the Qādiriyya in the region. The network of *zāwiya*s not only permitted the order to operate independently of religious institutions dominated by Qādirīs, but also provided it with a sacred landscape in a country where the main shrines were associated with combined Qādirī-Rifā'ī networks. Furthermore, the authority that the Shādhiliyya-Fāsiyya could draw from its association with elites in Mekka, Egypt, and the Ottoman Empire made the order more than capable to take on the established order, much as the connection with the western archipelagos, itinerant *taṅkaḷ*s, and a cherished but esoteric body of poetry had provided the Qādirī-Rifā'ī networks with the authority to integrate apparently autonomous Sufi lineages in the preceding centuries.

The discussion presented above has shown that the common assumption of Sufi orders—more specifically, the Qādiriyya—playing a central and more or less unchanging part in Muslim religious life in the Tamil-speaking parts of South India and Laṅkā for many centuries needs to be questioned and possibly modified. Rather, the data seem to suggest three distinct types of Sufi formations in the region. The earliest recognizable institution is the simple teaching lineage, by which doctrine and practices were passed on through the generations. Although these lineages may ultimately have traced themselves back to a common origin in a particular preceptor, there is relatively little in the material to suggest that. Rather, lineages may actually have been affiliated to different preceptors and the *ṭarīqa*s associated with them simultaneously so that what ultimately came to matter to an individual Sufi in the region in the earlier period was not so much the role as a member of a particular "order" but rather the particularized and localized participation in a teaching lineage through which multiple affiliations could be transmitted. The evidence for these lineages seems to suggest, furthermore, that they mattered only for those Muslims who were actively engaged in the study of religious knowledge, thus necessitating connection with an authoritative teacher for this purpose. There is little evidence of lay (if the term may be used) participation in Sufi practice during this earlier period. Sufism, in other words, seems to have been a part of Islamic learning that mattered to those who possessed or sought that learning, much like law or knowledge of the *ḥadīth*, whereas ordinary Muslims do not seem to have sought out initiation into any institutionalized Sufi lineage.

This situation seems to have been transformed by new developments starting around 1600. The period that followed saw the expansion of a new type of Sufi network from the western islands via Kerala to Tamil Nadu and Laṅkā—a network that was created by itinerant Sufis pledging allegiance to both the Qādiriyya and the Rifā'iyya but that was linked to settled society in the Muslim towns of the region primarily through the Qādiriyya. This network seems not only to have integrated local lineages, but also to have drawn a wider spectrum of local Muslim society into Qādirī devotionalism and commemorative practice, partly by forming an "interpretive community" around the textual corpus of Tamil songs of gnosis. In this network, with its itinerant preceptors, the actual Sufi lineage a person was initiated into seems to have been less important, thanks to its removal from the local scene. What mattered to the initiated layman was not so much the lineage but integration into the network created by these itinerant preceptors. It is only around the end of the eighteenth century that some lineages in this network seem to have risen to prominence and begun to form the nucleus of integrated "lineage orders" of the type that have often been assumed to be representative of Sufi orders. During the nineteenth century, such lineage orders formed the model not only for Qādirī practice, but also for those who challenged Qādirī dominance in the region, most notably the Shādhiliyya-Fāsiyya.

What does that mean for our understanding of Muslim history and the role of "orders" in the region more generally? What social developments were behind the transformations that took place between the sixteenth and nineteenth centuries, and which factors influenced these developments? Much more research is required to address these questions properly, but some observations can be made based on this initial study. Our knowledge of the situation preceding the late sixteenth century is, admittedly, still rather sketchy. However, the extension of a transregional Sufi network that integrated Muslim communities in the region from around 1600 onwards coincides with what appears to be an era of increased competition among religious groups in the region. The inroads made by European powers into both the economic and the religious organization of the central Indian Ocean was only one aspect of these transformations, though one that affected coastal Muslim communities significantly. Another interesting aspect is that the peculiar structure of the network, with its emphasis on the horizontal, integrative aspects of shared texts, interpretive practices, and recollection of a common heritage rather than the vertical hierarchy of the lineage, may have been one way of integrating the dispersed Muslim communities of the region in a situation where no central institution, such as a church or an empire, was able to effect such an integration. Whereas farther to the north Muslim empires may have favored certain Sufi lineages and in the kingdom of Kandy royal patronage supported the spread of the Siyam Nikāya among

Buddhist institutions, these Sufi networks of the Tamil regions spread without state patronage that could have supported the development of strong vertical integration through teaching lineages, as in the case of the Siyam Nikāya. The Qādirī network of the seventeenth and eighteenth centuries thus thrived not because it "Islamized" the local population but because it provided a means of social and religious integration for dispersed Muslim communities, operating as an integrative force in the absence of a centralizing Muslim state. The combination of strong vertical lineages with the horizontal integration of larger networks was fully achieved only when several developments made such integration feasible in the region. These included a stronger emphasis on the specificity and uniqueness of the lineage not only through common memory, but also through distinctive practices, a common political order that provided a more level playing field for religious groups competing with each other,[60] and technologies that facilitated the travel of individuals and the reproduction of texts to a far greater extent than had been possible earlier. It thus becomes clear that the history of religious "orders" needs to become far more cognizant of changes in the constitution of such institutions, their interaction, and integration into local society than has so far been achieved by historians of the region.

NOTES

1. "Katiṭam," *Muslim Nēcaṉ* 7.15 (12 Āṉi 1889): 60.

2. Following Anne M. Blackburn, *Buddhist Learning and Textual Practice in Eighteenth-Century Lankan Monastic Culture* (Princeton and Oxford: Princeton University Press, 2001), p. viii, I have chosen to refer to the island as "Laṅkā" rather than using the anachronistic name of the postcolonial nation-state "Sri Lanka."

3. "Katiṭiam," *Muslim Necaṉ* 7.16 (19 Āṉi 1889): 64.

4. The main exception is a massive but unfortunately still unpublished doctoral thesis on the Qādiriyya: Susan Elizabeth Schomburg, "'Reviving Religion': The Qādirī Sufi Order, Popular Devotion to Sufi Saint Muḥyīuddīn 'Abdul Qādir al-Gīlānī, and Processes of 'Islamization' in Tamil Nadu and Sri Lanka" (Ph.D. diss., Harvard University, 2003). See also Frederick de Jong, "Note sur les confréries soufies à Sri Lanka," in *Les ordres mystiques dans l'Islam: Cheminements et situation actuelle*, edited by Alexandre Popovic and Gilles Veinstein (Paris: Éditions de l'École des hautes études en sciences sociales, 1986), pp. 135–137; Muḥammad Yousuf Kokan, "Sufi Presence in South India," in *Islam in India: Studies and Commentaries*, vol. 2: *Religion and Religious Education*, edited by Christian W. Troll (Delhi: Vikas Publishing House, 1985), pp. 73–85; Dennis B. McGilvray, "Jailani: A Sufi Shrine in Sri Lanka," in *Lived Islam in South Asia: Adaptation, Accommodation and Conflict*, edited by Imtiaz Ahmad and Helmut Reifeld (Delhi: Social Science Press, 2004), pp. 272–289; Dennis B. McGilvray, *Crucible of Conflict: Tamil and Muslim Society on the East Coast of Sri Lanka* (Durham and London: Duke University Press, 2008), pp. 292–304.

5. Carl W. Ernst and Bruce B. Lawrence, *Sufi Martyrs of Love: The Chishti Order in South Asia and Beyond* (New York: Palgrave Macmillan, 2002), p. 11.

6. This is admittedly a tall claim and would need much further investigation. My preliminary assessment stems from the impression that the critique of existing sources developed

in this chapter can be applied to other South Asian contexts. First, it seems noteworthy how unclear or vague the *ṭarīqa* background of many venerated saints and vernacular Sufi poets seems to be. This includes personalities without *ṭarīqa* affiliation (e.g., Makhdūm ʻAlī of Mahim) or of unknown affiliation (e.g., Shāh ʻAbd al-Laṭīf of Bhīt). If we add cases where a somewhat obscure lineage seems retrospectively to have been interpreted as a full-fledged *ṭarīqa* (as in the case of the Maghribiyya in Gujarat) or where a *ṭarīqa* seems to be ascribed on the basis of an individual's peculiar traits (e.g., itinerant preceptors identified as Madārī or Rifāʻī), this covers a large number of South Asian Sufis. Second, it is noteworthy how rarely specific orders (in opposition to the basic meaning of *ṭarīqa* as part of the Sufi "path" in general) are mentioned in precolonial South Asian Islamic literatures apart from Persian. Important Sufi poets rarely mention their *ṭarīqa* affiliation, and the most central literary genre for the conceptual articulation of the Sufi order, the hagiography of local saints, seems strangely undeveloped in most vernacular Muslim literatures of South Asia, in striking contrast to both Muslim Persian and non-Muslim vernacular literature in the very same languages! This may suggest that Sufi orders were of greater importance as a discursive concept of Persianate political and historical discourse than as social institutions in South Asia.

7. The centrality of the Muslim state as an organizing trope characterizes otherwise very different works. Cf., for example, Raziuddin Aquil, *In the Name of Allah: Understanding Islam and Indian History* (Delhi: Penguin Books India, 2009); Jamal Malik, *Islam in South Asia: A Short History* (Leiden: Brill, 2008); Mohammad Mujeeb, *The Indian Muslims* (London: Allan and Unwin, 1967); Annemarie Schimmel, *Islam in the Indian Subcontinent* (Leiden: Brill, 1980).

8. The classic treatment of this trope is Simon Digby, "The Sufi Shaikh as a Source of Authority in Medieval India," *Puruṣārtha* 9 (1986): 57–77.

9. The connection between the initiatory "lineage" (*silsila*) and the "order" (*ṭarīqa*) is so close that some authors translate *silsila* as "order"; see, for example, Aquil, *In the Name of Allah*, p. 10.

10. Desai mentions a "Mosque of Shaikh Shādhilī" in Kozhikode, Kerala, which contains an inscription dating to 1727/1728. I have not been able to find out more about this mosque, whether the mosque already existed by the time the inscription was made, and whether it was already known by that name then; Ziyaud-Din A. Desai, *A Topographical List of Arabic, Persian and Urdu Inscriptions of South India* (Delhi: Indian Council of Historical Research and Northern Book Centre, 1989), p. 102 (no. 1065).

11. Concerning Abū Bakr Miskīn, see A. S. Satakkattullāh, "Ṣātuliyyā tarīkkāviṉ caṅkaimiku kalīpa," in *Paijul Aṉvār Arapik Kallūri veḷḷi viḻā ciṟappu malar* (Kadayanallur: Paijul Aṉvār Arapik Kallūri, 2000), p. 242; Tayka Shuʻayb, *Arabic, Arwi and Persian in Sarandib and Tamil Nadu: A Study of the Contributions of Sri Lanka and Tamil Nadu to Arabic, Arwi, Persian and Urdu Languages, Literature and Education* (Madras: Imāmul ʻArūs Trust, 1993), http://www.maqbara.com/tariqa.php (accessed March 16, 2014). On Laṅkā, see https://en.wikipedia.org/wiki/Ummu_Zavaya (accessed August 14, 2016); http://www.fassiyanews.com/fassiyathush-shazuliyya/baithul-fassi/ (accessed August 14, 2016). The latter article was purportedly written by Hatoon Ajwad Al Fassi, a descendant of Muḥammad al-Fāsī and currently associate professor of history at King Saud University, Riyadh, Saudi Arabia. De Jong, "Les confréries soufies à Sri Lanka," 135, erroneously claims that Macan Marikkar was the first to introduce the Fāsiyya to Laṅkā.

12. Regarding the Darqāwiyya and the Fāsiyya, see Thomas Eich, *Abū l-Hudā aṣ-Ṣayyādī: Eine Studie zur Instrumentalisierung sufischer Netzwerke und genealogischer Kontroversen im*

spätosmanischen Reich (Berlin: Klaus Schwarz Verlag, 2003), pp. 56–57, 166–168; J. Spencer Trimingham, *The Sufi Orders in Islam* (New York and Oxford: Oxford University Press, 1998 [first published 1971]), pp. 110–114 (Trimingham calls the Fāsiyya "Raḥmāniyya").

13. Shams al-Dīn al-Makkī apparently also initiated a few North Indian Muslims, as is evinced by a rhymed Persian *silsila* by one of his disciples published in Moradabad; Ḥashmat 'Alī Shāh, *Silsilat al-dhahabiyya a'nī shajarat al-shādhiliyya* (Moradabad: Maṭba' Gulzār Aḥmadī, ca. 1890).

14. Concerning Māppiḷḷai Leppai and his lineage, see Sayyid Muḥammad b. Aḥmad al-Qāhirī al-Kīrkarī, *Fat-ḥud-dayyān fi fiqhi khairil adyān* (A compendium on Muslim theology and jursiprudence) (Colombo: The Fat-ḥud-dayyān Publication Committee, 1963), pp. xviv–xxxvi; Shu'ayb, *Arabic, Arwi and Persian*, pp. 580–604, 627–640; Torsten Tschacher, "How to Die before Dying: Šarī'a and Sufism in a Nineteenth-Century Tamil Poem," in *Islâm: Collected Essays*, edited by Daniele Cevenini and Svevo D'Onofrio (Bologna: I libri di Emil, 2010), pp. 434–436.

15. McGilvray, "Jailani."

16. Desai, *Topographical List*, pp. 93–95 (nos. 977–994); Mehrdad Shokoohy, *Muslim Architecture of South India: The Sultanate of Ma'bar and the Traditions of the Maritime Settlers on the Malabar and Coromandel Coasts (Tamil Nadu, Kerala and Goa)* (London and New York: Routledge, 2003), pp. 275–289. For Sayyid Muḥyī al-Dīn, see Desai, *Topographical List*, p. 95 (no. 995); note that, although in the latter case ten generations of ancestors are mentioned, only Sayyid Muḥyī al-Dīn and his father carried "Qādirī" names but none in the earlier generations; for the contemporary situation in Kayalpattinam, see Schomburg, "Reviving Religion," pp. 193–196.

17. Desai, *Topographical List*, pp. 95–96 (nos. 1001–1002, from Kilakkarai); p. 115 (nos. 1201–1204, from Madurai); p. 128 (no. 1314, from Periyapattinam); p. 155 (nos. 1576–1579, from Valinokkam). All these inscriptions date to the fourteenth century except for the four inscriptions from Valinokkam, which date to the fifteenth century.

18. Torsten Tschacher, "Convention and Community: The Poetics of Prefaces to Early Islamic Tamil Literature," *Zeitschrift für Indologie und Südasienstudien* 28 (2011): 191.

19. Muḥammad Ismā'īl al-Nākafattanī, *Hidāyat al-sālikīn fī takhlīs al-hālikīn* (Madras: Matba' al-Qādiriyya, AH 1316), pp. 12–23.

20. Torsten Tschacher, "Circulating Islam: Understanding Convergence and Divergence in the Islamic Traditions of Ma'bar and Nusantara," in *Islamic Connections: Studies of South and Southeast Asia*, edited by R. Michael Feener and Terenjit Sevea (Singapore: Institute of Southeast Asian Studies, 2009), p. 55; cf. Azyumardi Azra, *The Origins of Islamic Reformism in Southeast Asia: Networks of Malay-Indonesian and Middle Eastern 'Ulamā' in the Seventeenth and Eighteenth Centuries* (Crows Nest: Allen and Unwin; and Honolulu: University of Hawai'i Press, 2004), pp. 16–20; Shu'ayb, *Arabic, Arwi and Persian*, pp. 496–498. The Naqshbandiyya's role in the region has similarly been ignored, though as late as the 1870s there were self-identifying Naqshbandīs among Tamil Sufis; Ṣākumukammatu Aptulkātiṟu Jeyiṉuttīṉ, *Muṟītuviḷakkameṉṉum irattiṉaccurukkam* (Singapore: Sayīti Yēntiracālai, 1878), [preface p. 1]; Sayyid Muḥammad al-Naqshbandī al-Qādirī, *Tab'īn al-ra'y al-qiyāsī min aqwāl Muḥammad al-Maghribī al-Fāsī* (Madras: Mu'ayyid al-Islām, AH 1327) (the fatwa on which this tract was based was completed in AH 1291 [1874/1875 CE], as can be gleaned from p. 196).

21. *Vētapurāṇam* 25.95: *nal paṟakkatt' ākum kātiriyyattaip piṭittukkoṇṭāl*. Periya Nūku Leppai, *Pūvāṟṟil aṭaṅki viḷaṅkum Periya Nūku Leppai Ālim Oliyullāh iyaṟṟi aruḷiya meyññāṉak*

karuvūlam Vēta Purāṇam, edited by Mu. Ceyyitu Muhammatu "Hasaṉ" (Chennai: Mu.Ki.Mu. Muhammatu Hasaṉ, 1999 [first published 1984]). In contrast, the term *ṭarīqa* is used in this and other texts only as a general technical term for a stage on the Sufi path and the connected practices, not with regard to specific orders; e.g., *Vētapurānam* 25.103.

22. McGilvray, "Jailani," pp. 276–283; McGilvray, *Crucible of Conflict*, pp. 297–304.

23. Shaik Abdul Azeez Saheb, "A 'Festival of Flags': Hindu-Muslim Devotion and the Sacralising of Localism at the Shrine of Nagore-e-Sharif in Tamil Nadu," in *Embodying Charisma: Modernity, Locality and the Performance of Emotion in Sufi Cults*, edited by Pnina Werbner and Helene Basu (London and New York: Routledge, 1998), pp. 63–65; concerning the Malangs, see Ute Falasch, *Heiligkeit und Mobilität: Die Madāriyya Sufibruderschaft und ihr Gründer Badīʿ al-Dīn Shāh Madār in Indien, 15.-19. Jahrhundert* (Münster: Lit Verlag, 2015).

24. British Library MS 26562/2, folio 56v.

25. McGilvray, "Jailani," pp. 276–280; also McGilvray, *Crucible of Conflict*, p. 299.

26. The manuscript was purchased at an Islamic bookstall in Nagore in August 2007. It contains 137 folios of texts in Arabic and Tamil, almost throughout in Arabic script. The first 120 folios are carefully written in black and red ink and contain three sets of texts: a couple of Arabic poems (folios 1v–31v), a Tamil prose version of the Tawaddud story from the Arabian Nights (folios 33r–65r), and the *Pismil Kuṟam*, a Tamil "Sufi" poem by Pīr Muḥammad of Takkalai. The following folios (122r–126r) are taken up by Arabic poems written in blue ink, the quality of writing indicating that they may have been the writing exercises of a child. The final pages (again in a more mature hand) include a Qādirī *silsila* (129r–130r), a Tamil text on the Qādirī *adab* of *dhikr* (131v–134r), and a single page mentioning the names and dates of birth of three boys born between 1933 and 1952, possibly the sons or grandsons of the woman who owned the manuscript (135v). This is the only page in the manuscript fully in Tamil script. That Balqīs Bī was the owner of the manuscript becomes clear from a marginal note to that effect in Tamil script on folio 5v.

27. Nile Green, *Sufism: A Global History* (Chichester and Malden: Wiley-Blackwell, 2012), p. 82.

28. Indira Peterson, "Tamil Śaiva Hagiography: The Narrative of the Holy Servants (of Śiva) and the Hagiographical Project in Tamil Śaivism," in *According to Tradition: Hagiographical Writing in India*, edited by Winand M. Callewaert and Rupert Snell (Wiesbaden: Harrassowitz Verlag, 1994), pp. 191–228; a somewhat similar case, with a late development of hagiographies of Muslim saints despite the existence of non-Muslim hagiographies and Muslim narrative literature about the prophets, seems to be provided by Bengali; Hans Harder, *Sufism and Saint Veneration in Contemporary Bangladesh: The Maijbhandaris of Chittagong* (London and New York: Routledge, 2011), pp. 106–112.

29. The inclusion of al-Shādhilī at such an early date (ca. 1700) is surprising; *Rasūl mālai* 76–77, 79, 89, 93 (in Muḥammad Yūsuf Labbay, ed., *Uṣūl al-asnā fī ḥuṣūl al-ḥusnā* [Madras: Maṭbaʿ Shāh al-Ḥamīdiyya, AH 1352], part 1, pp. 194–195).

30. For the two most important poems, Sām Shihāb al-Dīn's *Mīrān* (or *Mīrā*) *mālai* and Javātuppulavar's *Muhiyittiṉāṇṭakai Piḷḷaitamiḻ*, see Muḥammad Yūsuf Labbay, *Uṣūl al-asnā*, part 1, pp. 223–232; and Ku. Jamāl Muhammatu, *Collampu: Makāṉ Javātuppulavar* (Erode: Ku. Jamāl Muhammatu, 1999), pp. 59–113.

31. Regarding these poems and their literary context, see Tschacher, "Convention and Community"; Mahmood Mohamed Uwise, *Muslim Contribution to Tamil Literature* (Madras: Fifth International Islamic Tamil Literary Conference, 1990 [first published 1953]).

32. Muḥammad Ismāʿīl, *Hidāyat al-sālikīn*; Nūḥ b. ʿAbd al-Qādir al-Qāhirī, *Nafaḥāt al-ʿanbar fī manāqib al-quṭb al-akbar* (Bombay: al-Maṭbaʿ al-Gulzār Ḥasanī, AH 1320). Shuʿayb, *Arabic, Arwi and Persian*, pp. 274–289, 492–493, gives conflicting information on Nūḥ's lifetime; I have given the most likely dates. For early printed hagiographies, see J. B. Prashant More, *Muslim Identity, Print Culture and the Dravidian Factor in Tamil Nadu* (Hyderabad: Orient Longman, 2004), pp. 203–228.

33. More, *Muslim Identity*, p. 209; Mukammatu Mukiyittīṉleppai Hāji Pulavar, *Cātuli nāyakam*, 2nd edition (Jaffna: Mukammatu Mukiyittīṉ Hāji Pulavar, 1964 [first published 1914]).

34. The copy in my possession consists of three separate parts that may have been printed separately and only bound together later by a reader; the titles of the three parts are *Mawlid ʿaṭāʾ al-rasūl fī maḥtid sakhāʾ al-batūl*, *Hidāyat al-rabb al-matīn fī manāqib al-shaykh muʿīn al-dīn*, and *Manāʾiḥ al-qudsiyya fī siyar khulafāʾ al-chishtiyya*. Khwāja Muḥammad al-Kanjiwī, ed., *Mawlid ʿaṭāʾ al-rasūl fī maḥtid sakhāʾ al-batūl* (Madras: Maṭbaʿ al-Raḥmānī, AH 1333).

35. My understanding of "interpretive communities" is based on Blackburn's use of the term in her study on eighteenth-century Lankan monasticism; Blackburn, *Buddhist Learning*, pp. 89–90.

36. For Qādirī debates, see, for example, "Kaṭiṭa tāṟpariya viṭai," *Muslim Nēcaṉ* 7.22 (31 Āṭi 1889): 86; "Caṅkaiporuntiya muslim nēca pattirātipa ravarkaḷuk [*sic*] calām," *Muslim Nēcaṉ* 7.26 (28 Āvaṇi 1889): 103–104; "Cammāṅkōṭṭu ālimukku," *Muslim Nēcaṉ* 7.27 (4 Puraṭṭāci 1889): 107. For catalogs of Sufi orders, see Muḥammad Ismāʿīl, *Hidāyat al-Sālikīn*, pp. 266–273. Regarding the link between print and the production of hagiographies, see Nile Green, *Bombay Islam: The Religious Economy of the West Indian Ocean, 1840–1915* (Cambridge, UK: Cambridge University Press, 2011), pp. 92–104. On the use of print by Sufis in Southern Asia in general, see Green, *Bombay Islam*, chaps. 3 and 6; Michael Laffan, *The Makings of Indonesian Islam: Orientalism and the Narration of a Sufi Past* (Princeton: Princeton University Press, 2011), pp. 60–62, 143, 154.

37. Green, *Sufism*, p. 84.

38. Jamil M. Abun-Nasr, *Muslim Communities of Grace: The Sufi Brotherhoods in Islamic Religious Life* (New York: Columbia University Press, 2007), chaps. 5–7. At the same time, there has also been the opposite process of the transmission of Shādhilī texts outside Shādhilī institutions and contexts, such as the cases of al-Buṣīrī's *Burda* and Ibn ʿAṭāʾ Allāh's *Ḥikam* (personal communication by R. Michael Feener, Oxford, January 2016).

39. Leiden University Manuscript OR-7368, folio 5v; also Ph. S. van Ronkel, "A Tamil Malay Manuscript," *Journal of the Straits Branch of the Royal Asiatic Society* 85 (1922): 29–35. Most noteworthy, especially in a tract written by a student of Shaykh Ṣadaqatullāh, is the use of texts by al-Burhānpūrī and al-Qūshāshī, authors highly popular in Shaṭṭārī networks.

40. See Abdul Majeed Mohamed Sahabdeen, *The Sufi Doctrine in Tamil Literature* (Colombo: Abdul Majeed Mohamed Sahabdeen Trust Foundation, 1995 [first published 1986]); Susan Elizabeth Schomburg, "'Hey, Girl! Dance the *Kummi* Called "*Moṭcam*"!'": The Sufi Poetics of Iḷaiyāṉkuṭi Kaccippiḷḷaiyammāḷ," in *World Without Walls: Being Human, Being Tamil*, edited by R. Cheran et al. (Toronto: TSAR Publications, 2011), pp. 86–108; Schomburg, "Reviving Religion," pp. 383–424.

41. "Cammāṅkōṭṭu ālimukku," *Muslim Nēcaṉ* 7.27 (4 Puraṭṭāci 1889): 107.

42. See More, *Muslim Identity*, p. 57.

43. Sayyid Muḥammad b. Aḥmad al-Qāhirī al-Kīrkarī, *Fatḥ al-dayyān fī fiqh khayr al-adyān* (Bombay: Maṭbaʿ al-Shaykh Hasan b. Bahāʾ al-Dīn al-Khatīb al-Kōkanī, AH 1291),

part 1, p. 46; translated in Sayyid Muḥammad b. Aḥmad, *Fat-ḥud-dayyān*, p. 74. The respective stanza is from one of Mastān Ṣāḥib's *kīrttaṉais*, no. 18 (1074.1) in Mā. Vaṭivēlu Mutaliyār, ed., *Kuṇaṅkuṭi Mastāṉ Cākipu pāṭalkaḷ (uraiyuṭaṉ)* (Chennai: Mullai Nilaiyam, 2004), p. 398.

44. For a critique of this assumption, see Torsten Tschacher, "Can 'Om' Be an Islamic Term? Translations, Encounters, and Islamic Discourse in Vernacular South Asia," *South Asian History and Culture* 5.2 (2014): 199–203.

45. See again Blackburn, *Buddhist Learning*, for my use of the term "interpretive community."

46. Green, *Sufism*, p. 82.

47. Torsten Tschacher, "'Walls of Illusion': Information Generation in Colonial Singapore and the Reporting of the Mahdi-Rebellion in Sudan, 1887–1890," in *Singapore in Global History*, edited by Derek Heng and Syed Muhd Khairudin Aljuneid (Amsterdam: Amsterdam University Press, 2011), pp. 57–78.

48. Nūḥ b. 'Abd al-Qādir, *Nafaḥāt al-'anbar*, p. 8. For newspaper items, see, for example, "Cātiliyyā tarīkkattiṉ ceykunāyaka mavarkaḷuṭaiya maraṇam," *Muslim Nēcaṉ* 7.29 (18 Puraṭṭāci 1889): 116; "Cātuliyyāttarīka," *Carvajaṉanēcaṉ* 4.10 (March 23, 1889): 38; "Cātulimavulāṉā avarkaḷiṉ vapāttu," *Carvajaṉanēcaṉ* 4.30 (September 16, 1889): 118; "Cātiliyyā," *Carvajaṉanēcaṉ* 4.35 (October 30, 1889): 138.

49. British Library MS 26562/2, folio 53v; the word read as "Sorcery" here might also be "Larceny."

50. Ibid., folio 56v. A beautiful description of the way in which a Maldivian *taṅkaḷ* used his claim to be able to work miracles to gain patronage in a village in Kanniyakumari District early in the twentieth century can be found in one of the best-known Muslim novels in Tamil: Thoppil Mohammed Meeran, *The Story of a Seaside Village* (Hyderabad: Orient Longman, 1998).

51. See *Ciṉṉa Cīṟā* 11–12 (Paṉī Akumatu Maraikkāyar, *"Ciṉṉa Cīṟā" eṉṟu vaḻaṅkum Cīṟāp purāṇam: Hijrattuk kāṇṭam-2*, edited by Em. Saiyitu Muhammatu "Hasaṉ" [Chennai: Millat Piriṇṭars (P. S. M. Ahmatu Aptul Kātir), 1990]); *Tirumaṇakkāṭci* 31–32 (Vakutai Cēkāti Nayiṉārp Pulavar, *Tirumaṇak Kāṭci*, edited by Mu. Ceyyitu Muhammatu "Hasaṉ" [Chennai: Maraikkāyar Patippakam, 1990]). Regarding Cītakkāti, Māmu Nayiṉār, and Leppai Nayiṉār, see Lennart Bes, "The Setupatis, the Dutch, and Other Bandits in Eighteenth-Century Ramnad (South India)," *Journal of the Economic and Social History of the Orient* 44.4 (2001): 540–574; David Shulman and Sanjay Subrahmanyam, "Prince of Poets and Ports: Cītakkāti, the Maraikkāyars and Ramnad, ca. 1690–1710," in *Islam and Indian Regions*, edited by Anna Libera Dallapiccola and Stephanie Zingel-Avé Lallemant (Stuttgart: Franz Steiner Verlag, 1993), vol. 1, pp. 497–535, though these authors seem not to have been aware of the family connections between Leppai Nayiṉār, Ṣadaqatullāh, and Cītakkāti.

52. Green, *Sufism*, p. 175.

53. In addition to the two letters quoted at the beginning, see "Muslim Nēcap pattirātiparavarkalukku," *Muslim Nēcaṉ* 7.19 (10 Āṭi 1889): 76.

54. *Cātulināyakam*, *Kaṭavuḷ vāḻttu* 15–20; for the poems authored by Nūḥ, see Muḥammad Ismā'īl, *Hidāyat al-sālikīn*, p. 219; Shu'ayb, *Arabic, Arwi and Persian*, p. 629.

55. Muḥammad Ismā'īl, *Hidāyat al-sālikīn*, p. 229. At the same time, this book was printed at a printing press called al-Qādiriyya!

56. Sayyid Muḥammad al-Naqshbandī, *Tab'īn al-ra'y al-qiyāsī*; an online biography of al-Fāsī, apparently produced by a Syrian lineage gives the title of al-Fāsī's tract as *al-Futuḥāt al-rabbaniyya wa al-ijāza al-madaniyya*, "The Lordly Introductions and the Authorization of

the Madaniyya," and claims that it contains twenty-five arguments; http://privat.bahnhof.se/wb042294/Texter/bionotes/bio_m_fasi.html#10 (accessed March 10, 2014).

57. Christian Wagner, *Die Muslime Sri Lankas: Eine Volksgruppe im Spannungsfeld des ethnischen Konflikts zwischen Singhalesen und Tamilen* (Freiburg i.Br.: Arnold-Bergstraesser-Institut, 1990), pp. 83–85. For the general political context, see also M. N. M. Kamil Asad, *The Muslims of Sri Lanka under British Rule* (Delhi: Navrang, 1993); Wagner, *Die Muslime Sri Lankas*, pp. 63–98.

58. K. Kailasapathy, "The Writings of the Tamil Siddhas," in *The Sants: Studies in a Devotional Tradition of India*, edited by Karine Schomer and W. H. McLeod (Delhi: Motilal Banarsidass, 1987), p. 407.

59. E.g., *Vētapurāṇam* 25.82.

60. Green, *Bombay Islam*, pp. 8–23.

5

WHOSE ORDERS?

Chinese Popular God Temple Networks and the Rise of Chinese Mahāyāna Buddhist Monasteries in Southeast Asia

KENNETH DEAN

Anthony Reid has traced the religious revolutions of Southeast Asia during the fifteenth, sixteenth, and seventeenth centuries, as Theravāda Buddhist monastic orders and ritual traditions spread across mainland Southeast Asia and Islam competed with Christianity in the insular regions.[1] He has also noted the expanding role of Chinese merchants as middlemen in the British and Dutch colonies of Malaya and Indonesia. However, he makes little mention of the role of Chinese temples or of the spread of Chinese Mahāyāna Buddhism to Southeast Asia—although French travelers had already reported the presence of Chinese Buddhist monks in the Qingyunting (Pavilion of the Blue Clouds) in Malacca in 1698.[2]

The lack of a Chinese cultural context elsewhere in Southeast Asia would make the spread of Chinese Mahāyāna challenging and complex. Although the evidence on the spread of Mahāyāna Buddhism to Southeast Asia is sparse for the early modern era, we can trace the rise of full-fledged Mahāyāna monasteries and religious orders in the late nineteenth century. Reid briefly discusses the spread of Confucian culture and Chinese Mahāyāna within Vietnam, where a shared Chinese language and cultural context facilitated the spread of Buddhist orders.[3] At that time Chinese religious networks also expanded in the region through connections with traditions of Daoist ritual masters. Evidence for this includes a wooden "earth contract" from 1898 that was discovered during renovations to the Po Chiak Keng Tan Si Chong Su in Singapore. This ritual artifact demonstrates that Daoist ritual specialists conducted rites to exorcise the space of the temple and consecrate the new gods upon their installation and animation in diaspora Chinese contexts of the region.[4]

When scholars of religion speak of the spread of religious orders in Southeast Asia, however, they usually refer to the expansion of Theravāda

Buddhist monastic lineages, Islamic prophetic lineages (often related to Sufi teachers), or later lineages of Christian missionaries associated with Catholic monastic communities. What is strangely overlooked in these accounts is the long historical development of a vast network of Chinese temples in Southeast Asia dedicated to the gods of the regional pantheons of the different emigrant communities.

This chapter explores the expansion of a Chinese temple network that began in Fujian in the sixteenth century, spread across Southeast Asia in the seventeenth and eighteenth centuries, and accelerated its spread in the nineteenth century with the arrival of immigrants from multiple dialect regions. For centuries, Chinese temples and their native-place business offices provided the main institutional framework for the elaboration of trust networks holding long-distance trade together across the "Minnan coastal trading system."[5] These temples held rituals before the gods in which the two sides of a trading contract would swear to maintain their trust. Such rites (and institutions) were especially important because these were "merchants without empires,"[6] who were operating outside the legal protection of the Chinese state in treacherous environments. The temple business offices lent out funds and supervised credit pools watched over by the gods, which were designed to cover the costs of key life-cycle rituals for the members of the pool. Funds could be withdrawn for weddings, "cappings" (of young men come of age), or funerals and then returned with interest for the next person who needed them. The temple officers registered the marriages and deaths in their dialect communities, fulfilling ritual as well as bureaucratic roles. These temples were staffed by *miaozhu* (temple invokers), who were responsible for tending the incense and oil lamps, and assisting worshipers in making prayers and offerings. They were directed by temple management committees made up of Chinese leaders who held high positions in local society as wealthy merchants and traders. Because ritual roles were "differentially distributed" across Chinese society, these temple managers along with leaders of guilds, opera troupe directors, carpenters, and heads of households were all able to perform specific ritual roles.[7] Thus, larger rituals in temples could be conducted by the temple leadership, with one or more being selected annually to fill the ritual role of keeper of the incense burner, while other leaders in the community were assigned ritual roles as "leading families." Members of the temple committee could also serve as temporary masters of ritual ceremony (*lisheng*) during rites held in temples and ancestral halls.

These temples were transnational religious institutions linked by the division of incense marking generations of affiliations (see below). They were characterized by possession rituals that authorized expansion of the networks in new directions. Thus, although not defined by specific institutionalized lineages descending from a particular teacher or monastic adept, Chinese temples can be seen as transregional institutionally based religious orders in a broadly comparative sense. They are also transpersonal in the sense that different individuals rotated in and out of ritual roles and that spirit mediums were possessed by "outside" supernatural forces. The Chinese temples of Southeast Asia also invited in or temporarily housed representatives of more formal religious orders (defined by participation in specific lineages of monastics or masters) such as itinerant Buddhist monks and Daoist ritual specialists. Such itinerants performed rites of consecration of temples, animation of god statues, feasts for the gods or the ancestors, or funerals for individual members of the dialect communities. They also sometimes took care of the temple or the burial grounds of a particular dialect group. As will be seen below in the case of the Shuanglinsi (Double Grove Monastery) in Singapore, such itinerant monks were in some cases taking part in extended pilgrimages to Buddhist centers in Sri Lanka. These pilgrimages were an extension of the common process of *yunyou* (moving like a cloud), in which monks traveled from one monastery to another within China in search of an inspiring master and possibly a better position within a monastic organization. As for Daoist ritual specialists, many who are currently active in Southeast Asia are the descendants of men who emigrated for a wide range of reasons and who often worked in additional trades, only occasionally serving as Daoist ritual masters.

The Chinese temples of Southeast Asia are dedicated to a mixture of regional deities, mostly of Daoist derivation, as well as Buddhist gods such as Guanyin.[8] The diverse regional Daoist ritual traditions of Fujian coevolved along with the many regional pantheons of the dialect groups who founded these temples. Each dialect region along the coast of China (or inland in the case of Hakka regions) had its own topolect, distinctive temple architecture, regional pantheon, regional ritual traditions, food, clothing, and regional local customs. Each regional Daoist ritual tradition formed its own distinct lineage of groups of masters (and is thus referred to as a "formal religious order" above), although these were primarily transmitted through initiation rituals along paternal lines or between masters and disciples.

The Tianshifu (Celestial Master Headquarters) at Longhushan (Dragon Tiger Mountain) in northern Jiangxi was, at various times, a center for the coordination of regional Daoist ritual traditions and for the conferral of additional ordinations to the regional ritual specialists. However, integration across the wide range of distinct regional ritual traditions was minimal. For the most part, these localized Daoist orders were based in the homes of the Daoist masters and usually not in temples.[9] The regionally based Daoist ritual specialists did, however, contribute to the process of transforming many local god cults into regional, national, or transnational cult networks by writing up the invocations, legends, and miracles of the gods and then composing scriptures and liturgies for some of them, thus inscribing them within a shared "universal" Daoist liturgical framework. For centuries, starting with the large-scale migration of Han Chinese into Southeast China in the Tang, Five Dynasties, and Song eras, leaders of the local communal temples in different parts of Southeast China hired Daoist ritual masters to perform communal offerings (*jiao*) dedicated to the local gods on their feast days. Local communal temples were important centers of village life, forming the core of local self-governance of territorial communities.[10]

By the seventeenth century at the latest, branch temples from founding temples of the main gods of Fujian had spread to many parts of Southeast Asia. It is likely, however, that there were smaller shrines and temples in Chinese communities in Southeast Asia much earlier. Admiral Zheng He (1371–1433), for example, found over three thousand Chinese living in Palembang (Sumatra) in the early fifteenth century.[11] Most branch temples were established by means of a ritual of "division of incense" from the founding temple, and some have divided incense with newer third- or fourth-generation temples elsewhere in Southeast Asia, generating a network of affiliation, or a lineage. Often, small statues of the gods of the founding temples were carried overseas by emigrants (*fenling*, or division of the god's spiritual power). Some branch temples maintained strong ties with their founding temples in Southeast China.

Spirit mediums, a regular feature of the Southeast Chinese religious world, could become possessed by the gods of the regional pantheons back in China. These gods might insist (through the spirit medium) that their devotees build a temple to the deity in a new land in Southeast Asia. Spirit mediums flourished in these temples, perhaps because the Southeast Asian contexts lacked key features of the southern Chinese ritual sphere that restricted the space available to spirit mediums there, such as tightly interlocking strata of Confucian literati, localized lineages, strong traditions of Daoist ritual masters or Buddhist monasteries, and a hierarchy of local temples intersecting with the state cult at City God temples.

Of the many elements of the various regional ritual spheres of Southeast China that could be found in the Chinese temples of Southeast Asia, including temple managers acting in a ritual capacity, hired temple invokers, spirit mediums attached to a temple, itinerant Buddhist monks, and Daoist ritual specialists, only the latter two could be considered to be members of formal religious orders, and those of the regional Daoist ritual masters were often particularistic and fragmented. Nevertheless, careful procedures for the rotation and selection of temple management committees and annual keepers of the incense burners as well as the continuous production of spirit mediums ensured continuity of ritual practices within temple communities over hundreds of years. Even when formal religious orders were not present, we can identify what I refer to as "networked orders," shaped through the transpersonal transmission of ritualized roles within nodes of translocal networks rather than by individuals taking up vocations within a dedicated lineage in a stably institutionalized context.[12] This chapter presents a history of the rise and intensifying presence of formal religious orders in the Chinese religious context of Southeast Asia, a process linked to changes in temple environments, social functions of temple spaces, and the forms of social authority linked to Chinese temples. These changes occurred over several centuries. This chapter will trace particular strands of developments in the area that later became the British Straits Settlements.

I examine Chinese temple networks from a historical perspective, tracing the growth of the network of Hokkien (Fujian Minnan-speaking immigrants) temples from the seventeenth through the eighteenth centuries, followed by the rise of Teochew, Hakka, Cantonese, Hainan, and other regionally based and dialect-specific temple networks in the nineteenth century. Powerful emigrant communities from these different regions of Southeast China controlled the branch temples as well as the *huiguan* (native-place associations or business offices) housed within the temples. These temples/*huiguan* provided rooms for visiting Chinese business travelers from their regions of origin, loaned money to those linked to their associations, and managed graveyards for those unable to return to their points of origin.

The temples/*huiguan* were also at the center of intense and sometimes violent conflict between dialect groups (and among their business leaders) over control of the opium, alcohol, and prostitution farms (cartels, or monopoly rights) auctioned off by the colonial administration, which provided over half of the annual income of the Straits Settlement colonies.[13] The cartel business leaders were often the leaders of the temples/*huiguan*. They needed to have a strong enforcement apparatus to handle conflicts; administer monopoly control over the distribution of opium, alcohol, and prostitutes; and control the coolie trade within the mines and plantations across Southeast Asia. Many of the latter were owned and managed by the same Chinese leaders who served as managers of temples/*huiguan* within their dialect communities (which had specific residential zones, commercial territories, and economic niches). The sworn brotherhoods responsible for the enforcement of the cartels were often linked to the temples. These groups would later be stigmatized (and eventually criminalized) by the colonial authorities as Triads or secret societies.[14]

In the second half of the nineteenth century, there was a fundamental transformation in the structure and relative autonomy of temples/*huiguan* as Western colonial authorities made a deliberate attempt to separate these temples from their enforcement arms (secret societies/Triads). This was a long process, which took place in different colonial settings across Southeast Asia over the second half of the nineteenth century. Bureaucratic solutions and evolving imperial knowledge/power formations developed across the reach of the British Empire in Asia, through the itineraries of various colonial bureaucrats, officials, and governors, who experimented with different but converging policies over time across the empire to deal with the problem of the Chinese communities (that is to say, the temples/*huiguan*) and their secret societies. In different port cities at different times for different reasons, after gradually criminalizing the enforcement arm of the Chinese temples/*huiguan*, the colonial powers proceeded to regulate the finances and eventually the administrative structures and operations of the temple organizations—and this tended to continue into the postcolonial period. Leaders of the Chinese community realized that the ground rules had shifted and opted to focus more of their energies on emerging Chinese chambers of commerce. In some cases, they chose to cede control over some temples to more formal religious orders and to sponsor the establishment of local Buddhist monasteries. It is in this context that, at the end of the nineteenth century, we find evidence for the establishment of the first mainstream Buddhist monastery in Malaya, the Jilesi (Monastery of Extreme Joy) in Penang in 1905, followed by the founding of the Shuanglinsi (Double Grove Monastery) in Singapore in 1909.[15]

THE DEVELOPMENT OF THE OVERSEAS CHINESE TEMPLE NETWORK

In order to get a sense of longer-term Buddhist connections between Southeast Asia and China, one can turn to earlier travel accounts of monks, historical records, and stone inscriptions. Tansen Sen has discussed the flow of monks back and forth from India to China from the Han to the Tang/Song period.[16] Claudine Salmon has discussed religious exchanges between the Buddhist kingdom of Srivijaya (based in contemporary Palembang and Jambi in Sumatra) and Song China. The next period of intense contact between Chinese Buddhists and Southeast Asia began at the end of the Ming era and continued through the beginning of the Qing. During the Qing Manchu takeover of China, the entire coast of Southeast and South China endured a coastal evacuation policy, which lasted for up to twenty years (1660–1680) in some regions. Tens of thousands of villages were abandoned and destroyed along with many thousands of temples dedicated to popular gods and Buddhist monasteries. These measures were intended to eliminate any sources of support for the armies and navies of the Ming resistance, including those of Zheng Chenggong (1624–1662) and his son Zheng Jing (1642–1681) on Jinmen and later on Taiwan, and those of the Ming armies in the southwest. These policies drove many coastal residents to emigrate to Southeast Asia.

In the 1990s, Zheng Zhenman and I gathered inscriptions in temples and monasteries in the Quanzhou and Zhangzhou regions of Fujian.[17] We located an inscription dated 1697 at the Dragon Pool Buddhist monastery in Haicang, which revealed that this monastery had sent out Buddhist monks to Southeast Asia to raise funds for the reconstruction of the temple immediately after the Qing coastal evacuations. Leaders of the Chinese community in Batavia responded to their call and donated substantial sums toward the reconstruction of the temple. The Baosheng Dadi (Great Emperor Who Protects Life, a deified doctor from the Song named Wu Tao [979–1036]) temple nearby in Qingjiao,

Haicang, which dates back to the Song dynasty, also preserves a stele from the Kangxi period (also dated 1697) titled *Baguo yuanzhu beiji* (Stele record of the patrons from Batavia), describing how many of the same Chinese leaders in Batavia recorded on the Dragon Pool Monastery inscriptions agreed to donate two years of the income of their branch temple (presumably dedicated to Baosheng Dadi) to help pay for repairs to the temple.[18] Many other temples along the coast aimed to do the same.[19]

The Qingyunting (Pavilion of the Blue Clouds) in Malacca was one of the most important Chinese temples in Southeast Asia. This temple (not a monastery) was founded around 1673 by Ming loyalists including Zeng Qilu (1643–1718) and Lin Weijing (1614–1688).[20] Currently, the temple is dedicated to both Tian Hou (the Empress of Heaven, also known as Mazu, Goddess of the Sea) and Guanyin (the Mahāyāna Buddhist Bodhisattva of Mercy). The temple played a key role as the political command center for the Chinese community, with the pavilion director usually also serving as the Kapitan of the Chinese (appointed by the Dutch and later the English to administer the Chinese community). The temple also played a key role as a business center and social club for wealthy merchants who made up the temple management committee. They lent temple funds to smaller merchants and entrepreneurial immigrants, and maintained control over credit-pooling associations (for life-cycle ritual needs) housed inside the temple.

Reading through the epigraphy of this temple, we find early inscriptions praising the founders of the temple, Ming loyalist refugees from the Manchu takeover of China.[21] Some of the leaders inscribed steles at the Baoshanting (Precious Mountain Pavilion), a temple built at the foot of Sanbaoshan, the main Chinese cemetery in Malacca, which was sponsored and managed by the Qingyunting. Later inscriptions at the Qingyunting celebrate the success of the local merchant class. Other inscriptions continue to highlight the role of the leading Chinese merchant families of the region, with some early founders visited in dreams in order to display their virtuous natures.

From an early period, the Qingyunting temple hired Buddhist monks to conduct ritual services. One of the first accounts of the Pavilion of the Blue Clouds was provided in 1698 by the French voyager François Froger.[22] He describes visiting the temple and observing men in robes chanting over tables covered with offerings. Although he could not understand a word they said, he was certain that they were religious specialists (presumably Buddhist monks). He knew it was a temple because of the three icons on the altar. He also made a sketch of the temple, revealing that at that time it had only a single room, with statues of (Buddhist) deities on the altar at the back of the hall. The Qingyunting leaders also sponsored Buddhist rites at the nearby cemetery hill. The following inscription at the Precious Mountain Pavilion at the foot of the Hokkien cemetery hill was written by Cai Shizhang, who served as pavilion director of the Qingyunting, in 1801:

> The Precious Mountain Pavilion is a place where the secluded deceased are offered sacrifices with respect. . . . It is decided that of the entire year's rent from the property, 25 *wen* should be given to the monk[s] of this pavilion as "incense salary," 20 *wen* should be given to the master of the incense burner of that year so that he can separately set up offerings before the [main] spirit tablet[s] on days on which families make sacrifices. The remainder left over should be held on to and saved for use on future repairs.[23]

This passage reveals that, in the early period, the Buddhist monks connected to the Baoshanting Precious Mountain Pavilion were on a small salary from the Qingyunting. Similar indications can be found in inscriptions at several temples and cemetery shrines in Singapore.[24]

By the late eighteenth century, a shift occurs in the inscriptional record of the Qingyunting. We find a broader merchant class represented in steles and wooden plaques dedicated to Mazu or to Guanyin. In the nineteenth century, the temple was expanded, and new halls were added dedicated to the worship of the unrequited dead, with inscriptions outlining the development of a Pudu (Hungry Ghosts Universal Deliverance) Association. Here we see a shift from serving the top leadership or the merchant elite to a concern for the local Chinese community as a whole and their many deceased ancestors. This shift also implies the need for a broader range of ritual observances on the part of resident Buddhist monks.

THE MAIN EARLY TEMPLES OF THE SINGAPORE DIALECT COMMUNITIES

The earliest Hokkien temples and cemetery shrines in Singapore were built by leaders of the Qingyunting in Malacca, including Director of the Pavilion Si Hoo Keh (Xue Foji, 1793–1874), who helped sponsor the construction of the Tianfugong on Telok Ayer Street in Singapore in 1840. Si had first served as director of the Hokkien cemetery in Singapore, the Hengshanting (Pavilion of the Everlasting Mountain), founded in 1828. His sons succeeded him in this role, even after he returned to Malacca to take up the post of pavilion director once again. Several other Malacca *peranakan* (Southeast Asian-born Chinese) businessmen from Malacca banded together to build the Chongde (Worshiping Virtue) pagoda next door to the Tianfugong, and their descendants still worship their forefathers there on a triannual basis.

The formation of the old town of Singapore, at the mouth of the Singapore River, saw the rise of distinct dialect territories in which people from the same region in South or Southeast China gathered and built their temples, native-place and clan associations, as well as their shops that monopolized different trades and commercial activities. The boundaries of these dialect neighborhoods were preserved from the founding of Singapore in 1819 until the beginning of the urban development of Singapore island in the mid-1950s. Currently, only traces of these communities can be seen in the few temples left behind. The dialect communities have now been dispersed across the entire island into the HDB (Housing and Development Board) blocks built by the government in the satellite towns around Singapore island.

Each dialect group contains many subsections, based on combined principles of a common place of origin and dialect (as these can differ considerably by region within the broader dialect area). Often, within the same dialect and territorial subgroup, there are also divisions based on common surname, class, education, and gender. Thus, for example, the immigrants to Singapore from Jinmen divided into two groups, with the merchant leaders worshiping Chen Yuan (fl. 804), a Tang dynasty military founder of Chinese communities on the islands, and the lower-class dock workers who lived in coolie houses worshiping Liu Wangye (sometimes called a "plaque demon"), who is said to have been an officer under Chen Yuan in the Tang.

Stone inscriptions from the Heng San Ting (Eternal Mountain Pavilion) (built in 1828, burned down in 1997) and the Kim Lam (Golden Lotus) temple in Singapore provide some insight into the status of the monks attached to the major temples of the Chinese merchant communities in the period preceding the rise of organized monastic Buddhism and the later spread of Reform Buddhism.[25] In the *Five Regulations Agreed Upon though Discussion at the Eternal Mountain Pavilion*, dated 1836, we find the following:

> Third regulation: As for the splendid Mid-Autumn Festival, the funds raised by the Master of the Incense Burners and the Heads of the Families for ritual sacrifices and offerings can all be kept as blessed objects in the homes of the Master of the Incense Burner. When he wishes to invite all the Heads of the Families to partake in the blessed offerings, of whatever funds were raised, if there is any remainder, it should be given to the monks to cover the expenses of tobacco, old leaf [betel nut], and tea, and to cover the costs of his annual ritual expenses and of any occasional costs for the entertainment of visitors. Whomever takes turns and posts a proclamation for the two ceremonies of Qingming, and the monks should take care of and attend to. . . . If there are those who do not follow this regulation, they will receive ritual punishment or be sent away. Everyone must obey the public agreement, there being no exceptions for individual feelings.

This passage clearly indicates that the monks are receiving leftover funds from ritual offerings and that they are expected to be continuously on call and ready to provide ritual services to whomever asks to perform rites at the pavilion.

> Fourth regulation: On the festivals of Qingming, the seventh month Pudu, and the Mid-Autumn Festival, it is decided that extraneous idle people will not be allowed to set up gambling tables inside and outside of the Pavilion, as this would bring disruption to the order of the [Pavilion]. If there are any who disobey, we will invite the police to come and take them away to be punished by the Chief of Police. We also will not allow any Buddhist monk within the Pavilion to sell opium or to set up an opium den within or nearby the Pavilion. If there be anyone who disobeys and does not respect [this regulation], and who is then discovered by the people, then this monk will be expelled, and the opium den will be dismantled. There will be no mercy.

From the point of view of the temple leadership, the morals of the itinerant monks were suspicious. They were apparently thought likely to be involved in opium and gambling.

> Fifth regulation: As for the funds for incense [operational expenses] of the Mt. Heng Pavilion, each first and fifteenth day of the lunar month, the Buddhist monks should go down into Singapore to gather contributions. As for the Chinese, Thai, Vietnamese, or other foreign sailing boats or double decked boats that have safely reached Singapore each year, it is publicly agreed that each Chinese boat that belongs to someone from Quanzhou or Zhangzhou [prefectures] will make a contribution of four Spanish [(Lu)song, Manila Spanish] silver dollars. The sojourners on board these boats can make any [additional] contribution their hearts desire. As for Thai, Vietnamese, or other foreign sailing boats or double decked boats, and every other kind of boat, regardless of the size of the boat, so long as the boat belongs to a person from Quanzhou or Zhangzhou, it has been publicly decided that each boat will contribute two Spanish silver dollars. Should it happen that, during the annual contribution, a Singaporean boat has a captain [or owner] who refuses to obey, then if the captain or anyone else registered to his crew should happen to pass away, by public decision they will not be allowed to be buried in this cemetery. The Buddhist monks of this Pavilion should refuse them. If anyone from Quanzhou or Zhangzhou prefecture passes away and wishes to be buried in this cemetery, he or she must obtain a permit from the Master of the Incense of that year, which must be handed over to the monks of the Pavilion as evidence. Anyone who has not received a permit as proof should be refused by the monks.

As can be seen from the inscription above, the Buddhist monks working at the Chinese cemetery shrines were a floating population very much at the service of the temple leadership in contrast with later scenarios in which temples developed around monastics stably resident in a monastery linked to the Buddhist temple.

Another inscription from the Golden Orchid Temple sets out regulations concerning itinerant Buddhist monks and Daoist ritual masters and shows that the day-to-day activities of the temples were carried out by ritual specialists (temple keepers, or invocators, who would assist worshipers with their prayers and offerings, and tend to the incense and oil lamps in the temple). Monks and Daoist masters were not lodged permanently in these temples. The *Regulations of the Golden Orchid Temple*, dating to 1891, reveals that the itinerant Buddhist monks and Daoist ritual masters were under suspicion from the leadership for their tendency to make money on the side with gambling tables and the sale of opium. They were called on to provide ritual services at the temples on a regular basis and at the cemeteries during Qingming (sweeping of the graves) and Zhongyuan Pudu (universal deliverance of the hungry ghosts in the Middle Prime [lunar 7/15]), but they were expected to subsist on the leftovers from the sacrificial offerings. Other inscriptions from this period describe the (quite low) wages provided to monks, many of whom seem to have been largely peripatetic.

This was not the only scenario for monks' involvement with temples in nineteenth-century Singapore, as some temples contained monastic residents and granted monks more status. Some temples in Fujian dedicated to local gods maintained historical connections with Buddhist orders. This was also the case for the Hong San See (Fengshansi, lit., Phoenix Mountain Monastery), which was dedicated to Guangze Zunwang, the Reverent King of Broad Compassion (Guo Mingliang, 899–922). The mother temple of this god, one of the greatest of the Fujian local god cults, is located in Shishan township in upper Nanan County.[26] For centuries, the cult center has been maintained by Buddhist monks, although the god is best known for his highly Confucian filial piety, manifested in his visits to his parents' tombs (to apologize for becoming a Daoist immortal before they had died). The historical links with Buddhism at this temple center ensured that Buddhist monks were invited to its branch Fengshansi temple in Singapore (built in 1836), housed at the temple, and put in charge of the upkeep of the temple of the god's cult after it was moved to Mohammed Sultan Street. This progression can be seen from the epigraphy in the temple. The names of other Buddhist monks are also inscribed on steles revealing their roles in the running of the Linshanting Beijigong (Temple of the Northern Polestar of Unicorn Mountain Pavilion, built before 1866), another temple in charge of yet another Hokkien cemetery in Singapore. The Tianfugong, the main temple of the Hokkien community on Telok Ayer Street, also housed Buddhist monks at various times (such as Master Hong Choon, who resided there for several years in the 1930s). Nonetheless, it is important to note that even in these instances characterized by resident monks being offered greater status, these were all temporary institutional arrangements rather than permanent multigenerational monasteries. They thus left little scope for the training of future generations of monks.

JILESI IN PENANG AND THE TRANSFORMATION FROM SALARIED EMPLOYEES TO BUDDHIST ENTREPRENEURS

A major turning point in the rise of Chinese Mahāyāna monastic orders in Southeast Asia in the nineteenth century was the founding of the renowned Jilesi (Monastery of Extreme Joy) in Penang in 1898. The monastery was founded by the monk Miaolian (1824–1907), who had been sent in 1888 to Penang by the Gushan Yongquansi outside Fuzhou to raise money to repair his home temple. Miaolian set in motion a major transformation of local roles for Buddhist monks in the region. Miaolian worked with the local Penang Chinese temple leadership to develop a new system of financing for temples, with novel roles for the monks within the temple. The system changed the position of a Chinese Buddhist monk in Southeast Asia from a salaried itinerant to participant in a contract system wherein monks would handle all the finances of the temple, with any additional profits in temple income beyond the initial annual rental fee becoming their own.[27] Miaolian used these additional profits to begin the process of constructing a Mahāyāna monastery in Penang.

Before Miaolian's arrival, one finds scattered earlier records of Buddhist monks working in Penang on inscriptions within the Guangfu (Guangdong and Fujian) Temple, which had been founded in 1800. The 1824 *Chongjian Guangfu gong beiji* (Stele record of the reconstruction of the Guangfu Temple) states, "After we rebuilt the inner courtyard and buildings, and set up the images of the saints therein, then to the side we built quarters for monks to live in and made them complete."[28] However, within three decades a new monastic lineage began to take shape in Penang. The 1923 *Gazetteer of the Penang Crane Mountain Jile Monastery*, written by (Wei) Baozi, states,

> Formerly, in the *dinghai* year of the Qing [1888], Chan Master Miaolian came once more to Penang. The elite [merchants] Qiu Tiande, Hu Taixing, Lin Huacan, Tiao Xingyang, and so forth, invited him to become the abbot of the Guangfu Temple and charged him over 2,000 in gold for the annual rental [of the temple]. The name of this practice is called *baojuma* [contracting for annual temple income]. From this time on, the monks of the Gushan Monastery [near Fuzhou] became the leaders of the Guangfu Temple.

Although Miaolian left the Guangfu Temple within three years, he arranged for a series of his disciples to come from his Fuzhou home monastery, Gushan Yongquansi, to succeed him as abbots for over twenty-five years. Miaolian then began the process of establishing the Jilesi in a quiet spot outside of the crowded city center with support from local Chinese business leaders and eventually from the dowager empress of China.

Financial matters within the Guangfu Temple led to a government audit.[29] The entrance on the scene of a group of monks held together by strict master-disciple relations, having a specific code of conduct (internal regulations), and with an institutional base in an ancient, established Chan monastery back in Fujian (the Yongquansi is a renowned thousand-year-old Buddhist monastery outside Fuzhou City founded in 908) introduced a different set of relations between abbots and monks, on one hand, and between the monks and temple sponsors and everyday worshipers, on the other hand. Moreover, it reshaped relations between the temples (or monasteries) and the colonial authorities. These new monastic arrangements with the first establishment of a formal Buddhist order in Penang thus altered the religious ecology of the region.

An inscription written by Miaolian for the Jilesi dated 1907 outlines twenty-one detailed regulations for the conduct of the monks in the monastery.[30] He includes detailed rules on lines of authority (the abbot in the founding monastery in Fujian held decision-making power and exclusive rights to ordination of new monks), accounting procedures, and issuing of wages, and limitations on the hosting of "floating cloud" itinerant monks, who were restricted to a maximum stay of only one week. There were also warnings about not falling under the sway of local patrons and preserving Buddhist control over the monastery.

The Jilesi attracted considerable support and local funding from several of the wealthiest Hakka businessmen in Penang and across Southeast Asia. Five of them served as successive managing directors. These were (1) Zhang Bishi (cognomon Zhenxun, 1840–1916), a Hakka entrepreneur from Dapu, appointed Chinese consul in Penang and later consul general in Singapore; (2) Zhang Yunan (cognomon Rongxuan, fl. 1891–1912), from Meixian, who owned rubber plantations, was appointed Kapitan of Deli in Sumatra by the Dutch, and was named Chinese consul to Penang by the Qing imperial court; (3) Xie Rongguang (1846–1916) from Meixian, Kapitan under the Dutch and a consul in Penang, who served for over a decade as managing director of the temple; (4) Zheng Siwen, a mining magnate from Zengcheng County in Guangdong, who was made a Kapitan in Perak; and (5) Dai Chunru (d. 1919) from Dapu, another extremely wealthy managing director, renowned for his philanthropy, who established hospitals and schools, and contributed greatly to the monastery. Some of these patrons were major investors in the coastal railroad to Shantou in China. Other prominent patrons who merited special biographical notices in the *Gazetteer* include Zhang Hongnan (d. 1921), brother of Zhang Yunan, who also made his fortune in rubber plantations and was appointed major in Deli by the Dutch colonial government (he was a close friend of Buddhist monk Benzhong). Finally, Madame Lin, née Chen Xinan, made generous donations to the monastery, which were recorded in multilingual inscriptions.

An inscription dated 1906 reveals the vast transnational network of sponsors supporting this temple, who altogether contributed the sum of 210,030 yuan to the monastery. Sponsors include the businessmen listed above as well as individuals and native-place associations from all over Malaya, Singapore, and Indonesia, as well as patrons in Fujian and Jiangxi in China.[31] In response to this outpouring of support, a final unique set of plaques and inscriptions, including one by the dowager empress Cixi, details the transmission of a complete set of the Buddhist Canon (*Tripiṭaka*) from the Imperial Household via the (Folusi) Buddhist Registry Office to the Jilesi Monastery in Penang in 1904. This was the first *Tripiṭaka* to be sent to Malaysia, and the inscriptions (including one that was the inscribed record of a telegram from Beijing) make clear that these scriptures were intended for a foreign Southeast Asian audience.[32]

THE LIANSHAN SHUANGLINSI AND THE RISE OF BUDDHIST MONASTICISM IN SINGAPORE

The story of the founding of the first mainstream Buddhist monastery in Singapore revolves around a family of roaming Buddhist monks and nuns. However, in this case, they were Chinese Buddhist pilgrims who had traveled for several years in Sri Lanka and who were persuaded to stay in Singapore, where they stopped on their return trip to China. Low Kim Pong (Liu Jinbang, 1837–1909) donated land and set out to build a monastery (and a nunnery) for them. The mother of the founding monk wrote the following personal account of the tribulations of her family. Unfortunately, the original stele has been lost, but the text was preserved:

> I am from Huian county in Quanzhou prefecture [in Fujian, China]. My lay name is Xiao. My entire family united together and sought after the delights of Buddhism. As a result, my two sons became enlightened and floated through life as though it was a dream. They urged us to search out the truths of Buddhism, so in the *renchen* year [1892] I followed along with the entire family of men and women, twelve in all. We sailed by boat to Colombo and spent six years in the mountains in Sri Lanka. When it reached the *wuxu* [1898] year, in the spring we came down from the mountains and traveled all over the Buddhist kingdom. Later, we traveled to Penang and passed by Singapore, planning to return to our home country. We were greeted by the Patron Low, who graciously offered to donate this mountain [property to serve as a monastery]. Therefore, my eldest son, Xian Hui, built the Double Grove Chan Monastery here. He also planned to build a Zhulin [Pearl Gem] Nunnery behind the main hall of the monastery to provide a place for myself, my eldest daughter, Chan Hui, who was also nun, and my niece, Yueguang, who is also nun, so that all three of us could stay together. Unexpectedly, my son Xian Hui suddenly cast away his

> body of illusory transformations in the summer of the *xinqiu* year [1901] and entered into the realm of Nirvana. But at this time the construction was not complete, and life seemed to float like a dream: isn't that just the way things are! But since we, mother and son, had already been here for several years, I had a great desire to see the great work completed. Then above we could repay the Buddha's mercy. But now that things have come to this, what am I to say? Now my [second] son, Xing Hui, has already returned to the True, and it is no longer convenient for us three women to remain here. Therefore, I intend to give instructions that my second son Xing Hui's disciple, Great Master Mingguang, should manage what still needs to be done. Only by working hard will he be able to carry on the aspirations of his predecessors. [That he will] not let down the ancestral ways is what I earnest hope for. Now we will take the next boat back to our country, and I cannot help but feel emotional. So I have specially composed these few words and engraved then on fine stone, so that those of you who come passing by will know the origins [of this monastery] and also know that the Pearl Gem Nunnery is the Dharma hall, and the Dharma hall is the nunnery. On an auspicious day in the autumn of Guangxu *renyin* [1902], erected by Nun Cimiao.[33]

This touching and very personal inscription reveals that the founding monks of Lianshan Shuanglinsi (Lotus Mountain Double Grove Monastery) were itinerant monastics returning to China from a pilgrimage to Sri Lanka when they encountered the lay Buddhist patron Low Kim Pong. The decision to construct a full-fledged Buddhist monastery in Singapore at this point reflects a desire on the part of leading members of the lay Buddhist Singapore elite to localize Chan Buddhist orders from their founding monasteries in Fujian to Southeast Asia. Other mobile Buddhist monks also took advantage of changing circumstances, including changes in colonial policies toward religious institutions and the Chinese temple network, to set up smaller-scale temples in Singapore.[34]

THE COLONIAL REGULATION OF RELIGION

Looking back over developments within the Chinese religious sphere in Malaya and Singapore in the nineteenth century, one can see that colonial regulation of Chinese religion from the mid-1850s led to a gradual dismantling of central elements of the Chinese temple system, which combined communal leadership and enforcement in the form of secret societies. These colonial policies resulted in the creation of a new, autonomous category of "religion," as well as the separation among Chinese between a privatized sphere of religion and a public life based ultimately in chambers of commerce. Related colonial policies included the gradual elimination of Chinese cemeteries, the removal of hawkers from the five-foot ways, and other efforts to improve hygiene and regulate colonial space.[35] These transformations were facilitated by the rise of English-educated Chinese in mission schools, British universities, and government service. The rise of Chinese modern nation-state nationalism during the Republican period intensified the rejection of the earlier Chinese temple system among educated elite Chinese leaders.[36]

It is useful to analyze the impact of colonial conceptions and regulations of religion on the subsequent transformation of the Chinese dialect community temples. These policies were worked out across the British colonies, from colonial statements in India on religious tolerance, to bans in Madras on Thaipusam processions, to clashes in Penang, Hong Kong, and Singapore with secret societies. The colonial knowledge machine was creating and imposing categories as fast as it was absorbing and attempting to assess and categorize perceived new threats (such as the potential for the Kongsi in Borneo to become independent). The following regulations and policy changes enacted across the Straits Settlements had a major impact on Chinese temple networks in Malaya and Singapore as well as in Hong Kong:

1856: Penang riot over an opera stage

1867: Penang riot featuring feuding "secret societies"

1867: Peace Preservation Act: giving British authorities the right to banish undesirable individuals

1869: Dangerous Societies Suppression Ordinance: calling for the registration of all "secret societies" but only laxly enforced

1877: William Pickering appointed to the Chinese Protectorate in Singapore: working closely with the so-called secret societies, he argued for coordination with the colonial authorities

1887: Assassination attempt on Pickering

1890: Societies Ordinance Act: declaring sworn brotherhoods completely illegal and criminalizing such groups

1891: New prisons built in Singapore

1899: Chinese Advisory Board established: encouraging greater cooperation with the colonial authorities

1905: Mohammedan and Hindu Endowment Board established to coordinate these religious institutions with colonial authorities

1906: Singapore Chinese Chamber of Commerce established

With the prohibition of secret societies in 1890 (which took place later in Singapore than in Penang and Hong Kong), the enforcement arm of the temple and clan association business leadership was criminalized. At the same time, British authorities were intruding more and more into the financial side of temple administration. An example of this was noted earlier, in relation to the Guangfu Temple in Penang. An audit in 1890 led to the enforced reorganization of the temple's administrative structure and financial accounting procedures. This audit likely shaped the decision of temple leaders to transfer control over temple finances to the Buddhist monk Miaolian and his Chinese monastic order.

LAST STAND OF THE NINETEENTH-CENTURY CHINESE TEMPLE SYSTEM

Cheang Hong Lim (Zhang Fanglin, 1842–1892) was one of the preeminent leaders of the Singaporean Chinese community at the end of the nineteenth century. His engagement with the Chinese temple system represents a last effort to hold together the pieces of this rapidly changing system. Cheang was a major partner in the Great Opium Syndicate of 1890s Singapore, a position he inherited from his father, Cheang Sam Teo.[37] The vast fortune accumulated by controlling opium sales enabled Cheang to invest in property, diversifying his holdings. Over time, he built or restored six Chinese temples. Cheang first restored the temple established by his father dedicated to an obscure local god from his home region in Fujian called Qingzhen Yuanjun (Primordial Lord of Pure Perfection). He also built a temple at his seaside villa to house a boulder worshiped as an Earth God by local people. Later he restored the Golden Orchid Temple, which was a center of the secret societies of the Hokkien faction. In this context, he attempted to establish rules for this temple to enable its self-regulation, trying to keep a step ahead of colonial regulations forbidding secret societies. He also built a temple to the Jade Emperor, which attempted to transcend dialect boundaries and create the basis for new forms of Chinese leadership and alliances within Singapore. Bound closely to the Qing court and involved in disaster relief programs in Asia and beyond, Cheang received titles and honors from the Chinese imperial court as well as recognition and honors from the colonial authorities and other Asian governments. Most important here is Cheang's role as leader of the Chinese community in Singapore. According to his epitaph, he was regarded as the "chief libationer"—the head ritual specialist—of the entire Chinese community of Singapore. Cheang's activities as a patron of many Chinese temples and societies operated according to the earlier logic of Chinese temple administration marked by nonmonastic control and tight interconnections between ritual and commercial activities. At his death, Cheang was recognized in these terms by many associates and clients, yet this occurred as the Chinese temple system was undergoing massive transformations that eventually led to privileged Buddhist monastic leadership rather than that of nonmonastic entrepreneurs.

THE RISE OF MODERN(IST) TEMPLE LEADERS AND REFORMIST BUDDHIST MONKS

Despite the efforts of figures like Cheang Hong Lim, leadership based in the temples and associations would soon give way to modern forms of nationalism and capitalist networks. More and more, the Chinese leadership in Singapore was drawn into the process of building a Chinese modern nation-state. These leaders turned their energies away from the Chinese temple network that Cheang had worked so hard to preserve. Instead, they were content to allow Buddhist monks to run increasing numbers of monasteries.

Tan Kah Kee (Chen Jiageng, 1874–1961), leader of the Hokkien Huay Guan (native-place association) and founder of the Ee Ho Hean Club, was dedicated to supporting the revolutionary cause in China. He is an example of the new kind of leader who helped to develop newly emerging organizational forms. He raised large sums to support China in the first half of the twentieth century, founding modern educational centers such as Jimei College and Xiamen University. Other Singaporean Chinese leaders of the first half of the twentieth century, such as Lim Boon Keng (1869–1957), were closer to colonial rule, through English schooling in the missionary schools, scholarships to study in England, and government employment and honors. Later in his life, Lim turned to a reformed Confucianism as an alternative to Christianity as well as to Chinese popular religion. Negative attitudes toward Chinese popular religious practices—involving the temple network discussed at length above—can be seen in his editorials published in the leading Singaporean Chinese newspapers at the turn of the century.[38]

Such attacks led Singaporean Chinese Buddhist leaders to participate in reform movements designed to rationalize Buddhism and make it more compatible with the modern nation-state and its secular modernization projects (including its new definition of religion).[39] Taixu (1890–1947) and other Buddhist reform leaders came to Singapore in the Republican period to attempt to counter Japanese propaganda on the unity of the Asian races, the rise of the Pan-Asian Co-Prosperity Sphere, and the role of (Japanese state-linked) Buddhism within this vision.[40] These Chinese Reform Buddhism leaders also had a major impact on local Buddhist organizations within Singapore. They worked with Buddhist monks trained in China (primarily in the Fujian Chan Buddhist monasteries of Quanzhou, Xiamen, and Zhangzhou) to turn the major Buddhist centers in Singapore into centers of modern Reform Buddhism.[41] Reform Buddhism's emphasis on spirituality over ritual and on the cultivation of the self paralleled the emphasis of the Protestant missionaries, who established several mission schools in this period still considered top elite schools in Singapore. One can see these developments as instances of a "conversion to modernity."[42]

However, the rise of Reform Buddhism was not the only development in Buddhist circles in Singapore and Southeast Asia. Several other more traditional

Buddhist monastic networks had begun to extend into Southeast Asia in the Republican era and up to the early 1950s. One such network linked a series of temples across Southeast Asia to the Guanghuasi (Monastery of Broad Transformations, founded in 558 CE) in Putian. As soon as it was possible to return to China in the early 1980s, monks from this network (including those from the Singapore Guanghuasi) returned with suitcases full of cash to rebuild the Guanghuasi, which had been turned into a plastics factory and where several monks had committed suicide after refusing to eat meat and return to a secular life at the height of the Cultural Revolution.[43] Yet another such mainstream or unreformed Buddhist monastic network extends from the Guishansi (Turtle Mountain Monastery) in Huating, Putian, to the Qingyunting in Malacca, and from there to Muar, Penang, Singapore, Jakarta, and elsewhere. This network was able to mobilize related networks of Putian immigrants (spirit mediums, native-place associations, Mazu temples of fishermen/smugglers) to rebuild the founding temple and to use remaining funds to rebuild the home village in Huating of the Buddhist abbot Zhen Jing and to build an even larger temple across the street from the Qingyunting in Malacca.[44]

In the last Singapore census, conducted in 2010, over one million Singaporeans identified themselves as Buddhists.[45] Given the growing predominance of "socially engaged" or "human realm" Buddhist transnational organizations, such as the Ciji (Merciful Salvation) Foundation, Fagushan (Dharma Drum Mountain), and Foguangshan (Buddha's Light Mountain International Association) based in Taiwan, the history of twentieth-century Chinese Mahāyāna Buddhism is being rewritten as the inevitable triumph of Reform Buddhism.[46] This narrative leaves out many alternative lineages and developments in the region. Multiple networks link Buddhist monasteries and Chinese temples to their founding sacred sites in South and Southeast China. They provided another key vector for the spread of variant forms of Mahāyāna Buddhism into Southeast Asia within networks of sectarian lay-Buddhist movements.[47] Several of these networks maintain important but little studied traditions of Buddhist practice. For instance, lay-Buddhist groups in Southeast Asia such as the Xiantian Dao (Way of Prior Heaven) studied by Marjorie Topley set up *zhaijiao* (vegetarian retreat) centers for women. There are currently some thirty temples in Singapore linked to the Xiantian Dao, now under the leadership of the Kwan Im Thong on Waterloo Road.[48] These "vegetarian associations" were places of refuge for many Cantonese female laborers, spinsters, and orphans who moved to or were born in Singapore in the second half of the nineteenth century. This organization is now one of the wealthiest charities in Singapore.

Another important but more fragmentary network is made up of small nunneries spread across Southeast Asia, which often take in abandoned girls and perform a range of traditional Buddhist practices (reciting scriptures and making offerings to the spirit tablets of the deceased—often a female sponsor of the nunnery). This kind of quasi-private nunnery is also widespread in

Southeast China. A third lay-Buddhist Mahāyāna network is the Chaozhou Shantang (Halls of Merit) dedicated to the worship of the Song Buddhist monk Song Dafeng (1039?–1127?). This network of halls is of interest because most of the ritual activity is performed by the members themselves, without the intercession of Buddhist monks. The members of the temple don special robes and engage in group recitation. Many halls have set up *gongdetang* (halls of merit to worship ancestral tablets) as these tablets are being concentrated in such spaces. Halls of merit have evolved into charities that support medical clinics and other contemporary social needs. They constitute a tight, transnational business network.[49] These groups and others like them far outnumber the established Buddhist monastic orders or the new Reform Buddhist organizations, and they deserve further study. In such groups, we find that the relationship between Buddhist religious orders and their lay followers is blurred, inviting comparison to Chinese temple networks before their restructuring in the late nineteenth and early twentieth centuries under British colonial rule.

This chapter has examined transformations in the nature of the Chinese temple network of Southeast Asia from its early founding in the sixteenth century to its expansion in the seventeenth century after the Qing conquest of China and the consolidation of its central role in Chinese overseas life and transnational trust and trade networks in the eighteenth century. The nineteenth century witnessed exponential growth of the network with the sudden influx of laborers and the concomitant proliferation of temples and associations for dialect groups. For several centuries, Chinese temples and native-place business offices provided the main institutional framework for the elaboration of trust networks that facilitated long-distance trade across the Minnan coastal trading system. I have argued that such Chinese temples in Southeast Asia can be considered informal, transpersonal, translocal, networked religious orders, owing to their ties to founding temples in distinct regions of Southeast China and their provision of ritual frameworks for Chinese communities in Southeast Asia. I have also shown how they incorporated within their ritual frameworks representatives of more formal religious orders, such as itinerant Buddhists or Daoist ritual masters, for specialized ritual purposes. Finally, I have traced the rise of independent Chinese Mahāyāna Chan Buddhist monasteries in the Straits Settlements during the late nineteenth century that were linked to ancient founding monasteries in China by formal Buddhist orders of the time. This innovative moment in the Chinese religious life of the Straits Settlements was dependent on changes in colonial policy toward religion and, thus, on the effects that various projects of secularization had on Chinese societies in Southeast Asia.

In the second half of the nineteenth century, colonial authorities began to regulate and redefine Chinese religious institutions by criminalizing their violent enforcement arms and by forcing greater transparency, or at least accountability, in their management and fiscal accounting. These pressures along with the rise of modern nation-state nationalism and the spread of mixed forms of capitalism in the early twentieth century led many Chinese community leaders to channel their energies more into the emerging Chinese chambers of commerce than into existing temple networks.

We have seen how one Chinese leader in mid-nineteenth-century Singapore, Cheang Hong Lim, struggled to hold together the Chinese temple network framework, while many forces were working to undermine its central role in Chinese life. His life marked the end of an era. By the end of the nineteenth century, mobile Chinese Buddhist monks, moving through Southeast Asia on pilgrimage or in search of support for their home monasteries, took advantage of the opening created by the withdrawal of the Chinese leadership and the redefinition of the Chinese temples by the colonial authorities. Working with local business leaders but offering a complete system of temple management, they raised support for the construction of imposing monasteries. The turn of the twentieth century saw the collapse of the Qing dynasty and the rise of Chinese nationalism in Southeast Asia at precisely the moment that Chinese Mahāyāna monasteries were first established in Penang and Singapore.

These Buddhist monastic networks themselves became a site of contestation lasting into the middle of the twentieth century, as institutional debates led by Reform Buddhists like Taixu in China (in response to the widespread assault on popular religion) led to changes in the operations of Buddhist monasteries in Singapore and Malaya as well. As we have seen, the rise of formal monastic orders in Singapore and Malaya/Malaysia during the late nineteenth and twentieth centuries did not lead to a homogenization of Buddhist practice in the region. Many alternative forms of Buddhism, some syncretic and redemptive, others more traditional, continued to develop in Southeast Asia during the twentieth century. The larger Chinese temple network has persisted across time despite substantial changes in leadership and financing that occurred during the period considered here.

In recent decades, many temple communities in Southeast Asia have returned to China, helping to rebuild their founding temples. Hundreds of thousands of temples, monasteries, and ancestral halls have been rebuilt over the past three decades. A great deal of ritual knowledge had been preserved in the Chinese temples of Southeast Asia over the course of the Cultural Revolution, when many ritual traditions, temples, and religious practices were banned in China, in some areas for over two decades if not longer. Thus, the Southeast Asian Chinese temples (along with Taiwanese temples) played a crucial role in reviving, reinventing, and in some cases transforming ritual traditions in Southeast China, including rebuilding temple structures and ancestral halls, a cultural historical phenomenon largely overlooked. In this process, we can trace the role of a complex, historically evolved, transnational network of branch temples, native-place associations, ancestral halls, common surname associations, and Buddhist monasteries and lay movements scattered across Southeast

Asia. As these temple networks evolve and generate new possibilities, they will continue to draw in and circulate more flows of people, ritual knowledge, and capital, and develop new potentials for the expression of new identities and new aspirations within simultaneously transnational and localized circuits.

NOTES

1. For more on the spread of Theravāda Buddhism, see Stanley Tambiah, *World Conqueror and World Renouncer: A Study of Buddhism and Polity in Thailand against a Historical Background* (Cambridge, UK: Cambridge University Press, 1976); Richard Gombrich, *Theravāda Buddhism: A Social History from Ancient Benares to Modern Colombo* (London: Routledge and Kegan Paul, 1988); Donald Swearer, *The Buddhist World of Southeast Asia* (Albany: SUNY Press, 2011); Anne M. Blackburn, *Locations of Buddhism: Colonialism and Modernity in Sri Lanka* (Chicago: University of Chicago Press, 2010).

2. Anthony Reid, *Southeast Asia in the Age of Commerce 1450–1680*, vol. 2: *Expansion and Crisis* (New Haven: Yale University Press, 1993).

3. For further discussion of seventeenth-century Chinese Mahāyāna Chan missionary activity linking South China to Vietnam, see Claudine Salmon, "Réfugiés Ming dans les Mers du sud vus à travers diverses inscriptions (ca. 1650–ca. 1730)," *Bulletin de l'École française d'Extrême-Orient* 90–91 (2003): 177–227; Charles Wheeler, "Missionary Buddhism in a Post-Ancient World: Monks, Merchants, and Colonial Expansion in Seventeenth Century Cochinchina (Vietnam)," in *Secondary Cities and Urban Networking in the Indian Ocean Realm, c. 1400–1800*, edited by Kenneth Hall (Plymouth: Lexington Books, 2008), pp. 205–230; Charles Wheeler, "Buddhism in the Re-ordering of an Early Modern World: Chinese Missions to Cochinchina in the Seventeenth Century," *Journal of Global History* 3 (2007): 303–324; Charles Wheeler, "Re-thinking the Sea in Vietnamese History: Littoral Society in the Integration of Thuan-Quang, Seventeenth-Eighteenth Centuries," *Journal of Southeast Asian Studies* 37.1 (2006): 123–153; Charles Wheeler, "A Maritime Logic to Vietnamese History? Hoi An's Trading World, c. 1550–1830," in *Seascapes, Littoral Cultures and Trans-Oceanic Exchanges*, conference proceedings (Washington, DC: Library of Congress—The History Cooperative, 2003); Thich Thien-An, *Buddhism and Zen in Vietnam in Relation to the Development of Buddhism in Asia* (Rutland, VT: Charles Tuttle, 1975).

4. See Kenneth Dean and Hue Guan Thye, *Chinese Epigraphy in Singapore: 1819–1911* (Singapore: NUS Press, 2016).

5. The concept of "trust networks" is drawn from the works of Charles Tilly, e.g., *Trust and Rule* (Cambridge: Cambridge University Press, 2005). See also Kenneth Dean, "Ritual Revolutions," *Encounters: An International Journal for the Study of Culture and Society* 4 (2011): 17–42.

6. Wang Gungwu, "Merchants without Empires: The Hokkien Sojourning Communities," in *The Rise of Merchant Empires: Long-Distance Trade in the Early Modern World*, edited by James Tracy (Cambridge, UK: Cambridge University Press, 1990), pp. 400–422.

7. "Before the nineteenth century . . . religious knowledge and authority were differentially distributed, not only among several institutions and categories of clerics, but also among the laypersons who controlled most temples, forming highly complex social fields that did not include an autonomous space designated as 'religion.'" Vincent Goossaert and

David Palmer, *The Religious Question in Modern China* (Chicago: University of Chicago Press, 2011), p. 10.

8. Chinese popular religion (or local communal religion) blends Confucian morality with the worship of multiple deities, many with a Daoist derivation. Buddhist deities, especially Guanyin and the Goddess of Mercy, were often worshiped within these temples as well. For an account of the social organization and roles of the Three Teachings (Confucianism, Daoism, and Buddhism) within Chinese popular religion, see Goossaert and Palmer, *Religious Question*, pp. 22–23.

9. The home altars of the Zhengyi (Orthodox Unity) order of Daoist ritual masters contrast with the monastic orders of the Quanzhen (Complete Perfection) tradition. The latter tradition did not move to Southeast Asia until recent decades. Qing dynasty standard Chinese literary sources do not show a clear understanding of the technical terms relating to specific Daoist or Buddhist orders. See Vincent Goossaert, *The Taoists of Peking, 1800–1949: A Social History of Urban Clerics* (Cambridge: Harvard University Asia Center, 2007). These issues were of importance only within Daoist and Buddhist circles, however.

10. Kenneth Dean, *Taoist Rituals and Popular Cults of Southeast China* (Princeton: Princeton University Press, 1993).

11. Wang, *Merchants without Empires*.

12. This raises the important question of the position of the Chinese lineage within Southeast Asian Chinese society. Given the presence of dialect communities from many different regions of the southern and southeastern coast of China, there is no single common regional culture to provide integrated cultural unity in Singapore or elsewhere in the Straits Settlements. Whereas in the regional cultures of Fujian or Guangdong, powerful localized lineages linked up with prominent Daoist ritual masters and Buddhist monks to constrain new local forms of religious authority (such as locally based spirit mediums), this is not the case in Singapore and much of Southeast Asia, where spirit mediums have much more room to maneuver. In the classic model of the Chinese family lineage, in theory, the most important ritual role is assigned to the eldest son of the first line of descent (*zhangzi*). Such a role is a ritual function passed down within a lineage hierarchy. However, in practice, such rules of ritual priority were often bent or ignored, especially in Southeast Asia, where lineage forms were much more flexible than in South China. See P. Steven Sangren, "Traditional Chinese Corporations: Beyond Kinship," *Journal of Asian Studies* 43.3 (1984): 391–415. Some immigrant lineages mutated into temple communities, and others developed networks by combining into common surname groups and inventing a common ancestor. Rukang Tien, *The Chinese of Sarawak: A Study of Social Structure* (London: London School of Economics and Political Science, 1953).

13. Carl Trocki, *Opium and Empire: Chinese Society in Colonial Singapore, 1800–1910* (Ithaca: Cornell University Press, 1990).

14. The key Western sources on secret societies and Triads have been republished in a five-volume set. See Kingsley Bolton and Christopher Hutton, eds., *Triad Societies: Western Accounts of the History, Sociology and Linguistics of Chinese Secret Societies*, 5 vols. (London and New York: Routledge, 2002). For evolving academic views on the role of the secret societies, see Ching-hwang Yen, *A Social History of the Chinese in Singapore and Malaya, 1800–1911* (Singapore: Oxford University Press, 1986); David Ownby and Mary Somer Heidhues, eds., *"Secret Societies" Reconsidered: Perspectives on the Social History of Modern South China and Southeast Asia* (New York: M. E. Sharpe, 1993); David Ownby, *Brotherhoods and Secret Societies in Early and Ming-Qing China* (Stanford: Stanford University Press, 1996);

Jean DeBernardi, *Rites of Belonging: Memory, Modernity and Identity in a Malaysian Chinese Community* (Stanford: Stanford University Press, 2004). These groups practice elaborate initiations with complex ritual symbolism. While ter Haar demonstrates the continuities between the Triad "demonological" ritual paradigms and broader Chinese religious cosmology, Ownby places "brotherhoods" into the broader context of Chinese social institutions as self-help organizations for marginalized groups of young men. Barend ter Haar, *Ritual and Mythology of the Chinese Triads: Creating an Identity* (Leiden: Brill. 1998).

15. For compilations of Chinese epigraphic materials, see Ts'ung-i Jao, "Chronological Study of Some Chinese Tablet Inscriptions in Malaysia and Singapore" (in Chinese), *Shumu jikan* 5.12 (1970): 3–33; Chingho Chen and Tan Yoek Seong, *Xinjiapo huawen beiming jilu* (A collection of the Chinese inscriptions in Singapore) (Hong Kong: Chinese University Press, 1970); Wolfgang Franke and Ch'en Tieh-fan, eds., *Chinese Epigraphic Materials in Malaysia*, 3 vols. (Kuala Lumpur: University of Malaysia Press, 1980–1985); Wolfgang Franke, with the collaboration of Claudine Salmon and Anthony Siu and with the assistance of Hu Juyun and Teo Lee Kheng, *Chinese Epigraphic Materials in Indonesia*, 3 vols. (Singapore: Nanyang xuehui, 1988–1997); Wolfgang Franke, ed., *Taiguo Huawen mingke huibian* (Chinese epigraphic materials in Thailand) (Taipei: Xinwen fengchu bangongsi, Minguo 87 [1998]); Kenneth Dean and Zheng Zhenman, *Ritual Alliances*, 2 vols. (Leiden: E. J. Brill, 2010); Kenneth Dean and Zheng Zhenman, *Epigraphical Materials on the History of Religion in Fujian: The Quanzhou Region*, 3 vols. (Fuzhou: Fujian Peoples Publishing House, 2003); Kenneth Dean and Zheng Zhenman, *Epigraphical Materials on the History of Religion in Fujian*, vol. 1: *The Xinghua Region* (Fuzhou: Fujian Peoples Publishing House, 1995); Dean and Hue, *Chinese Epigraphy in Singapore*. For records of eminent Buddhist monks, see *Nanyou yunshui qing: Fojiao dade hongfa Xingma jishi 1888–2005* (Record of Chinese Buddhist missionaries to the South [lit., Feelings provoked by clouds and water in the southern journey]: Record of the great deeds of virtue in the spreading of the Dharma to Malaysia and Singapore, 1888–2005) (Penang: Poh Oo Toong Temple, 2010). These and other sources make it possible to trace some of the lines of development of a complex network of heterogeneous Mahāyāna Buddhist traditions, including the rise of twentieth-century Reform Buddhism. The 1923 *Gazetteer of the Penang Crane Mountain Jile Monastery* (10 *juan*), compiled by (Wei) Bao Ci, is one of the most complete early sources available for the establishment of the first Mahāyāna Buddhist monastery in Malaya. Chen Zhakang and Monk Baoci, *Gazetteer of the Penang Crane Mountain Jile Monastery* (Jiangsu: Guangling guji keyinshe, [1923] 1996); see also Baoci, *Heshan Jilesi zhi* (Gazetteer of the Crane Mountain Monastery of Extreme Joy) (Penang: Jilesi, 1923).

16. Tansen Sen, *Buddhism, Diplomacy, and Trade: The Realignment of Sino-Indian Relations, 600–1400* (Honolulu: University of Hawai'i Press, 2003); Tansen Sen, "The Intricacies of Premodern Asian Connections," *Journal of Asian Studies*, 69.4 (2010): 991–999.

17. These are recorded in Dean and Zheng, *Epigraphical Materials.*

18. Claudine Salmon, "Cultural Links between Insulindian Chinese and Fujian as Reflected in Two Late 17th-Century Epigraphs," *Archipel* 73 (2007): 167–194.

19. Salmon, "Réfugiés Ming."

20. Ibid.

21. Franke and Ch'en, *Chinese Epigraphic Materials.*

22. François Froger, "Relation du premier voyage des Français à la Chine en 1698–1700," manuscript preserved at the Bibliothèque d'Ajuda in Lisbon, with fifteen maps and plans, including one of the layout of the Qingyunting temple. See Salmon, "Réfugiés Ming."

23. Franke and Ch'en, *Chinese Epigraphic Materials*, vol. 1., p. 241.

24. More recently, in the mid-twentieth century, a group of Buddhist monks from the Guishansi (Turtle Mountain Monastery) in Huating near Putian, Fujian, established themselves within the Qingyunting. Disciples of the first monks from the Guishansi went on to establish branch temples in Muar, a port town some 100 kilometers to the south. In the 1990s, third-generation monks from this lineage gathered resources from across a wide range of Putian (Henghua) immigrant networks to rebuild the Guishansi in Putian. Additional funds were used to build the Xianglinsi Monastery of the Fragrant Grove across the street from the Qingyunting, and additional leftover funds were used to rebuild the entire home village (Yuantou cun) of the monk in charge of this project, Master Zhenjing. See Dean and Zheng, *Ritual Alliances*.

25. The texts blocks quoted below have been published in Dean and Hue, *Chinese Epigraphy*, chaps. 3–4.

26. Kenneth Dean, *Lord of the Three in One: The Spread of a Cult in Southeast Asia* (Princeton: Princeton University Press, 1998), chap. 4.

27. Wang Tanfa, "Huanchu 'Xiangzi' du zhongsheng: cong wenwu beiming tantuo 18, 19 shiji Maliujia haixia sanchi de Hua seng hudong" (Exchanging "incense salary" for saving souls: A discussion of the activities of Chinese monks in the three Straits Settlements in the eighteenth and nineteenth centuries from stone inscriptions) (online publication, 2004), http://www.xiao-en.org/cultural/magazine.asp?cat=34&loc=zh&id=662 (accessed January 21, 2013).

28. Franke and Chen, *Chinese Epigraphic Materials*, p. 532. J. D. Vaughan visited this temple in 1851 and commented that the monks there were mostly from Fujian, as were those he had seen in Singapore. Their funding mostly consisted of donations, but they could make a dollar by taking part in a funeral. They also received a dollar from every theater company that performed before the temple. Moreover, Vaughan was not impressed by the level of literacy or doctrinal knowledge of the Buddhist monks he encountered. See J. D. Vaughan, *The Manners and Customs of the Chinese of the Straits Settlements* (Oxford: Oxford University Press, 1977). This is the same temple that sent out the Chan master Kun Shan to Malacca some sixty years earlier, and it later sent Master Fachuan to Singapore, where he played an important role in the founding of the Guangmingshan Monastery. Penang is also the site of the tomb of a monk from Fujian dated to the seventh lunar month of 1854: "Chan Master of Xibin, Sramana Shun Ji of Kaiyuan(si)" (Jao, "Chronological Study").

29. *Penang Gazette Strait Chronicle*, February 2, 1888.

30. Franke and Ch'en, *Chinese Epigraphic Materials*, pp. 662–664.

31. Ibid., pp. 652–658.

32. Ibid., pp. 652–658. Miaolian is a controversial figure in the historiography of modern Buddhism. For a detailed account of the transmission of yet another set of the Buddhist *Tripiṭaka* by Master Xuyun from 1907 to 1910, starting from Beijing, then to Xiamen, and then by boat to Thailand, Penang, and Rangoon, and finally by land across Burma to a monastery on Jizu Mountain in Yunnan, see Xuyun, *Empty Cloud: The Autobiography of the Chinese Zen Master Xu Yun*, translated by Charles Luk, revised and edited by Richard Hunn (Shaftesbury: Element Books, 1988), pp. 94–119. Master Xuyun had been ordained by Master Miaolian, and he brought Miaolian's relics back with him to the Jilesi on this trip. For Miaolian's fundraising efforts in Taiwan, see Hsuan-Li Wang, "Gushan: The Formation of a Chan Lineage during the Seventeenth Century and Its Spread to Taiwan" (Ph.D. diss., Columbia University, 2014).

33. Kenneth Dean and Hue Guan Thye, *Chinese Epigraphy of Singapore: 1819–1911*, 2 vols. (Singapore: National University Press, 2017), p. 1127.

34. For an account of the regulation of Hindu and Islamic religious institutions under British colonial administrations, see Vineeta Sinha, *Religion State Encounters in Hindu Domains: From the Straits Settlements to Singapore* (Dordrecht and New York: Springer, 2011). On the establishment of Theravāda religious institutions in Singapore, see Anne M. Blackburn, "Ceylonese Buddhism in Colonial Singapore: New Ritual Spaces and Specialists, 1895–1935," ARI Working Papers Series 184 (National University of Singapore, 2012).

35. Brenda S. A. Yeoh, *Contesting Space in Colonial Singapore: Power Relations in the Urban Built Environment* (Singapore: NUS Press, 2012 [1996]).

36. For an insightful and in-depth analysis of the transformations of the Chinese temple and ritual system in Penang under the impact of forces of modernity, nationalism, and the hardening of ethnic boundaries, see DeBernardi, *Rites of Belonging.*

37. This section is based on Trocki, *Opium and Empire*, 116; Chen Zhakang and Monk Baoci, *Gazetteer of the Penang Crane Mountain Jile Monastery.*

38. On the changing discursive field in China and sinophone regions in the later nineteenth to mid-twentieth century, characterized by attacks on clericism, superstition, popular religion, and finally Buddhism, as well Daoism's role in supposedly preventing the modernization of China, see Goossaert and Palmer, *Religious Question.*

39. Goossaert and Palmer, *Religious Question*, pp. 201–209.

40. On Taixu, see Don A. Pittman, *Toward a Modern Chinese Buddhism: Taixu's Reforms* (Honolulu: Hawai'i University Press, 2001). On the period more broadly, see Holmes Welch, *The Buddhist Revival in China* (Cambridge, MA: Harvard University Press, 1968); Holmes Welch, *Buddhism in China: 1900–1969* (Cambridge, MA: Harvard University Press. 1969).

41. Khun Eng Kuah-Pierce, *Rebuilding the Ancestral Village: Singaporeans in China* (Hong Kong: Hong Kong University Press, 2011 [1993]).

42. See the discussion of this concept in Peter van der Veer, *Conversion to Modernities: The Globalization of Christianity* (New York: Routledge, 1996).

43. Dean and Zheng, *Ritual Alliances.*

44. Dean, "Ritual Revolutions," p. 15.

45. Kenneth Dean, "Parallel Universe: The Chinese Temples of Singapore," in *Handbook of Asian Cities and Religion*, edited by Peter van der Veer (Berkeley: University of California Press, 2015), pp. 257–289.

46. For a more critical perspective, see Julia C. Huang, *Charisma and Compassion: Cheng Yen and the Buddhist Tzu Chi Movement* (Cambridge, MA: Harvard University Press, 2009).

47. Another recent movement that has spread across Southeast Asia from its base in Taiwan is the Yiguandao. Francis Lim has examined the range of Yiguandao activities in Singapore. See Francis Lim, "'We Are Not a Religion': Secularization and the Religious Territory of the Yiguan Dao (Unity Way) in Singapore," in *Proselytizing and the Limits of Religious Pluralism in Asia*, edited by Julian Finucane and Michael Feener (Singapore: Springer, 2014).

48. See Marjorie Topley, *Cantonese Society in Hong Kong and Singapore: Gender, Religion, Medicine, and Money*, edited by Jean DeBernardi (Singapore: NUS Press, 2011).

49. Lee Chee Hiang, "Charity, Ritual and Business Networks of the Teochew Charity Halls in Singapore," *Asian Culture* 33 (2009): 37–55; Tan Chee Beng, "*Shantang*: Charitable Temples in China, Singapore and Malaysia," *Asian Ethnology* 71.1 (2012): 75–107.

6

SUFI "ORDERS" IN SOUTHEAST ASIA

From Private Devotions to Social Network and Corporate Action

MARTIN VAN BRUINESSEN

"Sufi order" is the most common English term for the formations called *ṭarīqa* (lit., "path"; Ar. pl. *ṭuruq*; Ind. *tarekat*), and, when thinking about "orders" in Muslim Southeast Asia, it is the *tarekat* that first come to mind. The term "Sufi order" may be deceptive, however, in suggesting more "order" than is warranted. The word *ṭarīqa* has, at different times and places, referred to a wide variety of manifestations, and this is also true of each individual Sufi *ṭarīqa*. Currently, the major Sufi *tarekat* active in Indonesia, such as the Naqshbandiyya Khālidiyya and the Qādiriyya wa'l-Naqshbandiyya, are corporate bodies with a well-defined core membership and a much larger and more fluid body of irregular followers who may be and at times have been mobilized for political purposes. It is tempting but probably misleading to assume that this has been characteristic of the *ṭarīqa* since their arrival in Southeast Asia. This chapter shows that the available sources tell us little about the social dimension of *ṭarīqa* in Indonesia and that only from the nineteenth century onwards do we see clear examples of corporate action. Further, I argue the *tarekat* were not the only "order"-like formations in Southeast Asia. Communities known as *putihan* (people in white), consisting of more strictly practicing Muslims and distinguishing themselves in dress and habitus from the population at large, for whom they (or some of them) performed roles as religious specialists and moral exemplars, may have been a more influential disciplining force among Muslims in the archipelago in earlier periods than the *tarekat* themselves.

SUFI ORDERS AND THE ISLAMIZATION OF SOUTHEAST ASIA

Settlements of foreign Muslim traders had been present in the port states of Southeast Asia for centuries, but only from the fourteenth century did significant indigenous communities begin to adopt Islam, and it took until the sixteenth century for most of the important island of Java to be Islamized. This period of transition in Southeast Asia coincided with a time when, in the "central lands" of Islam, Sufism had evolved from an elite movement of religious virtuosi to perhaps the dominant mode of religiosity. The more popularized Sufi orders of that period offered ordinary people more or less standardized methods of cultivating devotional piety and access to at least a glimpse of mystical experience. Belief in intercession by charismatic "friends of God" (*walī*) capable of working miracles (*karāmāt*) even after their death and the visiting (*ziyāra*) of such saints' graves were part and parcel of this dominant mode of religiosity, although there were also some *ʿulamāʾ* who, like Ibn Taymiyya (d. 1328), critiqued and opposed such beliefs and practices.

It is not surprising, therefore, that early Southeast Asian Islam was strongly colored by the forms of Sufism prevalent across the broader Muslim world at that time. Conversion myths from various parts of the region explicitly mention foreign miracle-working Sufi-like figures as the prime movers of conversion.[1] Several of the oldest extant Muslim texts from Southeast Asia appear infused with Sufi ethics or engage with Sufi concepts,[2] and the earliest Muslim authors who are known to us by name—Ḥamza Fanṣūrī, Shams al-Dīn Pasai, Nūr al-Dīn Rānīrī, ʿAbd al-Raʾūf Singkel, Yūsuf Makassar—were Sufis and wrote works of poetry and prose expressing Sufi religious ideas. The apparent dominance of Sufism in early (sixteenth- and seventeenth-century) Indonesian Islam does not, however, imply a lenient attitude toward sharīʿa obligations, as has often been assumed. Among the oldest extant manuscripts, in Java as well as Sumatra, we also find texts on Islamic law (*fiqh*), and several of the greatest early Sufi authors also wrote works on jurisprudence. Indeed, in 1638, Banten's rulers sent envoys to Mekka with a triple aim: to find authoritative answers to certain metaphysical questions of Sufi cosmology, to request the title of sultan for the ruler of Banten, and to invite a leading legal scholar to come and settle in Banten as the *qāḍī* (judge).[3]

Several scholars have speculated about a causal connection between the flourishing of Sufi orders in the heartlands of Islam and the spread of Islam to Southeast Asia. Anthony Johns, notably, suggested in several early articles that Sufi missionaries accompanying Muslim traders might have played a key role in the process.[4] Some conversion myths may be compatible with this hypothesis, but there is little other supportive evidence. It is only relatively late, from the seventeenth century onwards, that Sufi orders (*tarekat*) are explicitly mentioned in indigenous Indonesian sources, and they appear then in an environment that is already Muslim. The prolific author of Malay works Nūr al-Dīn Rānīrī fits the model of the foreign Sufi missionary best. He hailed from Gujarat and was of Ḥaḍramī Arab descent, belonged to the Rifāʿiyya Sufi order, and was active in Aceh as the leading Muslim scholar at the court until a conflict forced him to leave in 1644. However, he is especially known for his polemical campaign against the monistic Sufi teachings of earlier indigenous authors Ḥamza and Shams al-Dīn, whose works already reflected a sophisticated familiarity with learned Islamic discourse. Rānīrī's writings as well as those of Ḥamza and Shams al-Dīn addressed audiences with a considerable level of Islamic learning. Recent research has convincingly argued that Ḥamza flourished a half century earlier than had hitherto been assumed and died in Mekka in 1527.[5] This would mean that highly developed forms of Sufi poetry were being written in Malay more than a century before the earliest documented appearance of Sufi "orders" in the region. This chronology appears to make the hypothesis of Sufi orders as a major factor in the early Islamization of the region untenable, though they may well have played a crucial role in later stages.[6]

The most renowned Muslim scholars of seventeenth-century Southeast Asia—Nūr al-Dīn Rānīrī, ʿAbd al-Raʾūf Singkel, and Yūsuf Makassar—explicitly state their adherence to various *ṭarīqa* and also document their *silsila* (chains of transmission). Rānīrī's primary affiliation was with the Rifāʿiyya, into which he was initiated by another Arab of Ḥaḍramī descent resident in Gujarat, ʿUmar Bā Shaybān.[7] Nūr al-Dīn's uncle Muḥammad Jilānī Rānīrī had preceded him as a teacher in Aceh. (Nūr al-Dīn relates how his uncle, after having taught Islamic law in Aceh for a few years, traveled to Arabia to study Sufi metaphysics, because this is what the Acehnese demanded to learn, and returned then as a Sufi teacher.) When on his way from Makassar to Arabia, Yūsuf spent time in Aceh and was initiated into the Qādiriyya by either Nūr al-Dīn or his uncle (the names are conflated in Yūsuf's account).[8] The first part of Yūsuf's Qādiriyya *silsila* mentions the same ʿUmar Bā Shaybān, and for several generations it is practically identical with Rānīrī's Rifāʿiyya chain. Bā Shaybān's predecessors in that line belonged to the al-Aydarūs family, which had been resident in Gujarat for several centuries and appears to have been teaching both the Rifāʿiyya and the Qādiriyya as well as their own family *ṭarīqa*, the Aydarūsiyya. The presence of the Rifāʿiyya and Qādiriyya in Aceh in later years and their impact on popular religious practices are well attested, but it is not clear whether this is because of the influence of the Rānīrīs or from later incursions of the same *ṭarīqa*.

ʿAbd al-Raʾūf spent almost two decades in Arabia studying with the most prominent scholars of the time, and he was especially close with Aḥmad al-Qushāshī (d. 1661) and his successor Ibrāhīm al-Kūrānī (d. 1690), both of whom were widely regarded as the leading scholars of Medina. Both had reputations as *ḥadīth* scholars and taught a broad range of Islamic sciences, including several *ṭarīqa*. Qushāshī appointed ʿAbd al-Raʾūf as his *khalīfa* for the Shaṭṭāriyya, which he taught after his return to Aceh (probably in 1661), along with the metaphysical ideas associated with it. Qushāshī and Kūrānī figure prominently in all later Shattārī *silsila* found in Sumatra and Java. In some, the line passes through ʿAbd al-Raʾūf and one of his deputies; in others, a later

Indonesian student is connected with Kūrānī's son or grandson or a later successor in Medina. (Kūrānī also figures in Naqshbandī *silsila*, showing he initiated other Indonesians into this *ṭarīqa* rather than the Shaṭṭāriyya.)

Like ʿAbd al-Raʾūf, Yūsuf Makassar spent many years in Arabia studying with an equally impressive range of scholars from Yemen to Syria, and he was likewise initiated into several other *ṭarīqa*. Besides the Qādiriyya, he gives his *silsila* for the Naqshbandiyya, Shaṭṭāriyya, Bā ʿAlawiyya, and Khalwatiyya. His Shaṭṭāriyya teacher was Ibrāhīm al-Kūrānī, and his *silsila* therefore is practically identical with ʿAbd al-Raʾūf's. He became known primarily as a teacher of the Khalwatiyya, which he had taken in Syria, but he appears to have combined the specific techniques of this *ṭarīqa* with those of others, notably the Naqshbandiyya. He probably returned to Indonesia sometime in the 1660s; in 1672 we find him settled in Banten and rapidly gaining influence and power at the court. He appears to have taught his *ṭarīqa* only to members of the nobility of his own ethnic group, the Makassarese. Known as Khalwatiyya Yūsuf (to distinguish it from a later incursion of the order, Khalwatiyya Sammān), it is still present in South Sulawesi and retains its somewhat aristocratic character.[9]

There is one Indonesian source that hints at an earlier, sixteenth-century, arrival of Sufi orders, although this source is itself of a later date. The Banten court chronicle *Sajarah Banten Ranté-Ranté* or *Hikayat Hasanuddin*, which must have been compiled sometime between 1662 and 1725, relates how the founder of the Muslim polity of Banten, Maulana Makhdum alias Sunan Gunung Jati, spent decades studying in Mekka and Medina and was initiated there into several *ṭarīqa*: the Kubrawiyya, Shādhiliyya, Shaṭṭāriyya, and Naqshbandiyya. Most interestingly, this text lists the most important names of the *silsila* of two distinct Kubrawiyya branches as those of fellow students of Sunan Gunung Jati. The text lists no later representatives of this *ṭarīqa* than ʿAbd al-Laṭīf Jāmī, who visited Mekka in 1547–1548, and Aḥmad Shinnāwī (d. 1619), who was Qushāshī's predecessor as the leading scholar of Medina. This suggests that some Bantenese must have been aware of the Kubrawiyya and possibly initiated in it in Mekka and Medina at different points between 1547 and 1619.[10]

SUFI ORDERS IN THE CENTRAL LANDS OF ISLAM IN THE SEVENTEENTH CENTURY

In what still remains the major general overview of Sufi orders, J. Spencer Trimingham sketches their historical development as a simple linear progression along three stages of increasing systematization of spiritual techniques, increasing degree of organization, and incorporation of increasing numbers of followers. Trimingham associates the first stage with the *khānaqā*, or Sufi lodge, in which a master lived with his close disciples; the second with the *ṭarīqa* in the restricted sense, as "continuative teaching schools of mysticism" characterized by "new types of collectivistic methods of inducing ecstasy"; and the third stage with the emergence of "corporations" or "orders" proper, for which he uses the term *tā'ifa* (group, collectivity).[11]

Such a highly simplified model of major trends can be helpful as long as we are aware that in reality the developments were neither uniform nor unilinear. However, it may make more sense to look at the three ideal types of Trimingham's stages as different aspects of any single *ṭarīqa*: the physical institutions, the chain of transmission and standardized package of spiritual techniques, and the social organization. Sufi "lodges" (named *khānaqā*, *zāwiya*, or *tekke* in different contexts) remained important institutions until very recently, but there has always been wide variety in their functions.[12] Initially, the *khānaqā* and *zāwiya* were primarily associated with their founders (princes, governors, rich merchants) or the individual shaykhs heading them.[13] In later stages, they became associated with specific Sufi orders or lines of affiliation. It could happen that a lodge belonging to one order was taken over by (or handed over by the state to) another, but independent lodges were virtually nonexistent.

Trimingham's second stage was the crucial one in which chains of affiliation with the founders of distinctive spiritual traditions emerged. Virtually all *ṭarīqa* are named after the founder or a reformer of this tradition, and the masters and disciples of the *ṭarīqa* are connected by a *silsila*, a chain of master-disciple relations, to this founder and thence to the Prophet. Each of these paths consists of distinctive spiritual techniques, which can be carried out privately or collectively: recitation of the divine names (*dhikr*), litanies (*wird*, *rātib*), supplications (*du'ā'*), and various forms of meditation. The *silsila* is central to the concept of a Sufi order; it constitutes the genealogical legitimation of the master and his teachings, and it connects him with the saintly predecessors whose reputations define the spiritual tradition of the particular *ṭarīqa*.

The *silsila* is also a formative structural element of the social organization of the Sufi order. An influential shaykh who appoints several *khalīfa*, who in turn appoint their own to other places, is at the center of a network of local congregations, which is, as it were, a geometrical representation of the *khalīfa*'s combined *silsila*. Originally unconnected groups of devotees may, moreover, become part of the network by submitting themselves to the shaykh or a *khalīfa* and rearranging their *silsila* accordingly.[14]

Two other practices were important to the organizational aspect of the *ṭarīqa*: the *bay'a*, or vow of loyalty and obedience, which marks the formal moment of entry into the order, and the *ijāza*, or license to practice the techniques of the order. In most orders, there were different degrees of membership (Trimingham speaks of "adepts" and "affiliates") and a hierarchy of *ijāza* (to practice, to lead communal rituals, to induct new members into the order).

By the fifteenth century, several of the major Sufi orders—Qādiriyya, Khalwatiyya, Suhrawardiyya, and Rifā'iyya—consisted of networks of local groups of practitioners spread all over the central Islamic lands, from Egypt to India. The Kubrawiyya and Naqshbandiyya, then still Central Asian orders, rapidly expanded to the south and west in the sixteenth century, and the latter especially would henceforth be one of the most influential and most strongly connected orders.[15] The Chishtiyya and Shaṭṭāriyya were originally and long remained Indian orders and the Shādhiliyya, a North African order; they gained a presence in Mekka or Medina when scholars from these regions settled there as teachers. The degree of organization of these orders is difficult to gauge from the sources. Some were no doubt more like corporations than others.[16] Some of the orders were centralized, and the authority of the central lodge or supreme master was recognized by other local communities. This was especially the case where a state supported the central authority of the *ṭarīqa*. The major orders, however, transcended state boundaries and were at best partially centralized. Men like Shinnāwī, Qushāshī, and Kūrānī in Medina, who were among the most famous scholars of their time and who held teaching *ijāza* for a handful of different *ṭarīqa*, would not have been subjected to any one order's higher authority. It is not clear whether they actually headed *zāwiya* and regularly led collective rituals; since this would seem to imply a more unique affiliation with a single *ṭarīqa*, it may not have been the case.

WHAT CHARACTERIZED A *ṬARĪQA* IN SEVENTEENTH-CENTURY INDONESIA?

What the seventeenth-century scholars Rānīrī, ʿAbd al-Raʾūf, and Yūsuf write about their *ṭarīqa* is limited to their *silsila* and a few general prescriptions concerning the performance of *dhikr* and other ritual recitations. Yūsuf prescribes different recitations for beginners and the advanced, the latter progressing from the vocalization of the first sentence of the "profession of faith" ("There is no god but God"/Ar. *lā ilāha illā llāh*) to *Allāh, Allāh*, and finally *Hū Hū* ("Him, Him"), and explains how the syllables of the first-named *dhikr* should be "drawn" through the body, dragging a lengthened *lā* of negation from the navel up to the brain, then the *ilāha* to the right shoulder, with one pause briefly before moving to the left, hammering *illā llāh* into the heart with great force.[17] ʿAbd al-Raʾūf gives similar, but more elaborate, descriptions of *dhikr* in several of his treatises, while adding that oral instruction by the *murshid* (spiritual guide) is essential for correct practice.[18] He also describes the *wird* to be recited after the five daily prayers and the *rātib* litanies recited in meetings on the eve of Friday and Tuesday.[19]

ʿAbd al-Raʾūf's instructions for the *rātib* are the only indication that he adhered to collective Sufi rituals (the instructions are explicit about the alternating of the imam's singing and the congregation's response). There is reason to question, however, whether this collective ritual was specifically associated with the *ṭarīqa* and performed by initiated followers only. ʿAbd al-Raʾūf may have introduced it as a meritorious practice for the community at large. In later years, the *rātib*, in the louder and more ecstatic form associated with the Sammāniyya that reached Aceh a century later, eventually became a form of popular entertainment that lost much of its original Sufi devotional connotation.[20] In the late nineteenth century, as Snouck Hurgronje explicitly notes, these performances were very different from the less conspicuous Shattārī devotions, which were usually recited individually, not collectively.[21] He also notes that there were very few adepts of the Shaṭṭāriyya in Aceh, but there was a lively cult centered on ʿAbd al-Raʾūf's grave.[22]

ʿAbd al-Raʾūf appointed two deputies (*khalīfa*), whose graves also became major pilgrimage centers in the Indonesian archipelago: the Minangkabau scholar Burhān al-Dīn in Ulakan in Pariaman, West Sumatra, and the Javanese ʿAbd al-Muḥyī in Pamijahan, West Java. All three graves attract numerous visitors, but few of them are actually affiliated with the Shaṭṭāriyya.[23] In West Sumatra and in West and Central Java there are, however, a number of small congregations of Shaṭṭāriyya adepts and affiliates that trace their genealogies through one these two *khalīfa* and ʿAbd al-Raʾūf to Qushāshī. The relatively large number of Shaṭṭāriyya manuscripts containing *silsila* mentioning Burhān al-Dīn or ʿAbd al-Muḥyī indicates that both established self-perpetuating lines of Shaṭṭāriyya transmission. Other Shaṭṭārī *silsila* from Java reflect later initiations by descendants or successors of Ibrāhīm Kūrānī in Medina.[24]

In both Sumatra and Java, the name of the Shaṭṭāriyya is especially associated with popularized versions of the theory of divine emanation in "seven grades [of being]" (*martabat tujuh*) that, grafted onto indigenous cosmological ideas, became fundamental to numerous later esoteric movements as well as magical practices. Actual initiation into the *ṭarīqa* Shaṭṭāriyya, however, appears to have remained limited to small numbers of adepts and affiliates. In Java, the court of Cirebon stands out as the major center of Shaṭṭāriyya teaching. There appears to have been a direct connection between ʿAbd al-Muḥyī and the Cirebon court; some oral traditions claim he married a Cirebon princess, and several *silsila* in Cirebon manuscripts mention him as the fountainhead of the Shaṭṭāriyya in Java (but others claim a later introduction directly from Medina). The *ṭarīqa* later—in the late eighteenth or early nineteenth century—also began to be taught by the major *pesantren* (sites of Islamic learning) of the Cirebon region but until then appears to have remained restricted to court circles.[25]

The same appears to have been true of the other *tarekat* (*ṭarīqa*) appearing in Indonesia in the seventeenth century and well into the eighteenth. Nūr al-Dīn Rānīrī and ʿAbd al-Raʾūf were the leading Islamic scholars at the court of Aceh. Yūsuf Makassar came to play the same role at the court of Banten and corresponded with a prince of his native Gowa on matters of politics and mysticism. The most prominent *ṭarīqa* teacher of the mid-eighteenth century, ʿAbd Allāh b. ʿAbd al-Qahhār, who had received *ijāza* to teach the Shaṭṭāriyya and Naqshbandiyya from Ibrāhīm Kūrānī's second or third successor in Medina, was himself a member of Bantenese court circles. Cirebon court elites received Shaṭṭārī *ijāza* from him, but he also appointed three Naqshbandī *khalīfa* to the

Bogor-Cianjur region. The latter three were hajjis but may have been well-to-do commoners rather than court aristocrats.[26]

These men probably restricted their teaching of the *ṭarīqa* to those who had sufficient knowledge of Islamic doctrine and understanding of Sufi metaphysics. Courtiers may have had other reasons to prevent instruction in the *ṭarīqa* from reaching the masses. As the *Hikayat Hasanuddin* and the *Babad Cerbon* strongly suggest, the various *ṭarīqa* were considered as sources of occult knowledge (*ngèlmu*) that served to supernaturally support as well as to legitimize the ruler's control of his realm and to provide protection from all sorts of danger. In martial arts circles, it is still believed that the *ṭarīqa*-derived techniques of cultivating extraordinary strength (*tenaga dalam*) and invulnerability (*kekebalan*) were long jealously guarded as a monopoly of the courts.

All these men actively taught one or more *ṭarīqa* rather restrictively. They appointed only a few *khalīfa*, and did not induce large numbers of novices into their *ṭarīqa*. There are no references in our sources to *zāwiya* or similar physical institutions and no indication the *ṭarīqa* was a sort of association with members acting in concert (but we cannot conclude from the silence of our sources that collective rituals or other communal action did not take place). Judging by their extant writings, all of these men devoted more effort to the elucidation of mystical doctrines and their harmonization with Islamic orthodoxy than to instruction in the practical exercises of the *ṭarīqa*. There was clearly a local demand for authoritative explanations of these doctrines. As mentioned above, one of the tasks of the embassy the court of Banten sent to Mekka in the seventeenth century was to find such explanations.[27] A few decades later, Ibrāhīm Kūrānī wrote his *Itḥāf al-dhakī* in response to debates that had arisen in Indonesia over the interpretation of Burhānpūrī's widely read popularizing work on *waḥdat al-wujūd*.[28] Such writing was directed at an intellectual elite, which must have been mostly based at the courts.

After these Sufi authors' deaths, cults developed around their graves, and it became common to invoke their intercession and supernatural protection. These popular practices had but a tenuous link with the *ṭarīqa* they taught and practiced. It is perhaps significant that in late nineteenth-century Aceh, Nūr al-Dīn Rānīrī was not remembered for the *ṭarīqa* he had taught himself, but his name was invoked in a *rātib* associated with the Sammāniyya order, which represents a later phase in Indonesian Sufism.[29]

ENTER THE MASSES

The first indigenous reference to what looks like mass participation in *ṭarīqa* activity is in a Malay text from Palembang, the *Syair Perang Menteng*, which describes events that took place in 1819, when a Dutch military force commanded by the recently appointed governor Herman Warner Muntinghe ("Menteng") prepared to attack and conquer the sultanate. The *syair* describes how a large group of men dressed in white ("hajjis," according to the text) worked themselves into a trance by reciting *dhikr* ("hammering the words *lā ilāha illā llāh* into their hearts"), raised their frenzy by loudly shouting a *rātib*, and fearlessly attacked the militarily superior Dutch force. Invoking the most powerful of God's names, they fearlessly gave battle and dispersed the attackers.[30] The "hajjis" appeared to believe that the *dhikr* and *rātib* they recited loudly, accompanied by wild physical movements, gave them supernatural strength and virtual invulnerability.

As the Dutch expanded their territorial control of the archipelago in the nineteenth century, they repeatedly came up against similar "fanatical" resistance, in which people prepared themselves for battle by collective Sufi rituals of *dhikr* and *rātib*. In the 1860s, an anti-Dutch uprising in South Borneo reportedly became a more serious threat when people en masse performed *bay'a* with a *ṭarīqa* teacher, who taught them a *rātib* and gave them amulets for invulnerability. For decades, this *beratib beamal* movement, as it was locally known, was the major expression of common people's resistance to Dutch advances.[31]

Although the sources do not mention any specific *ṭarīqa* in this connection, it is almost certain that in both Palembang and South Borneo they were connected to the Sammāniyya, a "new" order known for its loud, rhythmic *rātib* and ecstatic *dhikr*.[32] Its founder, Muḥammad b. ʿAbd al-Karīm al-Sammān (d. 1775), was one of the great scholars teaching in Medina who developed a synthesis of various mystical traditions. His Sammāniyya is based on the Khalwatiyya, with the addition of various elements borrowed from other orders, notably the Qādiriyya and the Naqshbandiyya. It has some features unique to it, such as a loud *dhikr* beginning with divine names but then proceeding to apparently meaningless sounds.[33] After his death, he acquired a reputation for supernatural intervention only second to that of ʿAbd al-Qādir Jīlānī.

The Sammāniyya rapidly spread to many parts of Southeast Asia owing to the mediating role of the learned ʿAbd al-Ṣamad Palimbānī, a protégé of the Palembang court who spent most of his life in Arabia, studying, teaching, and writing Malay books that were to become the most widely read texts on Sufism in Southeast Asia. Numerous Southeast Asians who spent time studying in Arabia during the second half of the eighteenth century were ʿAbd al-Ṣamad's students, studying at least some texts of *fiqh* and other disciplines under his supervision.[34] He was also one of Sammān's *khalīfa* and must similarly have instructed many in the *dhikr* and *rātib* of the Sammāniyya or have pointed them to Sammān himself and later to his chief *khalīfa* in Medina, Ṣiddīq b. ʿUmar Khān. All three of these shaykhs appointed Muslims from Southeast Asia as *khalīfa*. The Palembang court patronized the Sammāniyya, and a year after Sammān's death the sultan of Palembang had a Sammānī *zāwiya* built in Jeddah for the benefit of his subjects who made the pilgrimage.[35] The construction of this *zāwiya* is mentioned in the Malay adaptation of the Arabic hagiography of Sammān that was probably composed in Palembang not long after his death and copied in many parts of the archipelago. Within decades, the Sammāniyya was known not only in Palembang, but also in Batavia and Banten, Aceh, Patani, South Borneo, and South Celebes (where it was known as Khalwatiyya-Sammān).[36]

The Sammāniyya had *bay'a*, but its *dhikr* and *rātib* were also recited by many who had no formal affiliation with the order. Membership was not a strict condition for participation. Some Indonesian teachers of the order appointed their own *khalīfa*, resulting in a certain hierarchy of organization and the possibility of corporate action. The Sammāniyya's role in anti-Dutch resistance made it more conspicuous, but in most places the collective *dhikr* and *rātib* were not connected with any form of political mobilization. The Sammāni *rātib* developed in some regions into a form of popular entertainment or folk performance; elsewhere it was adopted by martial arts groups as an invulnerability technique, in which Shaykh Sammān was called on along with 'Abd al-Qādir Jīlānī and Aḥmad Rifā'i to protect their devotees from the effects of cutting iron, scorching fire, and noxious poison.[37] Compared with the *ṭarīqa* of the seventeenth century, the Sammāniyya appears less aristocratic and more activist. Its networks spread more rapidly and more pervasively among the population at large, and in many places its rituals merged with popular culture.

In the second half of the nineteenth century, the Sammāniyya was gradually eclipsed by the Qādiriyya wa'l-Naqshbandiyya, a similar "new" *ṭarīqa* founded by the Mekka-based Malay scholar Aḥmad Khaṭīb Sambas (d. 1875) and successfully propagated in Java by three *khalīfa* based in Banten, Cirebon, and Madura. Like the Sammāniyya (and several other "new" *tarekat* emerging in the nineteenth century), this *ṭarīqa* combined a number of distinct traditions into a new synthesis.[38] Earlier scholars such as Qushāshī and Kūrānī had also taught a number of different *ṭarīqa*, but these remained distinct and had each its own *silsila*. Some students were taught one *ṭarīqa*, others a different one. Sammān and Aḥmad Khaṭīb, in contrast, taught an integrated package in which the components could no longer be separated. Another common trait is that both founders were legal scholars as well as mystics, and their new orders combined ecstatic practices with strict adherence to the sharī'a. Both orders also eventually found their major following outside court circles—whereas the Sammāniyya had initially been patronized by the Palembang sultanate, the Qādiriyya wa'l-Naqshbandiyya had no royal patrons. Aḥmad Khaṭīb's chief *khalīfa* in Banten and Cirebon may have belonged to families with historical court connections, but they were based in *pesantren* outside the center and spread the order among the rural population of the hinterland through a network of lower-ranking deputies.

As in the case of the Sammāniyya, much of our knowledge about the popular following of the Qādiriyya wa'l-Naqshbandiyya stems from the fact that the order was implicated in a number of uprisings against Dutch rule (or, rather, against the indigenous elite that collaborated with the Dutch). The great rebellion of Banten in 1888 occurred against a background of economic discontent and what the historian Kartodirdjo believed to be a religious revival, in which the Qādiriyya wa'l-Naqshbandiyya provided an institutional framework for communication and solidarity. The man who had been Aḥmad Khaṭīb's *khalīfa* in Banten, Shaykh 'Abd al-Karīm, was at that time residing in Mekka, where he had succeeded his teacher as the titular head of the order. Neither he nor his local deputies had been involved in the preparations for the uprising, but no doubt many of their followers took part in it. The loud *dhikr* and amulets made by *khalīfa* or other men of religion may have strengthened people's daring and belief in their invulnerability. We find the order in the background of several other revolts of the late nineteenth century as well.[39] In other regions, where there were no such uprisings connected to aspects of Sufism, it may well have also been present without being noticed. In the twentieth century, the Qādiriyya wa'l-Naqshbandiyya developed into three well-organized and centralized networks together covering all of Indonesia and Malaysia, with hundreds of thousands of followers and hundreds of local groups regularly meeting for collective *dhikr* and other rituals.[40]

IN SEARCH OF AN EXPLANATION: WHAT HAD CHANGED?

There are some remarkable differences between the manifestations of the Shaṭṭāriyya, Khalwatiyya, and Naqshbandiyya in the seventeenth and eighteenth centuries and those of the Sammāniyya and Qādiriyya wa'l-Naqshbandiyya in the nineteenth. Most notably, there appears to have been a pronounced increase in the degree of organization and popular participation. Here one cannot help being reminded of the second and third stages in Trimingham's three-stage model of the development of Sufi orders. All these orders were "continuative teaching schools of mysticism" that offered "collectivistic methods of inducing ecstasy" (as in Trimingham's second stage), but only the last two were to some extent "corporations" (third stage). A satisfying explanation for these apparent transitions and transformation, however, does not easily present itself. We have little sociological information about the earlier period, and it is conceivable that there was more organization and mass participation than was recorded in our sources for the earlier period. Assuming that the perceived differences cannot entirely be reduced to the uneven quality of our sources, however, explanation should be sought in either changes in the *ṭarīqa* as they functioned in Arabia or changes in Indonesian society that enabled the *ṭarīqa* to play new roles. I have pointed out some differences between the "new" orders and the older ones, but it is hard to see how these could have been the major cause of the former's greater popularity in Indonesia. Moreover, the Sammāniyya and the Qādiriyya wa'l-Naqshbandiyya did not experience a similar expansion elsewhere in the world (with the partial exception of the Sudan in the case of the Sammāniyya).

Therefore, it is necessary to seek relevant developments in Indonesian and Southeast Asian society generally that may have been causal factors. The obvious and most conspicuous change in Indonesian society was the colonial powers' expanding territorial control.[41] Colonial control brought in its wake a number of other changes that may have been more directly relevant for an expanding role of the Sufi orders. The various sultanates, which had been patrons of Sufis and scholars, lost much of their former power over the course of the nineteenth century. The sultanate of Banten was actually abolished in the early nineteenth century. Many others survived but were placed under Dutch suzerainty, and their control of land and people continued to decline. There were substantial changes in the infrastructure of the archipelago. Roads were built, and communications between previously isolated communities improved over the course of the nineteenth century. Scholars returning from study in Mekka established simple *pesantren* not at the court but in rural areas, interacting with a very different population. From the late eighteenth century through the nineteenth, the number of *pesantren* and their students gradually increased.[42] *Tarekat* and their teachers offered the rural population alternative sources of authority, partly replacing that of the court. There had always been persons and places of spiritual authority in the periphery, independent of the courts, but the development of *pesantren* significantly increased their number at a time of increasing colonial pressure on the authority of the archipelagic courts. The *pesantren* itself is, primarily, an institution in which children are taught to read *kitāb*, religious texts. Some of the same teachers also provided services for adults, in the form of communal rituals involving the reading of devotional texts, supplications, *rātib*, and *dhikr*.[43]

The expanding *pesantren* network in Southeast Asia was directly related to another development in Mekka: the emergence of a large community of resident "Jāwa," or Southeast Asians, many of them, but by no means all, scholars.[44] There is reason to believe, as I shall explain below, that the presence of a significant number of Jāwa teaching in Mekka was a relatively recent phenomenon, emerging not long before the nineteenth century. These scholars, even when teaching Arabic texts, would give explanations in Malay or Javanese. Their presence made it possible for men with limited command of Arabic to gain prestigious knowledge in Mekka quickly, within one or two years. Men like ʿAbd al-Raʾūf Singkel and Yūsuf Makassar had had to spend decades in Arabia before returning to Indonesia as teachers. The presence of Jāwa scholars (as well as Jāwa assistants to scholars and Sufis for the benefit of Jāwa students) made shortcuts possible for later generations. The number of Jāwa students increased, and on average they spent much less time in Arabia.

Intriguing indications about the dynamics of this community can be glimpsed from the chains of transmission (*isnād*) of the books they studied. The *isnād* are very much like the *silsila* of a *ṭarīqa* and have the same legitimating function. In the traditional educational setting, face-to-face contact was essential even in teaching written texts; a student who had completed the study of a particular text received an *ijāza* for this text from his teacher, usually with the *isnād*, the chain of preceding teachers, attached. It was not unusual for scholars to write intellectual autobiographies that consisted almost entirely of *isnād* for the major books they had studied and *silsila* of the *ṭarīqa* with which they were affiliated.[45] The man who was considered the leading Indonesian traditionalist scholar in Mekka in the late twentieth century, Shaykh Yāsīn Padang (d. 1990), was a great collector of *isnād* and published several books containing nothing but his *isnād* for all the major works of *fiqh*, *ḥadīth*, *tafsīr*, and other disciplines.[46] A preliminary analysis of this corpus yields some interesting findings relevant to the history of Indonesian *tarekat*. Shaykh Yāsīn had studied with many different teachers, and even books studied under the same teacher usually had quite different *isnād*, indicating that the previous generation of teachers also had sought knowledge with a variety of authorities. However, some of the same names recur in many *isnād*, suggesting that these were the leading authorities of their generation. During the entire nineteenth century, Southeast Asian names predominate among these authorities, with a sprinkling of famous Arabs, giving the impression of a tightly woven community of Jāwa scholars, mostly studying under other Jāwa and only a few of them directly under Arab scholars. In the mid-nineteenth century, for instance, the famous Nawāwī Banten constitutes a distinct node in the Jāwa scholarly networks. He taught many texts to numerous students. However, the key position in the networks belongs to ʿAbd al-Ṣamad Palimbānī of the earlier nineteenth century, who transmitted a wide range of texts, in all Islamic disciplines, from a variety of mostly Arab teachers to numerous Jāwa students. He appears to stand at the beginning of a self-perpetuating scholarly community of Jāwa in Mekka.

Back in the seventeenth century, ʿAbd al-Raʾūf Singkel and Yūsuf Makassar may also have acted as mediators for the other Jāwa studying in Arabia in their time. It is claimed that Yūsuf's future chief *khalīfa* had been with him in Arabia, for instance, and that ʿAbd al-Raʾūf communicated with Ibrāhīm Kūrānī on behalf of other Jāwa. However, the next few generations traveled to Arabia to study under the (non-Jāwa) successors of Kūrānī and his colleagues. The situation in the nineteenth century was quite different. The study of texts had become easier, as there were enough teachers who could give explanations in Malay, and practical training in the techniques of a *ṭarīqa* was also available in languages of Southeast Asia. There was a *zāwiya* of the Sammāniyya in Jeddah, where presumably Malay was spoken, and the learned founder of the Qādiriyya waʾl-Naqshbandiyya was himself a Jāwa resident of Mekka, Aḥmad Khaṭīb Sambas, who personally initiated "thousands of pilgrims and residents, from all parts of the East Indies."[47]

With the increasing numbers of pilgrims from Southeast Asia, many of whom wished to return home with an *ijāza* obtained in Mekka, there was such a demand for initiation in a *ṭarīqa* that by the mid-nineteenth century even some non-Jāwa teachers were beginning to specialize in training Jāwa students. The (Turkish and Daghistani) shaykhs of the Naqshbandiyya Khālidiyya order in Mekka had a staff of Malay, Javanese, and Sundanese assistants and translators in order to be able to serve as many customers as possible. Snouck Hurgronje, following his informants, writes in scathing terms of the Naqshbandī *zāwiya* in Mekka as a commercial enterprise in which quality was sacrificed to quantity. His judgment may, however, have been influenced by the fact that the first prominent Indonesian teacher belonging to this branch of the Naqshbandiyya, Ismāʿīl Minangkabawī, had been a "rather learned but very fanatical" man, that is, a fierce opponent of infidel rule over the Indies.[48] Be that as it may, the Naqshbandiyya Khālidiyya also experienced very rapid development in Indonesia and became perhaps the most highly organized of the orders there.

THE *ṬARĪQA* AS A CORPORATION: NAQSHBANDĪ VILLAGE OF BABUSSALAM, LANGKAT, NORTH SUMATRA

In this history of increasingly structured organization of Indonesian *tarekat*, one pivotal figure was Shaykh Sulaymān al-Zuhdī, who led the Naqshbandī *zāwiya* on the hill of Abū Qubays in Mekka during the last quarter of the nineteenth century. He was not the first Mekkan teacher of this order to gain influence in Southeast Asia, but he was the most prolific. His predecessors, Sulaymān al-Qirīmī and ʿAbdallah al-Arzinjānī, assisted by their Malay-speaking deputy Ismāʿīl Minangkabawī, had presided over the first expansion of the Naqshbandiyya Khālidiyya in Java and Sumatra, but it was especially al-Zuhdī who systematically appointed *khalīfa* to all parts of the archipelago.[49] A brief basic training followed by a twenty- or forty-day retreat (*khalwa* or *sulūk*) in the *zāwiya* under the close supervision by the shaykh or his assistants was apparently sufficient to warrant an *ijāza*. This abbreviated program of initiation proved to be a significant factor in the expansion and popularization of the order in the late nineteenth and early twentieth centuries.

Most of Sulaymān Zuhdī's Indonesian *khalīfa* only held *ijāza* to lead the *dhikr* and induce novices into the order but not to appoint their own deputies or successors. This meant that each new generation needed to request its *ijāza* from Mekka, which thereby remained the de facto center of the Southeast Asian Naqshbandī networks. A few trusted *khalīfa*, however, were also given *ijāza* to appoint their own deputies. One of them was a Malay from Central Sumatra who went on to become the most prolific Indonesian *ṭarīqa* teacher ever: ʿAbdul Wahab Rokan. He had studied under Shaykh Sulaymān al-Zuhdī, who had given him authority to develop the order over all of North and East Sumatra, from Aceh to Palembang, and this he did. He traveled extensively in this region, was welcomed everywhere as a man of special gifts, concluded strategic marriages with women of influential families, and inducted members of the local elites into the *ṭarīqa*. Between his return to Sumatra in 1868–1869 and his death in 1926, he married at least twenty-seven women, begot forty-three children, and appointed around 120 *khalīfa* in this region and across the straits in Malaya.[50] ʿAbdul Wahab gained the favors of many of the local rulers throughout the region, including the sultans of Langkat and Deli, who were the most prominent indigenous authorities on the east coast of Sumatra. Sultan Musa of Langkat, who was attracted to the religious life and who was affluent through his pepper plantations, became his chief benefactor. After a number of shorter visits, during which the shaykh had taught the *dhikr* and led retreats (*sulūk*), the sultan invited him in 1877 to settle permanently at the court in Tanjung Pura and a few years later endowed a large tract of land as *waqf* for the shaykh to develop as a center of the Naqshbandī order.

The shaykh had arrived with wives and children and a following of some 150 people from various parts of Sumatra, most of them Malay and Mandailing Batak. These were the first settlers of the village that was built on the *waqf* land, which the shaykh named Babussalam. The center of the village was (and is) the large *mandarsah* (lit., "school"), a brick mosque with a separate space for *dhikr* above the prayer hall. Separate from the *mandarsah* there were two *rumah suluk* (Ar. *sulūk*), houses for retreat, large wooden barracks partitioned by cloth screens into small cells where men and women from all over the east coast would come for the ten-, twenty-, or forty-day retreats that are a special feature of the Nashbandiyya Khālidiyya. As more followers of the shaykh continued arriving, the village grew to a size that was economically self-sustaining.

Under ʿAbdul Wahab's direction, the residents of Babussalam planted various cash crops on the *waqf* land—fruit trees, coffee, pepper, rubber—and raised animals. All had to contribute time and effort to the common enterprise, and the village economy flourished. The shaykh wrote an elaborate "constitution" (*peraturan-peraturan*) for the village, which stated that only active followers of the Naqshbandiyya could settle there, and access was completely denied to non-Muslims. All residents had to wear distinctive white headgear that made them stand out from the surrounding society. Space and time were patterned by voluntary work and devotions, as the entire village participated in the daily prayers and *dhikr*. At dawn and sunset, the call to prayer from the minaret was preceded by a long *munājāt* (supplication) invoking all the saints of the Naqshbandī *silsila*.[51]

As an economic enterprise, Babussalam was self-reliant and a contributor to the economic growth of the larger region, but it was also embedded in a network of economic transactions that reflected the hierarchical relations between teacher and disciple, and thereby the centralized structure of the Naqshbandiyya Khālidiyya *ṭarīqa*. ʿAbdul Wahab had been poor when he returned to Sumatra, but his reputation as a man of extraordinary qualities and patronage by the rich and powerful soon made him prosperous. He had earlier built a more modest village in Kubu, a district of Riau, from which he had begun his teaching. Disciples and visitors brought gifts in money and kind according to their abilities, which soon amounted to a considerable annual income. As soon as he could afford it, he sent each year large sums of money as gifts to his teachers in Mekka, especially Sulaymān al-Zuhdī.[52] Once he had gained the patronage of the rich Sultan Musa of Langkat, he persuaded the latter to perform the hajj and introduced him to al-Zuhdī. The sultan performed a retreat under al-Zuhdī and received an *ijāza* as *khalīfa*. He had a mosque built close to al-Zuhdī's *zāwiya*, which he donated to the shaykh, and houses for other teachers of ʿAbdul Wahab's network.[53]

The large *rumah suluk* in Babussalam attracted a steady stream of visitors who came to perform a retreat under the shaykh's guidance, bringing such gifts as they could afford. Especially in the quiet period following the harvest, villagers from far away traveled to Babussalam for ten- or twenty-day retreats. *Sulūk* or *khalwa* was a practice known in other orders too, but it had been adopted as one of the central practices for adepts of the Naqshbandiyya Khālidiyya order by the reformer Mawlānā Khālid.[54] It involved a regime of isolation, fasting, and entire days spent in *dhikr* and meditation. Whereas every *khalīfa* was allowed to lead communal *dhikr* sessions, the supervision of *sulūk* demanded a higher level of spiritual attainment recognized by a different type of *ijāza*. The network of ritual halls for these observances (*rumah suluk*) thus contributed to keeping the network of local Naqshbandī branches relatively centralized. There was, moreover, a hierarchy of *rumah suluk* and *khalīfa*, as was to be seen in the case of Sultan Musa's visit to Mekka. For ambitious adepts, spiritual progress corresponded with a rise along this hierarchy, from training by one or more local *khalīfa* to a number of retreats in Babussalam, and culminating in a retreat in the Mekkan *zāwiya* of Abū Qubays.

The centralized structure of the order was further underlined and maintained by the Naqshbandī meditation technique called *rābita* or *rābita biʾl-shaykh*, in which the *murīd* closes the eyes and visualizes the master, in order to establish a spiritual connection with the master and through him to the earlier masters of the *silsila* up to the Prophet. Mawlānā Khālid demanded that all disciples and even later generations perform the *rābita* directly with him (rather than with one of his *khalīfa*). Sulaymān al-Zuhdī, who was a third-generation *khalīfa* of Mawlānā Khālid, required his disciples and *khalīfa* to visualize Mawlānā Khālid. A notebook brought back by an Indonesian pilgrim who had received an initiation in Sulaymān al-Zuhdī's *zāwiya* contained, besides many other notes on Naqshbandī techniques, a brief description of Mawlānā Khālid's facial features as an aid to visualization.[55] All of ʿAbdul Wahab's disciples were instructed to visualize Mawlānā Khālid each time they meditated and thereby maintained a strong connection with the center. It was only after the ties with Mekka had been cut owing to the second conquest by the Wahhabis that Indonesian Naqshbandīs began visualizing Indonesian masters in the *rābita*.[56]

SUFI ORDERS, *PESANTREN TAREKAT*, AND *PUTIHAN* VILLAGE COMMUNITIES

Babussalam is a unique case because of the scale of ʿAbdul Wahab's successes in spreading the *ṭarīqa* and organizing agricultural production, but there were other cases of *ṭarīqa* teachers establishing village communities in the twentieth century. Such examples of institutionalizing *tarekat* highlight the transformations undergone by Sufi orders within the Indonesian archipelago during the nineteenth and twentieth centuries. A century before ʿAbdul Wahab, the Banjarese scholar Arshad al-Banjārī (d. 1812)—who had spent many years studying in Arabia and was probably affiliated with the Sammāniyya—similarly built a new village on a tract of wasteland granted to him by the sultan of Banjarmasin, which went on to become the major center of Islamic education in South Borneo. Arshad al-Banjārī together with his family and followers dug irrigation canals and opened up the land for cultivation, making the village a model for agricultural development in the region.[57] In ʿAbdul Wahab's time, other *khalīfa* of Sulaymān al-Zuhdī opened up their own villages in the forested interior of Java and Sumatra, and many more took up teaching the Naqshbandī devotions in existing mosques and *pesantren*.[58] Many of these *khalīfa* appointed their own deputies and established expanding networks of local groups of Naqshbandī affiliates. Two generations later, we find Naqshbandī shaykhs leading Sufi villages similar to Babussalam in South Aceh and Malaya.[59]

The rapid expansion of the Naqshbandiyya Khālidiyya was in part due to the reforms Mawlānā Khālid (d. 1827) had introduced into the order, the large number of *khalīfa* he appointed, and the missionary zeal he inspired in them. Its expansion in the Ottoman Empire preceded that in Indonesia and was even more rapid and spectacular. Shaykh Khālid had well over sixty *khalīfa*, in different parts of the Ottoman Empire, several of whom appointed numerous *khalīfa* of their own (although none may have been as prolific in this respect as ʿAbdul Wahab Rokan). Whereas in the Ottoman domains the Naqshbandiyya Khālidiyya was the only order that showed such dynamism in the nineteenth century, in Indonesia its expansion and activities had much in common with those of the two other recently arriving orders, the Sammāniyya and the Qādiriyya waʾl-Naqshbandiyya, which also had a number of regional networks with an internal hierarchy in Indonesia and a central authority based in Mekka or Medina.

The expansion of these centralized *ṭarīqa* networks in the nineteenth century was part of a broader development, the proliferation of rural (and occasionally urban) communities that signaled their stronger commitment and stricter adherence to Islam by wearing white headgear or dress, thus distinguishing themselves from their surroundings. There were various types of such communities, known in Java as *putihan* or *pamutihan* ("white ones"). Some consisted of families that guarded holy graves and could boast a long history; others had emerged more recently around a religious teacher or a village head of exemplary piety. Some, but not all, of these communities were exempted from certain taxes and other obligations in exchange for the religious services they provided for local rulers. Many *pesantren* found their origin in such *putihan* communities. The increase in the number of these communities was largely due to the increasing numbers of men returning from studies in Mekka and setting themselves up as teachers.[60]

Not all founders of *pesantren* and/or *putihan* communities had a Mekkan connection, however. One of the oldest extant *pesantren* of West Java is that of Buntet in Cirebon, founded in the late eighteenth century. The teachers, their families, and adherents there came to constitute a large *putihan* community. As oral tradition has it, before becoming a center of textual learning, Buntet was a *pesantren tarekat*, where adults came in search of supernatural power. The *ṭarīqa* that was taught here was the Shaṭṭāriyya, the same as that of the Cirebon court, but Buntet's first Shattārī teacher, known as Ki Buyut Kriyan, had taken his *ijāza* neither from court circles nor directly from Medina but from a Javanese teacher in Central Java, Kyai Ashʿarī of Kaliwungu (who had studied in Mekka but is not locally remembered as a *ṭarīqa* teacher, but rather as a representative of "Mataram Islam"—the Javanese-Islamic synthesis).[61] Unlike Babussalam, Buntet was not embedded in a larger *ṭarīqa* network, but the community appears to have carried out Shattārī devotions collectively. It was a *putihan* community not directly connected with Mekka but inspired by *tarekat* teachings embedded in Javanese culture. In the early twentieth century, however, facing competition from a nearby Qādiriyya wa'l-Naqshbandiyya *pesantren*, Buntet was the first in Indonesia to adopt and actively propagate the Tījāniyya *ṭarīqa*, in which one of the teachers, Kiai Anas, had been initiated during a stay in Arabia. This new development made the *pesantren* the center of a highly dynamic network of adepts and mobilized devotees recognizing a higher authority in Medina.[62]

These *putihan* communities and the *pesantren* that gained prominence in the nineteenth century constituted orderlike social formations that might be, but in many cases were not, affiliated with a regular *tarīqa* and connected to an external source of religious authority. Little detailed information on the *putihan* communities is available. Colonial surveys of *perdikan* (tax-exempted) villages were compiled relatively late and moreover probably missed newly founded *putihan* villages that did not have old tax privileges. The Javanese *santri lelana* literature (*Serat Centhini*, *Serat Jatiswara*, and so on) makes frequent mention of such communities but provides little concrete information, and local histories may give valuable information but are notoriously vague about chronology. There are, nonetheless, some indications that over the course of the "long" nineteenth century (beginning in the late eighteenth and continuing into the twentieth) the number of *putihan* communities significantly increased, and there was a significant shift of orientation. Although previously most of these communities had been connected with local centers of spiritual power such as holy graves, they increasingly came to be connected, via *silsila* and/or *isnād*, with authorities in Mekka or Medina.

Both the *ṭarīqa* and the *pesantren* were associated with *putihan* communities, but there was no simple or uniform relationship between these different social categories in nineteenth-century Java. Most *putihan* communities mentioned in Javanese texts performed various types of communal and individual devotions besides the obligatory prayers but may not have adhered to any specific *ṭarīqa*. Conversely, not all *ṭarīqa* followers belonged to *putihan* communities, even if most teachers did. The Shaṭṭāriyya was present in this period as a diffuse influence. Popular beliefs and magical practices were influenced by cosmological and metaphysical ideas once associated with this *ṭarīqa*. Most Shaṭṭārī teachers were a few generations removed from the last representatives of the learned line of teachers in Medina, and there appeared to be little uniformity in what they taught. The Qādiriyya wa'l-Naqshbandiyya and the Naqshbandiyya Khālidiyya (and later the Tījāniyya) were more centralized orders. Communities of followers were connected with one another and especially with the central authority in Mekka. Both orders also, at least in theory, demanded strict adherence to the sharīʿa and therefore some degree of textual knowledge.

The simplest *pesantren* only taught the Arabic script and memorization of some passages from the Qur'ān, although some also taught basic *fiqh* and doctrine, using simple textbooks. As the nineteenth century progressed, more *pesantren* emerged that also taught more sophisticated *fiqh* books and other *kitāb* in Arabic. Their founders were typically men who had spent years in Mekka in the teaching circles of established scholars, in most cases resident Jāwa *ʿulamā'* reading these *kitāb* under supervision and finally receiving *ijāza* to teach them. These men's relationship with their Mekkan teachers differed little from that of an Indonesian *khalīfa* of a *ṭarīqa* with his shaykh. In fact, although a scholar did not expect the same level of submission and obedience that the *ṭarīqa* shaykh demanded, the bond with him could even be stronger because of the protracted and intensive interaction that went with textual studies.[63] The *isnād* constituted a lasting link of authority and legitimation, like the *silsila*, the main difference being that most graduates from Mekka had multiple *isnād*, connecting them with more than one Mekkan teacher. Having studied under the same teachers in Mekka created bonds among the Javanese Islamic teachers (*kyai*) similar to those between adepts of the same *ṭarīqa*. Jointly, the community of Jāwa scholars resident in Mekka and their students who established (or taught at) *pesantren* in Southeast Asia constituted a sort of brotherhood, membership in which was not dependent on a formal *bayʿa* but on the *ijāza* proving the successful mastery of a body of texts.

By the mid-nineteenth century, this brotherhood of *kitāb* scholars and their students probably made up only a minor, but growing, proportion of all those classified by the Dutch as *geestelijken* ("clerics" who made their living by religion).[64] Many of the latter simply provided religious services such as leading *salāt* prayers or other devotions, taking care of the dead, guarding holy graves and overseeing grave visitation, reciting supplications (*du'ā'*) on behalf of clients, divination, and healing. Many also taught *dhikr*, *wird*, and various other formulae to be recited for magical purposes. Indeed the word *tarekat* was widely used to refer to magical practices even when there was no formal initiation into a specific *ṭarīqa*. The most significant shift taking place in the nineteenth century is that the two types of Mekka-based "orders," the new Sufi *tarekat* and the brotherhood of *kitāb* scholars, gradually became dominant in influence, if not in numbers, within the category of religious specialists.

To summarize, a *ṭarīqa* can be defined by three aspects. Each has, first, a distinct spiritual genealogy, or *silsila*, and, second, a repertoire of techniques and devotions that constitute its distinct "way." In addition, they can be associated with a specific pattern of social organization in which particular institutions may be diversely configured. Regarding the third aspect, a single *ṭarīqa* may show great variety over time and space.

The spiritual techniques of various established Sufi *ṭarīqa* have been taught in Southeast Asia since the seventeenth century and quite possibly since the second half of the sixteenth. Sufi thought and practice initially circulated primarily among the aristocratic elite of the indigenous sultanates. A lively interest in Sufi metaphysics and debates about the interpretation of the doctrine of *waḥdat al-wujūd* appears to have preceded the adoption of *ṭarīqa* as standardized ways of attaining the mystical experience. Actual adherence to a *ṭarīqa* long remained restricted, but at least in some regions certain practices of recitation (*dhikr*, *wird*, *rātib*) became part of popular devotion. The social organization of the *ṭarīqa* remains the most elusive aspect. The extant sources suggest that *ṭarīqa* teachers had but few *khalīfa* and that the numbers actually inducted into a *ṭarīqa* remained restricted.

Only from the nineteenth century onwards do we find reports of large numbers of people publicly taking part in collective *ṭarīqa* rituals. Besides greater concern on the part of Dutch colonial officials who cared to report on these activities, this may reflect two important changes in the relations between Southeast Asian Muslims and the symbolic center of the Muslim world—the holy cities of Mekka and Medina. Larger numbers of Southeast Asians were spending many years studying in the holy cities, which had become easier because the number of "Jāwa" scholars resident there who could serve as teachers for an increasing number of students from Southeast Asia had reached a critical mass. Moreover, new *ṭarīqa* had emerged that actively recruited among the Jāwa pilgrims and students, using the Malay language as a medium: the Sammāniyya in the eighteenth, and the Qādiriyya wa'l-Naqshbandiyya and Naqshbandiyya Khālidiyya in the nineteenth century. The *khalīfa* of these orders established rapidly expanding networks of local adepts and affiliates, turning the *ṭarīqa* into mass movements no longer associated with elite court culture.

There was during this same period a similar, albeit slower, expansion of schools where Islamic texts (*kitāb*) were taught. Mekka-trained scholars, united by common loyalty to the teachers to whom they owed their *ijāza*, constituted a sort of brotherhood that stood out among the class of professional religious and by the early twentieth century had become dominant among them. Scholars and *pesantren* teaching *kitāb* thus constituted parallel and potentially overlapping networks that were structurally similar to those of the new Sufi orders—as seen in the documentation of religious lineages in the parallel forms of *silsila* and *isnād*. For both, Mekka was the exemplary center where ultimate authority was located and where each new generation sought spiritual and scholarly perfection. Both also had secondary centers in different parts of Southeast Asia from which further expansion took place. The Saudi conquest of Mekka in 1924 was to result in changes in these networks again, notably a renewed indigenization of the *ṭarīqa* networks, but those developments are beyond the scope of this chapter.

NOTES

1. Russell Jones, "Ten Conversion Myths from Indonesia," in *Conversion to Islam*, edited by Nehemia Levtzion (New York: Holmes and Meier, 1979), pp. 129–158. One should not forget, however, that these myths are of much later date than the alleged conversion event.

2. G. W. J. Drewes, *Een Javaanse primbon uit de zestiende eeuw* (Leiden: Brill, 1954); G. W. J. Drewes, *The Admonitions of Seh Bari* (The Hague: Nijhoff, 1969).

3. The first mission was sent in 1638. Several later rulers sent similar missions upon accession. The metaphysical questions seem to refer to works written by Ḥamza and another, unknown author. Titik Pudjiastuti, "Sadjarah Banten: suntingan teks dan terjemahan disertai tinjauan aksara dan amanat" (Ph.D. diss., Universitas Indonesia, Depok, 2000), canto 37.7, 42.26; see also Hoesein Djajadiningrat, *Critische beschouwing van de Sadjarah Banten: Bijdrage ter enschetsing van de Javaansche geschiedschrijving* (Haarlem: Joh. Enschedé en Zonen, 1913), pp. 50, 174–175.

4. Anthony H. Johns, "The Role of Sufism in the Spread of Islam to Malaya and Indonesia," *Journal of the Pakistan Historical Society* 9 (1961): 143–160; Anthony H. Johns, "Sufism as a Category in Indonesian Literature and History," *Journal of Southeast Asian History* 2 (1961): 10–23.

5. Claude Guillot and Ludvik Kalus, "La stèle funéraire de Hamzah Fansuri," *Archipel* 60 (2000): 3–24; Claude Guillot and Ludvik Kalus, "En réponse à Vladimir I. Braginsky," *Archipel* 62 (2001): 34–38.

6. It has been claimed, on the basis of one of Ḥamza's quatrains, in which he declares that he received trusteeship of the exalted knowledge (*beroleh khilafat ilmu yang ʿali*) from ʿAbd al-Qādir al-Jīlānī, that he belonged to the Qādiriyya Sufi order and was in fact a *khalīfa*, a deputy representing the grand shaykh himself. Syed Muhammad Naguib Al-Attas, *The Mysticism of Hamzah Fansuri* (Kuala Lumpur: University of Malaya Press, 1970), pp. 10–11. This is one possible reading, and there are a few more references to ʿAbd al-Qādir in Ḥamza's works that indicate that he felt a special veneration for the Baghdadi saint. However, although there are frequent later references to Ḥamza's poetry and Sufi metaphysics, his name is never

mentioned in later chains of transmission of the Qādiriyya in Indonesia. For this and other reasons, I believe his teaching in Aceh did not include formal instruction in the *ṭarīqa*. For more on this, see the arguments presented in Martin van Bruinessen, "Shaykh ʿAbd al-Qâdir al-Jîlânî and the Qâdiriyya in Indonesia," *Journal of the History of Sufism* 1–2 (2000): 361–395, esp. pp. 362–364.

7. See Rānīrī's *silsila* as given in his *Jawāhir al-ʿulūm fi kafsh al-maʿlūm*, in Syed Naguib Al-Attas, *A Commentary on the Hujjat al-siddīq of Nūr al-Dīn al-Rānīrī* (Kuala Lumpur: Ministry of Culture Malaysia, 1986), pp. 14–15. On Bā Shaybān and Rānīrī's other teachers, see Azyumardi Azra, *The Origins of Islamic Reform in Southeast Asia: Networks of Malay-Indonesian and Middle Eastern ʿUlamāʾ in the Seventeenth and Eighteenth Centuries* (Leiden: KITLV Press, 2004), pp. 54–62.

8. Yūsuf gives the *silsila* of various *ṭarīqa* in his as yet unpublished *Safīnat al-najāh*. These *silsila* are reproduced in Abu Hamid, *Syekh Yusuf Makassar: Seorang ulama, sufi dan pejuang* (Jakarta: Yayasan Obor Indonesia, 1994), pp. 356–363. On Muḥammad Jīlānī Rānīrī and his Sufi teaching, see Azra, *Origins of Islamic Reform*, pp. 55–56.

9. Martin van Bruinessen, "The Tariqa Khalwatiyya in South Celebes," in *Excursies in Celebes*, edited by Harry A. Poeze and Pim Schoorl (Leiden: KITLV, 1991), pp. 251–269; Martin van Bruinessen, "Shariʿa Court, Tarekat and Pesantren: Religious Institutions in the Banten Sultanate," *Archipel* 50 (1995): 165–199, esp. pp. 180–182.

10. Martin van Bruinessen, "Najmuddin al-Kubra, Jumadil Kubra and Jamaluddin al-Akbar: Traces of Kubrawiyya Influence in Early Indonesian Islam," *Bijdragen tot de Taal-, Land- en Volkenkunde* 150 (1994): 305–329, esp. pp. 307–313, referring to the texts edited by Edel. See also J. Edel, *Hikajat Hasanoeddin* (Meppel: Brink, 1938). The Cirebon court chronicle *Babad Cerbon* also mentions Sunan Gunung Jati's studying the Shādhiliyya, Kubrawiyya, and Khalwatiyya in Mekka. See J. L. A. Brandes and D. A. Rinkes, eds., *Babad Tjerbon* (Batavia: Albrecht & Co.; The Hague: M. Nijhoff, 1911), pp. 66–67.

11. J. Spencer Trimingham, *The Sufi Orders in Islam* (Oxford: Clarendon Press, 1971), p. 103, summarizing the preceding historical discussion. Later scholars have been critical of some of Trimingham's analyses and claims, and there exists now a vast body of detailed and more sophisticated scholarship, but this remains the major synthesizing study. Two more recent major overviews are Alexandre Popovic and Gilles Veinstein, eds., *Les voies d'Allah: Les ordres mystiques dans le monde musulman des origines à aujourd'hui* (Paris: Fayard, 1996); Seyyed Hossein Nasr, ed., *Islamic Spirituality: Manifestations* (New York: Crossroad, 1991), both of which are rich in information about individual orders but do not attempt an overall synthesis.

12. Various aspects of the Sufi lodge are discussed in R. Lifchez, ed., *The Dervish Lodge: Architecture, Art, and Sufism in Ottoman Turkey* (Berkeley: University of California Press, 1992). For a description of different types of lodges in a single Sufi order in contemporary Egypt, the Khalwatiyya, see Rachida Chih, "What Is a Sufi Order? Revisiting the Concept through a Case Study of the Khalwatiyya in Contemporary Egypt," in *Sufism and the "Modern" in Islam*, edited by Martin van Bruinessen and Julia D. Howell (London: I. B. Tauris, 2007), pp. 21–38.

13. In his study of Sufism in Egypt and Syria in the Mamluk period, Eric Geoffroy suggests that the *khānaqā* was an institution defined by its powerful or rich founder, and the *zāwiya* was known for the Sufi master who led it. Eric Geoffroy, *Le soufisme en Égypte et en Syrie sous les derniers Mamelouks et les premiers Ottomans: Orientations spirituelles et enjeux culturels*

(Damascus: Institut français de Damas, 1995), pp. 116–175. Geoffroy's distinction may be valid for that period, but I do not believe it makes sense for other times and places.

14. This process is analyzed for the case of the Naqshbandiyya at a period of rapid expansion in nineteenth-century Kurdistan in Martin van Bruinessen, *Agha, Shaikh and State: The Social and Political Structures of Kurdistan* (London: Zed Books, 1992), pp. 224–228.

15. For Syria and Egypt, see Geoffroy, *Soufisme en Égypte et en Syrie*, which provides a detailed overview of the varieties of Sufi practice, institutions, and forms of association in the fourteenth and fifteenth centuries. For Asia Minor, important insights on the nature of Sufi and dervish groups of the same period are presented by Ahmet T. Karamustafa, *God's Unruly Friends: Dervish Groups in the Islamic Later Middle Period, 1200–1550* (Salt Lake City: University of Utah Press, 1994); and Mustafa Kara, *Türk tasavvuf tarihi araştırmaları: Tarikatlar—tekkeler—şeyhler* (Istanbul: Dergah, 2005). For South Asia, see Saiyid Athar Abbas Rizvi, *A History of Sufism in India*, vol. 1: *Early Sufism and Its History in India to 1600 AD* (New Delhi: Munshiram Manoharlal, 1978). On the expansion of the Naqshbandiyya from Central Asia to the west and south, Hamid Algar, "The Naqshbandi Order: A Preliminary Survey of Its History and Significance," *Studia Islamica* 44 (1976): 123–152; Dina Le Gall, *A Culture of Sufism: Naqshbandîs in the Ottoman World, 1540–1700* (Albany, NY: State University of New York Press, 2005); Saiyid Athar Abbas Rizvi, *A History of Sufism in India*, vol. 2: *From Sixteenth Century to Modern Century* (New Delhi: Munshiram Manoharlal, 1983).

16. Trimingham rightly observes that the term *tā'ifa* was also used for two other types of associations with a religious character that should be distinguished from the Sufi order although having similar patterns of organization: the trade guild and the *futuwwa* ("youngmanliness," or chivalry) association. The Kāzarūniyya, of which we know thanks to the early fourteenth-century Moroccan traveler Ibn Baṭṭūṭa, was yet another similar formation. Rizvi, *History of Sufism in India*, vol. 1, pp. 409–411, discusses it as a special type of Sufi order. Trimingham, *Sufi Orders in Islam*, p. 21, calls it a "Sufi insurance company." It consisted of a network of lodges dedicated to the eleventh-century Sufi Abū Isḥāq Kāzarūnī, patron saint and protector of sailors and merchants along the trade routes between the Persian Gulf and South China. Ibn Baṭṭūṭa visited the saint's shrine in Kāzarūn (Southern Iran) and the *khānaqā* in Cambay and Calicut in India, as well as the one outside the major South Chinese port of Zaytun, and notes that merchants vowed sums of money to the saint in exchange for protection. These sums were collected by the guardians of the various *khānaqā* (whose names were appended with the *nisba* Kāzarūnī, suggesting they were either biological descendants of Abū Ishaq or licensed representatives, *khalīfa*) on behalf of the central shrine and redistributed according to an intricate system that Ibn Baṭṭūṭa describes. There is, however, no mention of Sufi rituals or local followers of these *khalīfa*. They appear as agents of a financial institution rather than spiritual teachers. (See the summary of the functioning of this commercialization of Abū Ishaq's *baraka* in Trimingham, *Sufi Orders in Islam*, p. 236.)

17. Bruinessen, "Tarīqa Khalwatiyya in South Celebes," pp. 255–256, after Yūsuf's *Habl al-warīd li-sa'ādat al-murīd*. Cf. Abu Hamid, *Syekh Yusuf Makassar*, pp. 206–210.

18. D. A. Rinkes, "Abdoerraoef van Singkel: Bijdrage tot de kennis van de mystiek op Sumatra en Java" (dissertation, Leiden, 1909), pp. 64–75 (after 'Abd al-Ra'ūf's *'Umdat al-muhtājīn*); Oman Fathurahman, *Tanbih al-masyi: menyoal wahdatul wujud: Kasus 'Abdurrauf Singkel di Aceh abad 17* (Bandung: Mizan, 1999), pp. 66–74 (after *Tanbīh al-māshī*).

19. Rinkes, "Abdoerraoef van Singkel," pp. 74–75.

20. *Rātib* performances in late nineteenth-century Aceh are described in great detail in Christiaan Snouck Hurgronje, *De Atjèhers*, vol. 2 (Batavia: Landsdrukkerij; Leiden: Brill, 1893), pp. 220–265.

21. "The mysticism of the Shaṭṭāriyya reveals itself only in the observation of certain unspectacular, simple private recitations." Snouck Hurgronje, *De Atjèhers*, vol. 2, p. 221.

22. Ibid., pp. 16–20.

23. Ph. S. van Ronkel, "Het heiligdom te Oelakan," *Tijdschrift voor Indische Taal-, Land- en Volkenkunde* 56 (1914): 281–316; Azra, *Origins of Islamic Reform*, pp. 84–86; Oman Fathurahman, *Tarekat Syattariyah di Minangkabau, teks dan konteks* (Jakarta: Prenada Media Group/EFEO/PPIM/KITLV Jakarta, 2008), pp. 34–40; Rinkes, "Abdoerraoef van Singkel"; Tommy Christomy, "Shattâriyya Tradition in West Java: The Case of Pamijahan," *Studia Islamika* 8.2 (2001): 55–82. Azra and Fathurahman mention a few other alleged students of ʿAbd al-Raʾūf, but there is no evidence that these also came to represent the Shaṭṭāriyya.

24. Rinkes, "Abdoerraoef van Singkel," pp. 94–130; Aliefya M. Santrie, "Martabat (Alam) Tujuh: Suatu naskah mistik Islam dari desa Karang, Pamijahan," in *Warisan intelektual Islam Indonesia: Telaah atas karya-karya klasik*, edited by Ahmad Rifaʿi Hasan (Bandung: Mizan, 1987), pp. 105–129; Tommy Christomy, "Signs of the Wali: Narratives at the Sacred Sites in Pamijahan, West Java" (Ph.D. diss., Australian National University, 2003 [published as an e-book by ANU Press in 2008]), pp. 25–37; Fathurahman, *Tarekat Syattariyah di Minangkabau*, pp. 72–100.

25. Sharon Siddique, "Relics of the Past. A Sociological Study of the Sultanates of Cirebon, West Java" (Ph.D. diss., Bielefeld University, 1977), pp. 122–124; A. G. Muhaimin, "The Islamic Traditions of Cirebon: Ibadat and Adat among Javanese Muslims" (Ph.D. diss., Australian National University, 1995 [published as an e-book by ANU Press in 2006]), pp. 247–251. My interviews with *pesantren*- and court-based Shaṭṭārī teachers in Cirebon suggest that there was a considerable difference in practice between these two milieus.

26. Bruinessen, "Shariʿa Court, Tarekat and Pesantren," p. 182.

27. See note 3 above.

28. Oman Fathurahman, "*Itḥāf al-dhakī* by Ibrāhīm al-Kūrānī: A Commentary of *waḥdat al-wujūd* for Jawi Audiences," *Archipel* 81 (2011): 177–198; Anthony H. Johns, "Friends in Grace: Ibrāhīm al-Kūrānī and ʿAbd al- Raʾūf al-Singkeli," in *Spectrum: Essays Presented to Sutan Takdir Alisjahbana*, edited by S. Udin (Jakarta: Dian Rakyat, 1978), pp. 469–485. On Fadlullah Burhānpūri's *Al-Tuhfa al-mursala ila rūh al-nabī* and its Javanese and Malay adaptations, see Anthony H. Johns, *The Gift Addressed to the Spirit of the Prophet* (Canberra: Australian National University, 1965).

29. Snouck Hurgronje, *De Atjèhers*, vol. 2, p. 262.

30. The entire text of the *syair* is published in M. O. Woelders, *Het sultanaat Palembang 1811–1825* ('s-Gravenhage: Nijhoff, 1975), pp. 194–222 (Dutch translation at pp. 385–413).

31. P. J. Veth, "Het beratip beamal in Bandjermasin," *Tijdschrift voor Nederlandsch-Indië* 3.2 (1869–1870): 197–202; Helius Sjamsuddin, "Islam and Resistance in South and Central Kalimantan in the Nineteenth and Early Twentieth centuries," in *Islam in the Indonesian Social Context*, edited by M. C. Ricklefs (Clayton: Monash University Centre of Southeast Asian Studies, 1991), pp. 7–17. The *rātib* reported there was not the standard Sammānī *rātib*, but diverging versions have been reported from elsewhere too. The Sammāniyya is known to have been introduced into this region by Nafīs al-Banjārī, the author of the locally popular Sufi treatise *al-Durr al-nafīs*, and possibly by other returnees from Arabia as well.

32. In calling these synthetic orders "new," I refer to their recent emergence as distinct formations and am not alluding to "Neo-Sufism," a term that has been used to refer to too many different things and has so far caused more confusion than clarity (see the discussion in Martin van Bruinessen, "Sufism, 'Popular' Islam, and the Encounter with Modernity," in *Islam and Modernity: Key Issues and Debates*, edited by Muhammad Khalid Masud, Armando Salvatore, and Martin van Bruinessen [Edinburgh: Edinburgh University Press, 2009], pp. 125–157).

33. For an example of such a *dhikr*, see Syed Naguib Al-Attas, *Some Aspects of Sufism as Understood and Practised among the Malays* (Singapore: Malaysian Sociological Research Institute, 1963), p. 86.

34. On ʿAbd al-Ṣamad and his networks, see Azra, *Origins of Islamic Reform*, pp. 111–117; Martin van Bruinessen, "Studi tasawuf pada akhir abad kedelapan belas: ʿAbd al-Ṣamad al-Falimbani, Nafis al-Banjari, dan tarekat Sammaniyah," in Bruinessen, *Kitab kuning, pesantren dan tarekat: Tradisi-tradisi Islam di Indonesia* (Bandung: Mizan, 1995), pp. 55–87.

35. Aḥmad Purwadaksi, "Rātib Sammān dan Hikayat Syekh Muḥammad Sammān. Suntingan naskah dan kajian isi teks" (Ph.D. diss., Universitas Indonesia, Jakarta, 1992), pp. 335–336.

36. Bruinessen, "Tariqa Khalwatiyya in South Celebes," pp. 258–262; Bruinessen, "Studi tasawuf pada akhir abad kedelapan belas"; G. W. J. Drewes, "A Note on Muḥammad al-Sammān, His Writings, and 19th Century Sammāniyya Practices, Chiefly in Batavia, according to Written Data," *Archipel* 43 (1992): 73–87. Other well-known *ʿulamāʾ* affiliated with the Sammāniyya include M. Arshad al-Banjārī, Nafīs al-Banjārī, and Daūd al-Faṭānī (Patani). Besides Southeast Asia, the order spread only to Sudan and is virtually unknown elsewhere. On the Sammāniyya's development in Sudan, see Ali Salih Karrar, *The Sufi Brotherhoods in the Sudan* (London: C. Hurst and Company, 1992), pp. 43–49.

37. On the *rātib*: Purwadaksi, "Rātib Sammān dan Hikayat Syekh Muḥammad Sammān"; Al-Attas, *Some Aspects of Sufism*, pp. 68–88; Snouck Hurgronje, *De Atjèhers*, vol. 2, pp. 220–265; Veth, "Het beratip beamal in Bandjermasin."

38. In this case these were, as the earliest handbook of the order, *Fath al-ʿārifīn*, has it, the Naqshbandiyya, Qādiriyya, Ṭarīqat al-Anfās, Ṭarīqat al-Junayd, and Ṭarīqat al-Muwāfaqa. The same text makes the intriguing observation that this combination of *ṭarīqa* is identical (?) with the Sammāniya. A similar synthetic order with which Aḥmad Khaṭīb may have been well acquainted was the Khatmiyya, which became important in Sudan (see Karrar, *Sufi Brotherhoods in the Sudan*, pp. 64–66, 73–102).

39. Sartono Kartodirdjo, *The Peasants' Revolt of Banten in 1888* ('s-Gravenhage: Nijhoff, 1966); Sartono Kartodirdjo, *Protest Movements in Rural Java* (Kuala Lumpur: Oxford University Press, 1973); Christiaan Snouck Hurgronje, "Mystiek, magie, tarékats," in *Ambtelijke adviezen van C. Snouck Hurgronje, 1889–1936*, vol. 2, edited by E. Gobée and C. Adriaanse ('s-Gravenhage: Nijhoff, 1959), pp. 1182–1221; Bruinessen, "Shaykh ʿAbd al-Qâdir," pp. 378–381.

40. Sri Mulyati, *Peran edukasi tarekat Qadiriyyah Naqsyabandiyyah dengan referensi utama Suryalaya* (Jakarta: Kencana, 2010); Bruinessen. "Shaykh ʿAbd al-Qâdir," pp. 382–386.

41. This expansion had begun in a much earlier period. The reason Yūsuf of Makassar did not settle in his native Gowa on his return from Arabia but opted to live in Banten was that Gowa had been conquered by its Bugis neighbor Bone and the Netherlands East Indies Company. When the company later intervened in Banten too, replacing Sultan Ageng Tirtayasa with his more pliant son, Sultan Haji, Yūsuf firmly sided with the former and took to the mountains. Company troops captured him, and he was sent into exile in Ceylon.

42. Martin van Bruinessen, "Pesantren and Kitab Kuning: Continuity and Change in a Tradition of Religious Learning," in *Texts from the Islands: Oral and Written Traditions of Indonesia and the Malay World*, edited by Wolfgang Marschall (Berne: University of Berne Institute of Ethnology, 1994), pp. 121–146; M. C. Ricklefs, *Polarising Javanese Society: Islamic and Other Visions (c. 1830–1930)* (Singapore: NUS Press, 2007), pp. 49–74.

43. Several of the *pesantren* I have visited retain memories of previously having been *pesantren tarekat*, which meant they did not teach bookish knowledge but spiritual techniques, often for magical purposes.

44. This Jāwa community was famously described in the second volume of Snouck Hurgronje's *Mekka* (The Hague: Martinus Nijhoff, 1889).

45. Two famous examples are Aḥmad Qushāshī's *Al-Simṭ al-majīd* and Ibrāhīm Kūrānī's *Al-Umam li-iqāẓ al-himam*, both of which were printed in Hyderabad as recently as 1909–1910.

46. Shaykh Yāsīn was the director of the Indonesian college Dār al-ʿUlūm al-Islāmiyya in Mekka. He wrote at least ten such books, of which the most important are M. Yāsīn b. M. ʿĪsā al-Fadānī, *Al-ʿiqd al-farīd min jawāhir al-asānīd* (Surabaya: Dār al-Saqqāf, n.d.), and idem, *Nayl al-amānī fī baʿd asānīd al-shaykh Muḥammad Yāsīn bin Muḥammad ʿĪsā al-Fadānī* (Jakarta: Panitia Haul Syekh Moh. Yasin Isa al-Fadani, 1993).

47. Snouck Hurgronje, *Mekka*, vol. 2, p. 372. Snouck observes that both Aḥmad Khaṭīb and his successor ʿAbd Karīm Banten enjoyed the respect of all social classes, including even the most learned scholars, primarily the Jāwa but also scholars of local origin. He also makes some interesting observations on ʿAbd al-Karīm's teaching of the *ṭarīqa* and relations with different categories of affiliates; ibid. 372–379.

48. Snouck Hurgronje, *Mekka*, vol. 2, pp. 285–287, 380–381, 389 (on the Naqshbandī shaykhs), 355 (on Ismāʿīl Minangkabawī).

49. Martin van Bruinessen, *Tarekat Naqsyabandiyah di Indonesia: Survei historis, geografis, dan sosiologis* (Bandung: Mizan, 1992), chaps. 7, 10–12; Martin van Bruinessen, "After the Days of Abû Qubays: Indonesian Transformations of the Naqshbandiyya-Khâlidiyya," *Journal of the History of Sufism* 5 (2008): 225–228; Werner Kraus, "Some Notes on the Introduction of the Naqshbandiyya-Khālidiyya into Indonesia," in *Naqshbandis: Cheminements et situation actuelle d'un ordre mystique musulman*, edited by Marc Gaborieau, Alexandre Popovic, and Thierry Zarcone (Istanbul and Paris: Éditions Isis, 1990), pp. 691–706.

50. These *khalīfa* are listed, district by district, in H. A. Fuad Said, *Syekh ʿAbdul Wahab: Tuan guru Babussalam* (Medan: Pustaka Babussalam, 1983), pp. 136–139; for wives and descendants, see pp. 170–185. The author of this biography/hagiography is one of ʿAbdul Wahab's 207 grandchildren.

51. Description of life in Babussalam after Said's volume and my own interviews in the village in November 1993. See also Denys Lombard, "Tarekat et entreprise à Sumatra: L'exemple de Syekh ʿAbdul Wahab Rokan (c. 1830–1926)," in *Naqshbandis*, edited by Gaborieau, Popovic, and Zarcone, pp. 707–715.

52. According to the biography, ʿAbdul Wahab sent al-Zuhdī each year at least 400 *ringgit*, the equivalent of 1,000 Dutch guilders. See Said, *Syekh ʿAbdul Wahab*, p. 40.

53. Said, *Syekh ʿAbdul Wahab*, pp. 57–58.

54. See Butrus Abu-Manneh, "Khalwa and Rabita in the Khalidi Suborder," in *Naqshbandis*, edited by Gaborieau, Popovic, and Zarcone, pp. 283–302, on Mawlānā Khālid's emphasis on *khalwa* as a physical retreat from the world. This differed from the classical Naqshbandī principle of *khalwat dar anjuman*, the cultivation of an otherworldly attitude while

actively engaging with the world. Of the other orders, most branches of the Khalwatiyya (which owes its name to the practice) are said to have endorsed *khalwa*, but there is no unambiguous indication that it was ever introduced into Indonesia. (There is one intriguing account by the French missionary Nicolas Gervaise of what could be *khalwa* in a mosque in Makassar in the 1680s, but Gervaise had not been there himself and his description seems colored by his personal acquaintance with Thai Buddhism; see Christian Pelras, "La première description de Célèbes-sud en français et la destinée remarquable de deux jeunes princes makassar dans la France de Louis XIV," *Archipel* 54 [1997], pp. 63–80, esp. p. 67; Michael F. Laffan, *The Makings of Indonesian Islam: Orientalism and the Narration of a Sufi Past* [Princeton University Press, 2011], pp. 20–21.)

55. Snouck Hurgronje, "Mystiek, magie, tarékats," pp. 1182–1183. On the importance of the *rābita* in the Khālidiyya branch of the Naqshbandiyya, see Abu-Manneh, "Khalwa and Rabita in the Khalidi Suborder."

56. See also: Bruinessen, "After the Days of Abû Qubays."

57. Karel A. Steenbrink, *Beberapa aspek tentang Islam di Indonesia abad ke-19* (Jakarta: Bulan Bintang, 1984), p. 94; Azra, *Origins of Islamic Reform*, pp. 119–120.

58. Bruinessen, *Tarekat Naqsyabandiyah di Indonesia*, pp. 125–128 (West Sumatra), 162–167 (Girikusumo and Sokaraja in Java), and 162–172.

59. Ibid., pp. 143–146 (South Aceh), 158–160 (Selangor, Malaysia).

60. Insightful observations on the various types of *putihan* villages can be found in Christiaan Snouck Hurgronje, "Vrije desa's," in *Ambtelijke adviezen van C. Snouck Hurgronje, 1889–1936*, edited by E. Gobée and C. Adriaanse, vol. 1 ('s-Gravenhage: Nijhoff, 1957), pp. 722–735 (written in 1895), which supersedes older Dutch studies. A *putihan* lineage guarding holy graves in the Surakarta region is discussed in Stephen C. Headley, "The Islamization of Central Java: The Role of Muslim Lineages in Kalioso," *Studia Islamika* 4.2 (1997): 55–82. On *putihan* villages and *pesantren*, see Bruinessen, "Pesantren and Kitab Kuning." On the hajj and the proliferation of *putihan* communities, see Ricklefs, *Polarising Javanese Society*, pp. 49–74.

61. Muhaimin, "Islamic Traditions of Cirebon," pp. 249–250, and personal interviews in Buntet; the *silsila* names a Muḥammad Saʿīd Madanī as Ashʿarī's teacher and continues through "Tāhir Madanī," "Ibrāhīm," and another "Tāhir" to Ibrāhīm al-Kūrānī (various combinations of the same name, sometimes as Ibrāhīm b. Tāhir or Tāhir b. Ibrāhīm, occur in other Javanese Shattārī *silsila*). Local memories of Kyai Ashʿarī are compiled in Sholekhatul Amaliyah, "Peran Kyai Asy'ari (Kyai Guru) dalam berdakwah di Kecamatan Kaliwungu Kabupaten Kendal" (Walisongo State Islamic University thesis, Semarang, 2010).

62. G. F. Pijper, "De opkomst der Tidjaniyyah op Java," in Pijper, *Fragmenta Islamica* (Leiden: Brill, 1934), pp. 97–121; Martin van Bruinessen, "Controversies and Polemics Involving the Sufi Orders in Twentieth-Century Indonesia," in *Islamic Mysticism Contested: Thirteen Centuries of Controversies and Polemics*, edited by Frederick de Jong and Bernd Radtke (Leiden: Brill, 1999), pp. 705–728, esp. 720–722.

63. Thus ʿAbdul Wahab Rohan retained a lifelong loyalty to his chief teacher of *kitāb* in Mekka, H. M. Yunus Batu Bara. It had been Yunus who advised him to complement the theoretical study of Sufism through Ghazālī's *Ihyā* with practical experience under Sulaymān al-Zuhdī. ʿAbdul Wahab later sent annual gifts of money to both, and, when his patron, the sultan of Langkat, visited Mekka, he not only honored al-Zuhdī but showed equal respect to Yunus Batu Bara (Said, *Syekh ʿAbdul Wahab*, pp. 28–33, 58).

64. See the analysis of the statistics on *geestelijken*, hajjis, schools, and students in the 1860s through 1880s, from a variety of Dutch sources, in Ricklefs, *Polarising Javanese Society*,

pp. 63–72. Based on the differential geographic distribution of *geestelijken* and hajjis, Ricklefs gathered that most of the former, who outnumbered the hajjis everywhere but more so in the interior of Java, held religious views similar to the Javanese "mystic synthesis" embraced by the aristocracy, views that were challenged by the new ideas coming from Mekka. He perceives these two types of religious leaders as representing "diverging worlds of pious Islam." My own, slightly different, interpretation is that the divergence took place within the category of *geestelijken*. Only those hajjis who had pursued serious study in Mekka and on return became teachers made much of an impact.

7

SHAṬṬĀRIYYA SUFI SCENTS

The Literary World of the Surakarta Palace in Nineteenth-Century Java

NANCY K. FLORIDA

In February 1815, a poet from the central Javanese palace of Surakarta (Kraton Surakarta) found himself stranded in Aceh on the northern tip of Sumatra. He took the opportunity of this circumstance to render into classical Javanese verse form what he called the "secret" (*wadi*), "forbidden" (*linarangan*) teachings of his Sufi masters. The result was a poetic text known as *Suluk Acih* (Song of Aceh). The poet in question was one Mas Ngabéhi Ronggasasmita, a member of Java's most celebrated literary family. He was grandson to the renowned father of the so-called Surakarta literary renaissance, R. Ng. Yasadipura I (1729–1803), who is sometimes credited for having awakened Javanese literature from the darkness that had putatively covered it since the Muslim conquest of Hindu-Buddhist Java. Ronggasasmita's father was the renowned poet and statesman R. Ng. Yasadipura II (T. Sastranagara, 1756–1844). His brother was R. Ng. Ronggawarsita Sepuh (the Elder Ronggawarsita), the scholar and Muslim "revolutionary" whom the Dutch colonial government exiled to West Sumatra in 1828 for having conspired against them during the Dipanagara War (1825–1830). Manuscript evidence in the palace archive suggests that Ronggasasmita, our stranded poet, shared his brother's fate. The palace manuscript notes that the Elder Ronggawarsita and his younger brother "Mas Haji" were both exiled in punishment for their involvement in the rebellion of Prince Dipanagara.[1] Ronggasasmita's nephew—the Elder Ronggawarsita's son—was R. Ng. Ronggawarsita (1802–1873), the most celebrated of all Javanese poets. The younger Ronggawarsita, remembered today for his prophetic works, is considered "the last of the court poets" and famed as "the seal of the *pujongga*."[2]

Ronggasasmita was the author of several important Sufi songs, or *suluk*. The Arabic word *suluk* refers to the journey along the mystical path (*ṭarīqa* or, in the Malay world, *tarekat*); as a poetic genre in Java, *suluk* names a corpus of metaphysical texts composed in sung poetry that explore the nature of the relationship between God and His creation, especially the relationship between God and humanity. Of special interest in these texts are the nature of the human person (body and soul) and the potential for human perfection in and through God.

Suluk Acih, the *suluk* composed by our Javanese sojourner in Aceh, forms a compilation of about sixteen or seventeen mystical poems, two of which are "signed" by Ronggasasmita—the 324-line *Suluk Acih* "proper" and the 340-line *Suluk Martabat Sanga* (Song of the nine grades of being).[3] These two poems will form the focus of the present chapter. Ronggasasmita's *suluk* appears to have been widely disseminated in the middle and later years of the nineteenth century, especially among the Surakartan court elite. Today seventeen manuscript witnesses of the *Suluk Acih* or portions of it are extant in the three royal archives of Surakarta, that is, the libraries of the Kraton Surakarta, the Pura Mangkunagaran, and the Radya Pustaka Museum.[4] There are at least fourteen additional witnesses scattered through public and private collections in Indonesia, the Netherlands, and Great Britain.[5]

The poems that make up *Suluk Acih* concern, among other things, the celestial composition of the human body, the generation (spiritual and corporeal gestation) of each and every human being, the nine levels of Reality manifest in the Prophet Muḥammad, the relationship between God and humanity, the nature of creation, the descent from and return to God, the discipline of human perfection, and the discipline of perfect death. The *suluk* also reveals the movement of a particular Javanese Sufi practitioner through both local and transregional religious networks; it contains brief though fascinating accounts of the author's sojourn in distant Aceh and of his early educational journey through a series of spiritual guides in Java. The text also provides the poet's spiritual genealogy (Ar. *silsila*; Jv. *silsilah*).[6] This genealogy reveals that the secret teachings that Ronggasasmita exposes in his *suluk* belong to the heritage of the Shaṭṭāriyya (Jv. Syattariyah) *tarekat*. Although *tarekat* (Ar. *ṭarīqa*) is usually translated as "order," in the context of early nineteenth-century Java, the word is better understood as "path," "discipline," or "lineage." The manuscript evidence from that time suggests that the *tarekat* did not form an "order" in the sense of a corporate body or horizontal brotherhood, but rather that it indicated a tradition of knowledge and practice that was passed vertically from individual masters to their students. In Java, the *tarekat* only appear to have become congealed into more formalized orders in the later years of the nineteenth century.[7]

The Shaṭṭāriyya forms a Sufi discipline that arose out of the Bistami ecstatic Sufi tradition in fifteenth-century Persia and was brought to Mughal India by Shah ʿAbd Allah (Jv. Sèh Ngabdullah Satari) (d. 1485).[8] Thence it spread to the holy cities of the Hijaz in the sixteenth century, and then on from there to the Malay world in the second half of the seventeenth century. The Shaṭṭāriyya, a minor order in Indonesia today, was the dominant Sufi lineage in the Malay world for nearly two centuries—from the time of its introduction there during the 1660s until the middle of the nineteenth century.[9] The Shaṭṭāriyya is characterized by the quick speed and relative ease with which its initiates may attain dissolution in God (*fana*). According to Rizvi, the definitive practices and the emotional and metaphysical frameworks that define the Shaṭṭāriyya were set by its sixteenth-century South Asian shaykh, Muḥammad Ghawth (Jv. Sèh Muhammad Gos) (d. 1562/3).[10] Ghawth provided travelers along the mystical path with contemplative practices involving recitations in remembrance of God (*zikir*; Ar. *dhikr*) that were performed with bodily discipline, including breath control. All of these were to be practiced under the guidance of a shaykh.[11]

In the Shaṭṭārī texts of the premodern Malay world, the traveler would begin his or her journey at the highest level of manifest divinity and from there descend (*tanazul*) from Divine Perfection through multiple (usually seven) levels of being in order to perform the return (*tarki*) to God, which she or he would attain on realization of the final and seventh level of being, that of the Perfect Man (*insān kāmil*). That realization, in both senses of the word, brought to pass the perfection (body and soul) of the traveler's person or self (*awak, sarira*).[12] The ultimate goal was not, however, *fanā*ʾ (dissolution of the self into the Godhead) but rather the stage called *fanā*ʾ *al- fanā*ʾ (the extinction of the extinction), which would deliver the traveler to the higher station of *baqā*ʾ, the ultimate return marked by the self-conscious reintegration of his or her person (body and soul) with the divine. At this stage of the journey, the traveler, experiencing the truth of having always already arrived, would be in a conscious state of everlasting abiding in God, even as he or she, thus empowered, continued to move through life in the phenomenal world.

This chapter will introduce the history of the Shaṭṭāriyya path in the Indies with a focus on its place among the literary and political elite of the palace of Surakarta in the early nineteenth century.[13] An understanding of the *tarekat* within these palace circles will be drawn from an exploration of a selection of manuscripts containing Shaṭṭārī teachings, most of which are stored in the Surakarta archives. I will touch on some of these Shaṭṭārī teachings as they appear in the two Ronggasasmitan *suluk*, with the hope that this may provide some sense of the *tarekat*'s teachings in the specific Javanese literary contexts to which they belong. Finally, I will briefly remark on the apparent decline in the status of the Shaṭṭāriyya *tarekat* within court circles and elsewhere in Java after 1830.

A BRIEF HISTORY OF THE SHAṬṬĀRIYYA IN THE MALAY WORLD WITH A FOCUS ON SURAKARTA

The Shaṭṭāriyya was brought to the Malay world by one of Ronggasasmita's spiritual forefathers, that is, the remarkable Sufi scholar ʿAbd al-Raʾūf Singkel (ca. 1620–1693), whose family hailed from Aceh's west coast. He was initiated into the lineage in the holy city of Medina around the middle of the seventeenth century, having come to the Hijaz around 1642 to perform the hajj and to pursue advanced studies of Islam. This was a time of significant conflict among Aceh's Muslims: the Sufi teachings of ʿAbd al-Raʾūf's "elder kinsman," the poet-scholar Ḥamza Fanṣūrī (d. 1527?), along with those of Fanṣūrī's epigone Shams al-Dīn Pasai (a.k.a. al-Sumaṭrāʾī/al-Sumaṭrānī, d. 1630), were under assault at the Acehnese court.[14] The teachings of both Ḥamza and Shams al-Dīn, which had been ascendant in Aceh during the reign of Sultan Iskandar Muda (r. 1607–1636), were ruled heresy by his successor Iskandar Thani, under the influence of a new arrival among the Islamic scholars at his court, Nūr al-Dīn al-Rānīrī (d. 1658; in Aceh 1637–1644). The next few years formed the high point, or, perhaps better, the low point, of the controversy over the metaphysical teachings that had come to be known as *wahdatul wujud* (Ar. *waḥdat al-wujūd*, "the oneness of Being").[15] Books were burned and followers who refused to recant were put to death. It is not at all unlikely that the young ʿAbd al-Raʾūf made for the holy lands at this precise moment in part to escape the unpleasantness, if not the purge. ʿAbd al-Raʾūf spent almost twenty years in Arabia, where he received the teachings of the Shaṭṭāriyya from the renowned Medinan Sufi scholar Shaykh Aḥmad al-Qushāshī (1583–1661).[16] After his return to Aceh in the early 1660s, ʿAbd al-Raʾūf remained in contact with the then-Shaṭṭārī shaykh in Medina, the well-known Ibrāhīm al-Kūrānī (1614–1690).[17] While firmly establishing the Shaṭṭāriyya in late seventeenth-century Aceh, ʿAbd al-Raʾūf disseminated among his students one of its most characteristic teachings, that of the seven levels of being (*martabat tujuh*) articulated in the Self-Manifestation (*tajallī*) of God.[18] He also produced the first complete Malay *tafsīr* (interpretation) of the Qurʾān, translated a number of Sufi and other works into Malay, composed his own original works in both Malay and Arabic, and served as the *qāḍī*; (chief judge and minister) of the sultanate.

Among ʿAbd al-Raʾūf's students was Shaykh Haji Abdul Muhyi (ʿAbd al-Muḥyī, ca. 1640–ca. 1715) of Karang, a Javanese Muslim scholar from the central Javanese kingdom of Mataram, who, sometime after receiving the Shaṭṭāriyya teachings from ʿAbd al-Raʾūf, removed himself to the kingdom of Banten and settled in the hills of southwest Java not too far from the coast.[19] ʿAbd al-Muḥyī was probably a student of ʿAbd al-Raʾūf in Aceh following the shaykh's return to Sumatra in the early 1660s. Nevertheless, as ʿAbd al-Muḥyī himself was a hajji, it is at least possible that the two met and studied together in the holy land.[20] Manuscript witnesses of ʿAbd al-Muḥyī's teachings, which include elaborations on the seven grades of being, can be found in the Surakartan royal manuscripts.[21]

Some have suggested that ʿAbd al-Muḥyī's son Fakih Ibrahim may have served as the chief religious official in the Surakartan court under Pakubuwana

II (r. Surakarta, 1745–1749) and Pakubuwana III (r. 1749–1788).[22] That Pakubuwana II sought and ultimately failed to reign as an exemplary Sufi king in Kartasura before removing his palace to Surakarta has been explored in detail by Merle Ricklefs in his *Seen and Unseen Worlds in Java*.[23] Ricklefs' fascinating study reveals, among many other things, the central role that the king's grandmother Ratu Pakubuwana (d. 1732) played in this endeavor. Ratu Pakubuwana was queen to the first of the Pakubuwanas ("Axes of the World"), a royal name that was no doubt created to recall the *wali kutub* (Ar. *quṭb*), the hidden "axial saint" of the age on whom all phenomenal existence metaphysically depends. In the sole (surviving) literary text attributed to Pakubuwana II, however, we find none of the Shaṭṭārī-scented metaphysical speculations that characterize Javanese *suluk* literature. This Pakubuwanan text is a moralistic-didactic poem that emphasizes the necessity of strict adherence to Islam's ritual obligations and that contains sharp criticisms of any who dare stray from the sharīʿa (Islamic law).[24] The writings of his son and successor, Pakubuwana III (r. 1749–1788), do, however, reverberate with echoes of Shaṭṭārī metaphysical teachings. Among the *suluk* composed by Pakubuwana III is *Suluk Martabat Wahdat Wakidiyat*, a song that lingers on the seven grades of being that were elaborated by ʿAbd al-Raʾūf and ʿAbd al-Muḥyī. The text composes a particularly subtle meditation on the second and third grades (*waḥda* and *wāḥidiyya*) that form the most sublime levels of God's self-manifestation within Himself and on the dissolution of the self into the godhead that is experienced in perfect gnosis.[25]

If no clear genealogy from ʿAbd al-Muḥyī to these Pakubuwanan kings has yet been uncovered in the archives, I have found a tiny handful of manuscript witnesses in which the Shaṭṭārī spiritual lineages of other noble Surakartan literati are explicitly traced to this saint. All but one of these are witnesses of Ronggasasmita's *Suluk Martabat Sanga*, one of the songs comprising *Suluk Acih*. In the Ronggasasmitan genealogy that begins with the Prophet Muḥammad, it is attested that the teachings passed from ʿAbd al-Muḥyī to his son, Dalem Bojong, and then on to his son, Kyai Mas, and then on to Kyai Talabudinu of Banyumas, who passed them to Syakh Muhammad Salim of Madahab, Ronggasasmita's teacher.[26] The sole exceptional manuscript is a prose handbook of Shaṭṭārī practices and thought that was composed by a prominent Surakartan statesman, probably around the turn of the nineteenth century.[27] This statesman, Kyai Tumenggung Arungbinang, traces his Shaṭṭārī lineage to ʿAbd al-Muḥyī through a different line of masters. The Shaṭṭārī teachings that Arungbinang received passed from ʿAbd al-Muḥyī to another of his sons (or, perhaps, grandson), one Mas Bagus Muhyidin.[28] Bagus Muhyidin then passed them to Kyai Mufid of Kedhung Lo, Roma, who taught Abdul Gani of Tersana, Kedhu. Abdul Gani was Arungbinang's teacher.[29] Arungbinang provides this *silsila* in the preface to *Bab Dérah ing Ngèlmi Tarèk Wiriding Dikir* (On diagrams of *tarekat* knowledges and *zikir* litanies/practices), the treatise of

Shaṭṭāriyya knowledge that he compiled. It is notable that what appears to be the only extant witness of this early nineteenth-century treatise was inscribed in 1864 for a prominent Surakartan prince in a manuscript that also includes a witness of Ronggasasmita's *Suluk Acih*, of which *Suluk Martabat Sanga* is part.[30] Arungbinang, a courtier of I.S.K.S. Pakubuwana IV (r. 1788–1820), was a well-connected statesman in the late eighteenth- and early nineteenth-century Surakartan palace. In addition to his own service to the king, he was also the father of the Surakartan *patih* (vizier) Sasradiningrat III (in office 1846–1866) and the step-grandfather of K.G.P.H. Cakradiningrat (d. 1882), the also very well connected Surakartan noble who commissioned the copy of the 1864 manuscript containing Arungbinang's treatise of Shaṭṭāriyya knowledge and Ronggasasmita's *Suluk Acih*.[31]

The Arungbinang Shaṭṭārī treatise is an extensive prose treatise on the *tarekat*'s thought and practice. It is, in effect, a manual to instruct and enlighten the traveler along the mystic path, providing a detailed guide to the Shaṭṭārī initiation ritual and a great number of *zikir* texts with recitation instructions that include breathing practices and bodily postures.[32] The greater portion of the text forms a treatise on Shaṭṭārī metaphysics, with extensive meditations on cosmology and on "anthropology"—in the sense of teachings on the metaphysics of the human body, the mysteries of human gestation, and the means by which to open the body's metaphysical potentials (a number of these provided with diagrams, or *dérah*). As would be expected in a Shaṭṭārī text, discussions of the seven grades of being and the seven levels of the soul's attainments figure prominently. Also of interest are teachings concerning the relations of teachers and students and on the different categories of students. In addition to this extraordinary compilation of Shaṭṭārī knowledge, Arungbinang is also known to have composed a remarkable *suluk* that forms an extended metaphysical meditation on the nature of ritual prayer, or *salat* (Ar. *ṣalāt*), culminating in reflections on the perfection of *salat* in its eternal and everlasting form (*salat daim*).[33]

Another particularly striking Surakartan initiate into the Shaṭṭāriyya appears to have been the Surakartan king, I.S.K.S. Pakubuwana IV (r. 1788–1820), whom Arungbinang served. Pakubuwana IV is celebrated as an author, most notably of the didactic text *Wulang Rèh* (Teachings on rule), a moral handbook for members of the ruling class that he composed in 1809. It has gone almost unnoticed, however, that he also composed a number of *suluk*. The king composed these *suluk* over a period of nearly forty years—from the time that he was a young crown prince until the year preceding his death. These Pakubuwanan *suluk*, concerned especially with the metaphysical and cosmological natures of the human body, are redolent with the scent of Shaṭṭārī teachings.[34] It is also of note that Pakubuwana IV chose the name Radèn Ayu Satariyah (i.e., Shaṭṭāriyya) for his first daughter from a queen; he named his second daughter from the same queen Radèn Ayu Kisbandiyah (i.e., Naqshbandiyya), suggesting that the king was also affiliated with the Naqshbandiyya *tarekat*.[35]

Muhammad Arif of Banjar was Pakubuwana IV's teacher and probably his Shaṭṭāriyya master. We learn this in the very truncated spiritual genealogy that M. Ng. Tepasonta II, one of Pakubuwana IV's courtiers, provides in his 1820 redaction of *Suluk Martabat Sanga.*[36] In this version, which by today's standards would count as plagiarism, Tepasonta repeats Ronggasasmita's teachings—and his educational biography—verbatim while usurping Ronggasasmita's place as author.[37] Dispensing with the Shaṭṭāriyya lineage from the Prophet Muḥammad through numerous generations of masters down to Ronggasasmita that belongs to this poem and its teachings, Tepasonta instead begins his genealogy with Muhammad Arif—his own guru. He compensates for this erasure of lineage by noting that Pakubuwana IV was his fellow student under Muhammad Arif and by adding other biographical and genealogical notes—these concerning his own court position and those of his ancestors.

Another Kraton Surakarta text redolent with Shaṭṭārī teachings is the *Serat Centhini*, among the most celebrated of all works of Javanese literature. The *Centhini* was commissioned by the then–crown prince of Surakarta, who would later reign as I.S.K.S. Pakubuwana V (1820–1823) in January 1815—exactly one month before Ronggasasmita would commence his writing in Aceh.[38] Composed by a team of court poets that was led by Mas Ronggasutrasna, Ki Ng. Sastradipura, and R. Ng. Yasadipura II (Ronggasasmita's father), along with the crown prince himself, the 722-canto *Centhini* is often called an encyclopedia of Javanese knowledge. The *Centhini* incorporates a large body of *suluk* literature, and recognizably Shaṭṭārī teachings, though usually unattributed, pervade these *suluk*. Given the apparent prominence of the Shaṭṭāriyya among Surakartan literati at the time of its composition, it is not at all surprising that Shaṭṭārī teachings are so pervasive in the *Centhini*—and that it was not deemed necessary to attribute them. In addition to the unattributed teachings, Shaṭṭārī practices are explicitly mentioned a number of times in the *Centhini*—notably as the spiritual practice of Amongraga, the "hero" of the poem. These practices are usually conjoined with those of the Naqshbandiyya, as "Satariyah Isbandiyah," indicating that the discipline of the character Amongraga, like that of Pakubuwana IV, seems to have formed an amalgam of the practices of both *tarekat*.[39]

There is very strong evidence that the historical figure Kyai Maja (ca. 1792–1849), a figure whose ties with the Surakarta palace are often overlooked, was also a disciple of the Shaṭṭāriyya.[40] Kyai Maja is remembered today as the principal religious advisor of Prince Dipanagara (1785–1855), the charismatic Yogyakartan prince who led the rebellion against Dutch authority that later became known as the Dipanagara War (1825–1830).[41] That ultimately failed rebellion formed the last stand of Javanese royal power against the Europeans. Maja had been a teacher in a rural religious establishment endowed by the Surakarta palace, and he was known to have been very close to members of its royal family.[42] Among his intimate associates was Pakubuwana IV's brother Buminata, the prince who, after his brother's death in 1820, led the crown prince's administration in which Ronggasasmita and his kinsmen served.[43] Kyai Maja stood at the center of the powerful network of Islamic teachers that provided the core backing for Dipanagara's rebellion. It would not be far-fetched to presume that this network was a Shaṭṭāriyya one. Furthermore, with Kyai Maja as his spiritual guide, it is not surprising that Prince Dipanagara, too, appears to have been an adherent of Shaṭṭārī knowledge and practice.[44] With the failure of the rebellion and the exiles of Kyai Maja in 1828 and of Dipanagara and Surakarta's king Pakubuwana VI in 1830, the old royal order of Java was over.

The year 1830 was a watershed year in Javanese social and political history: it marked the end of indigenous royal political power and the beginning of high colonialism in Java. The defeat also appears to have delivered a blow to the ascendance of the Shaṭṭāriyya at the Surakarta court, on which I will elaborate further in the conclusion of this chapter. There is reason to believe that the Shaṭṭārī court poet Mas Ronggasasmita—along with the *pujongga* Ronggawarsita's father—were among the casualties of that war. To my knowledge, no new Shaṭṭārī texts were composed at the court after the war—although the older Shaṭṭāriyya manuscripts continued to be copied, redacted, and circulated.[45]

THE WRITING OF *SULUK ACIH*

Some ten years before the outbreak of the Dipanagara War, the Javanese court poet Ronggasasmita composed his collection of Shaṭṭārī Sufi poems in far-off Aceh. Ronggasasmita almost certainly composed this work in the course of an interrupted pilgrimage to Mekka. Stranded in Aceh, the so-called Veranda of Mekka through which pilgrims from the archipelago often passed, the poet, speaking in the third person, notes that his writing

> [10] Was at the time that he was cast adrift by God
> Separated from his companions
> In the land of Aceh overseas
> Just the two of them, he and his uncle Yakir.
>
> [11] But his uncle, fallen ill with a fever
> Weeks on end, sorrowful of heart
> Could not be drawn to speak.
> The writing began on a Friday, in the month of Rabinguawal
>
> [12] On the seventh day, in the year Jé, in the seventh season
> Rendered in chronogram:
> "Pure Countenance of the Priest King" [17 February 1815].[46]
> (*Suluk Acih*)[47]

For pilgrims from south-central Java in the era before the steamship, performing the hajj in Mekka entailed, to be sure, an arduous journey.[48] We do not know how long the preparations had taken for our two pilgrims' voyage or how long they might have waited for this opportunity. We do know that the Haramayn had been under Wahhābī control from 1806 to 1813, which would have made Mekka less than conducive to Sufi practitioners.[49]

Ronggasasmita and his uncle probably set sail from the port of Semarang on Java's north coast in the fall of 1814 to journey westward and northward for over 1,300 miles—across the north coast of Java and then up through the Straits of Malacca to Aceh. The pilgrims would have needed to embark from Aceh sometime between late December and early February in order to catch the monsoon winds for the 4,000-mile trip across the Indian Ocean in order to arrive in time for the hajj season in November 1815.[50] Ronggasasmita began composing his *suluk* on February 17, 1815; owing to his uncle's illness, he had just missed the boat. We do not know whether he waited in Aceh for the next season's boat out to Aden or if he and his ailing uncle tarried there until they could catch a boat back to Java—though I am inclined to think that the poet did bide his time in Aceh, writing, and that he likely did make the hajj the following year, for, as I suggested at the opening of this chapter, I am also inclined to think that he was the "Mas Haji" who was exiled along with his elder brother in 1828. Until evidence is unearthed to prove or disprove my supposition, all that we know for sure is that in February 1815 the poet was cast off, stranded, and despondent over the interruption in his pilgrimage. At this time of intense disappointment—indeed, of a broken heart—Ronggasasmita decided to divulge in poetry the teachings of his Shaṭṭārī masters. And so he set himself to writing:

[6] The elect knowledge of Reality
The truth that
Brings perfection to life
The knowledge that is forbidden

[7] Secreted by the prophets, the saints, and the faithful.
In former times there was none
Who dared render it in verse;
For so secret is this knowledge.

[8] The first to render it in verse, in Pucung meter
Is Dyan Ronggasasmita
Charging headlong, revealing the secret
All the teachings of his master[s]

> [9] All those bound in *primbon* books[51]
> Here are set to verse
> To be a journey of knowledge [*suluking ngèlmi*]
> Deliverance for a broken heart
> (*Suluk Acih*)[52]

The *suluk* forms a poetic journey along the mystical path, and that path was a Shaṭṭārī one. Was this journey, in part, to replace the journey to the holy land that the poet was forced to defer? What form of secret teachings could salve the wound that this interruption in the poet's pilgrimage had inflicted? Before touching on the nature of the secret teachings that Ronggasasmita so boldly reveals in his *suluk*, a word on his background is in order.

THE BACKGROUND OF THE WRITER: FAMILY AND EDUCATION

Ronggasasmita belonged to one of the most distinguished and powerful literary families in Java. His grandfather, R. Ng. Yasadipura I (1729–1803), is among the most renowned of Javanese literati. Yasadipura I is most remembered for his translations of the Old Javanese classics (e.g., the Ramayana and the Mahabharata) into modern Javanese verse. However, his writings are not restricted to just the Indic classics: he is also credited with a masterful history that chronicles the war of the division of Java (1746–1757) through which he lived,[53] a poetic history of an important case of Islamic polemics in eighteenth-century Java,[54] a voluminous poetic rendering of the adventures of the Prophet's uncle Amīr Ḥamza,[55] the renowned Déwaruci tale of the Mahabharata hero Bima's mystical journey in search of the water of life (notably classified as a *suluk* in the Kraton Surakarta archives),[56] and at least one other poem that is more easily recognizable as *suluk*.[57] Yasadipura I was also an avid reader of *suluk* literature, as Ronggasasmita attests in his *Suluk Martabat Sanga*, and a close confidant of Surakarta's king I.S.K.S. Pakubuwana III (r. 1749–1788), who, as noted above, was himself an author of *suluk* infused with Shaṭṭārī thought.

Yasadipura I's son and Ronggasasmita's father, R. T. Sastranagara (a.k.a. Yasadipura II, 1756–1844), was both a prolific writer and a major statesman, serving as the senior minister of the Surakarta palace's Kadipatèn from 1826 to his death.[58] Sastranagara produced a range of literary works: in addition to participating in the composition of the encyclopedic *Centhini*, he also wrote historical chronicles, commentaries on good and bad statecraft, moralistic manuals for the ruling class, translations of the Old Javanese classics into modern Javanese poetry (and, conversely, translations of modern Javanese poetry into Old Javanese classical meters), voluminous histories of the Islamic prophets (*Serat Ambiya*), and, perhaps most relevant here, at least two *suluk*. One of those admonishes his children to study, to work with written materials and with properly qualified masters in order to achieve perfection, especially perfection in death; the other *suluk* provides a sense of what that perfection might mean, and that would appear to be the perfect embodiment of spirit in both life and death.[59]

Ronggasasmita seems to have followed his father's directions in seeking out a spiritual education, though he was not always entirely successful in this endeavor; we learn this in an unprecedented narrative that is tucked away in one of the poems that compose his *Suluk Acih*. In the section of *Suluk Martabat Sanga* immediately following the secret teachings on the nine grades of the Prophet Muḥammad's being, which open the *suluk*, and immediately preceding the poet's Shaṭṭāriyya genealogy, Ronggasasmita provides a concise autobiographical narrative of his early educational journey. I should note that this is the only such first-person narrative on a Javanese subject's spiritual education that I have encountered in any traditional Javanese text. The narrative begins with a specific prohibition: Ronggasasmita instructs his students and children to conceal the esoteric teachings that he has newly disclosed to them from what he calls the "sharīʿa folk" (Jv. *ahli sarak*), the community of those whose main concern is Islamic Law, a community to which he himself once belonged:[60]

> [38] Keep this hidden, fenced away closed tight
> Those belonging to the sharīʿa folk [*ahli sarak*]
> Are forbidden [*siriken*], let it not be known to them.
> Even with others, you must take care.
>
> [39] I give so strong a warning because
> It has been truly demonstrated:
> I myself did once become
> One of the sharīʿa folk, but not as learned as the *'ulamā'*
> [accomplished religious scholars]
>
> [40] Still stupid [*maksih busuk*], nevertheless I took a guru
> [*anggeguru*].
> And this first time
> It did not penetrate my heart,
> So I took another guru, the second time still
>
> [41] My heart was confused: like yes, like no
> Scored by sharīʿa
> Terrified of death.
> Again I took a guru, this then was my third.
>
> [42] At last I began to understand,
> But still not rid of
> The traces of sharīʿa, troubled
> Day and night my heart did roil in argument.

[43] Over and again my position I turned
On the secret knowledge [*rahsiya*]
Lost in twisted argument [*kapulintir*]
In frustration, I took no heed

[44] Heedless, again a guru I took.
This then was my fourth.
And there my heart, now strong [*gagah*]
Received the revelation [*wahyu*], the gift of grace [*nugraha*],

[45] Completed, opened and cleansed was my heart.
No longer was it shrouded
Gone were all the screens
Mad, ecstatic, now assured.

[46] Ever stronger, my passion [*birahèningsun*] for knowledge
Ceaselessly seeking teachers [*puruhita*]
From them to learn of that within [*batin*].
Now wholly dedicated, I did not spare expense.

[47] The taking of gurus I took to its end:
Within [*batin*] I was untroubled
But outwardly [*lahiré*] I did conceal that
Ritual performance [*angibadah*] was useless [*tanpa pédah*] then for me

[48] Like a *dul*, my *zikir* knew no set times[61]
My *ratib* and *sama*, ceaseless[62]
I gathered all the hajjis
Finally then impoverished by hosting all those feasts.

[49] All ye, young and old, my followers all
Know ye all
The lineage of my gurus
This exceeds in excellence reading the Qur'ān.

[50] My gurus were not many, only twenty-three
But I am counting only
The lineage of but one:
Whose foundation came from our Master

[51] For it was first the Messenger of God who taught
Sayidina Ali
The son of bin Talib.
Then Sayidina Ali taught . . .
(*Suluk Martabat Sanga*)[63]

The Shaṭṭāriyya spiritual genealogy that begins with the Prophet Muḥammad continues on through twenty-eight generations of gurus before coming to Ronggasasmita's Shaṭṭārī master, Shaykh Muhammad Salim of "Madahab," that one guru whose lineage "counted."[64] Ronggasasmita was, then, the thirtieth in the lineage.

It is no doubt significant that the poet chose to preface his distinguished Shaṭṭāriyya genealogy with an outline of what had been his sketchy educational journey as a young spiritual seeker. In doing this, Ronggasasmita seems to be both censuring and celebrating the educational failures he experienced at the start of his quest and the excesses in which he indulged toward the end of his journey—and to be doing so in the interface between revealing the deepest esoteric knowledge of the Prophetic Reality and authorizing that knowledge with the pedigree of his Shaṭṭārī heritage. At the end of his (preliminary) journey, he is like a *santri dul*, mad and ecstatic in his embrace and his practices; he impoverishes himself by holding feasts for all the religious. Did these excesses precede or succeed Ronggasasmita's entrance into the Shaṭṭāriyya? Where is Shaykh Muhammad Salim of Madahab, that one teacher that counted, located in this narrative? Is he the favored fourth guru under whose guidance Ronggasasmita's heart was opened to the revelation, an experience that was followed by the poet's indulgence in unregulated "mystic excess"? Or was he perhaps one of those hajjis who enjoyed Ronggasasmita's largesse? Or did Shaykh Muhammad Salim come into the poet's life after his impoverishment—after the feasting was over? At the least, I should note that the excesses Ronggasasmita describes here are not consistent with the teachings in the rest of *Suluk Martabat Sanga* or with the teachings of almost all the other poems normally included in the *Suluk Acih* compilation.[65]

Ronggasasmita notes that it was only after having been frustrated in his study of sharīʿa, and still in a state of ignorant stupidity (*maksih busuk*), that he turned to the world of (Sufi) gurus (*anggeguru*). Narrating the difficulties he encountered on the path, he may then be describing the pitfalls into which one who is too steeped in the petty details of sharīʿa—though not truly learned like the ʿ*ulamā*ʾ—may fall when confronted with esoteric Sufi knowledge. He does, after all, explicitly cite his own stumbling experience with his gurus as evidence of the impediments to Sufi practice faced by a half-baked student of sharīʿa. But is this the prime reason that the secret knowledge is forbidden to the sharīʿa folk? Or is this prohibition rather a warning to his students to keep what he has taught them secret lest they be misunderstood and perhaps punished by the sharī'a folk? There is, in Javanese historical texts as well as in *suluk*, a tradition of writings concerning such misunderstandings and punishments, most notably in narratives of the martyrdom of the "heretic" saint Sèh Sitijenar that is thought to have taken place in fifteenth- or sixteenth-century Demak.[66] Ronggasasmita does note that, after he finally saw the light, he concealed within himself what had been revealed to him and continued to perform the outward ritual devotions required by Islam (*ibadah*), something that Sitijenar failed to do. But at the same time Ronggasasmita evaluates that performance as useless or devoid of merit (*tanpa pédah*). And in the very next stanza—the last before turning to his pedigree—Ronggasasmita describes his very public ecstatic Sufi (Shaṭṭārī or not) practices that fall outside the bounds of prescribed ritual practice, practices that fall out of time (*tanpa mangsa*) and are marked by an immoderation that eventually beggars him.

RONGGASASMITA'S ADMONITIONS TO THOSE WHO WOULD COME AFTER

The final portion of *Suluk Martabat Sanga*, directly following the poet's Shaṭṭāriyya *silsila*, turns on Ronggasasmita's admonitions to his students and his readers, and these are four. The first two of these are dispatched quickly. Ronggasasmita first admonishes those who will come after him "to keep it fast" (*dèn-agemi*), that is, to conceal the secret teachings from the many; second, he admonishes them "to be scrupulous" (*dèn-nastiti*), by which he means to be attentive in study and unwavering in conviction. Ronggasasmita lingers, however, on the interconnected third and fourth admonitions. The third admonition is "to be diligent" (*dèn-taberi*); by "diligence" he means diligence in reading practices, and that which is to be read are *suluk*. It is here that Ronggasasmita provides the only extended critical reflections on the practice of reading that I have encountered in Javanese manuscripts. These self-conscious, at times almost ethnographic, notes on reading are, I think, unprecedented. For Ronggasasmita, diligent reading entails a kind of critical engagement that is the result both of sufficient understanding of the Javanese Sufi corpus and a dialogical interaction with the text, through which the well-informed reader participates in its production of meaning.[67] Passive, uncritical reception fails to meet the mark: the practice of diligent reading that he calls for entails the active and informed interpretive practice of the enlightened reader. Such true "diligence" in reading makes it possible for students to distinguish between true and false gurus, a critical distinction for travelers along the mystical path. Finally, Ronggasasmita's fourth admonition to his students is that they "take care" (*dèn-ati-ati*) in their reading practices. He goes on to explain that "taking care" means attending carefully to the complexity of meaning found within the *suluk* that are the objects of their study. Every student needs to work actively toward the apprehension and experience of these meanings—of this complexity—but, Ronggasasmita cautions, he or she must do so under the guidance of a qualified guru. "Taking care," then, is a function of having already practiced "due diligence."[68] Only the diligent reader who has taken sufficient care is open to the experience of knowledge.

In this final section of the *suluk*, Ronggasasmita describes the exemplary reader (and presumably guru) and contrasts his practice and knowledge with that of the charlatans. For Ronggasasmita, the exemplary perfected reader was his own grandfather, R. Ng. Yasadipura I. He tells of watching his grandfather, notably one who was already imbued with knowledge (*ahli ngèlmu*), pore over texts almost every night, and those texts, he says, were *suluk* and other Sufi texts.

> [76] I myself did see him in the deep of night
> When he had no guests
> Once resting from his writing
> There was nothing other seen by him
>
> [77] Save *suluks* and other Sufi works . . .
> (*Suluk Martabat Sanga*)[69]

Ronggasasmita goes on to compare Yasadipura's reading practices with those of the false gurus "nowadays" who dare to teach without a foundation of diligent reading. These rascally teachers (*guru bérnakal*) even go so far as to offer interpretations of metaphysical poems that they themselves do not understand, and by "understanding" he means the experiential spiritual understanding that is *ngèlmu*. They may be clever (*bér-ngakal*), but their cleverness is built on shaky (if rational) foundations, their interpretations of *suluk* are trivial, and their teachings lead their students astray. For this, Ronggasasmita tells us, they deserve to have their mouths stuffed with seven fists full of rocks.[70] As Ronggasasmita reminds us at the close of *Suluk Martabat Sanga*, if these poems were of no benefit or merit (again *tanpa pédah*), the saints would never have written them. No, they were written in days of old as teachings for the future. Hence, we must take care in our reading of them.[71]

THE POET'S SHAṬṬĀRIYYA TEACHINGS

This introduction to the articulation of the Shaṭṭāriyya among the literati of the early nineteenth-century Kraton Surakarta would be hollow without some attention to the Shaṭṭārī teachings their writings comprise. My discussion here will be brief and restricted to just some of the teachings that are found in just two of the poems that compose Ronggasasmita's *Suluk Acih* (*Suluk Acih* "proper" and *Suluk Martabat Sanga*). Both *suluk* at heart form reflections on *tawhīd* (the absolute unicity and uniqueness of God), on the nature of creation, and especially on the nature of humanity, the most perfect manifestation of God in creation. Although there is no explicit reference in either text to the *insān al-kāmil*, the "Perfect Man" who forms the final (seventh) and most sublime self-manifestation of God in the Shaṭṭārī discourses of the Malay world, both poems can be understood as explorations of human perfection in and through God. The most perfect of Perfect Men is the Prophet Muḥammad. In Shaṭṭārī teachings, it is through the Prophet's light that creation itself emerges, and it is in his person (both body and soul) that all the potentials of the created universe are realized most completely. Ronggasasmita explores this embodied perfection most explicitly in his *Suluk Martabat Sanga* with the poetic meditation on the nine grades of created and uncreated being encompassed by the Prophetic Reality with which he opens his song.

Having already discussed the middle and end of Ronggasasmita's *Suluk Martabat Sanga*, I turn at long last to the opening section of the work and the secret teachings that the poet cautioned should be hidden from the people of sharīʿa. These teachings with their elaborations on the very being of the Prophet provide an exemplar of the kind of knowledge that Ronggasasmita tells us is so easy to misinterpret, the kind of knowledge that he says was written to be of benefit in the future. The first thirty-six stanzas of the poem form an intricate reflection on the unfolding of God in creation through the person of Muḥammad, the most perfect of Perfect Men. The *suluk* moves through the nine levels of God's self-manifestation in the Prophetic Reality, each of which is perpetually re-created in Muḥammad's perfect human form in the punctual eternal moment "from before there were heaven and earth straight through unto now." In this song, Ronggasasmita celebrates the Prophet in his perfectly realized form as the one who gathers into presence both the infinite potentials of the cosmos and the form of the man Muḥammad.[72] He reflects on the Prophetic Reality reflexively in a way that invites careful readers to join in the reflection and to share in the experience of that eternal moment.

The reflection begins with the Divine Face, unchanging and eternal and made fully manifest in the Prophet, as the palace (*kraton*) of God that lies within each of us. The journey through the nine levels of the Prophetic Reality descending from the first grade, that of the Face, to the ninth, that of the fixing of the Prophetic form in the person of Muḥammad, is an exploration both of the creation of the world and of the generation of humanity, that is, of the gestational process of each and every human being from conception until birth. Ronggasasmita tells us that to follow this journey under the guidance of a perfect teacher is to attain knowledge of the "palace of the self," that is, to learn to "see" the self under the aspect of the divine. The task of the traveler on the mystical path is, then, to follow the Prophet's realization.

Suluk Acih too lingers on the Prophetic Reality. Ronggasasmita both opens and closes *Suluk Acih* with a version of the well-known Sufi metaphor of the mirror. The knowledge of reality is to be discerned in the knot that this metaphor forms. In his extended interpretation of the metaphor that opens the *suluk*, Ronggasasmita identifies the Perfect Man (that is, the Prophet Muḥammad) as the perfect reflection of God in the mirror of the universe, wherein the One who gazes is identical with the reflection on which He gazes. The subject and object of vision are one. The created universe (the mirror) is the reality of negation (*nafi*). God (the One who sees and His seeing) is the reality of affirmation (*isbat*). The reflection is the manifestation of God's self-affirmation in the form of the Prophet Muḥammad. Finally, in the closing stanzas of the same *suluk*, Ronggasasmita affirms that whatsoever man or woman completes the journey along the path (*suluk*), whosoever realizes his or her return, is indistinguishable in his or her reality from the reality of the Prophet, the manifestation of God's essence abiding in the oneness of God's Face.[73] And, in the end, "the one who is called 'Allāh' in truth/is he who utters '*Allāhu akbār*.'"[74]

Both *Suluk Martabat Sanga* and *Suluk Acih* "proper" are exemplars of *wujūdī* thought. That is, both are extended explorations of the "oneness of being" that explore the absolute unicity of an absolutely transcendent God who is nevertheless immanent in His creation. The *suluk* turn on the relation of the One to the many, God to His creation, and humanity to God, through reflections on the multiple levels of being, potential being, and potential nonbeing through which God eternally discloses himself in His creation along with reflections on the central position of humanity within that creation. Ronggasasmita's *suluk* articulate the unity of being, which is ultimately only God's Being, in a manner that can neither be dismissed as vulgar pantheism nor argued to be an abstract monism.[75] This is effected, in part, by the wit, nuance, and economy of Ronggasasmita's poetic language. There is a terseness of expression in the metaphysical articulations of the being of God and that of humanity that opens Ronggasasmita's poetry not only to multivalent interpretation, but, more important in the context of *suluk*, to perplexity, to the knowledge of unknowingness (Jv. *éram*, from the Arabic *ḥayra*, "perplexity").

The Javanese language seems particularly suited to the generation and exploration of metaphysical puzzlements. In his rendering and evocation of these moments of wonder, Ronggasasmita plays to maximum effect the ambiguity of Javanese personal pronouns, where a single pronoun (*sira*) can and does mean "He," "he," and "you"; and another pronoun (*kita*) can mean both —and at the same time—"I" and "we" and often "you" as well. He makes deft use of the semantic indeterminacy of a number of other critical words in Javanese mystical discourse, such as words that denote "the self"; for example, the word *awak* is at the same time "self," "person," and "body." The senses of words, then, slip between and among multiple possible meanings, setting off a movement of undecidability that beats in reverberation and opens to wonder. In Javanese poetic phrasing, the agent of an action often remains ambiguous. Ronggasasmita plays with this feature of poetic language to effect productive perplexities that cross and sometimes confound the lines of poetry.

This is notable, for example, in his reflections on the creative will in the generation of the universe, where the subject of the verb "to will" (and this is the Divine Will) is willfully obscured. Finally, Javanese verbs do not mark tense. Ronggasasmita plays this feature of language, too, to maximum effect, thereby to slip with ease between past and present, time and eternity.

> [6] . . . .
> Who stands in Junun Mukawiyah ["the Face unfurling in the wide world"]?
>
> [7] Yea, the Reality of My Life [*sajatiné urip ingsun*: the life of God and that of the Prophet, but also that "palace of the self" that is the secret interior "I" of the *suluk*'s writer and of its reader]
> Before there did exist
> Heaven and earth straight through unto now
> As for the will, what is it that was/is willed?
>
> [8] Yea, its name is Maklum Suksma
> *Maklum* means "knowledge"
> *Suksma* is "the will
> Not yet to will, but just to know"
>
> [9] Who then stands within Maklum?
> Who indeed is it but
> The All High, the All Pure
> Yea, truly it is my life itself, our lives themselves [*iya iku nyata urip kita dhawak*: and/or "Yea, the reality of my Life itself, our lives themselves"; and/or "Yea, the manifestation of my life itself, our lives themselves"; and/or "Yea, the Truth of my/your own life"; and so on]
>
> [10] When the heavens and earth were yet to exist
> Straight through unto now
> And then there was/is another will . . .
> (*Suluk Martabat Sanga*)[76]

Finally, I would like to say a word or two on how Ronggasasmita, the writer who is foremost a seeker, understands the relation between the written word and human action. Both *suluk* take an interest in the status of the written word, of writing itself. Each of them lays claim to participating in distinctive Islamic discursive traditions, and both valorize writing and reading as Sufi practice. *Suluk Acih* begins by referencing classical theological sources, the

Ibn Abbās tradition of Qur'ānic interpretation and the renowned eleventh-century theologian al-Ghazālī's (d. 1111) most famous work, the *Iḥyā' 'ulūm al-dīn* (Revivification of the religious sciences).[77] It continues with translations from Arabic sources that form reflective interpretations of Qur'ānic passages, along with several well-known *ḥadīth* and classical Sufi utterances. *Suluk Martabat Sanga* also opens in dialogue with the Islamic theological tradition of *kalām*, and it does so through the sometimes-singular translations of Islamic theological terminology—or of what is taken to be Islamic theological terminology—through which it elaborates the nine grades of the Prophetic Reality.[78] After completing its intricate exercises of translation, the poem then moves into reflections on knowledge transmission, recording the poet's educational biography (stanzas 39–48), his Shaṭṭāriyya lineage (stanzas 49–67), and his advice on reading and teachers (stanzas 67–84). Finally, the *suluk* concludes by emphatically locating itself as heir to and participant in the Sufi literary traditions of Java, traditions of merit (Jv. *pédah*) whose teachings point to a kind of knowledge that is not finally subject to the constraints of the logical mind (Jv. *akal*).

While valorizing writing, both *suluk* at the same time prioritize the supra-discursive knowledge that proper reading practices can cultivate. In *Suluk Acih*, Ronggasasmita cautions his readers repeatedly not to be carried away by the written word, but to bring the word to life, in practice. Similarly, in *Suluk Martabat Sanga*, readers are warned against the slavish rationality that precludes the experience of unknowingness that marks humanity's ultimate return to God. In their relation to the Islamic written word, both *suluk* take a critical stance toward the science of jurisprudence. Although neither is hostile to the sharī'a itself, both are critical of the overinflation of the law and especially of the narrow interpretations of those who are carried away by an incessant focus on *fiqh*, the science of sharī'a. *Suluk Acih* is more measured in its criticism than is *Suluk Martabat Sanga*, which, as we have seen, seems to imply that a focus limited to the law can form an impediment to success along the mystical path. In *Suluk Acih*, Ronggasasmita is particularly critical of those who think that the final, ultimate wisdom is to be found in the study of jurisprudence at the level of the book—as an academic discursive practice. This, he says, strays into the domain of idolatry of the written word, which he condemns as a form of *syirk* (polytheism).[79]

For Ronggasasmita, the ultimate wisdom is not to be discovered in academic exercises, but rather realized through other forms of practice, including not only specifically Shaṭṭāriyya ritual and knowledge practices, but also the social action that the fully realized man or woman will perform in the course of his or her everyday life. This complex of praxis culminates in the supra-discursive experience of *ma'rifa* (gnosis), in which the perfected practitioner then abides. The mark of one who has come to Real knowledge—who has achieved the divine end (and simultaneously the divine beginning) of his or her mystical journey—is not the mastery of writing but to have been dissolved into all writing slates and all writing—to have been dissolved into all life.[80] In Ronggasasmita's *suluk*, the end is not in disembodied abstraction, but in the dissolution of the perfectly realized man into life. His *suluk*, like those composed by his ancestors whether by blood or by spirit, were written to be useful—to have *pédah*. The *suluk* were composed to draw those who could read them carefully toward a state of productive perplexity, a space out of which they could move from venal worldliness to the realization of a form of worldly perfection like that most perfectly embodied by the Prophet—to lead them to experience what it is to "die before you die" and to sustain that experience in lives of purposeful action. The final lines of *Suluk Martabat Sanga* read:

> [83] . . . .
> It is impossible that the saints would have
>
> [84] Written the *suluk*s were they without merit [*pédah*]
> Nay, they were created
> As teachings for the future
> So by "taking care" I mean
>
> [85] Don't drown in the life of this world
> Within your lives of valor [*kawiryan*]
> Live in practiced mindfulness [*prihatin*]
> To die before dying—in life!
> (*Suluk Martabat Sanga*)[81]

THE SHAṬṬĀRIYYA IN JAVA AFTER 1830

I will conclude this cursory introduction to the Shaṭṭāriyya in the literary world of the Kraton Surakarta with some preliminary notes on the shifting position of the *tarekat* after 1830. An examination of manuscripts now stored in the three royal repositories of Surakarta suggests that the composition of new Shaṭṭārī-scented *suluk* by the court's literati came to a near standstill with the close of the Dipanagara War. This apparently sudden shift in literary practice was no doubt a consequence, in part, of the vicissitudes of that war. Prince Dipanagara and his spiritual advisor, Kyai Maja, were both disciples of the Shaṭṭāriyya, as no doubt were many, if not most, of the Islamic teachers who provided the core support of the rebellion. With their defeat and with the shifting policies of the colonial government toward "political Islam" in the wake of that war, Shaṭṭārī Sufism as a subject for literary composition may well have become an uncomfortable, if not dangerous, prospect for court literati.[82] As we have seen, several members of Surakarta's Yasadipuran literary family, almost certainly including Ronggasasmita, had disappeared into exile in the course of that war. The apparent decline of the Shaṭṭāriyya after 1830 was not, however, confined to the literary circles of the Surakarta palace and was not merely a function of local political developments.

By the second half of the nineteenth century, it was a newly invigorated Naqshbandiyya that was becoming ascendant across Java as the Shaṭṭāriyya was fading into the background. Reflecting developments that were sweeping across the Muslim world, the Naqshbandiyya of this period bore distinct "reformist" characteristics: it appears to have placed more emphasis on observation of the five pillars of Islamic practice than had the Shaṭṭāriyya—or, for that matter, the earlier Naqshbandiyya.[83] It also attracted a more popular following than appears to have been the case for the earlier *tarekat*.[84] Surviving manuscript evidence suggests that the earlier Naqshbandiyya and the Shaṭṭāriyya may have been reserved to more elite circles (royals, high officials, and religious teachers—including those in the countryside, many of whom, like Kyai Maja, were associated with the court).[85] No doubt the reformed Naqshbandiyya generated both new lineages and new, more expansive, networks.

The success of the Naqshbandiyya in its competition with the Shaṭṭāriyya for adherents in the Malay world was no doubt accelerated by the increased flow of ideas and pilgrims to and from the Hijaz and the archipelago made possible by the advent of steam travel and the opening of the Suez Canal in 1869. Malay pilgrims were always highly attuned to developments in the Haramayn, and, by the later years of the nineteenth century, the Shaṭṭāriyya had become unfashionable in Mekka. The aspirant Sufi practitioners from the Jāwī world sojourning in the Haramayn were instead flocking to the Naqshbandiyya—as well as to the new Qādiriyya wa'l-Naqshbandiyya order.[86] The greatly expanded body of returning pilgrims brought the newly ascendant Naqsyabandiyya and Qādiriyya wa'l-Naqshbandiyya teachings back to Java with them. It is not at all surprising that it was these lineages and disciplines, then, that found favor among the spiritual seekers of Java who revered and followed these hajjis.

The prominence of the Naqshbandiyya at the Surakarta court (and other royal circles) in the early 1880s is well documented in Michael Laffan's study of changing Dutch perceptions of Islam in Java.[87] However, by the end of the century the Naqshbandiyya, too, appear to have faded from the palace scene.[88] At the very least, there is manuscript evidence from 1885 attesting that there were members of court society who heavily censured the Naqshbandīs and their practices, prescribing instead even more recently "reformed" models of Islamic practice.[89] Although *suluk*, including Shaṭṭārī *suluk*, continued to be copied and circulated in manuscript form among Surakartan elites up through the early twentieth century, a survey of *suluk* texts in the Surakarta palace suggests that there was a sharp drop in this manuscript production at the court after 1886. Fewer *suluk* were copied, and almost no new *suluk* were composed.

After that time, the (notably few) new "mystical" manuscripts that were produced in court circles had taken a turn toward what was thought a specifically Javanese mysticism (*kejawèn*) that was sometimes colored by theosophical speculations.

Perhaps anticipating this turn to what were to be understood as specifically Javanese knowledges, in 1850 Ronggasasmita's celebrated nephew, the *pujongga* Ronggawarsita (1802–1873), compiled his prose treatise of Muslim mystical doctrine and practice that he titled *Wirid Hidayat Jati* (Litany of true guidance).[90] Many of the knowledges presented in this treatise bear resemblance to those found in Shaṭṭārī texts. But there are also significant differences. The teachings are not attributed to a Shaṭṭārī tradition that traces its lineage back to the Prophet Muḥammad; rather, the teachings provided in this *True Guidance* are said to have originated in Java, to have been first composed by eight of the usually nine saints (*wali*) credited with having brought Islam to Java.[91] According to Ronggawarsita, each of these Javanese saints created his own school of mystical knowledge. But, while establishing these schools as specifically Javanese, Ronggawarsita was also careful to emphasize that each of them was based firmly in the four principal sources of Islamic law: the Qur'ān, *ḥadīth*, *ijmā*ʿ, and *qiyās*. These eight "schools" progressed through four generations of eight Javanese saints, finally to be brought together as one under the guidance of Sultan Agung, who ruled the kingdom of Mataram in the first half of the seventeenth century.[92] It is the eight combined as one by the king that form the "True Guidance." Toward the close of his treatise, Ronggawarsita differentiates this true guidance from other lesser forms of knowledge (*ngèlmu*). These lesser forms are instrumental knowledges concerned, he says, with performing miracles (*ngèlmu talèk*) and unlocking the spirit world (*ngèlmu patah*). Ronggawarsita enumerates nine forms of *ngèlmu patah*.[93] Among the knowledges that he categorizes as forms of "spiritism" are, shockingly, the teachings of the Shaṭṭāriyya—along with those of the Naqshbandiyya, Majalis, Sufi, Khahfi, and Patahulrahman. The less than positive evaluation of the remaining three *ngèlmus* is less surprising as they are more recognizable as what could be considered magical-mystical forms of knowledge. None of the nine, he emphasizes, is congruent with true spiritual knowledge, and all of them can lead to argument and thus ultimately to unbelief.[94]

And yet there is evidence suggesting that Ronggawarsita himself was a Shaṭṭārī master. A solitary manuscript witness of his uncle Ronggasasmita's *Suluk Martabat Sanga* that was inscribed in Surakarta in 1872, a year before the *pujongga*'s death, continues Ronggasasmita's Shaṭṭārī genealogy for two more generations. According to this witness, Ronggasasmita passed the Shaṭṭārī teachings on to none other than said nephew Ronggawarsita, who in turn guided two lower-level Kraton Surakarta courtiers along the path.[95] Although Ronggawarsita is not—and apparently would not have been pleased to be—remembered as a disciple (much less a *murshid*) of the Shaṭṭāriyya, this manuscript evidence suggests otherwise. Perhaps the "seal of the *pujongga*" felt it necessary to disguise his Shaṭṭāriyya genealogy in the wake of the Dipanagara War that had claimed his father, the elder Ronggawarsita, and his uncle, the hajji Ronggasasmita who authored the *suluk* that has been at the heart of this chapter.

NOTES

I am grateful to Anne Blackburn and Michael Feener for their helpful comments on earlier drafts of this chapter. Any mistakes and shortcomings remain my own.

1. That the elder Ronggawarsita was exiled is sufficiently well known; that his younger brother was exiled along with him, however, appears to have vanished from historical memory. An entry in a prose dynastic history composed in the Surakarta palace around 1831 records the exile of the two brothers: "Mas Ronggawarsita, Mantri Lurah Carik of the crown prince's administration, was exiled by the Dutch government along with his younger brother, Mas Haji, in punishment for their involvement in the rebellion of Prince Dipanagara on Friday, the 24th of Sawal Alip 1755 [May 9, 1828]" (*Serat Babad Sangkala kang Urut saking Kagungan Dalem Serat Babad* [composed and inscribed in the Kraton Surakarta, ca. 1831], ms. Kraton Surakarta [henceforth KS] 1 C [6 Ta], p. 127). For a comprehensive history of the Dipanagara War, see Peter Carey's *The Power of Prophecy: Prince Dipanagara and the End of an Old Order in Java, 1785–1855* (Leiden: KITLV Press, 2008).

2. A *pujongga* is a poet-scholar who has received the revealed divine power (*wahyu*) of prophecy. It also names an office in the palace of the Kraton Surakarta. Yasadipura I, Yasadipura II, and the younger Ronggawarsita were the last three to hold this office. After his death, Ronggawarsita was known as the seal (*panutup*) of the *pujongga*, echoing the Prophet Muḥammad's distinction as the "seal of the prophets" (*nabi panutup*). For more on this literati family and on the problematic of the Surakarta "literary renaissance," see Nancy K. Florida, "Writing Traditions in Colonial Java: The Question of Islam," in *Cultures of Scholarship*, edited by S. C. Humphreys (Ann Arbor: University of Michigan Press, 1997), pp. 187–217.

3. The overwhelming majority of texts belonging to Javanese manuscript literature are anonymous. R. T. Sastranagara, Ronggasasmita's father, was one of the very few early nineteenth-century authors who identified himself in some of his works. From around the middle of the nineteenth century, a practice known as *sandiasma* appeared in which some authors—notably the *pujongga* Ronggawarsita—signed their compositions in acrostics embedded in the opening lines of their works. The style of Ronggasasmita's "signatures" in these two *Suluk Acih* texts is truly exceptional. In *Suluk Acih* "proper" he not only identifies himself, but also notes the historical circumstances of the poem's composition. In *Suluk Martabat Sanga*, Ronggasasmita identifies himself in the uniquely versified Shaṭṭārī *silsila* that he provides following the extremely rare—that is, the only one that I am aware of—narrative describing his early educational experiences.

4. For descriptions of these manuscripts, the oldest of which was inscribed in 1845 and the youngest in the early twentieth century, see Nancy K. Florida, *Javanese Literature in Surakarta Manuscripts*, vols. 1–3 (New York: Cornell University SEAP, 1993, 2000, 2012).

5. On the Leiden manuscripts and for preliminary philological notes on the *suluk*, see Edwin Wieringa, "Aanvullende gegevens over de Suluk Acih van Ranggasasmita," *Bijdragen tot de Taal-, Land- en Volkenkunde* 149.2 (1993): 362–373.

6. Ronggasasmita provides his Shaṭṭārī *silsila* in *Suluk Martabat Sanga*, a text that is almost invariably included in *Suluk Acih* compilations. There are numerous manuscript witnesses of this text, several of which will be referenced in this chapter. My primary sources will be the *Suluk Martabat Sanga* texts in *Serat Suluk Warni-warni tuwin Wirid Syattariyah* (inscribed in Surakarta for K.G.P.H. Cakradiningrat by R. Panji Jayaasmara, 1864), ms. Museum Radya Pustaka [henceforth RP] 333, pp. 83–95; and in *Serat Suluk Acih* (inscribed in the Kraton Surakarta for Pakubuwana IX, 1867), ms. KS 502 (15 Ca), pp. 46–57.

7. In this, developments in Java appear to parallel broader historical trends across the region. See Chapter 1 in this volume by Anne Blackburn and Michael Feener.

8. K. A. Nizami, "Shaṭṭāriyya," in *Encyclopaedia of Islam, Second Edition*, edited by P. Bearman, Th. Bianquis, C. E. Bosworth, E. van Donzel, and W. P. Heinrichs (Brill Online, 2012), http://referenceworks.brillonline.com/entries/encyclopaedia-of-islam-2/shattariyya-SIM_6869, accessed May 13, 2015.

9. On the spread of the Shaṭṭāriyya in Southeast Asia, see Oman Fathurahman, *Tarekat Syattariyah di Minangkabau* (Jakarta: Prenada Media Group, 2008), pp. 25–40; and Fakhriati, *Menelusuri Tarekat Syattariyah di Aceh lewat Naskah* (Jakarta: Departemen Agama RI, 2008).

10. Sèh Muhammad Gos is included in the *silsila* that Ronggasasmita provides in *Suluk Martabat Sanga* and is cited as an authority of Shaṭṭārī discipline in the most extensive textbook of the practice and doctrine of the *tarekat* now extant in the Surakartan archives (R. T. Arungbinang, *Bab Dérah ing Ngèlmi Tarèk Wiriding Dikir*, in *Serat Suluk Warni-warni tuwin Wirid Syattariyah* [inscribed by R. Panji Jayaasmara for K.G.P.H. Cakradiningrat, 1864], ms. RP 333, p. 326).

11. Saiyid Athar Abbas Rizvi, *A History of Sufism in India*, vol. 2 (New Delhi: Munshiram Monoharial, 1983), pp. 159–160. For more on Muḥammad Ghawth and his place in the formation of Shaṭṭārī Sufi traditions, see Carl Ernst's "Persecution and Circumspection in Shaṭṭārī Sufism," in *Islamic Mysticism Contested: Thirteen Centuries of Controversies and Polemics*, edited by de Frederik Jong and Bernd Radtke (Leiden: Brill, 1999), pp. 416–435; and Scott Kugle's "Heaven's Witness: The Uses and Abuses of Muḥammad Ghawth's Mystical Ascension," *Journal of Islamic Studies* 14.1 (January 2003): 1–36.

12. The Javanese word *awak*, which can be translated as "self," means "body." The word *awakku* (my body) translates as "I" or "me"; *awakmu* (your body), as "you." *Sarira* (self) is also glossed as "body," "person," and "you." Fortuitously, owing to its sound (that is, like the Arabic *sirr*), *sarira* also and at the same time suggests "the inmost secret (self)." The Old Javanese *śarīra*, again denoting body, self, and person, is from the Sanskrit *śarīra*, a word that in Buddhist terminology designates "a sacred relic"—in particular a relic from the mummified remains, or the cremains, of a Buddhist saint.

13. Whereas the presence of the Shaṭṭāriyya *tarekat* among court circles in the Cirebon palace has received considerable scholarly attention, the prominence of the *tarekat*'s teachings in the Surakartan court has been heretofore overlooked. On the Shaṭṭāriyya in Cirebon, see Martin van Bruinessen's contribution to this volume and Abdul Ghoffir Muhaimin, *The Islamic Traditions of Cirebon: Ibadat and Adat among Javanese Muslims* (Jakarta: Ministry of Religious Affairs, 2004).

14. Without exception, the Javanese Shaṭṭāriyya *silsila*s that I have seen always identify ʿAbd al-Raʾūf as belonging to the family, or "the people," of Ḥamza Fanṣūrī ("Sèh Ngabdul Raup, putra Ngali ingkang [a]bangsa Sèh Kamjah Pansuri"). See, for example, the *silsila*

published in: Oman Fathurahman, *Shaṭṭāriyah Silsilah in Aceh, Java, and the Lanao area of Mindanao* (Tokyo: Research Institute for Languages and Cultures of Asia and Africa, Tokyo University of Foreign Studies, 2016). The connection between Ḥamza and Abd al-Ra'ūf may, however, have been less direct than this would imply; see Oman Fathurahman, *Tanbih al-Masyi Menyoal Wahdatul Wujud: Kasus Abdurrauf Singkel di Aceh Abad 17* (Bandung: Mizan, 1999), p. 26. On the date of Ḥamza Fanṣūrī's death, see L. Kalus and C. Guillot, "La stèle funéraire de Hamzah Fansuri," *Archipel* 60 (2000): 3–24. Although Kalus and Guillot's argument for the 1527 date is convincing, it has been contested by V. I. Braginsky in his "On the Copy of Hamzah Fansuri's Epitaph Published by C. Guillot & L. Kalus," *Archipel* 62 (2001): 21–33. For more on this theological conflict at the Acehnese court, see Syed Muhammad Naguib Al-Attas, *Rānīrī and the Wujūdiyyah of 17th Century Aceh* (Singapore: MBRAS, 1966).

15. The teachings that came to be known as *waḥdat al-wujūd* (or sometimes *wujūdiyya*) are rooted in the intricate and sometimes ecstatic cosmological metaphysics that was developed by the great Andalusian Sufi master Ibn 'Arabī (1165–1240). Ibn 'Arabī 's metaphysics explores the multiple levels of being and potential nonbeing through which God eternally discloses Himself in His creation. The disclosure moves from God's absolute unknowable, immutable, eternal essence through real being in the creative Reality of the Light of Muḥammad, to possible/relative being as God eternally impresses Himself onto nonbeing (that which-is-not), thus to make manifest His Reality in creation.

16. See 'Abd al-Ra'ūf, "Autobiographical Codicil to 'Umdat al-Muhtajin,'" in *Transferring a Tradition: 'Abd al-Ra'ūf al-Singkili's Rendering into Malay of the Jalalayn Commentary*, edited by Peter Riddell (Berkeley: University of California Centers for South and Southeast Asian Studies, 1990), pp. 222–238. In addition to his Shaṭṭāriyya *silsila*, the "autobiographical codicil" also provides 'Abd al-Ra'ūf's Qādiriyya *silsila* along with a listing of the great number of other scholars and Sufis with whom he studied in the Arabian peninsula.

17. On this relationship, see Anthony H. Johns, "Friends in Grace: Ibrahim al-Kurani and 'Abd al-Ra'uf al-Singkeli," in *Spectrum: Essays Presented to Sultan Takdir Alisjahbana*, edited by S. Udin (Jakarta: Dian Rakyat, 1978), pp. 469–485.

18. It was Shams al-Dīn Pasai who first introduced these teachings into the Malay world; for a wonderful essay on Shams al-Dīn's major work on the *martabat tujuh*, see Anthony H. Johns, "Shams al-Dīn al-Sumaṭrā'ī," in *Essays in Arabic Literary Biography, 1350–1850*, edited by Joseph E. Lowry and Devin J. Stewart (Wiesbaden: Harrassaowitz Verlag, 2009), pp. 357–371. As Shams al-Dīn's writings had been suppressed and many of his works destroyed during the purge in the early 1640s, it was 'Abd al-Ra'ūf who reintroduced and disseminated the *martabat tujuh* teachings among the Jāwa. His teachings had no doubt gained elaboration from his Shaṭṭārī *murshid*, Aḥmad al-Qushāshī. For more on textual traditions of "seven-grade" Shaṭṭārī Sufism in Southeast Asia, see A. H. Johns, *The Gift Addressed to the Spirit of the Prophet* (Canberra: Australian National University, 1965). Johns' book is a translation and commentary on an eighteenth-century Javanese poetic interpretation of the Arabic *Tuḥfa* that was composed by Muḥammad b. Faḍlillāh (d. 1620) in Gujarat. The *Tuḥfa* was highly influential in seventeenth-century Aceh. Internal textual evidence indicates that the Javanese poetic interpretation was produced by its anonymous author on commission of the ruler of Cirebon.

19. Ngabdul Muhyi ('Abd al-Muḥyī) is buried in Pamijahan (or Safarwidi, Karang) in the Tasikmalaya district of West Java. His tomb was described by D. A. Rinkes in 1910 in his article "De maqam van Sjech 'Abdoelmoehji," *Tijdschrift voor Indische Taal-, Land- en Volkenkunde* 52 (1910): 556–574. H. M. Froger's English translation of the article can be found in D. A.

Rinkes, *Nine Saints of Java* (Kuala Lumpur: Malaysian Sociological Research Institute, 1996), pp. 1–14. The tomb remains an important shrine today and still attracts many pilgrims.

20. For more on ʿAbd al-Muḥyī, see Werner Kraus, "An Enigmatic Saint: Sheykh Haji Abdul Muhyi Waliyullah Pamijahan (?1640–1715?)," *Indonesian Circle* 65 (1995): 21–31; Tommy Christomy, *Signs of the Wali: Narratives at the Sacred Sites in Pamijahan, West Java* (Canberra: ANU E Press, 2008).

21. See, for example, the saint's teaching on the seven levels of the human soul in *Wasiyat saking Ngabdul Mukiyi Pajang*, in *Serat Suluk Warni-warni* (compiled and inscribed in Surakarta, 1886), ms. RP 332, pp. 116–117, and other more "magical" teachings attributed to him (and to ʿAbd al-Raʾūf) in *Èsmu: Waris saking Tuwan Sèh Ngabdul Rakub* (compiled and inscribed in Surakarta, [mid-nineteenth century]), ms. RP 334, pp. 20–26.

22. Christomy, *Signs of the Wali*, pp. 103–104. See also R. Ng. Ronggawarsita, *Serat Sarasilah: Urutipun Panjenengan Nata ing Tanah Jawi Awit Panjenengan Ratu Prabu Déwatacengkar, Medhangkamulan* (compiled Surakarta, mid-nineteenth century; inscribed Surakarta, 1878), ms. Mangkunagaran [henceforth MN] 245 (Rekso Pustoko B 84), pp. 45–46.

23. Merle C. Ricklefs, *The Seen and Unseen Worlds in Java 1726–1749: History, Literature and Islam in the Court of Pakubuwana II* (St. Leonards, Australia: Allen and Unwin, 1998).

24. Pakubuwana II, *Serat Wulang-Dalem Sampéyan-Dalem Ingkang Sinuhun Kangjeng Susuhunan kaping II* (composed Panaraga? ca. 1742 and Surakarta 1845; inscribed in the Kraton Surakarta for the future Pakubuwana X 1885/1886), ms. KS 367 (210 Na-B).

25. Pakubuwana III, *Suluk Martabat Wahdat Wakidiyat* (composed Surakarta, late eighteenth century), in *Serat Suluk: Jaman Karaton Dalem ing Surakarta* (inscribed in the Kraton Surakarta by Ng. Hawikrama, 1870), ms. KS 481 (244 Na), pp. 30–35.

26. Ronggasasmita, *Suluk Martabat Sanga*, stanzas 59–61, in *Serat Suluk Acih*, ms. KS 502 (15 Ca), p. 54.

27. Kyai T. Arungbinang, *Bab Dérah ing Ngèlmi Tarèk Wiriding Dikir* (composed Surakarta, early nineteenth century), in *Serat Suluk Warni-warni tuwin Wirid Syattariyah* (inscribed in Surakarta by R. Panji Jayaasmara for K.G.P.H. Cakradiningrat, 1864), ms. RP 333, pp. 300–471.

28. Although Arungbinang's *silsila* clearly marks Bagus Muhyidin as ʿAbd al-Muḥyī's son (*Bab Dérah ing Ngèlmi Tarèk Wiriding Dikir*, ms. RP 333, p. 312), Tommy Christomy identifies him as ʿAbd al-Muḥyī's grandson (*Signs of the Wali*, p. 105).

29. In addition to Shaṭṭārī metaphysical thought and practice, Abdul Gani also taught the "external knowledges" (*ngèlmu lahir*) that had been handed down to him from "Panembahan Kawis" (ʿAbd al-Muḥyī). These "external knowledges" comprise formulae (*ngèlmu, ismu*) and prayers (*donga*) that are designed to enhance the adept's powers in the phenomenal world—when they are recited in accordance with the designated conditions. Among these knowledges are formulae to activate one's shadow self (Makdum Sarpin), to protect oneself from iron weapons, to enhance one's invulnerability (*kateguhan, katimbulan*), and to make oneself invisible to enemies (Arungbinang, *Bab Dérah ing Ngèlmi Tarèk Wiriding Dikir*, ms. RP 333, pp. 423–445). The final section of Arungbinang's *Bab Dérah* comprises a translation of an extended excerpt from al-Ghazālī's *Bidayāt al-Hidāya* (Beginning of guidance) (ms. RP 333, pp. 446–471).

30. Arungbinang, *Bab Dérah*, in *Serat Suluk Warni-warni tuwin Wirid Syattariyah*, RP 333.

31. For Cakradiningrat's astounding web of genealogical connections with Surakartan kings and nobles along with his connection to the most celebrated of Surakartan literati, see Florida, *Javanese Literature in Surakarta Manuscripts*, vol. 3, p. 241.

32. The word *zikir* (Ar. *dhikr*), or "remembrance," indicates the practice of remembering God through the repetition of formulae or utterances among travelers on the mystic path.

33. *Ṣalāt* is the ritual practice of devotion that every Muslim is required to offer to God five times a day. *Salat daim* knows no time; it is perpetual. Arungbinang's *suluk* is *Suluk saking Kitab Markun*, which is to be found in *Serat Suluk: Jaman Karaton Dalem ing Surakarta*, ms. KS 481 (244 Na), pp. 243–258.

34. Among these *suluk* are *Suluk Dhudha tanpa Sekar*, *Suluk Purwaduksina*, *Suluk Dumunung in Manah*, *Suluk Dumunung ing Toya*, *Suluk Dumung ing Siti*, and *Suluk Kitab Usul-mubin*; manuscript witnesses of these *suluk* are found in *Serat Suluk: Jaman Karaton Dalem in Surakarta*, ms. KS 481 (244 Na), pp. 39–80. For other *suluk* attributed to Pakubuwana IV, see the listings in my *Surakarta Literature in Javanese Manuscripts*, vols. 1–3.

35. The princesses' mother was K. Ratu Kencana II. Later elevated to the position of R. Ayu Sekar Kedaton and then to that of K. Ratu Pembayun, R. Ayu Satariyah was the highest-ranking princess at Pakubuwana IV's court. Ki Padmasusastra and R. Ng. Wirapratana, *Sejarah Ageng in Karaton Surakarta* (composed Surakarta, 1900), ms. MN 670 (B 77), pp. 96–97.

36. M. Ng. Ronggasasmita and M. Ng. Tepasonta II, *Suluk Martabat Sanga*, in *Suluk Acih Tepasantan* (composed Surakarta, 1820; inscribed Surakarta, 1845), ms. MN 304 (A 90), pp. 52–53. The Teposantan manuscript is (or was), to my knowledge, the oldest surviving *Suluk Acih* witness. Sadly, when I last visited the Mangkunagaran in 2012, this manuscript appeared to be no longer extant in the Rekso Pustoko library.

37. Although reproduction and redaction of earlier texts without attribution were common practices among "classical" Javanese writers, this case was exceptional because of the unusual nature of Ronggasasmita's text: in his reproduction of Ronggasasmita's text, Teposanta effectively appropriated Ronggasasmita's personal autobiographical narrative (and experience) as his own.

38. The poem was first published in its entirety just a little over twenty years ago. This edition (in twelve volumes) was produced by the tireless Yogyanese scholar of Javanese literature Kamajaya (a.k.a. Partono K. Kartokusumo). *Serat Centhini*, vols. 1–12, edited by Kamajaya (Yogyakarta: Yayasan Centhini Yogyakarta, 1985–1991).

39. For explicit mention of these practices, see the following stanzas in the Kamajaya edition of the *Centhini*: canto 354, stanza 66 (*Centhini*, vol. 5, p. 154); canto 360, stanza 4 (6:56); canto 362, stanza 12 (6:105); canto 365, stanza 49 (6:157); canto 366, stanza 42 (6:165); canto 368, stanza 2 (6:204); canto 368, stanza 31 (6:208); canto 383, stanza 218 (7:120); canto 383, stanza 241 (7:123); canto 667, stanza 96 (11:173); canto 672, stanza 145 (12:224); canto 675, stanza 16 (12:244); canto 708, stanza 485 (12:224). On the fusion of Shaṭṭāriyya and Naqshbandiyya practices, see also Martin van Bruinessen, *Tarekat Naqsyabandiyah di Indonesia: Survei Historis, Geografis dan Sosiologis* (Bandung: Mizan, 1992), pp. 43–45.

40. Dipanagara, "Salasilah Kiai Mojo Tondano," Menado 15-12-1919, ms. LOr (Leiden Oriental) 8652k, cited in Carey, *Power of Prophecy*, p. 111.

41. The Dipanagara War (also known as the "Java War") was no small-scale rebellion. At a time when the population of the entire island of Java numbered some seven million, the war claimed at least 200,000 Javanese lives; Yogyakarta's population was reduced by half. Fifteen

thousand colonial troops (seven thousand of whom were "Indonesians") also perished in the war. Merle C. Ricklefs, *A History of Modern Indonesia since c. 1200*, 3rd edition (Stanford, CA: Stanford University Press, 2001), p. 153.

42. Kyai Maja's father, Kyai Badheran (Ngabdul Arif), was installed as *'ulamā pradikan* of Badheran, and later of Maja, by Pakubuwana IV. He was tasked with, among other things, praying for the welfare of the realm of Surakarta and coming to court to attend the state meetings convened by the palace's leading religious official (the Pengulu). Like his son, Kyai Badheran had great influence and a large number of pupils in the Surakartan palace. Peter Carey, *Babad Dipanagara: An Account of the Outbreak of the Java War (1825–1830)* (Kuala Lumpur: Malaysian Branch of the Royal Asiatic Society, 1981), pp. 261–262, n. 110.

43. On Buminata, see note 58 below.

44. Carey, *Power of Prophecy*, pp. 90–114.

45. Among the most copied of these was Ronggasasmita's *Suluk Acih.* In the mid-1880s there appears to have been a spike in the number of *suluk* copied in the Surakartan palace—a number of these for the crown prince who would later reign as Pakubuwana X; see my *Javanese Literature in Surakarta Manuscripts*, vol. 1, pp. 264–279. Several later nineteenth-century texts produced at the palace do carry faint scents of Shaṭṭārī thought. One of these is a prose treatise attributed to Pakubuwana VIII (1789–1861; r. 1858–1861), which is said to form the king's mystical manual (*wirid*). The text, which is largely preoccupied with locating particular Sufi concepts and terms in particular human body parts, contains a smattering of Shaṭṭāriyya terminology but no systematic metaphysics. This text was apparently also used by Pakubuwana X (1866–1939; r. 1893–1939) as the manual that he employed to instruct his own students (*Serat Wirid-dalem Sampéyan-dalem Ingkang Sinuhun Kangjeng Susuhunan Pakubuwana ingkang kaping VIII, Bab Ngèlmu Kasampurnan* [compiled Surakarta, mid-nineteenth century; inscribed at court of Pakubuwana X], ms. KS 524 [68 Sa]). In the poetic instructions that he delivered to his son, the then ten-year-old crown prince, Pakubuwana IX advises him to find teachers with knowledge of the "writing of the body" from the "four *tarekat*," suggesting specifically that he learn from them the knowledge of the "seven and nine grades of being." Again, the poem does not provide any metaphysical elaborations (Pakubuwana IX, *Wulang Putra* [Surakarta, 1976], in *Piwulang-dalem Warni-warni* [inscribed in the Kraton Surakarta for Pakubuwana X, 1913], ms. KS 336 [256 Ca], p. 1177).

46. Dates of composition and inscription in Javanese manuscripts, when they are provided, are almost always composed through *candrasangkala* (or chronograms), aphoristic phrases whose words when read backwards signify—by a logical system of associative conventions—various numerical values. For example, words associated with eyes mean "two." Words associated with fire mean "three," because *guna*, "fire" or "ability," also means "three" in Sanskrit. The present *sangkala* is *Naya Suci Pandhita Aji*: "Countenance" (2) "Pure" (4) "Priest" (7) "King" (1) = 1742. The seventh of Rabinguawal Jé 1742 fell on the seventeenth of February 1815.

47. *Suluk Acih*, stanzas 10–12, ms. KS 502 (15 Ca), p. 2.

48. In another of his poetic works (no doubt drawing on his own experience), Ronggasasmita wrote of the sea voyage of another small group of Muslim pilgrims, that is, of the saints who are said to have brought Islam to Java in the fifteenth century. The narrative is vivid, telling, for example, how the pilgrims persuaded a trader to take them on his vessel, the time spent in trading ports along the way, the trader's inconstancy, and a shipwreck. Ronggasasmita, *Serat Walisana*, edited by Tanoyo (Surakarta: Sadubudi, 1955), pp. 5–11.

49. The conquest of the Haramayn by the Wahhābīs in the first decade of the nineteenth century had interrupted the pilgrimage and had certainly made Mekka unconducive to Sufi practitioners. It was only in 1813 that Mekka and Medina were wrested from the Wahhābīs by Egyptian troops in the Ottoman reconquest. I am presuming, then, that Ronggasasmita and his uncle would have been dissuaded from performing the hajj during this Wahhābī interval.

50. I am grateful to both Michael Feener and Sebastian Prange for their assistance concerning the seasonal sailing schedules between Aceh and the holy lands. Pilgrims would embark from Aceh during the winter monsoon (late December to the beginning of February) to catch the westerly currents across the Indian Ocean. The voyage would take at least six weeks but could be much longer depending on the route (via the Bay of Bengal, the Maldives, or straight for Aden via Laṅkā). On the return voyage, pilgrims would set off from Aden during either the long monsoon (mid-March to early May) or the short monsoon that began in mid- to late August (Michael Feener and Sebastian Prange, personal communication, January 2013).

51. *Primbon* (from *rimbu*, Kawi for "to secrete, to save away") designates a body of texts that form compilations of various forms of esoteric knowledge, with Sufi knowledge figuring prominently among them. Ronggasasmita is straightforward and, as it turns out, completely honest in the description of his project. For we find in Arungbinang's Shaṭṭārī treatise what appears to be a witness of the very *primbon* text that was selectively rendered into nuanced poetry by Ronggasasmita to compose his *Suluk Acih* (*Bab Dérah ing Ngèlmi Tarèk Wiriding Dikir*, ms. RP 333, pp. 389–398).

52. *Suluk Acih*, stanzas 6–9, ms. KS 502 (15 Ca), pp. 1–2.

53. Yasadipura I, *Babad Giyanti*, 21 vols. (Batavia: Balai Poestaka, 1937–1939).

54. For a textual edition and English translation of this work, see S. Soebardi, *The Book of Cabolèk* (The Hague: Martinus Nijhoff, 1975).

55. Yasadipura I, *Serat Ménak*, 25 vols. (Batavia: Bale Pustaka, 1933–1937).

56. R. Ng. Yasadipura I, *Suluk Déwaruci* (composed Surakarta, 1793/1794), in *Serat Suluk: Jaman Karaton-Dalem ing Surakarta*, ms. KS 481 (244 Na), pp. 198–242.

57. Yasadipura I's *Suluk Makmun Nurhadi Salikin* is a metaphysical Sufi poem that bears within it traces of Shaṭṭārī teachings. It also calls explicitly for strict adherence to the sharīʿa, as do many, but not all, other Shaṭṭāriyya-tinged texts of the late eighteenth- and early-nineteenth-century Surakartan palace (R. Ng.Yasadipura I, *Suluk Makmun Nurhadi Salikin* [composed Surakarta, late nineteenth century], in *Serat Suluk: Jaman Karaton-Dalem ing Surakarta* [inscribed in the Kraton Surakarta by Ng. Hawikrama, 1870], ms. KS 481 [244 Na], pp. 190–197, 305–309).

58. The Kadipatèn was the governing institution within the Kraton Surakarta normally associated with the crown prince. From 1820 to 1858, there was no crown prince, however. G. P. Adipati Buminata, a younger brother of Pakubuwana IV and a patron of the Yasadipura-Ronggawarsita family, headed the Kadipatèn from 1820 until his death in 1834. As noted above, Buminata had been a confidant of the Shaṭṭāriyya teacher and revolutionary Kyai Maja.

59. The first *suluk* is *Suluk Panduking Dudunungan*; the second is *Suluk Burung*. Both are to be found in *Serat Suluk: Jaman Karaton-Dalem ing Surakarta*, ms. KS 481 (244 Na), pp. 259–266. In another of his works, it is significant that Sastranagara praises ʿAbd al-Muḥyī, the Shaṭṭāriyya shaykh of Karang, as the paragon of learning in contrast to the radical teachers

who had gotten Pakubuwana IV into so much trouble during the early years of his reign (R. T. Sastranagara, *Serat Wicara Keras* [Kedhiri: Tan Khoen Swie, 1926], p. 9). On those troubles, the so-called Pakepung affair, see Merle C. Ricklefs, *Jogyakarta under Sultan Mangkubumi, 1749–1793: A History of the Division of Java* (London: Oxford University Press, 1974), pp. 285–340.

60. The word "sharīʿa" (the Way) is sometimes translated as the "sacred law of Islam." By the "sharīʿa folk" (*ahli sarak*) Ronggasasmita must be referring to the students and/or practitioners of jurisprudence whose task it is to attempt to divine God's Way in order to make their determinations of law (*fiqh*) as to which human actions are required, which advisable, which neutral, which inadvisable, and which forbidden.

61. The *santri dul* were ecstatic Sufis said to be given to excess and licentiousness. They are described in the *Centhini* and appear to be of the *malāmatiyya* (blame seeker) Sufi tradition. For more on the *santri dul*, see Merle C. Ricklefs, *Polarising Javanese Society: Islamic and Other Visions c. 1830–1930* (Singapore: NUS Press, 2007), pp. 36–38.

62. *Ratib* and *sama* are Sufi devotional practices involving music and dance, or voice and movement.

63. Ronggasasmita, *Suluk Martabat Sanga*, stanzas 38–51, in *Serat Suluk Warni-warni tuwin Wirid Syattariyah*, ms. RP 333, pp. 88–90. In the 1867 witness of the poem that was inscribed for Pakubuwana IX (ms. KS 502 [15 Ca]), the stanza numbered 43 here is missing.

64. Though "Madahab" appears to indicate a place name, it may signify here "*the* destination" or, perhaps, "the way out." The Arabic word *madhāhib* (sing. *madhhab*), which often refers to the four "schools" of Islamic jurisprudence, can also indicate more generally the "place one goes to," "way out," or "manner followed." The place of Ronggasasmita's shaykh, then, was the disciple's most favored destination and, at the same time, the way out of his difficulties. I am grateful to Ali Hussain and Michael Feener for these suggestions.

65. The great majority of *Suluk Acih* compilations do, however, include the truly excessive *Suluk Lebé Lonthang*. On this wildly irreverent and simply wild poem, see Nancy K. Florida, "Sex Wars: Writing Gender Relations in Nineteenth-Century Java," in *Fantasizing the Feminine in Indonesia*, edited by L. J. Sears (Durham and London: Duke University Press, 1996), pp. 207–224.

66. On this "tradition" of writing, see S. Soebardi's *The Book of Cabolèk*, pp. 35–45. For a discussion of Sitijenar's "trial" and execution, see Nancy K. Florida, *Writing the Past, Inscribing the Future: History as Prophecy in Colonial Java* (Durham and London: Duke University Press, 1995), pp. 358–366.

67. For a more extended discussion of what Ronggasasmita might mean by diligent reading, see my *Writing the Past, Inscribing the Future*, pp. 1–6. I would be remiss, however, if I did not note that my recent discovery of variant renderings in variant manuscript witnesses of the stanzas that form the basis of my earlier analysis could provide somewhat different senses concerning what defines proper reading practice.

68. *Suluk Martabat Sanga*, stanzas 67–83, in *Suluk Warni-warni*, ms. RP 333, pp. 92–95.

69. *Suluk Martabat Sanga*, stanzas 76–77, in *Suluk Warni-warni*, ms. RP 333, p. 94.

70. *Suluk Martabat Sanga*, stanzas 77–83, in *Suluk Warni-warni*, ms. RP 333, pp. 94–95.

71. *Suluk Martabat Sanga*, stanzas 83–85, in *Suluk Warni-warni*, ms. RP 333, p. 95.

72. I am grateful to Ali Hussain for his suggestion that the poem appears, in the tradition of Ibn ʿArabī, to be describing the Reality of the Prophet (*al-haqīqa al-muḥammadiyya*) as the "presence of gathering" (*ḥaḍrat al-jamʿ*), manifesting perfectly within his presence all the

divine attributes, negative and positive, the entire cosmos in *potentia* (personal communication, February 5, 2013).

73. *Suluk Acih*, stanzas 59–71, ms. KS 502 (15 Ca), pp. 9–10.

74. *Suluk Acih*, stanza 73, ms. KS 502 (15 Ca), p. 10.

75. Ronggasasmita explicitly addresses the potential accusation of pantheism: "Let none of you ever dare/to call Allah the entirety of the material universe. For to call Allah such/is still to see/two beings indeed/and this is unbelief in all four schools of thought" (*Suluk Acih*, stanzas 22–23, ms. KS 502[15 Ca], p. 4). The accusation of monism is addressed in the poet's concern with embodiment, seen perhaps most clearly in his treatment of the being of the Prophet that he elaborates in *Suluk Martabat Sanga*.

76. *Suluk Martabat Sanga*, stanzas 6–10, in *Suluk Warni-warni*, ms. RP 333, p. 84.

77. *Suluk Acih*, stanza 13, ms. KS 502 (15 Ca), p. 2.

78. Ronggasasmita's translations of the Arabic terms are at times nonstandard—if not idiosyncratic. He calls the highest of the nine grades of the Prophet's being *junun mukawiyah*, which he identifies as the stage of the undifferentiated void (*awang-awang, uwung-uwung*). The poet then proceeds to translate the word *junun* as *tata* ("manifestation" or "spreading forth," but also "order"). He then splits the word *mukawiyah* into *muka* and *wiyah*, translating *muka* as *rarahi* (the Face) and *wiyah* as *jagad jembar* (the wide world). *Suluk Martabat Sanga*, stanzas 3–5, in *Suluk Warni-warni*, ms. RP 333, pp. 83–84.

79. *Suluk Acih*, stanza 55, ms. KS 502 (15 Ca), p. 8.

80. *Suluk Acih*, stanza 72, ms. KS 502 (15 Ca), p. 10.

81. *Suluk Martabat Sanga*, stanzas 83–85, in *Suluk Warni-warni*, ms. RP 333, p. 95.

82. On these shifting policies and their effects, see my "Writing Traditions in Colonial Java."

83. For a concise and cogent discussion of these developments, see Ricklefs, *Polarising Javanese Society*, pp. 74–79; see also Martin van Bruinessen's contribution to this volume.

84. This appears to have been especially true for the Qādiriyya wa'l-Naqshbandiyya, which became widespread in the later years of the nineteenth century. This was a new order coming out of Mekka whose practices combined those of the Qādiriyya and the Naqshbandiyya.

85. For more on the connections between the court and rural Islamic scholars, see my "Writing Traditions in Colonial Java."

86. C. Snouck Hurgronje, *The Achehnese*, vol. 2 (Leiden: Brill, 1906), pp. 18–20; C. Snouck Hurgronje, *Mekka in the Latter Part of the 19th Century* (Leiden: Brill, 1931). The Qādiriyya wa'l-Naqshbandiyya order was established in Mekka in the mid-nineteenth century, probably by the "Indonesian"-born scholar Aḥmad Khātib b. ʿAbd al-Ghaffar Sambas (see Bruinessen, *Tarekat Naqsyabandiyah di Indonesia*, pp. 89–97).

87. Michael F. Laffan, "'A Watchful Eye': The Mekkan Plot of 1881 and Changing Dutch Perceptions of Islam in Indonesia," *Archipel* 63 (2002): 79–108.

88. This may have been in part a function of Dutch intervention (ibid.).

89. See Muhammad Azali Ibnu Sulaéman's advice poem that was composed in Malay and inscribed in Javanese script—apparently for Pakubuwana IX (*Nasékat Manyanyi* [composed and inscribed in Surakarta, 1885], ms. KS 540).

90. Ronggawarsita's treatise was published in Javanese script in 1908 with the title *Serat Wirid Nyayariyosaken Wewejanganipun Wali 8* (Surakarta: Albert Rusche and Co., 1908). This publication is provided in facsimile, transliterated into Roman script, translated into

Indonesian, and analyzed in Simuh's *Mistik Islam Kejawen Raden Ngabehi Ranggawarsita: Suatu Studi Terhadap Serat Wirid Hidayat Jati* (Jakarta: University of Indonesia Press, 1988).

91. Although the saints who are credited with the Islamization of Java are invariably nine in number (hence their name, the *wali sanga*, or "the nine saints"), *which* nine saints are thought to have composed this group varies considerably. In some texts there are eight (again variably named) axial saints with the ninth of their number being the princely saint (*wali ngumran*), that is, the king who was recognized ruler of Java at the time that they were active. See, for example, my *Writing the Past, Inscribing the Future*, pp. 156–157. In the Ronggawarsitan text, the eight saints who are named as the originators of the teachings that he reveals are Sunan Giri Kadhaton, Sunan Tandhes, Sunan Majagung, Sunan Bénang, Sunan Wuryapada, Sunan Kalinyamat, Sunan Gunungjati, and Sunan Kajenar (probably naming the "heretic" saint, Siti Jenar, a saint not usually included in the enumeration of the nine) (Simuh, *Mistik Islam Kejawen Raden Ngabehi Ranggawarsita*, p. 170).

92. Simuh, *Mistik Islam Kejawen Raden Ngabehi Ranggawarsita*, pp. 170–172.

93. The nine *ngèlmu*s are in this order: (1) *ngèlmu* Makdum Sarpin, (2) *ngèlmu* Patariyah [Satariyah = Shaṭṭāriyya], (3) *ngèlmu* Sirasab, (4) *ngèlmu* Karajèk, (5) *ngèlmu* Majalis, (6) *ngèlmu* Patakurrahman, (7) *ngèlmu* Supi [Sufi], (8) *ngèlmu* Khapi [khahfi], (9) *ngèlmu* Nakisbandiyah [Naqshbandiyya] (Simuh, *Mistik Islam Kejawen Raden Ngabehi Ranggawarsita*, p. 201). The Satariyah and Nakisbandiyah name the two dominant *tarekat* of early nineteenth-century Java. *Majālis* refers to a gathering of those on the path to perform *dhikr* and *sama*. *Khahfi* (spelled *khapi*) refers to the innermost secret or consciousness. *Patahulrahman* (spelled *patakurrahman*) is the title of the eighteenth-century Javanese adaptation of al-Anṣārī's *Kitāb Fatḥ al-Raḥmān* (and Raslān's commentary on it) that is transliterated, translated, and analyzed in G. W. J. Drewes' *Directions for Travellers on the Mystic Path* (The Hague: Martinus Nijhoff, 1977). The other three *ngèlmu patah* are Makdum Sarpin (conjuration of the shadow spirit associated with a person's four spiritual birth brothers: the amniotic fluid, placenta, blood of birth, and naval cord), *ngèlmu sirasab* (?), and *ngèlmu karajèk* (a knowledge apparently having to do with the science of twitches). There is a typographical error in the 1908 published edition that Simuh used as his source text, where "Satariyah" is erroneously written as "Patariyah." The earliest witness known to me of Ronggawarsita's text is one excerpted in a Kraton Surakarta manuscript that, judging from the hand, was inscribed in the late nineteenth century. This manuscript correctly writes the name of this lower instrumental knowledge as "Satariyah" (*Serat Panatagama sarta Wirid* [inscribed Surakarta, late nineteenth century], ms. KS 523 [13 Ca-B], p. 132).

94. Simuh, *Mistik Islam Kejawen Raden Ngabehi Ranggawarsita*, p. 202.

95. This originally Surakartan manuscript is now stored in the Sono Budoyo Museum in Yogyakarta (Ronggasasmita, *Suluk Martabat Sanga*, in *Serat Suluk Warni-Warni* [*Suluk Acih*] [inscribed Surakarta, 1872], ms. Sonobudoyo PB C.33 258 [Behrend P167]). The *silsila* naming the *pujongga* Ronggawarsita as a Shaṭṭāriyya master is to be found on page 56 verso of the manuscript. The names of his students were Ngabéhi Surakéwuh and Mas Metajaya.

8

NEGOTIATING ORDER IN THE LAND OF THE DRAGON AND THE HIDDEN VALLEY OF RICE

Local Motives and Regional Networks in the Transmission of New "Tibetan" Buddhist Lineages in Bhutan and Sikkim

AMY HOLMES-TAGCHUNGDARPA

In the summer of 1953, visitors gathered in the village of Rinchenpong in the eastern Himalayan kingdom of Sikkim to bid farewell to a local luminary. These visitors, who represented a variety of ethnic and religious groups in the state and came from different classes, including aristocrats and local villagers, were unified in their devotion to Risung Rinpoche (Ri gsung rin poche),[1] a Buddhist teacher who had been based in an old retreat house at the top of Rinchenpong hill for almost three decades. They mourned a beloved teacher who had traveled throughout Sikkim to perform rituals commemorating life-cycle rites and to celebrate festivals, who had been called upon as an astrologer and healer, and who was known for his talents as a teacher. Even as his health failed when he reached his eighties, Risung Rinpoche would still travel wherever he was invited, carried on a palanquin on the shoulders of faithful patrons. Among those gathered at his funeral were many of the students who had studied with him in the jungles of Rinchenpong, a site rendered powerful through its status as a cremation ground that was considered haunted and appropriate only for the most dedicated *tantrika*s. After several days of rituals, Risung Rinpoche's remains were interred in a distinctive stone reliquary in the jungle.

The outpouring of emotion over the loss of a meditation teacher based in a distant rural retreat center indicates the continued importance of Buddhism in Sikkimese culture at a time of striking change for the small state. Other monasteries remained important sites of cultural belonging and identity after the British departure from the subcontinent, as the local government negotiated new relationships with the new government of India and looked north to the new People's Republic of China with some concern. However, although Risung Rinpoche's exalted position in Sikkim appears indicative of local forms of community and identity, his biographical narrative demonstrates the transregional histories characteristic of Sikkimese Buddhism. Risung Rinpoche was originally from the neighboring kingdom of Bhutan. And, although both Sikkim and Bhutan had been anxious about Christian missionaries entering and influencing their communities, Risung Rinpoche's arrival in Sikkim had been celebrated and enthusiastically supported, just as his passing was deeply mourned.

Risung Rinpoche was one of many teachers crossing borders in the eastern Himalayas during the late nineteenth and early twentieth centuries, engaging in broader networks of trans-Himalayan Buddhist connectivity cultivated through shared histories, trade links, and the emergence of innovative new lineages. These new lineages did not involve any radical breaks with preexisting traditions or the introduction of new social identities, as Christianity did. However, they introduced new sources of authority into the Himalayan kingdoms at a time when enormous change was already under way. This change was propelled by contact with the global commercial networks facilitated by the British Empire. This chapter will explore the complex motivations behind the introduction of a specific Vajrayāna Buddhist lineage into the kingdoms of Bhutan and Sikkim around the turn of the twentieth century. In doing so, it will draw attention to the fruitfulness of analyzing the geographic extension of Buddhist lineages and Buddhist orders in relation to individual life stories and smaller-scale analyses of institution building and patronage.

The lineage of the eastern Tibetan meditation teacher Tokden Shakya Shri (Rtogs ldan Śā skya Śrī, 1853–1919) presents a salient case study for understanding the processes through which lineages were and are transferred within the broader Tibetan and Himalayan Buddhist networks of practitioners and institutions. Shakya Shri spent his life on the peripheries of Tibet, in the eastern Sino-Tibetan borderlands of Kham (Khams) and later at the southeastern pilgrimage site of Tsari (Rtsa ri). He is not representative of figures usually studied as emblematic of lineage and authority in the Tibetan Buddhist world, as he was not an incarnation of a famous historical teacher (*sprul sku*) or the head of a vast monastic estate. These are the most commonly invoked institutional forms in Tibetan Buddhism. Instead he became known throughout the Himalayas through his personal reputation, developed through narratives that were spread by word of mouth along the Himalayan trade routes traveled by his students and later disseminated widely through the creation of a textual biography published by his children and students.[2]

In this chapter, I will focus on the other side of this narrative, outlining the motives of Shakya Shri's students and patrons in the adoption and dissemination of his lineage. This approach highlights the complexities involved in the acceptance of new lineage transmissions in historically Buddhist areas of the Himalayas. These new lineage transmissions introduced new practices and teachers into local pantheons but were rarely perceived as problematic because the modes of transmission, including textual forms and genres, ritual vocabulary, and cosmology, were seen as belonging to preexisting Buddhist traditions.

These Buddhist traditions are often labeled as "Tibetan," as they are believed to have originated historically from Tibet, to share narrative traditions with Tibetan Buddhism, and to use Classical Tibetan as the language of their recorded canons. The organization of these traditions into what we might call "orders" is, however, complex in the Tibetan cultural world. In Tibet, the concepts of the monastic order (*dge 'dun*) and the teaching lineage (*bla brgyud*, lit., "the lineage of lamas/teachers") are distinct. Monastic orders are maintained through ritual ordination ceremonies, ritual initiations (*dbang*) into liturgy and meditation practices, and shared behavioral expectations. In Tibet and the Himalayas, these orders are affiliated with teachers and landed institutions, such as monasteries. Teaching lineages, in contrast, are more intricate. Distinctive teaching lineages have their own texts and practices. They are often attached, but not confined, to several major traditions of Tibetan Buddhism—the Nyingma (Rnying ma), Kagyü (Bka' brgyud), Sakya (Sa skya), Geluk (Dge' lugs), and, more recently, the Jonang (Jo nang)—that have grouped together historical practitioners according to certain lineage ancestors.[3] This chapter will explore the idea of lineages, distinguishing them from Himalayan monastic orders and thereby bringing into view more diverse forms of institutional formation and affiliation. Buddhism was not only based in monasteries in Tibet and the Himalayas. Other institutional forms included monastic schools, meditation retreat centers, and ritual centers or temples that included nonmonastic as well as monastic practitioners. The relationships between these forms can be understood as facilitating networks of practitioners in Buddhist exchange of knowledge, ritual, and friendship.

As well as detailing the transmission and acceptance of Buddhist lineages, I will also examine their distinctive elements and interactions in different parts of the Himalayas. Labeling local forms of Buddhism in the Himalayas as "Tibetan" does not capture the complexity of these traditions or their interrelationships on a regional level and incorrectly assumes that they all look to Tibet as their source of authority. Although acknowledging their Tibetan origins does help to differentiate them from other forms of Himalayan Buddhism, particularly the Newar form practiced in the Kathmandu Valley (which has its own distinctive history as well as some overlap with Tibetan traditions), it may veil the local agency involved in the creation of these traditions.[4] Therefore, in addition to outlining the motives of local agents in the establishment of Shakya Shri's lineage, this chapter critically considers the issue of terminology in light of the complex relationship networks that have influenced the reception and dissemination of Buddhism in different parts of the Himalayas.

I review concepts of "lineage" as distinct from "order" in the Tibetan-Himalayan Buddhist world as a starting point for examining the issue of the reintroduction or revitalization of Buddhism in areas where it has previously been present. Here I consider local motives, such as participating in prophetic narratives and identity, securing patronage relationships and legitimacy, and revitalizing older traditions. I outline some of these local motives more fully through case studies of students and patrons of Shakya Shri from Bhutan and Sikkim. In particular, I look at the local conditions that allowed for Shakya Shri's lineage to be accepted in specific locations at the turn of the twentieth century as well as the shared forms of cosmology that granted Shakya Shri cultural legitimacy in these areas. This interweaving of local needs and conditions with a shared sense of history allowed new lineages such as that of Shakya Shri to function and thrive in the Himalayas and, later, on a global stage as well. This study of the mobility and localization of Shayka Shri's lineage will demonstrate the negotiability of authority within Buddhist and other communities as well as the need to consider both vernacular and cosmopolitan impulses in their expansion.

DEMARCATING AUTHORITY THROUGH ORDER AND LINEAGE

As we shall see, the terminology related to Tibetan and Himalayan orders and lineages reflects many geographic and institutional distinctions. Tibetan Buddhism is a prominent and visible Asian religion practiced on a global scale today. However, it is also commonly misrepresented as a singular, homogeneous tradition, in part owing to the visibility of the Fourteenth Dalai Lama Tenzin Gyatso (Bstan 'dzin rgya mtsho) as a representative figure of authority for the Tibetan (and wider) Buddhist community. This misunderstanding is also partly the result of the geopolitics of the nineteenth and twentieth centuries that saw the creation of a distinct state called Tibet on colonial maps, only to have it banished and subsumed within another entity called the People's Republic of China in the mid-twentieth century. Yet, historically, what was considered to be "Tibet"—or, as it is known in central Tibetan dialect, Böd (Bod)—was variously interpreted and sometimes overtly contested.

To some scholars both within and outside of the Tibetan Buddhist scholastic tradition, Böd incorporates a wide area of Inner Asia, stretching into the Himalayas in South Asia and including the geographic reaches of the Tibetan plateau. What binds these people together has also been a point of negotiation. Some scholars argue for the importance of a shared Tibeto-Burman dialect; others identify staple food practices and the centrality of barley, or *tsampa* (*rstam pa*).[5] According to others, it is the practice of distinctive forms of Buddhism with shared historical narratives that distinguishes these communities as a Tibetan cultural world. Some critics argue, however, that historically Böd referenced only a small part of central Tibet until the seventeenth century, when communities throughout the plateau and the Himalayas were united by the Fifth Dalai Lama and his Mongol patrons into a new centralized state, the Galden Phodrang (Dga' ldan pho brang).[6]

All of the arguments above have their own problems, which are related to a central point: they all flatten and homogenize the diversity of cultural and political forms within this area. The last argument particularly ignores other crucial political changes in the seventeenth-century Himalayas, as new states also developed. Two of these states were the kingdoms of Bhutan and Sikkim. They had much in common in terms of their cultural narratives. The leaders that led their respective kingdoms in the seventeenth century were Tibetans who united local populations, some of whom were considered to be earlier immigrants from Tibet and others of whom were indigenous inhabitants. In both cases, these leaders used forms of Buddhism derived from the Tibetan plateau to create coherent state narratives.

They were not unique in choosing to do so. Since its inception in South Asia, Buddhism has been connected with politics, statecraft, and community identity. In the centuries following the Buddha's death, this community became an organized corporate body of monastics regulated by a code of conduct, the Vinaya. The *saṅgha* were supported by the laity, for whom there were far less distinct rules but who asserted their role within Buddhist institutions through their ritual relationships with the *saṅgha*. Both lay and monastic Buddhists followed the path of the Buddha and could reach awakening/enlightenment. In early Buddhist India, only monastics, however, participated within institutionally marked and managed intergenerational student–teacher/preceptor relationships. Over time, in diverse parts of the Southern Asian Buddhist world, Buddhist communities developed a variety of approaches to the organization and administration of monastic ordinations and transmission, and a variety of local nomenclatures used to refer to student–teacher/preceptor lineages within the monastic sphere. In some cases, Buddhist communities chose to celebrate and record nonmonastic student-teacher lineages as well, particularly following the emergence of Mahāyāna and Vajrayāna communities.[7]

The role of nonmonastic practitioners in the continuation of the Buddhist tradition—that is, the teachings of the Buddha and the communities that came after him—was therefore historically complex. Nonmonastic transmission lineages became distinct from monastic orders. Monks also took part in lineages organized around nonmonastics and thus held multiple affiliations, which can be understood as contributing to interacting networks. In this chapter, "lineage" will refer to practices and teachings transmitted from teacher to student, irrespective of monastic status, and will be treated as distinct from a monastic "order." Recording and investigating teaching lineages—who transmitted which elements of religious instruction to whom—provides an alternative to usual *saṅgha*-centric narratives of Buddhist history. These teaching lineages became very important in the reception of Buddhism in Tibet, as a number of crucial early translators and teachers were not members of the *saṅgha*.[8] Teaching lineages can supplement—or be encompassed by—the lineage ancestors claimed by any of the four major Tibetan Buddhist traditions mentioned earlier (Nyingma, Kagyü, Sakya, and Geluk). In addition, teaching lineages are also sometimes identified with particular meditation traditions, especially Dzokchen (Rdzogs chen, or The Great Perfection) and Mahāmudrā (Phyag chen, or The Great Seal). Teaching lineages associated with a meditation tradition are characterized by distinctive transmission practices: teacher-disciple connections are consolidated by swearing vows of loyalty (Skt. *samaya*; Tib. *dam tshig*) and require initiation through ritual (such as Skt. *abhiṣeka*; Tib. *dbang*). Thus, teaching lineages may be—but need not be—associated by their participants with one of the major Tibetan Buddhist traditions and/or one of the central meditation traditions. They also may or may not be tied to specific landed institutions, and so understanding them in a looser sense as networks, inhabited and disseminated by individual practitioners, can be a productive way to think about their relationships.[9]

In the Tibetan Buddhist world, practitioners—lay and monastic—can belong to multiple teaching lineages at the same time. These lineages need not be traced to Sakyamuni Buddha. Instead, they may be traced to other buddhas, bodhisattvas, or members of the Buddhist pantheon. One striking, unique, and influential form of teaching lineage in the Tibetan Buddhist world is the *terma* (*gter ma*) tradition, in which lineages are understood to derive from discovered texts or objects found by practitioners who are destined through karmic ties to identify them. These *terma* lineages are traced to the time of Guru Rinpoche (Skt. Padmasambhava), the Tantric sorcerer and Tibetan cultural hero who is believed to have helped introduce Buddhism to Tibet in the eighth century. *Terma* lineages include their own distinctive canons, featuring ritual instructions, invocation prayers to specific Tantric deities, meditation instructions, and other forms of yogic practice. The practitioners who discovered them were responsible for mastering these traditions in isolation before passing them on to students.[10]

Tokden Shakya Shri's lineage was made up of *terma* of this type. He studied with a number of renowned teachers based in eastern Tibet during his day and passed on the practices of these traditions. In addition, he had his own visionary experiences that led him to "reveal" new cycles of teachings that were held to have been hidden by the saint Guru Rinpoche during the period of the introduction of Buddhism into Tibet for discovery at a later time of need.[11] He mastered these cycles during years of meditation and transmitted them to his students, who included both lay Buddhists and monastics. It was this relationship of transmission that consolidated such lineages, as opposed to participation in physical institutions or shared ritual practices. The students of the founder of a *terma* lineage, or a "treasure revealer" as they were called, would then go on to teach these traditions and establish temples, monasteries, and other institutional homes for them. Their itineraries were often explained through Guru Rinpoche–related narratives. Shakya Shri's students often harked back to other related narratives in their activities, which were used as explanations for and justification of their promulgation of Shakya Shri's lineage in certain places.

One idea that was particularly resonant was the narrative traditions of "Hidden Lands" (*sbas yul*), sacred demarcated spaces that were believed to be efficacious sites for spiritual practice and safety during times of persecution. As with his *terma*, Hidden Lands were also waiting to be opened by treasure revealers who had karmic connections to Guru Rinpoche and who would rediscover these sealed spaces for Buddhist practitioners at a predestined future time.[12]

The demarcation between the monastic order and the transmission lineage found in Tibetan Buddhism allowed for the participation of a diverse range of practitioners in areas where Tibetan-derived Buddhism spread, including these Hidden Lands. Some of the participants in these lineages were ordained monastics, but others were not. Some were ritual specialists, affiliated with monasteries; others were itinerant ritualists, supported by local communities. Still others were yogis, living for years in retreat, or regular laypeople, who had taken initiation while integrating rituals or prayers into their daily routines alongside agricultural or trade pursuits. Shakya Shri was known especially for his acceptance of a wide range of people within his teaching lineage and for his ability to teach different forms of practice to different individuals according to their needs. Though he was associated with the Drukpa Kagyü ('Brug pa bka' brgyud) tradition of Tibetan Buddhism, he held transmission lineages for both Dzokchen and Mahāmudrā meditation, and had studied with teachers from a variety of Tibetan Buddhist traditions. The social diversity and location of Shakya Shri's teacher-student community reflected these differences. Tulku Urgyen Rinpoché, a twentieth-century teacher, described the impressions that his uncle Samten Gyatso (called Uncle Tersé below), a student of Shakya Shri, had of the community. Shakya Shri's students did not live in a monastery but in a valley where his students modified the landscape in order to create living spaces near their teacher.

> "Shakya Shri lived with about seven hundred disciples in Kyipuk," Uncle Tersé told me. "His disciples had dug caves all around the two surrounding slopes, while others stayed in tiny tents made of either canvas or yak-felt. Shakya Shri himself lived on a meadow in the only house around, which was a simple structure of stamped mud with one large window." . . .
>
> Even though so many disciples had gathered around him, Shakya Shri didn't teach year round but only at particular times during summer and winter. . . .
>
> Shakya Shri told some of his disciples, "You belong to the Mahāmudrā side of the valley," while to others he said, "You belong to the Dzokchen side." And so he divided them up in two groups and gave instructions in Mahāmudrā and Dzokchen in accordance with each follower's disposition.[13]

Communities such as Shakya Shri's were not rare in the Tibetan Buddhist world, but their histories have been neglected. This is partly because of the political prominence of the megamonasteries that were spread throughout central Tibet and retained large territories that supported their monastic communities.[14] These megamonasteries were not only dominant in their localities, however. They were also part of larger networks that linked them to the political centers of Lhasa and Beijing, where their patrons were. Moreover, they were self-replicating, as monastic authorities could dispatch representatives to establish satellite monasteries in the borderlands of the Tibetan world.[15] In time, the traffic between the megamonasteries and their satellites was not just unidirectional, as practitioners from these borderlands also traveled to the megamonasteries to study in the centers of spiritual education of their day. These institutions were therefore very diverse, as students from throughout Inner Asia, China, and the Himalayas using a wide range of languages also traveled to the megamonasteries to study and master their curricula. Some of the talented would become part of the monastic hierarchy; others returned home or traveled elsewhere to disseminate their lineages.

However, other, smaller communities had similar patterns of geographic extension and translocal linkages. Shakya Shri had students from throughout the Himalayas who traveled to study with him. The nature of transmission in these communities is not straightforward. The majority of these students came from areas with previous Buddhist connections to Tibet. They were not new converts to Buddhist traditions. Therefore, these networks of travel and transmission cannot be seen simply as the result of missionary activity emanating from the institutional and teaching center of Shakya Shri's lineage. Instead, as Elisabeth Stutchbury, who studied the lineage of Shakya Shri in the western Himalayan region of Karzha in Lahul (in contemporary Himachal Pradesh, India), has argued, these cases indicate a more intricate process of cyclical renewal and rejuvenation for Buddhist communities. New teachers and lineages did not disturb the religious landscape of these places. Instead, their arrival and the transmission of their new lineages were seen to be part of a continuous, ongoing transmission.[16] They were developed around historical connections between certain religious centers both within Tibet and in its borderland regions, which had been facilitated through trade networks throughout the Himalayas. Although it was based outside of large landed monastic establishments, Shakya Shri's lineage was also disseminated through these networks. Its agents of transmission in Bhutan and Sikkim looked to older cultural narratives of connectivity as well as changes in the contemporary landscape to explain and support their travel and teaching.

LOCAL FACTORS IN THE TRANSMISSION OF TOKDEN SHAKYA SHRI'S LINEAGE

By the late nineteenth century, Bhutan and Sikkim had already shared a long history of interaction, conflict, and negotiation in the forging of the eastern

Himalayan political order. However, both kingdoms were also experiencing in very different ways the enormous change brought by European interest in the Himalayas, and their negotiations with colonial modernity had strikingly different outcomes. It is this diversity of experience as well as connection through networks of practitioners and historical narratives that make Bhutan and Sikkim generative sites for the exploration of lineage and network development.

The small kingdom of Sikkim had been significantly compromised by British incursion into the eastern Himalayas. It was originally consolidated as a state in the mid-seventeenth century. The kings of the Namgyal (Rnam rgyal) dynasty were challenged by incursions into their territories by Gorkhas and Bhutanese in the eighteenth century. British interest in the Himalayas grew during this time with the desire to discover new markets as well as to discover more accessible and profitable sources for tea.[17] The East India Company was also interested in finding suitable locations for sanatoria that could provide British subjects in India respite from the heat of the plains.[18] They found both in Darjeeling and after a diplomatic scuffle took over the area in 1835, though nominally continued to "rent" it from the king of Sikkim. After further incidents with rulers of Nepal and Tibet, the British inserted a political officer in Sikkim in 1889, theoretically to assist with international affairs and administration. In reality, this action led to the king and his ministers losing most of their authority until the early twentieth century.[19] Political officers were distinct from the British Residents in Nepal established in 1802, as in Sikkim they had more direct power. This was therefore a time of great change, during which local historical forms of political power were compromised and undermined by colonial incursion.

The kingdom of Bhutan at this time was undergoing centralization after decades of rule by the Druk Desi ('Brug sde srid), or prime ministers, who acted as regents in lieu of the Zhabdrung (Zhab drung), the incarnations of the seventeenth-century unifier of Bhutan, Ngawang Namgyal (Ngag dbang rnam rgyal, 1594–1651). After civil war in the 1870s, the leader of this movement for unification was the innovative and intelligent Ugyen Wangchuck (U rgyan dbang phyug, 1862–1926), the Pönlop (*dpon slob*, or minister) of Trongsa (Krong gsar). His astute leadership led him to become a crucial intermediary between the British and Tibetan governments but also ensured that Bhutan retained its sovereignty. In a move to consolidate centralized power and peace in the state, he was elected hereditary king of Bhutan in 1907.[20]

Although the state religion of the Zhabdrung had been part of the Drukpa Kagyü Tibetan Buddhist tradition, Ugyen Wangchuck shifted affiliations in favor of the Nyingma tradition of Tibetan Buddhism. However, he was eclectic in his generous patronage of sacred site building, artworks, and printing projects.[21] From at least the 1880s onwards, Ugyen Wangchuck became a generous supporter of Tokden Shakya Shri. This patronage relationship is demonstrated in the colophon of a text that appears in the *Collected Works* (*Gsung 'bum*) of

Shakya Shri, which is dedicated to Ugyen Wangchuck the Trongsa Pönlop, "ruler among men."[22]

Why did the Ugyen Wangchuck choose to support this meditation teacher from Kham? Evidence from the period suggests that he originally learned about Shakya Shri while traveling in Tibet working as a mediator for the British. He heard about Shakya Shri's abilities as a teacher and miracle worker, and decided to sponsor him along with a number of other lamas (religious teachers) in the eastern Tibetan region of Kham. He also sent a number of Bhutanese students to study in Kham.[23] He saw this sponsorship of Buddhist practice as a means to consolidate peace and happiness in Bhutan.[24] The reference to peace and happiness was in response to Bhutan's unstable political situation in the nineteenth century, which Ugyen Wangchuck and his supporters were working to alleviate after a century of internal fighting. The idea of religious patronage as a tool able to unite communities in a peaceful way (thereby helping to create a strong state identity) was not new in the Buddhist world, but its use here is interesting given the political transformations under way in Bhutan.

One possible explanation for Ugyen Wangchuck's patronage of Shakya Shri could have been his desire to support an alternate transmission lineage of the Drukpa Kagyü tradition in Bhutan, distinct from that of the earlier Zhabdrung ruler incarnation, who had developed his own lineage when he originally arrived in Bhutan in the seventeenth century. This lineage had been used to unite the country and create a strong state. Before the seventeenth century, there had been a number of waves in the transmission of Buddhist orders and lineages in Bhutan, and Bhutanese Buddhism had come to incorporate eclectic forms, including the Nyingma and Kagyü traditions.[25] The Zhabdrung's Drukpa Kagyü lineage was consolidated through the introduction of hegemonic forms of state ritual and religious institutions.[26] Support of an alternate lineage was beneficial for Ugyen Wangchuck as he worked to unify the state at a time when he had received both local and British support to establish himself as the first king of Bhutan. The new monarchy was designed by Wangchuck to create stability and centrality, and to replace the Zhabdrung. However, although this motive may appear logical to us looking back from the present, the situation on the ground was more complicated. Transmission lineages could not be demarcated so easily. Ugyen Wangchuck continued to try to align himself with the Zhabdrung in the early twentieth century, thereby demonstrating a conciliatory and ecumenical attitude toward different Buddhist lineages.[27] However, the Shakya Shri lineage was one he was especially interested, in perhaps as an alternative, to help downplay the political function the Zhabdrung had enjoyed.

Wangchuck's effort to maintain peace with the Zhabdrung was demonstrated in his patronage of an important student of the Zhabdrung named Mönlam Rabzang (Smon lam rab bzang, 1878–1945). Their close relationship is demonstrated through the story of how Mönlam Rabzang originally went to study in Kham, which also provides clues to how Ugyen Wangchuck learned about Shakya Shri. Ugyen Wangchuck's wife, Rinchen Pémo (Rin chen pad mo), became gravely ill in 1896. In line with tradition, Ugyen Wangchuck spared no expense to treat her, bringing in doctors and also sponsoring large rituals. However, she did not recover, and she passed away in 1900. Ugyen Wangchuck decided to give offerings in her name to all the major sacred sites and monasteries of central Tibet and so sought out a trusted and capable emissary in the person of Mönlam Rabzang.

Originally from the Tsangkha (Mtshang kha) village of Tangsibi (Stang si bi) in the Mangde (Mang sde) valley, Mönlam Rabzang was recognized at a young age as an incarnation of an acclaimed yogi. He received a broad monastic education in many of the great monastic and religious institutions of the time in Trongsar, Wangdu Phodrang (Dbang 'dus pho brang), and Punakha (Spu na kha), and with many of the great Bhutanese teachers, including the Fifth Zhabdrung Tuktrul Jikmé Chögyal (Zhabs drung thugs sprul 'jigs med chos rgyal, 1862–1904). He became most well known as an artistic savant, skilled in painting, sculpture, and other arts. These talents brought him to the attention of Ugyen Wangchuck, who commissioned a number of works from him, which led to the development of a strong relationship between the two. Therefore, it is no surprise that, at a time of personal need, Ugyen Wangchuck selected Mönlam Rabzang to travel on his behalf to Lhasa. On arriving there, Mönlam Rabzang heard tales about a famous meditation teacher in Kham named Tokden Shakya Shri and, after asking permission from Ugyen Wangchuck, traveled to study with him instead of returning to Bhutan.[28] Mönlam Rabzang stayed with Shakya Shri for several years and gained a reputation in the community as a master of Mahāmudrā. Shakya Shri eventually instructed him to return to Bhutan, where Mönlam Rabzang taught and continued to carry out his artistic projects in Tashigang.[29]

Thus, Ugyen Wangchuck's support of Shakya Shri was not simply a political effort to disseminate lineages of Buddhism alternative to those of the Zhabdrung. These efforts also reflected his personal relationships and beliefs.

Sikkim also had a strong tradition of state Buddhism, dating from the seventeenth century. Such particular motivations and factors of local context help to explain the success of Shakya Shri's lineage in Sikkim. There, unlike the Bhutanese Zhabdrung, the kings of the hereditary Namgyal dynasty did not derive their authority directly from religious status, but instead through the age-old method of patronizing Buddhist teachers and ritual specialists. This idealized patron-lama relationship (*mchod yon*) was an integral part of the narrative of the founding of the Sikkimese state, which, according to Sikkimese traditions, had taken place through a Tibetan *terma* revealer. Lhatsün Namkha Jikmé (Lha btsun nam mkha' 'jigs med, 1597–1653) had received visions leading him to Sikkim. Sikkimese traditions recall that he, along with two other visiting Tibetans, identified the first king, Phuntsok Namgyal (Phun tshogs rnam rgyal), based on a prophecy. State traditions were sponsored by the king and disseminated through monastic institutions. The major monastic institution was the Pemayangtsé Monastery (Pad ma yang rtse) located in Sikkim, which had lineage ties to the Nyingma institution of Mindroling (Smin sgrol gling) in central Tibet.[30]

These state traditions connected to Lhatsün's *terma* lineage and the Tibetan Nyingma tradition had remained strong over the centuries that followed, the lamas serving as valued advisors to the kings. However, as British interest in Sikkim deepened, colonial authorities grew concerned about these relationships, particularly as the lamas were skeptical of British motivations. After a series of border skirmishes in the mid-nineteenth century, the government of India sent a political officer to oversee the affairs of the state in 1889, as mentioned earlier. The king—a minor at the time—was marginalized, as were the lamas, who were no longer given prominence in the state council. Their relationships with other monastic institutions in Tibet were also carefully monitored, and it became increasingly difficult for Pemayangtsé lamas from Sikkim to travel to Tibet for study, as they had done in the past.[31]

This situation opened up the opportunity for alternative lineages and institutional forms of Buddhism to flourish in Sikkim. This was evidenced particularly by the popularity of local ritual specialists and meditators. From the 1890s to 1910s, a number of these meditators traveled to study with Shakya Shri, who was then residing in Kham.[32] They originally learned of Shakya Shri through word of mouth, from traders and pilgrims who had heard of him in their travels elsewhere in the Buddhist world. The technologies of colonial modernity, particularly the train, revitalized pilgrimage networks, especially within India. Many Sikkimese Buddhists visited the Buddhist center of Bodh Gaya after its rediscovery and reinvigoration through the efforts of the Ceylonese Buddhist reformer Anagarika Dharmapala (1864–1933).[33] The British apparently did not see these visits to India as problematic, as they brought the Sikkimese into the centers of British imperial power and introduced them to the idea of the British as benevolent patrons of Buddhist restoration. Pelling Ani Wangdzin (Pad gling a ni dbang 'dzin, ca. 1870–1925), a female practitioner from West Sikkim, was one of these visitors and apparently took part in a state-sponsored pilgrimage to Bodh Gaya in the early 1910s. While there, she heard about Shakya Shri and decided to enrich her Tantric education by traveling to Kham and studying with him. It was only through participation in broader educational networks that she could have had this opportunity, as there were no state-sponsored nunneries or Buddhist educational institutions for women in Sikkim at the time. Some women studied with their male relatives where they could, but most were heavily involved in other agricultural and mercantile activities that occupied their time. Pelling Ani Wangdzin came from a wealthy family and had a supportive father who provided her with the financial means to pursue a religious vocation. When she returned from her time in Kham, her brothers and relatives became her patrons and built her a meditation hut above Pelling, where she taught yogic traditions to dozens of students who represented the many Buddhist ethnic and cultural groups present in Sikkim, including Bhutias, Lepchas, Tamang, and Gurung.[34] Students of Shakya Shri in Sikkim such as Pelling Ani Wangdzin indicate how this alternative transmission lineage provided opportunities for religious education for those outside of state monastic institutions that were being monitored by British authorities.

The cases of Mönlam Rabzang in Bhutan and Pelling Ani Wangdzin in Sikkim represent the very different local situations in these kingdoms that facilitated the spread of Shakya Shri's lineage. In Bhutan, the tradition became part of broader state traditions that were in formation during the introduction of the new monarchy. Sikkim was also being fundamentally altered by interactions with colonial modernity, but a fragile royal state under pressure from British projects facilitated heterogeneity as opposed to the homogenization of state traditions.

SHARED LEGACIES IN CONSTRUCTING THE BUDDHISM OF TOKDEN SHAKYA SHRI

Although local conditions are important considerations in the motives of patrons and practitioners in introducing new lineages into an area, regional affiliations and shared sense of identity were also influential. These regional affiliations are often glossed through labeling the Buddhisms of Bhutan and Sikkim as "Tibetan-derived" or "closely-related" to Tibetan Buddhism.[35] Looking more closely at the details of such affiliations, however, helps us to understand how and why local communities supported students of Shakya Shri. There are a number of factors that could strengthen or alternately undermine these affiliations, which included shared languages and print media. The shared use of Classical Tibetan for the production and dissemination of textual traditions was a key factor,[36] especially in the case of this lineage, since the students of Shakya Shri were from geographically diverse areas that often spoke mutually unintelligible dialects of Tibetan or Tibetan-related languages. To overcome these differences, a shared written language was important. The Shakya Shri tradition contains a number of apocryphal stories of how students spontaneously overcame language differences and could innately understand teachers who spoke different dialects when meeting with them for the first time. Shakya Shri is said to have encountered the problem of language differences even in Kham, where the geographic extremities of the mountainous landscape had led to the development of very different dialects. Oral narratives recount his first meeting with Adzom Drukpa (A 'dzom 'brug pa, 1842–1924), one of his teachers, who later also studied with him as a student:

> Upon merely meeting, guru and student felt their minds merge, becoming one. The guru Drukpa Rinpoché, being a nomad from Washül Tromtar

> [Wa shul trom tar], said in the dialect of that region, "To experience the true nature of great perfection, just rest straight out, just rest. I don't suppose there's anything else but that." Shakya Shri understood what the guru was saying to him, that there was nothing to this enlightened intent other than resting naturally, without contrivance. Adzom Drukpa transferred to Shakya Shri the enlightened intent of *dharmakāya*, unbiased timeless awareness as the naked unity of awareness and emptiness. Distinguishing between his ordinary mind and pure awareness, Shakya Shri attained the realization of great perfection in a quantum leap, having been directly introduced to it in the immediacy of his own true nature.[37]

This was an example of a "mind transmission," a narrative trope used to explain how language differences were negotiated in these communities. It seems likely that students who traveled to Shakya Shri and stayed with him for longer periods of time were responsible for facilitating discussions by serving as translators. Students were then able to absorb the teachings and put them into their own local languages to facilitate the acceptance of these teachings by local communities.

Another important factor shaping the absorption of new lineages within historically Tibetan Buddhist areas was the existence of powerful historical affiliations that were linked to historical narratives about the shared Buddhist past. Particularly, this history was focused on the very earliest periods of Buddhist interaction with the landscapes of the eastern Himalayas and was specifically remembered through stories tied to the eighth-century saint Guru Rinpoche, who was held to have been integral to the introduction of Tantric Buddhism in Tibet. He remains a popular figure revered throughout different areas of the Himalayas for his magical prowess and for performing miracles that allowed Buddhism to be introduced to specific places.

Acknowledging these narratives as forms of continuity helps to explain the enthusiastic acceptance of lineages such as that of Shakya Shri. It also helps to avoid some of the problems noted by Elisabeth Stutchbury, who cautions scholars not to rely on missionizing discourse to explain the dissemination of Buddhism. Instead, it is useful to look for connections between new lineages and older cultural narratives.[38] Stutchbury found that the Shakya Shri lineage was able to enter Kardang in the western Himalayas through established Drukpa Kagyü ties as well as through narrative traditions about Guru Rinpoché and other local saints. It is tempting to interpret the entrance of new lineages into the Himalayas in the nineteenth and twentieth centuries as part of the many changes wrought by colonial modernity in the Himalayas. This was indeed part of their attraction. However, as Anne Blackburn has argued, it is important to consider how these lineages have retained markers of continuity with precolonial forms of Buddhism. They cannot simply be explained as modern, as they do not draw on "developmentalist discourse that approached social problems and their solution through a self-conscious reflection on [their] own era as one that required a compensatory imitation of new forms of political order, ritual and devotion, or education," approaches explicitly presented as appropriate to "modern" times.[39] Instead, such lineages were closely related to and thereby naturalized by earlier disseminations of Buddhist tradition and lineage, which paved the way for and legitimated new forms. Annabella Pitkin's characterization of these shared values and narratives as an alternative form of Himalayan cosmopolitanism is also helpful here in considering the integral role of travel and how it facilitated a union of different local histories to create a shared vision of the Buddhist past for practitioners in traditions such as that of Shakya Shri.[40]

Narratives related to Guru Rinpoche are found throughout the Himalayan borderlands. Guru Rinpoche was a key figure for the dissemination of Tantric Buddhism in Tibet and the Himalayas. Stories tell of his subjugation and taming of local spirits and their conversion to Buddhism. These tales can be read largely as an account of the spread of Buddhism as it came into contact with and subjugated local traditions. Guru Rinpoche was also central to the *terma* tradition described earlier, as he had hidden original texts to be discovered at later, appropriate times by predestined individuals. Shakya Shri enjoyed a special relationship with the guru as well, through his identity as one such *terma* revealer.[41] These links with the guru also helped created itineraries for the dissemination of Shakya Shri's lineage. Both Sikkim and Bhutan were considered part of the Hidden Land geographies. For example, all of Sikkim was traditionally known as the "Bayul Démojong" (Sbas yul 'bras mo ljongs), the Hidden Land of Rice. Its opening took place over the visits of several treasure revealers, including Lhatsün Namkha Jikmé.[42] Bhutan was also believed to be home to several Hidden Lands.[43] Such narratives often helped practitioners to situate themselves and their followers within a sacred landscape possessed of a deep history when they left their teacher's community and went out into the world to practice or teach.

An example of a more complex transregional connection facilitated by such a narrative is that of Risung[44] Rinpoche Jikmé Kunzang Chöpel (Ri gsung rin po che 'Jigs med kun bzang chos 'phel, 187?–1953). Risung Rinpoché was a Bhutanese teacher who traveled from eastern Bhutan to study with Tokden Shakya Shri and eventually settled in West Sikkim, rather than returning to his homeland as many of his Bhutanese peers did. Risung Rinpoche was originally from the Sharchop ethnocultural community in eastern Bhutan. Little is known about how he traveled to Kham, but, after staying for a number of years in Shakya Shri's community, he decided to move to Sikkim to continue his practice of Shakya Shri's lineage. He chose Sikkim for its reputation as a Hidden Land and ended up living at Risung in the area of Rinchenpong in West Sikkim. West Sikkim had particularly powerful cultural resonance for a Bhutanese expatriate, as it was believed that Péma Lingpa (Pad ma gling pa, 1450–1521), the great Bhutanese treasure revealer, had visited and practiced in the area.

A number of sites remain associated with Péma Lingpa in Sikkim, including the town of Pelling, which is said to be named after him, and Rinchenpong. Risung was situated in a flat area of forest that had been used as a cremation site and that was regarded as being especially efficacious for Tantric practice. Risung Rinpoche initially moved there in the early 1910s with his consort, a Sharchop woman known as Risung Sangyum, and her daughter. The local landlord, the Pönchung Thikidar, allowed him to live in a small temple that had already been built on the land,[45] and Risung Rinpoche and his family became responsible for carrying out rituals for the Thikidar. Word soon spread of his ritual prowess, and he gained a number of aristocratic sponsors who invited him to different parts of Sikkim to carry out rituals related to a number of needs, including rituals for health and building consecration. Students also began to gather around him at Risung, living in simple tents and makeshift huts on the slopes below the temple. As with Pelling Ani Wangdzin's community, these students represented a number of different ethnocultural groups from the eastern Himalayas, including Bhutias, Lepchas, Tamang, Gurung, and other Bhutanese, who traveled to Sikkim to study with Risung Rinpoche. They also represented a number of institutions, including both monastic orders and teaching lineages. Some were itinerant practitioners, traveling from teacher to teacher. Others were associated with local monastic institutions and came to travel with Risung Rinpoche as a kind of apprenticeship in the rituals and meditative traditions he taught. They were varied in their level of commitment as well. Whereas some students remained at Risung for years, others passed through for a few months. As Risung Rinpoche's reputation grew, students increasingly came to stay just to gain an association with his name. They studied in a number of fields. Some of the students would travel with Risung Rinpoche, setting up their tents at patrons' houses and assisting in rituals. As Risung Rinpoche got older and his health declined, they would carry him on a type of palanquin, assisted by local patrons who would come to meet him. Other students remained in the forests at Rinchenpong, meditating during the day and practicing the dance of Chöd (Gchod) and the yoga of the winds (*rtsa rlung*) at night, and would later be dispatched by their teacher to undertake intensive individual retreats. In addition to the narrative memory linking Risung Rinpoche's Sikkim sites to a deep Bhutanese Buddhist past, retreat areas favored by his students were typically connected with stories about the activities of Guru Rinpoche and the early dissemination of forms of Tibetan Buddhism within Sikkim.[46]

What allowed this Bhutanese expatriate teacher to become so renowned in this small kingdom, which had its own distinctive Buddhist traditions? A major factor was Risung Rinpoche's association with both Dzokchen and Mahāmudrā meditation traditions. He was therefore accepted as a teacher who could bring together different networks. He was a Dzokchen master in the local Nyingma traditions as well as a teacher who could accept students with different needs and different order and lineage affiliations. His recognition of the shared history of Guru Rinpoche was also key to this acceptance and demonstrated the shared regional affiliations held by the Shakya Shri lineage. His students went on to hold many different roles in the historical development of Buddhism in modern Sikkim. Linguistic or cultural differences between Risung Rinpoche and his lineage, and with his Sikkimese students were not seen as detrimental. This is even more striking in its specific historical context. By the early twentieth century, the demarcation of identity, especially along national lines, was becoming increasingly influential in the Himalayas, undermining historical forms of cosmopolitanism.[47] However, the history of the Shakya Shri lineage in Sikkim reveals transregional manifestations of Buddhism that survived across revised state boundaries and that flourished despite a rise in new forms of nationalist discourse.

INTERPERSONAL NETWORKS AND THE COMPLEXITIES OF AFFILIATION IN THE DISSEMINATION OF SHAKYA SHRI'S LINEAGE

The final factor that facilitated the dissemination of Shakya Shri's lineage in Bhutan and Sikkim is very simple yet often overlooked: interpersonal relationships and the broader networks that arose out of them. These interpersonal connections were often consolidated through economic and political networks. Trade routes throughout the broader Himalayas were especially influential, as they allowed for a certain amount of mobility, as did the pilgrimage traditions discussed earlier. They allowed for people with otherwise diverse forms of affiliation to meet over shared interests and to disseminate information before text traditions were consolidated. In other words, patronage relationships were a key factor in the creation of opportunities for the expansion of lineages across the Himalayas and the development of transregional education within lineages like that of Shakya Shri.

Considering interpersonal interaction as a site for the dissemination of lineage also allows for some of the more intangible elements of dissemination to be taken into account. These could include perceptions of personal charisma and magnetism that lead students to study with teachers. Such qualities are present in the Shakya Shri lineage. The Bhutanese student Tenzin Gyatso (1883–1966) provides an example. Born in Paro (Spa gro), Tenzin Gyatso began his formal study of Buddhism at a young age, when he was dispatched to live with his uncle, who was an accomplished monk. He excelled in his studies, undertaking courses in many of the great educational institutions of Bhutan. During his studies, he had the opportunity to meet with Artsa Lama (A rtsa bla ma, dates unknown), who told him about his amazing teacher the meditator from Kham: Tokden Shakya Shri. Tenzin Gyatso's hagiography states that, when Tenzin heard these tales, "the hair on his arms rose up."[48] His imagination inspired, he traveled to Kham with Artsa Lama under the patronage of Ugyen Wangchuck to study with Shakya Shri. This patronage again reinforces Ugyen Wangchuck's personal connection to the lineage, as well as his material contributions by sending students to study with Shakya Shri. Tenzin Gyatso eventually returned to Bhutan, where he became an important teacher within the country, serving as an attendant to his uncle, who rose to become the preeminent master of Bhutan, the Jé Khenpo (Rje mkhan po), and later an important teacher and practitioner in his own right.[49]

Artsa Lama also visited other communities in the Himalayas, including Karzha, where he was said to have been dispatched after Shakya Shri dreamed that he had students who were living there but whom he had not yet met.[50] Artsa Lama's invitation to Karzha students led to batches of students traveling to study with Shakya Shri, to the establishment of new religious institutions in the area, and, eventually, to the forging of personal relationships that contributed to the decision by one of the grandchildren of Shakya Shri to settle there in the 1950s.[51]

Another example of a Bhutanese student who came to study with Shakya Shri through Artsa Lama is that of Mémé Lama Sönam Zangpo (Mes mes bla ma bsod nams bzang po, 1892–1982), a key figure in the Shakya Shri lineage due to his publication of Shakya Shri's *Collected Works* in the 1970s (reprinted in 1998). His case is a powerful representation of Ugyen Wangchuck's personal commitment to Shakya Shri and his sponsorship of students to study in eastern Tibet. It also demonstrates the entrance of print technology into the dissemination of lineage. Sources indicate that Sönam Zangpo was related to Ugyen Wangchuck, with some even suggesting he was an illegitimate son. He was born in Kurtoe (Kur stod) into a family descended from Péma Lingpa and was a deeply religious youth, which led to his being recognized as the incarnation of two different lamas.[52] When he was twelve, a number of members of his community decided to visit Shakya Shri in Kham. He was desperate to join them after hearing about Shakya Shri and feeling deeply inspired. He begged his mother, who at first refused but eventually gave in and went to see Ugyen Wangchuck to request support. Ugyen Wangchuck was moved by Sönam Zangpo's commitment to Buddhism at such a young age and offered to provide him with offerings for Shakya Shri and other provisions for the long journey to Kham.[53] Sönam Zangpo then set off to join his comrades and became the youngest of the Bhutanese students sent to Kham. He remained there for many years, eventually rising to become a leader of Shakya Shri's community at Tsari. He returned to Bhutan in the 1930s, when he moved with an itinerant community of yogic practitioners between different sites associated with Guru Rinpoche and the religious history of Bhutan, staying nowhere for more than three years and developing a reputation for his service to villagers as well as to the royal family.[54] His relationship with Ugyen Wangchuck as well as his mother's commitment and connections not only facilitated his own education, but also played a crucial part in the development of Shakya Shri's textual legacy far beyond the Himalayas.

There is a famous proverb in Tibetan: "Every lama has his own religious tradition and every valley its own dialect." This saying is often used to demonstrate the diversity of language in Tibetan cultural areas of the plateau and the Himalayas. It also makes an important point about religion in these areas, as it addresses the remarkable diversity found throughout the region. This diversity manifests in a multitude of institutional, ritual, and practice lineages whose participants represent networks of multiple affiliations. It also raises important questions about the use of "Tibetan Buddhism" or even "Tibetan-derived Buddhism" as an analytic category. Acknowledging local agency and thinking about Tibetan or Himalayan Buddhisms on smaller scales is important for creating more representative histories for this area and for bringing to light the processes through which Buddhist lineages expanded and were localized in the wider Himalayan region.

Although framing histories of Himalayan Buddhism as part of the history of Tibetan Buddhism or Tibetan-derived Buddhism effaces much of the diversity, analysis from the perspective of technologies of transmission, such as lineages, orders, and networks, can help expand our gaze from the local contexts in the Himalayas to other spaces and religions. It is fruitful to examine specific small-scale technologies of transmission and the circulation of specific teaching lineages in the Himalayas as opposed to the more formal institutions of orders. This perspective includes diverse forms of practitioners beyond the monks formally associated with orders. Thinking about the different elements that frame participation in lineages across space and time, such as shared cultural narratives, interpersonal relationships, concepts of sacred space, and print technologies as well as distinctive meditative and ritual practices, helps to explain how new lineages are spread. These elements underpin affective affiliations and help to explain local-scale motives for the adoption of new lineages in areas where Buddhist traditions are already strong.

The eastern Himalayan kingdoms of Bhutan and Sikkim are both home to distinctive forms of Buddhism that share cultural forms with Tibet but have their own histories. The adoption of the lineage of Shakya Shri, embodied by the descendants of practitioners who studied in eastern Tibet with him and his disciples, is now found in a variety of religious institutional forms in different guises. Practices from this lineage are continued by scholars and members of monastic orders in large monasteries and Buddhist educational institutions in urban centers such as Thimphu and Gangtok. At the same time, lineage participants serve as patrons and supplicants at local temples throughout the countryside as wandering yogis and meditators, and even as young laypeople who adorn their cellphones and car windshields with sticker images of Shakya Shri and his students. Such varieties of connections demonstrate the ongoing adaptability of lineage in the Himalayas and its ability to meld different local and regional ideologies that hold together the orders and itineraries that create religious communities within and beyond national and regional boundaries.

NOTES

I would like to acknowledge the generosity of all the people who have provided materials and stories used in the research for this chapter, especially Dorji Penjore; Khenpo Shedup Tenzin; Lama Thinley Namgyal; surviving members of the Risung community, particularly H. E. Dorlop Chewang Rinzin Tagchungdarpa and Mellipa; and my family in Sikkim. Anne Blackburn and Michael Feener made invaluable suggestions. I dedicate this article to the memory of my teacher Elisabeth Stutchbury, whose brilliant work on the Shakya Shri lineage in the western Himalayas continues to inspire me. I will always be grateful for her guidance, wisdom, and compassion.

1. In this chapter, Tibetan words will be transliterated according to the Tibetan and Himalayan Library system, followed by Wylie spelling in parentheses on their first appearance. In circumstances where individuals or authors are known widely by another spelling, however, their preferences will be retained.

2. This biography is Kaḥ thog si tu chos kyi rgya mtsho, *Rje bstun bla ma rdo rje 'chang chen po Śākya shrī dznya' na'i rnam thar me tog phreng ba* (originally published by Gangtok: Sherab Gyaltsen, Palace Monastery, 1990); reprinted in *Shakya Shri's Collected Works*, pp. 17–230. A critical study of the life of Shakya Shri and his lineage is included in Amy Holmes-Tagchungdarpa, *The Social Life of Tibetan Biography: Textuality, Community and Authority in the Lineage of Tokden Shakya Shri* (Lanham, MD: Lexington, 2014). A full translation of his biography can be found in Elio Guarisco, trans., *Togden Shakya Shri: The Life and Liberation of a Tibetan Yogin* (Merigar: Shang Shung Publications, 2011).

3. Tibet's indigenous religion, Bön, is also sometimes affiliated with this system of organization of lineages.

4. This flattening of Himalayan diversity is noted in Karma Phuntsho, *The History of Bhutan* (Noida: Random House, 2013), pp. xii–xiii, and can also be seen in general surveys related to Tibetan and Himalayan Buddhisms that often only include Tibet in the title, such as John Powers, *Introduction to Tibetan Buddhism* (Ithaca: Snow Lion, 2007); and Geoffrey Samuel, *Introducing Tibetan Buddhism* (New York: Routledge, 2012). The latter does include discussion of diverse forms of Buddhism in Bhutan, Nepal, and Ladakh as well. The terminology used to classify forms of Buddhism has recently been a topic of critical inquiry in Theravāda studies and is represented in Peter Skilling and Jason Carbine, eds., *How Theravada Is Theravada? Exploring Buddhist Identities* (Chiang Mai: Silkworm Books, 2012).

5. For more on these discussions, see Sam van Schaik, *Tibet: A History* (New Haven: Yale University Press, 2011), preface. On the discussion of *tsampa* and what unites Tibetan identity, see Tsering Shakya, "Whither the Tsampa Eaters?" *Himal* 6.5 (1993): 8–12.

6. An accessible overview of Tibetan history, in the broader sense of the word, can be found in van Schaik, *Tibet: A History*. A recent study that disputes centralized representations of Tibetan history is Yudru Tsomu, *The Rise of Gönpo Namgyel in Kham: The Blind Warrior of Nyarong* (Lanham, MD: Lexington, 2014).

7. See Ronald M. Davidson, *Indian Esoteric Buddhism* (New York: Columbia University Press, 2002), for more on these communities and forms of affiliation.

8. The complex process of Buddhism's entrance into Tibet is outlined in Ronald M. Davidson, *Tibetan Renaissance: Tantric Buddhism in the Rebirth of Tibetan Culture* (New York: Columbia University Press, 2005).

9. For more on the historical development of the four schools and the Vinaya transmission, see Davidson, *Tibetan Renaissance*. Powers, *Introduction to Tibetan Buddhism*, and Samuel, *Introducing Tibetan Buddhism*, which also use the four-school system to explicate Tibetan Buddhism.

10. Accessible introductions to the *terma* tradition can be found in Tulku Thondup, *Hidden Teachings of Tibet: An Explanation of the Terma Tradition of Tibetan Buddhism* (Boston: Wisdom Publications, 1986); Janet Gyatso, *Apparitions of the Self: The Secret Autobiographies of a Tibetan Visionary* (Princeton: Princeton University Press, 1998).

11. Popular Tibetan historical narratives about the guru state that he visited Tibet initially in the 760s at the invitation of King Trisong Detsen (r. 755–794). However, he does not appear as a major figure in historical documents from the period. For more on his historical status, see van Schaik, *Tibet: A History*, pp. 34–35; and Jacob Dalton, "The Early Development of the Padmasambhava Legend in Tibet: A Study of IOL Tib J 644 and Pelliot Tibétain 307," *Journal of the American Oriental Society* 124.4 (2004): 759–772. For more on his development into a major cultural hero for Tibetans after the late twelfth century, see Davidson, *Tibetan Renaissance*, p. 213.

12. Franz-Karl Ehrhard, "The Role of 'Treasure Discoverers' and Their Search for Himalayan Sacred Lands," in *Sacred Spaces and Powerful Places in Tibetan Culture: A Collection of Essays*, edited by Toni Huber (Dharamsala: Library of Tibetan Works and Archives, 1999), pp. 227–239.

13. Tulku Urgyen Rinpoche, *Blazing Splendor: The Memoirs of Tulku Urgyen Rinpoche*, edited by Erik Pema Kunsang and Marcia Schmidt (Kathmandu: Rangjung Yeshe, 2005), pp. 129–130.

14. Melvyn C. Goldstein, "The Revival of Monastic Life in Drepung Monastery," in *Buddhism in Contemporary Tibet: Religious Revival and Cultural Identity*, edited by Melvyn C. Goldstein and M. T. Kapstein (Berkeley: University of California Press, 1998), p. 15. The term "megamonastery" comes from Brenton Sullivan, "The Mother of All Monasteries: Gönlung Jampa Ling and the Rise of Mega Monasteries in Northeastern Tibet" (Ph.D. diss., University of Virginia, 2013). The dissertation provides a detailed overview of these institutions.

15. Beatrice D. Miller, "The Web of Tibetan Monasticism," *Journal of Asian Studies* 20.2 (1961): 197–203.

16. Elisabeth Stutchbury, "The Making of Gonpa: Norbu Rinpoche from Kardang and Kunga Rinpoche from Lama Gonpa," in *Tantra and Popular Religion in Tibet*, edited by Geoffrey Samuel, Hamish Gregor, and Elisabeth Stutchbury (New Delhi: International Academy of Indian Culture and Aditya Prakashan, 1994), p. 188.

17. Kalzang Dorjee Bhutia, "An Evaluation of the Role of Buddhism as an Anti-Colonial Force as Depicted in the History of Sikkim" (Ph.D. diss., University of Delhi, 2014). For the impact of British incursion in the eastern Himalayas more generally, see Indrani Chatterjee, *Forgotten Friends* (Delhi: Oxford University Press, 2014).

18. Nandni Bhattacharya, "Leisure, Economy and Colonial Urbanism: Darjeeling, 1835–1930," *Urban History* 40.3 (2013): 442–461.

19. P. Kumar Jha, *History of Sikkim, 1817–1904: An Analysis of British Policy and Activities* (Calcutta: OPS Publishers, 1985).

20. Phuntsho, *History of Bhutan*.

21. Phuntsho outlines a number of these projects in his chapter on Ugyen Wangchuck: "The Emergence of Ugyen Wangchuck and End of Civil War," in Phuntsho, *History of Bhutan*.

22. Śākya shrī et al., *Grub dbang Śākya shrī dznya' na'i gsung 'bum* (Kathmandu: Ven. Khenpo Shedup Tenzin and Lama Thinley Namgyal, 1998), p. 673.

23. Phuntsho, *History of Bhutan*, p. 495.

24. Khenpo Phuntsok Tashi, *Nyi ma shar gyi phyogs las shar ba'i skar ma rnam gsum* (Thimphu: Mtsho skyes rdo rje gzhi tshogs, 2013), p. 50.

25. Gyaltsen Dorji, "The Lho-Druk Tradition of Bhutan: The Arrival and Spread of Buddhism," in *Bhutanese Buddhism and Its Culture*, edited by S. Kumagai (Kathmandu: Vajra Books, 2014), pp. 61–72.

26. Dorji Penjore, "Rows of Auspicious Seats: The Role of Bzhugs gral phun tshogs pa'i rten 'brel Ritual in the Founding of the First Bhutanese State in the 17th Century," *Journal of Bhutan Studies* 24 (2011): 1–41.

27. Phuntsho, *History of Bhutan*, pp. 481–482.

28. Elisabeth Stutchbury, "Rediscovering Western Tibet: Gonpa, Chorten and the Continuity of Practice with a Tibetan Buddhist Community in the Indian Himalaya" (Ph.D. diss., Australian National University, 1991).

29. Gyaltsen, *Dran gtam zla ba'i bdud rtsi*.

30. Stutchbury, "Rediscovering Western Tibet."

31. Bhutia, "Evaluation of the Role of Buddhism."

32. Studies of these practitioners include Holmes-Tagchungdarpa, *Social Life of Tibetan Biography*; Annabella Pitkin, "Cosmopolitanism in the Himalayas: The Intellectual and Spiritual Journeys of Khu nu bLa ma bsTan 'dzin rgyal mtshan and His Sikkimese Teacher, Khang gsar bLa ma O rgyan bstan 'dzin Rin po che," *Bulletin of Tibetology* 40.2 (2004): 5–24; and Marilyn Silverstone, "Five Nyingmapa Lamas in Sikkim," *Kailash* 1.1 (2003):. 9–17.

33. Dharmapala's print venue, the *Journal of the Mahabodhi Society*, records a number of visits by Himalayan Buddhists during this period. For more on the history of Bodh Gaya, see Alan Trevithick, *The Revival of Buddhist Pilgrimage at Bodh Gaya (1811–1949): Anagarika Dharmapala and the Mahabodhi Temple* (Delhi: Motilal Banarsidass, 2006); Stephen Kemper, *Rescued from the Nation: Anagarika Dharmapala and the Buddhist World* (Chicago: University of Chicago Press, 2015). For more on Tibetan interactions with Bodh Gaya, see Toni Huber, *The Holy Land Reborn: Pilgrimage and the Tibetan Reinvention of Buddhist India* (Chicago: University of Chicago Press, 2008).

34. Amy Holmes-Tagchungdarpa, "Excavating the Stories of Border-Crossing Women Masters in Modern Buddhism: The Oral Biography of Pelling Ani Wangdzin and Her Family," in *Understanding Buddhism through Biographies of Buddhists*, edited by Todd Lewis (Oxford: Wiley-Blackwell Publishers, 2014), pp. 257–264.

35. For examples, see Powers, *Introduction to Tibetan Buddhism*, p. 27.

36. Holmes-Tagchungdarpa, *Social Life of Tibetan Biography*, and Andrew Quintman, *The Yogin and the Madman: Reading the Biographical Corpus of Tibet's Great Saint Milarepa* (New York: Columbia University Press, 2013), provide critical studies of the role of text in the dissemination of lineage. Ricci's study of the dissemination of an Islamic textual tradition through South and Southeast Asia, and its assimilation into local vernacular languages and cultures also demonstrates this role; see Ronit Ricci, *Islam Translated: Literature, Conversion and the Arabic Cosmopolis of South and Southeast Asia* (Chicago: University of Chicago Press, 2011).

37. Nyöshul Khenpo Jamyang Dorje, *A Marvelous Garland of Rare Gems: Biographies of Masters of Awareness in the Dzogchen Lineage (A Spiritual History of the Teachings of*

Natural Great Perfection), trans. Richard Barron (Junction City, CA: Padma Publishing, 2005), pp. 442–443.

38. See Stutchbury, "Making of Gonpa," p. 188. See also Linda Learman, ed., *Buddhist Missionaries in the Era of Globalization* (Honolulu: University of Hawai'i Press, 2005), for a series of critical studies related to Buddhist missionary activities.

39. Anne Blackburn, *Locations of Buddhism: Colonialism and Modernity in Sri Lanka* (Chicago: University of Chicago Press, 2010), p. 212.

40. Pitkin, "Cosmopolitanism in the Himalayas."

41. This is discussed in his biography and in Holmes-Tagchungdarpa's *Social Life of Tibetan Biography*, chap. 4.

42. Thuthop Namgyal and Yeshe Drolma, *The History of Sikkim* (Gangtok: Tsuklhakhang Trust, 1908 [2003]).

43. Dorji, "Lho-Druk Tradition of Bhutan," pp. 63–65.

44. An alternate spelling of Risung is Risum (Ri gsum), literally meaning "three peaks," which refers to the three peaks of the area.

45. My thanks to the contemporary descendants of the Pönchung Tikidhar and the Gyatso family for their reminiscences of Risung Rinpoche.

46. My thanks to two of this community's few surviving members, HE Dorlop Chewang Rinzin Lama and Mellipa, for generously sharing their memories of Risung Rinpoche.

47. For more on nationalism and these changes, see Bhutia, "Evaluation on the Role of Buddhism," and Phuntsok, *History of Bhutan*.

48. Amy Holmes, "The Making of a Bhutanese Buddha: Preliminary Remarks on the Biography of Tenzin Gyatso, a Bhutanese Scholar-Yogi," *Journal of Bhutan Studies* 17 (2007): 16.

49. Ibid.

50. Stutchbury, "Rediscovering Western Tibet."

51. See Stutchbury, "Making of Gonpa," for further discussion.

52. Tashi, *Nyi ma shar gyi phyogs las shar ba'i skar ma rnam gsum*, p. 42.

53. Ibid., p. 49.

54. Nyöshul, *Marvelous Garland of Rare Gems*.

CONTRIBUTORS

Ismail Fajrie Alatas is assistant professor of Middle Eastern and Islamic studies at New York University. He holds a Ph.D. in anthropology and history from the University of Michigan, Ann Arbor; an M.A. in history from the National University of Singapore; and a B.A. (Hons) from the University of Melbourne, Australia. His research explores the intersections of religious authority, social formation, mobility, semiotics, and communicative practice with a focus on Islamic Law, Sufism, and the Ḥaḍramī diaspora in Indonesia (that is, those who trace their origins to the Ḥaḍramawt valley of southern Yemen). He has published articles in *Comparative Studies in Society and History*, *Indonesia and the Malay World*, *Journal of Islamic Studies*, *Die Welt des Islams*, and *Studia Islamika* as well as written several entries for *The Encyclopedia of Islam*.

Anne M. Blackburn is professor of South Asia studies and Buddhist studies in the Department of Asian Studies at Cornell University and has served as director of the Cornell University South Asia Program. She taught at the University of South Carolina before joining Cornell's faculty. She received her B.A. from Swarthmore College and M.A. and Ph.D. degrees from the University of Chicago. Blackburn studies Buddhism in Southern Asia, with a special interest in Buddhist monastic culture and Buddhist participation in networks involving Sri Lanka before and during colonial presence in the region. Her publications include *Buddhist Learning and Textual Practice in Eighteenth-Century Lankan Monastic Culture* (Princeton, 2001), *Approaching the Dhamma: Buddhist Texts and Practices in South and Southeast Asia*, coedited with Jeffrey Samuels (BPS Pariyatti Editions, 2003), and *Locations of Buddhism: Colonialism and Modernity in Sri Lanka* (Chicago, 2010). She is working on a new project, "Making Buddhist Kingdoms across the Indian Ocean, 1200–1500," supported in part by an ACLS Fellowship.

Martin van Bruinessen is professor emeritus of comparative studies of modern Muslim societies at Utrecht University. He is an anthropologist with a strong interest in politics, history, and philology, and has conducted extensive fieldwork in Kurdistan and Indonesia.

Kenneth Dean is Raffles Professor of Humanities, head of the Department of Chinese Studies, and Religion and Globalisation Research Cluster leader in the Asia Research Institute of the National University of Singapore. He is the author of several books and articles on Daoism and Chinese local communal religion, religious epigraphy, and Chinese temple networks in Southeast Asia. He directed a documentary film titled *Bored in Heaven* about ritual sensation (2010). His most recent publication (with Hue Guan Thye) is *Chinese Epigraphy in Singapore, 1819–1911* (2 vols.) (NUS Press, 2017).

R. Michael Feener is the Sultan of Oman Fellow at the Oxford Centre for Islamic Studies and Islamic Centre lecturer in the History Faculty at the University of Oxford. He was formerly leader of the Religion and Globalisation Research Cluster at the Asia Research Institute and associate professor in the Department of History at the National University of Singapore. He has also taught at Reed College and the University of California, Riverside, and held visiting professor positions and research fellowships at Harvard, Kyoto University, École des hautes études en sciences sociales (Paris), the University of Copenhagen, the Doris Duke Foundation for Islamic Art (Honolulu), and the International Institute for Asian Studies (IIAS) in Leiden, the Netherlands. He has published extensively in the fields of Islamic studies and Southeast Asian history as well as on postdisaster reconstruction, religion, and development.

Nancy K. Florida, professor of Javanese and Indonesian studies at the University of Michigan, is a historian whose work concerns Javanese and Indonesian history, historiography, and literary studies. She was director of the university's Islamic Studies Program (2010–2012). Her publications include *Writing the Past, Inscribing the Future: History as Prophecy in Colonial Java* (Duke, 1995) and *Javanese Literature in Surakarta Manuscripts*, 3 vols. (Cornell SEAP, 1993, 2000, 2012).

Amy Holmes-Tagchungdarpa is associate professor of religious studies and Asian studies at Occidental College. She received her B.A. from Victoria University, Wellington, New Zealand, and her Ph.D. from the Australian National University. She researches the cosmological and material encounters that have shaped trans-Himalayan cultures and their global connections, with a focus on Buddhist communities, language, gender, and material culture. Her first book was *The Social Life of Tibetan Biography: Textuality, Community, and Authority in the Lineage of Tokden Shakya Shri* (Lexington, 2014), and her current project explores printing, language, and materiality in the making of Himalayan communities.

Alexey Kirichenko is assistant professor at the Institute of Asian and African Studies, Moscow State University, Russia. He received his doctorate in history from Moscow State University in 2003 with a thesis focused on the study of Burmese chronicles. His primary research focus is on field and archival work in Burma dealing with monastic Buddhism, manuscript culture, Buddhist religious infrastructure, historiography, and cultural memory. His latest publications include *La vie du Bouddha: Peintures murales de Haute-Birmanie* (with Cristophe Munier-Gaillard and Minbu Aung Kyaing; Éditions Findakly, 2017); "Historiography: Burma," in Brill's Encyclopaedia of Buddhism, vol. 1 (Brill Academic Publishers, 2015); and "Dynamics of Monastic Mobility and Networking in Seventeenth- and Eighteenth-Century Upper Burma," in *Buddhist Dynamics in Premodern and Early Modern Southeast Asia*, edited by D. Christian Lammerts (Institute of Southeast Asian Studies, Singapore, 2015).

Torsten Tschacher is junior professor of Muslim culture and society in South Asia at Freie Universität Berlin, Germany. His research focuses on the history and textual traditions of Tamil-speaking Muslim societies in South India, Sri Lanka, Singapore, and Malaysia. He is currently engaged in a study of early Islamic textual cultures in Tamil between 1572 and 1842. His most recent publications include "Can 'Om' Be an Islamic Term? Translations, Encounters, and Islamic Discourse in Vernacular South Asia," *South Asian History and Culture* 5 (2014); "From Script to Language: The Three Identities of 'Arabic-Tamil,'" *South Asian History and Culture* 8 (2017); an edited volume (with Deepra Dandekar), *Islam, Sufism and Everyday Politics of Belonging in South Asia* (Routledge, 2016), and a monograph titled *Race, Religion, and the "Indian Muslim" Predicament in Singapore* (Routledge, 2018).

INDEX